IN SEARCH OF
PAUL

IN SEARCH OF
PAUL

*How Jesus's Apostle Opposed
Rome's Empire with
God's Kingdom*

A NEW VISION OF PAUL'S WORDS & WORLD

John Dominic Crossan
and Jonathan L. Reed

HarperSanFrancisco
A Division of HarperCollins*Publishers*

HarperCollins books may be purchased for educational, business, or sales promotional use. For information please write: Special Markets Department, HarperCollins Publishers, Inc., 10 East 53rd Street, New York, NY 10022.

HarperCollins Web site: http://www.harpercollins.com

HarperCollins®, ♛®, and HarperSanFrancisco™ are trademarks of HarperCollins Publishers, Inc.

FIRST EDITION

Library of Congress Cataloging-in-Publication Data available on request.
ISBN 0–06–051457–4 (cloth)

Book design by RLF Design

04 05 06 07 08 RRD(H) 10 9 8 7 6 5 4 3 2 1

For
Kris Ashley
and
John Loudon

Contents

CHAPTER 7
One World Under Divine Justice

EPILOGUE
The Lure of a Global Empire

Preface

Paul for a New Millennium

Paul has been called by many names, most of them nasty. He was an apostate who betrayed Judaism, or he was an apostle who betrayed Jesus. He is not an open and affirming theologian, so why bother to read him today? Some say, as compliment or indictment (wrong either way), that he was the actual founder of Christianity. On the one hand, thirteen of the twenty-seven books in the New Testament are attributed to him, and his story dominates one other book, the Acts of the Apostles. On the other hand, books about Paul could fill a library, so why one more on an overworked subject? What's *new* here?

First, this book is *new* in both form and content. Its form is an equal and integrated study by a field archaeologist and a textual exegete of the world and word of the apostle Paul. That has not been done before. At least one of us has been to every place we discuss, and both of us have been several times to certain places. We want, however, not just to emphasize our presence at this or that site, but to invite you to imagine yourselves in those locations. That is why we open major sections with a "you are there" format. Gustav Adolf Deissmann, professor of New Testament exegesis at the University of Berlin, knew that "you are there" value over a hundred years ago. He called his groundbreaking volume *Light from the Ancient East,* but intended "light" not just as a metaphor for information, knowledge, or wisdom. He meant it literally, like this:

> On the castled height of Pergamum observe the wondrous light bathing the marble of Hellenistic temples at noonday. . . . If you have ancient texts to decipher, the sunbeam will bring stone and potsherd to speech. If you have sculptures of the Mediterranean world to scrutinise, the sunbeam will put life into them for you—men, horses, giants, and all. And

if you have been found worthy to study the sacred Scriptures, the sunbeam will reanimate the apostles and evangelists, will bring out with greater distinctness the august figure of the Redeemer from the East, Him whom the Church is bound to reverence and to obey. And then, if you speak of the East, you cannot help yourself: made happy by its marvels, thankful for its gifts, you must speak of the light of the East. (xv)

Something special happens, we are convinced, when you stand on the heights of Priene in the Mediterranean sunlight and read that huge fallen beam from a temple once dedicated to the "Imperator Caesar, the Son of God, the God Augustus." There and elsewhere, on Pauline and non-Pauline sites, we ask you to stand with us, possibly on location, but certainly in imagination.

Second, this new approach from integrated archaeology and exegesis breaks *new* ground as it relates the apostle Paul to the Roman imperial world that surrounded him, the Jewish covenantal religion that formed him, and the Christian faith that enthralled him.

PAUL AND THE ROMAN EMPIRE. Although we will of course travel to cities Paul actually visited, we will also study sites he never saw, but sites that tell us much about the world in which he lived. Our *new* question is this: Where does archaeology uncover most clearly Rome's imperial theology, which Paul's Christian theology confronted nonviolently but opposed relentlessly? In Paul's lifetime Roman emperors were deemed divine, and, first and foremost, Augustus was called Son of God, God, and God of God. He was Lord, Redeemer, and Savior of the World. People knew that both verbally from Latin authors like Virgil, Horace, and Ovid and visually from coins, cups, statues, altars, temples, and forums; from ports, roads, bridges, and aqueducts; from landscapes transformed and cities established. It was all around them everywhere, just as advertising is all around us today. Without seeing the archaeology of Roman imperial theology, you cannot understand any exegesis of Pauline Christian theology.

Some scholars of Paul have already emphasized creatively and accurately the confrontation between Pauline Christianity and Roman imperialism. That clash is at the core of our book, but we see it incarnating deeper and even more fundamental strains beneath the surface of human history. What is *newest* about this book is our insistence that Paul opposed Rome with Christ against Caesar, not because that empire was particularly unjust or oppressive, but because he questioned *the normalcy of civilization itself,* since civilization has always been imperial, that is, unjust and oppressive.

Paul's essential challenge is how to embody communally that radical vision of a *new creation* in a way far beyond even our present best hopes for freedom, democracy, and human rights. The Roman Empire was based on the common principle of *peace through victory* or, more fully, on a faith in the sequence of *piety, war, victory,* and *peace*. Paul was a Jewish visionary following in Jesus' footsteps, and they both claimed that the Kingdom of God was already present and operative in this world. He opposed the mantras of Roman normalcy with a vision of *peace though justice* or, more fully, with a faith in the sequence of *covenant, nonviolence, justice,* and *peace*. A subtext of *In Search of Paul* is, therefore: To what extent can America be Christian? We are now the greatest postindustrial civilization as Rome was then the greatest preindustrial one. That is precisely what makes Paul's challenge equally forceful for now as for then, for here as for there, for Senatus Populusque Romanus as for Senatus Populusque Americanus.

PAUL AND THE JEWISH COVENANT. In an ancient world divided between Jews and Gentiles, there was also a third, in-between category of pagans sympathetic to Judaism. In the New Testament, the Acts of the Apostles calls them "God-fearers" or "God-worshipers." They remained pagans, but they admired Jewish culture, attended synagogue services on the Sabbath, and were a very important buffer zone against any localized anti-Judaism. What is *new* in this book is our claim that those pagan sympathizers are absolutely crucial for understanding both Paul's mission and message.

We argue that Paul went to Jewish synagogues not to convert Jews (despite those stories in the Acts of the Apostles), but to "unconvert" their pagan sympathizers. That convert poaching was inflammatory in the highest possible degree. He was, where successful, stripping a local synagogue of some or all of its most important religious, political, social, and financial defenders, all still operating fully in the urban civic world. That central focus explains many big questions about Paul.

First, his gentile converts could readily understand his theology, because they were already familiar with Jewish practices, traditions, and scriptures. Second, such convert poaching would have generated stiff opposition, not only from other local Jews, but also from those local sympathizers who stayed loyal to Judaism. Third, that explains Paul's polemical descriptions of Judaism in his letters. In his fight to obtain and hold on to his God-worshipers, Paul fiercely but unfairly—is polemics ever fair?—attacks the quite normal Judaism of his opponents. Fourth, that explains why Paul could move so fast from one major provincial capital to another and could consider his work in the eastern Mediterranean finished when he wrote his letter to the Romans in the mid-50s. He was setting up small cells around those now Christian God-worshipers and letting them bring in other, purely pagan, converts. The Pauline express thundered along on God-worshiper rails, and Paul moved fast because he did not have to lay track.

PAUL AND THE CHRISTIAN COMMUNITY. In 1906 a small cave was discovered cut into the rock on the northern slope of Bülbül Dag, high above the ruins of ancient Ephesus, just off the mid-Aegean coast of Turkey. To the right of the entrance and beneath layers of plaster, Karl Herold, of the Austrian Archaeological Institute, uncovered two sixth-century images of St. Thecla and St. Paul (Figure 1).

They are both the same height and are therefore iconographically of equal importance. They both have their right hands raised in teaching gesture and are therefore iconographically of equal authority. But although the eyes and upraised hand of Paul are untouched, some later person scratched out the eyes and erased the upraised hand of Thecla (Figure 2). If the eyes of both images had been disfigured, it would be simply another example of iconoclastic antagonism, since that was believed to negate the spiritual power of an icon without having to destroy it completely. But here only Thecla's eyes and her authoritative hand are destroyed (Figure 3). Original imagery and defaced imagery represent a fundamental clash of theology. An earlier image in which Thecla and Paul were equally authoritative apostolic figures has been replaced by one in which the male is apostolic and authori-

FIGURE 1.
Inside the Grotto
of St. Paul at
Ephesus.

tative and the female is blinded and silenced. And even the cave's present name, St. Paul's Grotto, continues that negation of female-male equality once depicted on its walls.

We take that original assertion of equality and later counterassertion of inequality as encapsulating visually the central claim of this book for Christianity itself. The authentic and historical Paul, author of the seven New Testament letters he actually wrote (Romans, 1–2 Corinthians, Galatians, Philippians, 1 Thessalonians, Philemon), held that *within Christian communities* it made no difference whether one entered as a Christian Jew or a Christian pagan, as a Christian man or a Christian woman, as a Christian freeborn or a Christian slave. All were absolutely equal with each other. But in 1 Timothy, a letter attributed to Paul by later Christians though not actually written by him, women are told to be silent in church and pregnant at home (2:8–15). And a later follower of Paul inserted in 1 Corinthians that it is shameful for women to speak in church, but correct to ask their husbands for explanations at home (14:33–36).

Those pseudo-Pauline, post-Pauline, and anti-Pauline obliterations of female authority are the verbal and canonical equivalent of that visual and iconographic obliteration of Thecla's eyes and hand in that hillside cave. But both defacements also bear witness to what was there before the attack. Pauline equality was negated by post-Pauline inequality. Our book is about the actual and historical Paul, about the radical apostle who was there before

FIGURE 2. Byzantine fresco of Paul (*Paulos*) and Thecla (*Theokli[a]*), inside the grotto.

the reaction, revision, and replacement began. He did not think in terms of political democracy or universal human rights. He only said what Christianity has never been able to follow, that *within it* all are equal and this is to be its witness and challenge to the world outside.

We put on our front cover an artist's creative restoration of that frescoed point-counterpoint from the Cave of St. Thecla and St. Paul. Paul is in the center under full spotlight, just as the church's post-Pauline tradition has always placed him. Thecla is of equal height, with open eyes intact and upraised hand untouched, but she is on the very edge of the cover. She is half on and half off. But here are our questions. Is Thecla still departing or now returning? Does a search for Paul push female leadership, authority, and apostolicity off to the side and finally off that cover, or does a search for Paul bring Thecla, women, and equality back steadily and inevitably into the light until female and male stand together side by side in the full life of the center?

Back to the Roman Empire. In Matthew's powerful parable, Pilate's wife sent him this message as he sat in judgment on Jesus: "Have nothing to do with that innocent man, for today I have suffered a great deal because of a dream about him" (27:19). That is all Matthew tells us about the interchange, but imagine what might have happened later that day. When Pilate returned to his private quarters, he told his wife that he had received her advice but had condemned Jesus to death in any case. "But this," he said, "is what I cannot understand. Why do these people oppose us? We have brought them law and order. We have brought them peace and prosperity. We have brought them culture and civilization. We have brought them free trade and international commerce. Why do they hate us so?"

FIGURE 3.
Fresco of Thecla,
with eyes gouged
out and hand with
teaching gesture
scratched off and
burned.

Prologue

The Hope of
a Peaceful Earth

The interest of Rome lies in its imperialism. It was one of the most successful conquering states in all history, but it was *the* most successful *retainer* of conquests. Rome institutionalized the rule of its legions more stably and over a longer period than any other society before or since. . . . This empire of domination eventually became a true *territorial* empire, or at least had about as high a level and intensity of territorial control as could be attained within the logistical constraints imposed on all agrarian societies. . . . What Rome acquired, Rome kept . . . and in so doing it produced the highest level of ideological, economic, political, and military collective power yet seen in the world. . . . Rome was thus the first territorial empire, the first predominantly nonsegmental extensive society, at least in its highest reaches.

—Michael Mann,
The Sources of Social Power (1986)

Roman civilization eventually appeared everywhere, as one single thing, so far as it was ever achieved. The degree of achievement, however imperfect, remains a thing of wonder, familiar to everyone. . . . Never, however, was there greater progress made toward one single way of life, a thing to be fairly called "Roman civilization of the Empire," than in that lifetime of Augustus. . . . The natives would be taught, if it was not plain enough on its face, that they could better rise into the ranks of the master race by reforming themselves—by talking, dressing, looking, and in every way resembling Romans. They would and did respond as ambition directed. They pulled Roman civilization to them—to their homes, their families, their world.

—Ramsay MacMullen,
Romanization in the Time of Augustus (2003)

On the Acropolis of Philippi

You stand on the heights of Philippi and look down at a dead city. The ruins sit astride the modern road that runs in Macedonian Greece north from Kavalla to Drama, loops west around the Phalakro and Menikio mountains, and heads north up the Strymon Valley to the Bulgarian frontier. The ancient city also sat astride a road, but then it was an east-west road across the Balkan peninsula, and Philippi guarded the narrows where the Via Egnatia, Rome's all-weather route from the Adriatic to the Aegean, was pinched between southern marshes and northern mountains. There is now a medieval tower on Philippi's acropolis atop a jutting spur of Mt. Lekanis. You ignore it and the ruins below. You look to the southwest and golden Mt. Pangaion (Figure 4), replacing in imagination those marshes drained and reclaimed in the 1930s, and seeing instead a late October day in the fall of 42 B.C.E., when Brutus and Cassius, Julius Caesar's assassins, waited there between swamps and foothills for the attack of Antony and Octavian, Julius Caesar's avengers.

The structural weakness that was but the other side of Rome's governmental strength was already lethally evident. The system of two annual consuls, twin kings for a year, avoided the danger of royal tyranny, but invited the danger of social anarchy if and when aristocrats, consuls, or generals-become-warlords fought with one another. Roman civil war, with battle-hardened legions on either side, devastated farms, ruined cities, destroyed families, and dispossessed, proscribed, exiled, or slaughtered enemies. Athens had learned that you could have a democracy or an empire, but not both. Rome would learn, that fall day at Philippi, that you could have a republic or an empire, but not both. That lesson would be certified off Actium on the opposite side of Greece on another fall day a decade later.

The Republican battle positions were excellent and, like Philippi itself, they straddled the road. Cassius's forces were south with marshes behind; Brutus's were north with mountains behind. The Gangitis River ran in front of both and, through the narrows behind their positions, the Republicans held the city and a secure supply route eastward to their fleet off coastal

Neapolis, modern Kavalla. The Caesarian legions lacked all of that, but they had, in Antony, the best general and, in Octavian, a *divi filius,* the divine son of the deified Julius Caesar. The outcome was by no means inevitable, although you might claim, with infallible hindsight, that the Republicans fought for a past already gone, the Caesarians for a future already present.

You see, in imagination, those two separate battles at Philippi and, at the end, Cassius dead, a suicide too soon; Brutus dead, a suicide too late; and Antony and Octavian victorious despite that bloody confusion of a general too many. A little over a decade later Antony and Octavian finally faced one another, not as allies, but as enemies. On the morning of September 2, 31 B.C.E., Antony's squadrons moved out from the Ambracian Gulf on the northwestern coast of Greece, for breakout if possible, for battle if necessary, for victory if imaginable. They rowed past the narrows of Cape Actium with Cleopatra's fleet forming up behind Antony's battle line. Octavian and his admiral-general, Agrippa, waited for them out in the Ionian Sea, and both sides maneuvered to turn each other's flank by means of the rising northwesterners. It was all over before it began, and by day's end defeat,

FIGURE 4. Philippi, looking southwest onto the valley where Antony and Octavian defeated the Republican forces.

defection, and despair sent Antony back on Cleopatra's flagship to another double suicide, this time at Alexandria. Never in the field of human conflict has so much been changed for so many by so little.

Octavian now stood alone as *princeps,* "leading citizen" or "first among equals," but with all the other equals dead. The long civil wars were over, internal peace was restored, the Golden Age was at hand. And Octavian, later named Augustus, had done it. He was Lord, Savior, Redeemer, and Liberator. He was Divine, Son of God, God, and God from God. And none of that was simply one-way propaganda enforced unilaterally. It was fully two-way ideology accepted multilaterally. It was Roman imperial theology, the ideological glue that held the empire dynamically together.

On the Road to Damascus

Still on Philippi's acropolis, look now in the opposite direction and imagine, almost a hundred years later, not Octavian coming eastward, but Paul coming westward. According to the New Testament's Acts of the Apostles, Paul's first European landfall was at nearby Neapolis, today the quiet seaside resort of Kavalla on Greece's northeastern Aegean coast. But it had all started some twenty years earlier and much farther east at Damascus.

A FERVENT JEW. Both Paul's letters and Luke's Acts of the Apostles agree that Paul was a fervent Jew. "I was," says Paul, "circumcised on the eighth day, a member of the people of Israel, of the tribe of Benjamin, a Hebrew born of Hebrews; as to the law, a Pharisee . . . as to righteousness under the law, blameless" (Phil. 3:5–6). Furthermore, "I advanced in Judaism beyond many among my people of the same age, for I was far more zealous for the traditions of my ancestors" (Gal. 1:14). He asks polemically about some Jewish opponents, "Are they Hebrews? So am I. Are they Israelites? So am I. Are they descendants of Abraham? So am I" (2 Cor. 11:22). He concludes, "I myself am an Israelite, a descendant of Abraham, a member of the tribe of Benjamin" (Rom. 11:1). Even when he talked about his opponents, he did not say "Jews" and "Gentiles," but spoke of "danger from my own people (*genous*), danger from Gentiles" (2 Cor. 11:26). Paul was Jewish born and bred, understood Hebrew, was a Pharisee, and was proud of all that lineage. He identified himself as a Jew within Judaism.

Luke in the Acts of the Apostles agrees with that general picture, but he also adds some details better taken as enthusiasm rather than as history. He has Paul declare, "I am a Jew" (21:39); "I am a Jew, born in Tarsus in Cilicia, but brought up in this city [Jerusalem] at the feet of Gamaliel, educated strictly according to our ancestral law, being zealous for God, just as all of you are today" (22:3); "I am a Pharisee, a son of Pharisees" (23:6); and, finally, "I have belonged to the strictest sect of our religion and lived as a Pharisee" (26:5). It is probably safer to bracket Pharisaic ancestry and especially Jerusalem education as a Lukan upgrading of Paul's status and as part of his theme that everything starts from Jerusalem. Another Lukan upgrading of Pauline status concerns his Tarsian citizenship in Acts 9:11; 21:39; 22:3 (impossible?) and his Roman citizenship in Acts 16:37; 22:27–28; 23:27 (improbable?). In any case, Paul himself never mentions that latter status, and, if his Roman beatings are any indication, he was never a Roman citizen. Those are first warnings about distinguishing the Pauline Paul from the Lukan Paul by separation and discrimination rather than by combination and conflation. To that we will return in Chapter 1 below and quite often thereafter.

A ZEALOUS PERSECUTOR. Paul and Luke agree that he persecuted the early church, but, once again, some Lukan details require bracketing. Paul mentions this point twice with a close conjunction between violent persecution and religious zeal. "I was violently persecuting the church of God and was trying to destroy it. . . . I was far more zealous for the traditions of my ancestors" (Gal. 1:13–14). And again, "As to zeal, [I was] a persecutor of the church" (Phil. 3:6). He also notes, "I am the least of the apostles, unfit to be called an apostle, because I persecuted the church of God" (1 Cor. 15:9). "Zeal" indicates religious vigilantism based on personal and individual responsibility after the model and in the tradition of Phineas, who, in Numbers 25:6–8, slew an Israelite and the Midianite woman he had married. That is how, for example, the treatise *The Special Laws* by the contemporary Jewish philosopher Philo understands such religious "zeal." It allows *any* outraged person "to exact the penalties offhand and with no delay without bringing the offender before jury or council or any kind of magistrate at all" (1.55).

Luke agrees on Paul as persecutor, but adds that he went from the high priests at Jerusalem with authority to punish Christians at Damascus (Acts 9:1–2). Still, apart from the historical implausibility of such Jewish authority exercised in Nabatean Damascus, Acts has the same combination of zeal and violence (or zeal as violence) found in Paul. Luke has Paul say, "Being zealous for God . . . I persecuted this Way up to the point of death by binding both men and women and putting them in prison" (22:3–4).

Neither Paul nor Luke tells us exactly what precise aspect of Christianity made Paul want to "destroy it." What was it? Our best guess, and it can be no more than that, is that Paul persecuted precisely that to which he was later called. He reacted violently to those fellow Jews who claimed that pagans could now be full and equal members of God's people alongside Jews—without circumcision for males or purity rules for anyone. In other words, he converted 180 degrees from his former to his latter position. He could have simply stayed a fervent Jew and left Christian Jews alone, or converted from Pharisaic Judaism to Christian Judaism (as, for instance, James and the members of the Jerusalem church did), or proclaimed Jesus as Messiah only to his fellow Jews. Instead, he converted *not from Judaism to Christianity,* of course, but *from violent opponent and persecutor of pagan inclusion to nonviolent proponent and persuader of pagan inclusion.* That which he persecuted *for* God was exactly that to which he was called *by* God.

A CHOSEN APOSTLE.   Both his own letter to the Galatians (1:17) and Luke's Acts of the Apostles (9:3; 22:6; 26:12) agree that Damascus was the inaugural moment of apparition, revelation, conversion, and vocation for Paul. But after that initial agreement, we proceed very cautiously, remembering that general warning about the Pauline Paul versus the Lukan Paul and bracketing that specific instance of Paul's high-priestly authority from Jerusalem against Damascus.

To emphasize a story's importance Luke often repeats the entire narrative. For example, God's revelation to Peter that all foods are equally pure is told fully and twice in Acts 10:1–11:18. But God's revelation to Paul of his gentile apostolate is even more important and is told fully not twice, but thrice. Luke's account of Paul's conversion and call on the road to Damascus is well known from both biblical text and artistic image and is a superb example of Luke's literary imagination at work in Acts. He emphasizes with compositional creativity this crucial subject as you read or hear, first, a third-person account (9:3–16), then a first-person version by Paul in Jerusalem's Temple (22:6–15), and, finally, another first-person account by Paul in Caesarea's palace (26:12–18). But watch how Luke repeats this triple account without boring his audience.

Jesus to Ananias (9:15)	*Ananias to Paul* (22:14–15)	*Jesus to Paul* (26:16–18)
But the Lord said to him [Ananias], "Go, for he [Paul] is an instrument whom I have chosen to bring my name before Gentiles and kings and before the people of Israel."	Then he [Ananias] said, "The God of our ancestors has chosen you [Paul] to know his will, to see the Righteous One and to hear his own voice; for you will be his witness to all the world of what you have seen and heard."	"I [Jesus] have appeared to you [Paul] for this purpose, to appoint you to serve and testify to the things in which you have seen me and to those in which I will appear to you. I will rescue you from your people and from the Gentiles—to whom I am sending you to open their eyes so that they may turn from darkness to light and from the power of Satan to God, so that they may receive forgiveness of sins and a place among those who are sanctified by faith in me."

In Luke's elegant literary climax, Paul's vocational mandate is first told by Jesus to Ananias (long), then by Ananias to Paul (longer), and finally by Jesus directly to Paul (longest).

Paul himself, however, tells a rather less dramatic and much less photogenic story, but he agrees with Luke on the essential point, namely, that apparition and revelation begot conversion and vocation.

For I want you to know, brothers and sisters, that the gospel that was proclaimed by me is not of human origin; for I did not receive it from a human source, nor was I taught it, but I received it through a revelation

of Jesus Christ. . . . God, who had set me apart before I was born and
called me through his grace, was pleased to reveal his Son to me, so
that I might proclaim him among the Gentiles. (Gal. 1:11–12, 15–16)

In Acts, Luke's famous scenario emphasizes the light of God, the voice of
Christ, and the blindness of Paul (9:8; 22:11). Paul himself says nothing
about a blindness, but instead emphasizes sight. He asks rhetorically, "Have I
not seen Jesus our Lord?" (1 Cor. 9:1) and replies, "Christ . . . appeared [lit-
erally, was seen] also to me" (1 Cor. 15:8). We understand, of course, that
Luke underlines for *later converts* that symbolic sequence of disbelief and
blindness, voice and faith, sight and baptism. Paul also tells *later converts,*
"Faith comes from what is heard, and what is heard comes through the
word of Christ" (Rom. 10:17). But here is the question. What did Paul actually *see* in that vision at Damascus? Did Paul *see,* as Luke says, a heavenly
light that blinded him? Or did Paul *see,* as he himself says, a heavenly figure
that he recognized as Jesus? But how could Paul, even in vision, recognize a
Jesus he had never met?

We can only imagine one answer, and it emphasizes that Paul already
knew enough about the life, death, and resurrection of Jesus to persecute his
followers for proclaiming its implications to their fellow Jews in Damascus.
In Christian gospel, art, and mysticism, the risen Christ retains the wounds
of historical crucifixion even or especially on his glorified and transcendental body. Those wounds do not heal or fade. They are forever there. To take
seriously Paul's claim to have *seen* the risen Jesus, we suggest that his inaugural vision was of Jesus's body simultaneously wounded *and* glorified. Such a
stunning vocational vision would already contain the message of Paul's faith
and theology, the meaning of Paul's life and death. We propose, therefore,
that in reading the Lukan accounts of Paul's inaugural conversion and vocation experience, we bracket that blinded-by-light sequence and imagine instead a vision in which Paul both *sees* and hears Jesus as the resurrected
Christ, the risen Lord. It need not be added that, then as now, dreams and
visions are hard-wired possibilities of the human brain. But, of course and
always, their value depends on contents and results, purposes and intentions,
means and ends.

A footnote. Millennia of Christian art have lingered lovingly over that
Lukan scenario and engraved it indelibly on Western imagination. And, of
course, it added to Luke's account a horse for Paul. That was utterly appropriate in a world where upended pride was best symbolized by a fallen hero

looking up his horse's rump. So we must face not just Luke's texts but, for example, Caravaggio's paintings (Figures 5 and 6). Around 1600 that artist produced two very different versions of that scene and their differences remind us that a visual artist can vary details just like a literary one. In one, Paul is young, beardless, fully clothed, and with normal hair. In the other, he is older, bearded, naked above the waist, and definitely balding from the front. But here is the key difference. In the former, the heavenly light shines down upon his blinded eyes through the whitened section of his skewbald horse. In the latter painting, there is no light, but a quite visible and angel-supported Christ reaches down his hand toward the blinded Paul (no wounds, by the way). Once again, we have the same question. Did Paul see *light,* with Luke's account and Caravaggio's former painting, or *Lord,* with Paul's account and Caravaggio's second painting?

You look down, then, one final time from Philippi's high acropolis. The view southeast is not as open as southwest, but you hold together, as if in a simultaneous moment of time, both Octavian and Paul on the Via Egnatia to west and east of the city. Any comparison seems absolutely ludicrous. But with Paul, with dusty, tired, much-traveled Paul, came Rome's most dangerous opponent—not legions but ideas, not an alternative force but an

FIGURE 5. Caravaggio's *Conversion of St. Paul* in Rome's S. Maria del Popolo.

FIGURE 6. Caravaggio's *Conversion of St. Paul* in Rome's Coll. Odescalchi Balbi di Piovera.

alternative faith. Paul too proclaimed one who was Lord, Savior, Redeemer, and Liberator. He announced one who was Divine, Son of God, God, and God from God. But Paul's new divinity was Christ, not Caesar. His was a radically divergent but equally global theology.

Two Sons of Two Gods

It is a profound if standard mistake to dismiss Roman imperial theology as empty rhetoric, poetic hyperbole, or pragmatic flattery. It was, actually, the ideological core of Roman imperial power, the theological heart of Roman global rule. In 1906 and 1909 Gustav Adolf Deissmann, then at the University of Heidelberg and later at the University of Berlin, searched Western museums and Eastern sites to show the importance of *nonliterary* written memorials from the Roman Empire in the first century C.E. for a proper understanding of earliest Christianity. By *nonliterary* he meant texts on stone, metal, wax, papyrus, parchment, wood, or ceramic recently discovered by archaeological excavation.

That search began, according to his classic *Light from the Ancient East,* after he read the title "Son of God" used for the emperor Augustus.

> It was the *theou yios* [Son of God] in No. 174 of the *Berliner Griechische Urkunden* that stimulated me, all in a flash, to a considerable part of the work that has occupied my life as a scholar. Some thirty years ago I happened to see the unbound volume in the hands of Wilhelm Schulze in the [University of] Marburg library. Looking over his shoulder, I noticed the text, which caught my eye owing to its being an autograph reproduction. I was arrested, fascinated by the *theou yios* and found myself, as I continued to turn the leaves, everywhere in the world of the New Testament and the world surrounding it. (346)

He was reading the language of Augustan imperial theology and hearing the counterlanguage of, say, Pauline Christian theology.

> I remember discussing with a librarian friend of mine the fact that in many inscriptions and papyri of the Greek east Augustus and (with the name of their divine father inserted) his successors are called "the son of a god." My friend, a classical scholar, smiled benignly and said there could be no significance in that, "for" it was a translation of the Latin *divi filius.* I do not think that a Christian out of one of St. Paul's

churches would have smiled at the expression or have considered it non-significant. (346)

Note, by the way, that Latin makes a distinction between *deus,* an eternal god like Jupiter, and a *divus,* a deified human like Julius Caesar. But Greek translates both terms with the same word, *theos.* Latin titles like *dei filius* ("Son of a God") and *divi filius* ("Son of a Divine One") appear, therefore, alike in Greek as *theou yios* or *theou hyios* ("Son of God").

Christians must have understood, then, that to proclaim Jesus as Son of God was deliberately denying Caesar his highest title and that to announce Jesus as Lord and Savior was calculated treason. We may have to translate those titles and their effects differently for now, but their ancient challenge is still the same. What divinity and what divine incarnation runs this world? Is that ruling divinity one of force and violence or of justice and love? If, in the early 1930s, some German Christians had called Jesus *der Führer,* we would know why they died at Dachau. But what if contemporary American Christians spoke of a *divine* world order, would we understand how it opposed a *new* world order?

At the start of the past century Deissmann was quite explicit on that clash between Christ and Caesar:

The cult of Christ goes forth into the world of the Mediterranean and soon displays the endeavour to reserve for Christ the words already in use for worship in that world, words that had just been transferred to the deified emperors (or had perhaps even been newly invented in emperor worship). Thus there arises a polemical parallelism between the cult of the emperor and the cult of Christ, which makes itself felt where ancient words derived by Christianity from the treasury of the Septuagint and the Gospels happen to coincide with solemn concepts of the Imperial cult which sounded the same or similar. In many cases this polemical parallelism, which is a clear prophecy of the coming centuries of martyrdom, may be established by very ancient witness. (342)

From the heights of Philippi, then, you think about two contests. One is a clash of armies between Republicans and Caesarians, the other a clash of beliefs between Caesarians and Christians. And, as you climb down from the Mt. Lekanis foothills, you think about these questions. What were the structural and systemic differences between the God incarnate in Augustus and the God incarnate in Christ? What were the religious and political differences between Caesar Augustus as Son of God and Jesus Christ as Son of God? What were the ethical and economic differences between a world grounded in Caesar and a world founded on Christ?

At the start of this century the clash and challenge are still the same, but now we must ask this with a far more terrible clarity: What is the structural and systemic character of Christ and how precisely does it clash with the structural and systemic character of Caesar? How does the gospel of the divine Caesar differ from that of the divine Christ? How does it differ not just in name, but in content, and not just in theory, but in practice? And this above all: Who now is Caesar, and where now is Christ?

I

Jewish Faith and
Pagan Society

The influence of Judaism on non-Jews in the Roman Empire was profound and lasting. This is paradoxical. For the exclusiveness of Jewish worship, and the strictness of the Jewish food laws, served as a barrier between Jew and gentile. Moreover the Jews do not as a rule appear to have actively propagated their religion. So evidently there was something in the nature of Jewish religion, and of the Jewish community, which satisfied a need felt by many within and even beyond the frontiers of the Empire.

—Wolf Liebeschuetz, "The Influence of Judaism
Among Non-Jews in the Imperial Period" (2001)

Judaism throughout the Hellenistic and Roman periods and even after the triumph of Christianity showed tremendous vigor not only in strengthening itself internally with the development of that remarkable document, the Talmud, but also in reaching out to pagans and later to Christians and winning large numbers as proselytes and as "sympathizers.". . . Even after the three great revolts of 66–74, 115–17, and 132–35, the Jews were hardly powerless and indeed continued to win proselytes and especially "sympathizers." In short, the lachrymose theory of Jewish history, highlighting the weakness and suffering of the Jews, would not, on the whole, seem to apply to the ancient period.

—Louis H. Feldman, *Jew and Gentile in the Ancient World* (1993)

Judaism, by the early third century, may well have been a more popular religion among the pagans, and therefore a more powerful rival to Christianity in the race for the soul of the Roman world, than we have had any reason to think until now. This helps us understand the tension between the Church and the Synagogue in the first few centuries A.D.

—Robert F. Tannenbaum, "Jews and God-Fearers
in the Holy City of Aphrodite" (1986)

cᴀᴏ   cᴀᴏ   cᴀᴏ

In the City of Aphrodite

Overture

You come to Aphrodisias on a full-day visit from Denizli, in southwestern Turkey. As you leave that city its innumerable modern textile factories continue the area's ancient importance for the manufacture of cotton, linen, and woolen garments. So also do the flocks of sheep and goats that take right-of-way across the narrow roads as you shortcut through the mountains off the main Denizli–Antalya road. It is a beautiful mid-September day in 2002, cool and cloudy, with an odd shower early and late, so not really inconvenient.

Two thousand years ago, Octavian, the not-yet Augustus, said, "Aphrodisias is the one city from all of Asia I have selected to be my own," and the citizens carved that accolade on the archive wall of their theater. Since the Greek goddess Aphrodite was the Roman goddess Venus, from whom the Julian line was allegedly descended, the city was most fortunately named at that precise historical moment. Millennia later, in *Aphrodisias: City of Venus Aphrodite,* the frontispiece poem by L. G. Harvey says,

when all paper words
are turned to ash
there will remain
one scarred hillside
beautiful enough to last
forever.

Kenan Erim, of New York University, the city's Turkish-born excavator and that book's author, spent his professional life there and is now buried most

FIGURE 7. Theater at Aphrodisias and overview of the archaeological excavations by New York University.

appropriately beside the reconstructed gate to Aphrodite's temple. He said that "of all the Graeco-Roman sites of Anatolia, Aphrodisias is the most hauntingly beautiful" (1). Agreed.

The hamlet of Geyre once sat atop the ancient site, but was removed and rebuilt in its nearby location after an earthquake in the 1960s. That opened the site for archaeology, but the old village square still underlies the new entrance plaza ringed by restrooms (very elegant), a restaurant (very limited), and a museum (very beautiful). You get there around 11:30 A.M. and have the site almost totally to yourself. The morning tour buses heading west from Hierapolis and the hot-spring pools of Pamukkale are just leaving, and those reversing that itinerary will not arrive until much later. You sit high up in the once thirty-thousand-seat theater, eat a quiet picnic lunch, admire the stands of stately poplars amid the marbled ruins (Figure 7), and look east to where the seven-thousand-foot tip of Baba Dag emerges periodically from scudding cloud cover. At the foot of that mountain are the marble quarries that gave the city ready material for sculpture or inscription and made its products famous far beyond its own borders. The Dandalaz tributary, fed from the snows of that eastern mountain range, circled the city's south side and took sculptures northwestward to the ancient Meander, the modern Büyük Menderes, which carried them westward to the coast and the world.

Overview

What text do you read to see most clearly Paul's life, and what site do you visit to see most clearly Paul's world—even, or especially, if Paul himself neither wrote that text nor visited that site? In this chapter two chosen sites, the city of Aphrodisias, now in southwestern Turkey, and the island of Delos, now in mid-Aegean Greece (Figure 8), frame two contradictory aspects of the chosen text, Luke's Acts of the Apostles, now a prelude to Paul's letters in the New Testament.

We begin this chapter at Aphrodisias because it illustrates most forcibly two major themes of this book, the relationship of Paul to Roman imperial theology and to his Jewish religious tradition. The former theme focuses here on the Sebasteion, or Augusteum, whose elegant gate, three-storied facing porticoes, and high-stepped imperial temple celebrated the Roman Julio-Claudian divinities by inserting them among and above the ancient gods and traditions of Greece. The latter theme focuses here on a Jewish inscription that explicitly distinguishes Jews, converts, and a third category of "God-worshipers," with rather surprising numbers in each category.

We continue by considering the New Testament's Acts of the Apostles as a most ambiguous source for understanding Paul's life and work, mission and message. We presume, by the way, that the same author wrote that two-volume work that is now separated into the Gospel According to Luke and the Acts of the Apostles, but we do not presume that author is "Luke, the beloved physician" from Colossians 4:14 (we use "Luke" simply for convenience). On the one hand, Luke emphasizes certain elements with regard to Christians, pagans, Jews, and Roman authorities that reflect his own, much later views rather than Paul's much earlier experiences. On the other, he emphasizes the presence of "God-fearers" or "God-worshipers" in Jewish synagogues and underlines Paul's controversial successes among them. Those pagan sympathizers, not full Jews but no longer pure pagans, will be crucial for this book's understanding of Paul's polemics with those fellow Jews on whose domain he was confrontationally convert poaching. Luke, in summary, both knows much about Paul's time and place, but also interprets it according to his own time and place. Both those elements must be carefully and critically assessed in reading Paul through Lukan eyes.

We finish this chapter on another site that Paul never visited, Delos, amid the Cycladic Islands of the Aegean. We chose it for two reasons. First, it was a microcosm of Paul's world, a miniature crucible of that world's political,

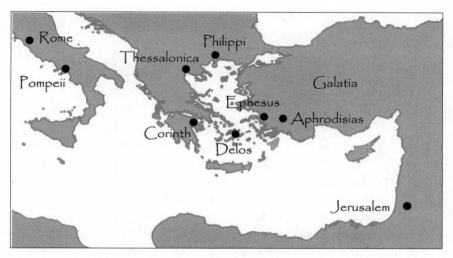

FIGURE 8. Key archaeological sites in search of Paul.

economic, social, and religious ferment. Second, it is today an entire island preserved for archaeological study. In its many temples, shrines, and synagogues we see both Roman theology spreading eastward from Rome, but also Eastern religions spreading westward toward Rome. We recognize in both cases the absolute conjunction between religion and politics. We catch glimpses of the voluntary associations that organized religion and economics within Greco-Roman commercial life. Above all, we see the ancient tradition of Judaism moving powerfully among Greeks and under Romans. It was only amid that mobility and because of its possibility and security that Paul could operate so successfully.

The Sculptures of the Imperial Sebasteion

Imagine what Paul *would* have seen *had* he visited Aphrodisias. Imagine you are walking in the middle of that city on a busy street and turn in under one of the arches of a beautiful two-story marble monumental gate. You slow down for a moment in its shade, but soon rejoin the sun's glare on a glistening east-west plaza, 46 feet wide, 40 feet high on both sides, and 300 feet long (Figure 9). It is like entering a roofless funnel as long as a football field. To your left and right are parallel three-story-high galleries lined with bulky Doric columns on the bottom level, sleek Ionic columns on the middle level, and ornate Corinthian columns on the third and upper level. Your eyes are drawn up along those columns toward the terra-cotta roof tiles that contrast with the deep blue sky. But they are drawn even more forcibly along the length of the plaza's funnel to the temple at its far end. It sits on a high podium and can be reached only by a flight of stairs to a front emphasized by six Corinthian columns, taller, larger, and more imposing than those all along the third story to your left and right. Walking toward the temple past civic officials, ministering priests, and people from all walks of life, you look up at those high galleries on either side and see something that is unique in all the Greco-Roman world. Between the columns on the upper two levels of both sides are 180 5-by-5-foot panels sculpted in high relief.

To your left, on the upper level of the north gallery, are universalizing Hellenistic allegories such as Day and Night or Land and Sea, which locate the entire sculptural program within the widest ambience of time and place from Greek mythology. On the middle level, history is absorbed into that mythical framework above it by a series of conquered peoples, personified as elegantly dressed females standing on inscribed bases, extending across the entire sweep of the Roman Empire and emphasizing military victories under Augustus. To your right, in the south gallery's two upper levels, is the same celebration of war and conquest, the same absorption of history into

FIGURE 9. Reconstruction of the imperial cult's Sebasteion at Aphrodisias.

myth, the same creation of Roman imperial theology. But now the juxta-position is reversed. In the upper story are important members of the divine Julio-Claudian dynasty, from Augustus and Livia to Nero and Agrippina. In the middle story are various scenes and divinities from Greek mythology such as Zeus, Aphrodite, Poseidon, and Asclepius. But among them are also Aeneas's flight from Troy and the She-wolf suckling Romulus and Remus, the two mytho-historical stories of Roman and Augustan origins.

An inscription dedicates the complex to "Aphrodite, the *Theoi Sebastoi,* and the People." The *Theoi Sebastoi* are the Augustan gods (*Sebastos* is Greek for the Latin *Augustus*), the family of the Julio-Claudian divinities (minus Caligula!). There are no panels on the bottom level, only on the two upper levels of both sides. You are forced constantly to swivel from left to right and consistently to look upward until your neck begins to hurt. Your body gets the message even before your mind catches up. That panorama of Roman imperial theology smoothly controls them both.

The Sebasteion, begun under Tiberius and finished under Nero, was damaged by an earthquake even as it was being built and was eventually de-stroyed by another one afterwards. The northern gallery was quarried for building materials, but the southern one survived without that indignity. But the overall sculptural program can be reconstructed from the many sur-viving panels that Kenan Erim first discovered in 1979. Two examples con-tain Roman imperial theology in striking summaries.

A first panel is iconographically simple and still somewhat historical (Fig-ure 10). It depicts an idealized world-conquering Julio-Claudian emperor, not armored but naked except for a back cloak, standing in the center. To his right is a battle trophy above a kneeling and weeping barbarian prisoner whose hands are tied behind her back. To his left is a female figure, either the Roman people or the Senate, crowning him with an oak wreath. A sec-ond panel is iconographically more complex and much more cosmic (Fig-ure 11). Claudius, nude as was that preceding figure and all other male imperial figures in the Sebasteion (save an armored one of Nero), strides forcibly forward with his cloak billowing in a wide semicircle above his head. On his right a female earth figure has given him a cornucopia, symbol of control over earth's fertility—no more wars. On his left a female sea fig-ure has just given him an oar or rudder, symbol of control over ocean's safety—no more pirates. It displays divine control of both Land and Sea. Nudity, of course, was the Greek and Hellenistic way of iconographically indicating divinity; imperial nudity meant imperial divinity.

FIGURE 10.
Sculptural relief of
an idealized Julio-
Claudian emperor
and a barbarian
prisoner, from the
Sebasteion at
Aphrodisias.

FIGURE 10. Sculptural relief of an idealized Julio-Claudian emperor and a barbarian prisoner, from the Sebasteion at Aphrodisias.

What is most interesting, however, is how that Sebasteion fused Roman and Greek elements and styles, although its relief-clad galleries were neither, but unique. The temple's placement was not approachable from all sides in the Greek egalitarian manner, but had a single procession-like approach that exuded imperial authority in the Roman hierarchical style. The emperors' portraits, whether those of Augustus, Claudius, or Nero, closely copied the imperial models distributed by Rome. Their bodies and scenes did not rely on Roman models, however, but were local creations and represented a Greek interpretation of Roman imperial rule. The galleries represent, as a whole, the idea that Greek myth and history were destined to unfold into Roman rule under the divine Roman emperors.

The city of Aphrodisias, left free and independent by Rome, was not coerced into setting up that magnificent building. But since the relationship between Rome and Aphrodisias was mutually beneficial, it is no surprise that the civic council endorsed the Sebasteion's construction and that it was financed by two wealthy Aphrodisian families. Two brothers, Menander and Eusebes, paid for the monumental gate and northern gallery, which were

FIGURE 11.
Relief from the
Sebasteion at
Aphrodisias of the
Roman emperor
Claudius depicted
cosmically con-
trolling Land and
Sea.

restored by Eusebes's wife, Apphias, and her daughter Tata after an earthquake. The temple and southern gallery were built by two other brothers,
Diogenes and Attalus, but since Diogenes died in the planning stages, it was
completed by his wife, Attalis Apphion, and then restored after the earthquake by his son Tiberius Claudius Diogenes, who had a Roman name and
presumably Roman citizenship. Those citizens were certainly attracted to
the imperial favors that inevitably followed imperial honors, including of
course Roman citizenship, and they understood the material blessings that
accompanied Augustan and Julio-Claudian rule for those who positioned
themselves appropriately.

Those blessings extended beyond the elites, as the vast figural program on
the Sebasteion makes clear. The number of masons, craftsmen, and sculptors necessary for this enormous enterprise was substantial, and most workshops in the city received commissions. The sudden demand for skilled labor
led to the hasty promotion of marble cutters to figural sculptors. Many a
new apprentice took up mallet and chisel for on-the-job training, as is apparent from the uneven quality of carving. Designers and foremen disguised

that fact from viewers by having novices cut the panel's lower portions, which were less visible from the plaza, and having experts work the upper and more visible portions, especially the imperial portraits. Roman imperial rule energized Aphrodisias's sculptural workshops and was a boon to the local economy. Any potential criticism of the elite's attraction to the Roman imperial family would certainly be muted by those many prospering shops and increased incomes.

The construction of a Sebasteion with a temple for the Roman imperial cult was a seductive proposition for any city, and its attraction is easily explained. "Victory and conquest were felt to be an important justification of imperial rule," as R. R. R. Smith, the city's current excavator, notes in his article "The Imperial Reliefs from the Sebasteion at Aphrodisias," but "it is always victory over barbarians of various kinds: Britons, Armenians, and the like. The conquest of the Greeks is long forgotten. That was before the emperors. The Greeks were now partners, not subjugated recalcitrants" (98). He concludes,

> The Aphrodisian Sebasteion gives material evidence of the imperial cult that is both different in kind and greater in quantity than anything known before. . . . The relief panels as a whole present a detailed and broadly expressed vision of the fortunate position of the Greek world under Roman imperial rule, such as we have nowhere else. The atti-

FIGURE 12 *(right)*. Inscribed marble column from the entrance to the Jewish synagogue at Aphrodisias.

FIGURE 13 *(opposite)*. Face *b* of the synagogue inscription, listing Jews at the top and "God-worshipers" at the bottom.

tudes to the Roman emperor found here were common to the other cities of Asia Minor in the first century A.D., but the grand and elaborate manner in which they are expressed in marble in the Sebasteion is so far unique. (137–38)

It is indeed clear that the Greek Aphrodisians became Roman enthusiasts even as the Roman emperors became Greek gods in that Sebasteion's city.

The *Theosebeis* of the Jewish Synagogue

GOD-WORSHIPERS. Imagine now the entrance to a Jewish building at Aphrodisias a century later in the early 200s C.E. There are two square marble columns on either side of the doorway. Focus on the right-hand one. Three of its sides are smoothed and visible as you enter (faces *a, b, c*), but the fourth one is unsmoothed and backs against the entrance wall (face *d*). It was, ironically, when the Aphrodisian museum's foundations were being dug in 1976 that the right-hand column was discovered (Figure 12). The left-hand one, on the presumption of a pair, is still lost and could be anywhere, still under the ground undiscovered or relocated as part of the foundation of some farmer's house. As you entered the building you could read the right-hand column's face *b* (in front as you approached) and then its face *a* (to right as you passed inside). Those two faces contain 126 named individuals who organized or funded that edifice's construction. The building itself has not been discovered, and its function is not totally clear, but then not even a quarter of the city has been excavated. It might, possibly, have been a charitable soup kitchen for the poor or, more probably, the actual Jewish synagogue of Aphrodisias. Our present concern, in any case, is with those 126 donors and supporters on faces *a* and *b* of that recovered 6-foot-plus honorific column.

Here are the statistics. Face *a* lists 19 names as members of the "decany," or leadership, of the project.

Of those, 14 are Jewish names, 3 are called proselytes, and 2 are called God-worshipers (*theosebeis*). Those latter 5 are interspersed among the former 14 with the God-worshipers set together, but the proselytes separated. Face *b* has a top list of 55 names divided clearly and spatially from a bottom list of 52 names (Figure 13). The former are Jewish, the latter pagan. And, most significantly, they are prefaced with the phrase "and such as are God-worshipers" (*kai hosoi theosebeis*). This is the longest Jewish inscription from antiquity and indicates close cooperation between Jews (proselytes included) and pagan sympathizers. Here, more clearly and certainly than anywhere else, are those enigmatic "God-worshipers" from Luke's Acts of the Apostles carved in stone.

Think about those statistics for a moment. We did not know before 1966 that there were any Jews or any Jewish buildings in Aphrodisias. We now know of 126 donors to one such building in these proportions: 69 individuals, or 55 percent, Jews; 3 individuals, or 2 percent, proselytes; and 54 individuals, or 43 percent, God-worshipers. Those are rather extraordinary proportions, and even though generalizing from this one random discovery is surely precarious, how can you not? Was Aphrodisias an absolute exception or a standard example for the numerical proportions of Jew and God-fearer in part or all of the Roman Empire's cities?

Some footnotes. That column is the clearest archaeological and inscriptional evidence we have for the existence of those God-worshipers as pagan sympathizers who were neither Jews nor converts. But it dates from the early third century. We will, however, see further archaeological and inscriptional evidence for their presence from as early as 16 C.E. and throughout the first and second centuries in Chapter 4.

Only one woman is mentioned among those 126 names, but she is the first one cited in the decany leadership on face *a*, lines 9–10. She is called Jael, after the Jewish heroine in Judges 4:17–22 and 5:24–27. She is described as a *prostatēs,* which means a protector or patron when found in such Jewish inscriptions. She was, as Paul Trebilco concluded in his book *Jewish Communities in Asia Minor,* "a prominent leader of the Jewish community at Aphrodisias. She was either a patron of the community and represented their interests to the wider society or the president or leader who directed community affairs" (110). Indeed, as he notes, that fits well with other evidence about women in that general area. Women, whether as pagan priestesses, Jewish leaders, or female God-worshipers, were high-profile religious leaders in Asia Minor, just as they would be important apostles later for Paul.

The first 9 names in face *b*'s list of 52 God-worshipers are noted as members of the *boulē,* the council or governing body of the city. That 17 percent is another very high and striking proportion of important to ordinary people among that group.

The names are generally followed by a family appellation and/or commercial activity. For 27 individuals trades are designated, and of those 10 are Jews and 17 are God-worshipers. In general, the occupations of the God-fearers seem somewhat better than those of the Jews but, apart from those city councilors, they are all quite ordinary. The major categories are production and sale of goods: food, textiles, leather, wood, stone, construction, and other miscellaneous trades. Among the Jews are a secondhand clothes dealer, a grocer, and a goldsmith. Among the God-fearers are an athlete, a sculptor, and a purple-dyer.

One final question. Why were some pagans attracted enough to Judaism to become "God-fearers" or "God-worshipers"—semi-Jews by whatever name one chooses to call them? Apart from social, political, economic, or personal reasons, there was one very special religious factor. Greek and then Roman thinkers appreciated and admired Jewish *aniconic monotheism,* that is, the belief that there was but one transcendent and un–image-able divinity.

Marcus Terentius Varro is described in Menahem Stern's *Greek and Latin Authors on Jews and Judaism* as "the greatest scholar of republican Rome and the forerunner of the Augustan religious restoration" (1.207). Varro's *Res Divinae* was written between 63 and 47 B.C.E., but this citation is preserved only in St. Augustine's *City of God:*

> [Varro] also says that for more than one hundred and seventy years the ancient Romans worshiped the gods without an image. "If this usage had continued to our own days," he says, "our worship of the gods would be more devout." And in support of this opinion he adduces, among other things, the testimony of the Jewish race. And he ends with the forthright statement that those who first set up images of the gods for the people diminished reverence in their cities as they added to error, for he wisely judged that gods in the shape of senseless images might easily inspire contempt. (4.31)

Similar praise appears in Strabo of Amaseia in Pontus, who lived between 64 B.C.E. and 21 C.E. In his *Geography,* written under the emperors Augustus and Tiberius, he says,

Moses . . . one of the Egyptian priests . . . went away from there to Judaea, since he was displeased with the state of affairs there, and was accompanied by many people who worshiped the Divine Being. For he said, and taught, that the Egyptians were mistaken in representing the Divine Being by the images of beasts and cattle, as were also the Libyans; and that the Greeks were also wrong in modelling gods in human form; for, according to him, God is the one thing alone that encompasses us all and encompasses land and sea—the thing which we call heaven, or universe, or the nature of all that exists. What man, then, if he has sense, could be bold enough to fabricate an image of God resembling any creature amongst us? Nay, people should leave off all image-carving, and, setting apart a sacred precinct and a worthy sanctuary, should worship God without an image. (16.2.35)

No doubt there were many other reasons ranging from social supports to moral ideals that attracted pagans to Jewish customs and traditions. But aniconic monotheism must be given full emphasis as that which most deeply attracted some and, of course, most deeply repelled others.

COUNTERFACTUALS. At the start of this book we look at those two column faces with their harmonious integration of Jews and God-worshipers and ask two questions. They are not hypothetical questions about what might transpire in the future, but counterfactual questions about what did not transpire in the past. Each is a "what if" that never was. This exercise in virtual history is intended not as academic play, but as mental therapy. Since we know what happened in the past, it is easy to think that it was necessary, that it was fated, that it was providential, that it was inevitable. But what if, for example, Cleopatra and Antony had defeated Octavian and Agrippa at the battle of Actium? What then, what there? Such counterfactual questions and the virtual history derived from them remind us of the contingencies, decisions, and accidents that are always involved in what actually happened. It could always have been otherwise.

Our first counterfactual question is this: *What if Judaism rather than Christianity had become the religion of Rome? What if the Roman Empire had become Jewish rather than Christian?* An immediate answer might be, How absolutely ridiculous! How can you even suggest a Jewish Roman Empire in the face of so much anti-Jewish criticism and contempt, accusation and rejection, libel and slander in Greco-Roman life and literature? But that is precisely why we have asked it, and we now add to it a second question. *Do those re-peated attacks indicate that Judaism was a joke or a threat, a widely rejected impossi-bility or a broadly attractive possibility? Did Greco-Roman anti-Semitism indicate Judaism's too obvious failure or Judaism's too great success?*

Note, for example, the oscillation between approval and disapproval when Greeks and Romans discussed Jews and Judaism. A few decades ago, Menahem Stern's three-volume *Greek and Latin Authors on Jews and Judaism* published all the extant texts with translations and commentaries. It is quite fascinating and very instructive, especially in the light of our two questions, to read straight through his entire collection from beginning to end. Louis Feldman, in his book from which we took an epigraph at the start of this chapter, gave these general statistics on Stern's collection: "In volume 1, from Herodotus in the fifth century B.C.E. through Plutarch in the first cen-tury C.E., 47 notices are favorable (16 percent), 69 are unfavorable (24 per-cent), and 165 are neutral (60 percent). In volume 2, covering the period from the second through the sixth century, 54 are favorable (20 percent), 61 are unfavorable (21 percent), and 174 are neutral (59 percent)" (498, n. 4). The third volume, by the way, consists of appendixes and indexes. In other words, cumulatively, "According to my count, 101 (18 percent) of the com-ments by pagans in Stern's collection are substantially favorable, 339 (59 per-cent) are more or less neutral, and only 130 (23 percent) are substantially unfavorable" (124).

It is precisely those relatively balanced statistics that warrant at least asking our two questions. *Was there a serious chance for a Jewish Roman Empire? And was it that chance that bred both approval and disapproval among pagans?* It is nec-essary, therefore, to hold this first chapter's opening section constantly in mind until we return to it in the final chapter's opening section. As we think about Paul among Jews, with Greeks, and under Romans in that first-century's imperial globalization, we will not argue directly for a positive or negative response to those two counterfactual questions. Instead, we use them as silent but permanent undertones throughout this book in order to monitor our answers, to observe the presuppositions they reveal, and to assess the principles they presume.

A Tale of Two Pauls

As far as we know, Paul never visited Aphrodisias, but we began there to em-phasize in one place the two most basic elements in this book's understanding of his vision and program, namely, Roman imperial theology in the Greek cities and pagan God-worshipers in the Jewish synagogues. We turn now from archaeology to exegesis, but not yet to Paul's own letters. We look first, within the New Testament, at the Acts of the Apostles to see how its author connects Paul with both urban Roman authorities and synagogal pagan God-worshipers.

The problem is not that Luke lacked Pauline sources and simply made up an apostolic novel. Many of the places mentioned in Paul's letters line up alongside those cited in Luke's Acts. Even a cursory survey shows that Paul wrote to the Galatians, Philippians, Corinthians, Thessalonians, and Romans and that Luke's Acts locates him in Galatia (13:14–14:24; 16:1–6), Philippi (16:12–40), Thessalonica (17:1–9), Corinth (18:1–17), and Rome (28:15–31). And, even if he did not write to the Ephesians, Luke has him at Ephesus (19:1–20). Notice, however, that Luke never mentions Paul's letters. But, in any case, the geographical terrain and maybe even the sequence of its places are basically the same for the Pauline Paul and the Lukan Paul.

Luke's problem is not that he lacks sources on Paul. He has excellent sources, but although he knows many correct details, accurate places, and even travel sequences, he also seems to care very little about the purposes, intentions, and meanings that Paul himself emphasizes in his own letters. That puts the problem negatively. Put positively, it is this: Luke's Acts was written in the 80s or 90s, several decades after Paul's time, and Luke gives him an overall interpretation from within his own geographical situation, historical understanding, and theological vision. In the Acts of the Apostles, Paul becomes a Christian not of his own time and place, but of Luke's. Here are four examples that will have ramifications throughout the book. They concern Christians, pagans, Jews, and Romans, that is, just about everyone in Luke's world.

Pauline Subordination

Luke describes a consistently harmonious agreement between Paul and authoritative figures like James or Peter. All of them, for example, are in perfect accord over Paul's pagan mission at their Jerusalem and Antioch meetings in Luke's Acts 15, despite far more discord than accord and disagreement than agreement as Paul tells the same story in Galatians 1–2. Luke describes Paul as a missionary sent from Jerusalem through Antioch, and he cannot imagine that Paul could seriously clash with those to whom he was subordinate. But, in all his letters, Paul sees himself as an apostle sent from God through Christ. The very vocation for which Paul lives and dies is denied him by Luke. He is, to be sure, an important missionary sent out from and living in complete accord with Jerusalem. But he is not an apostle equal with the Twelve.

Luke insists in Acts 1 that, after Jesus's resurrection, there were still, always, and only "the twelve apostles." Further, they were all male since the replacement for Judas had to be chosen from among "the *men* who have accompanied us during all the time that the Lord Jesus went in and out among us, beginning from the baptism of John until the day when he was taken up from us," and so Matthias "was added to the eleven apostles" (1:21–22, 26). For Luke, Paul is simply not an apostle. Without Matthias's explicit selection, one might have imagined that Luke's Paul was at least implicitly Judas's replacement as the twelfth apostle. With it, Luke implies that Paul was not an apostle and could never be one. He had never been with the earthly Jesus and had not been selected by God through lots cast in community. He could be and was, for Luke, a vitally important missionary through whom the Holy Spirit moved headquarters from Jerusalem to Rome, but he could never be the one thing Paul always insisted that he was, namely, an apostle sent by God through a revelation of the risen Lord. He could be a missionary sent by Jerusalem through Antioch, but not an apostle sent by God through Jesus. At stake is not just name but status, not just title but authority.

Notice how Paul, in contrast to Luke, identifies himself in the formal openings of those letters in which his authority may be in question, and especially in the letter to the Galatians, where it was under frontal assault:

- Paul an apostle—sent neither by human commission nor from human authorities, but through Jesus Christ and God the Father, who raised him from the dead (Gal. 1:1)
- Paul, called to be an apostle of Christ Jesus by the will of God (1 Cor. 1:1)
- Paul, an apostle of Christ Jesus by the will of God (2 Cor. 1:1)
- Paul, a servant of Jesus Christ, called to be an apostle, set apart for the gospel of God (Rom. 1:1)

There is an even more explicit emphasis in 1 Corinthians 15:5, 7, where Paul distinguishes Peter and "the Twelve" from James and "all the apostles." He then insists in 1 Corinthians 15:8–10 that he is one of the latter, since the risen Lord appeared not only to them, but also, "last of all, as to one untimely born, he appeared also to me. For I am the least of the apostles, unfit to be called an apostle, because I persecuted the church of God. But by the grace of God I am what I am, and his grace toward me has not been in vain. On the contrary, I worked harder than any of them—though it was not I, but the grace of God that is with me."

In other words Paul does not think that "the twelve *apostles*" exist as a closed group. Instead, there is the closed and highly symbolic group "the Twelve" and then there are also "all the apostles" including himself and, as we shall see later, others, including women. Apostolicity derives from revelation and vocation by the risen Lord and not by presence with the earthly Jesus. Luke's interpretation took from Paul what was most precious to his understanding, most vital to his independence, and most important to his authority. But Luke muted thereby the actuality of severe disagreement between Paul and other leading Christians.

Pagan Greed

All is peaceful and harmonious, then, in Luke's Acts among Christian communities and between Christian leaders. Any problems, disputes, or even riots are the fault not of Christians, but of pagans or Jews. And that fault furnishes the second and third major themes that run throughout Luke's Acts.

Riots about Christianity are caused by pagan greed judging it bad for normal business. At Philippi there was "a slave girl who had a spirit of divination and brought her owners a great deal of money by fortune-telling." Paul exorcised her, and "when her owners saw that their hope of making money was gone, they seized Paul and Silas and dragged them into the marketplace before the authorities." The disturbance spread as "the crowd joined in attacking them" (16:16–22). Later, at Ephesus, there was an even greater disturbance by the silversmiths who made images of Artemis/Diana lest "this trade of ours may come into disrepute" (19:23–29), with Pauline converts ignoring or despising their city's famous temple.

In other words, Paul and Christianity were bad for pagan business. And that, of course, is not exactly false. It was also mentioned as a socioreligious problem around 112 C.E. when Pliny the Younger, the emergency governor of Bithynia-Pontus on the Black Sea's southern coast, reported back to the emperor Trajan. In his *Letters* he says that he had moved against Christianity, "for this contagious superstition is not confined to the cities only but has spread through the villages and rural districts." But he is curing the problem, he reports, so that temples are again frequented, festivals again celebrated, and "there is a general demand for sacrificial animals, which for some time past have met with but few purchasers" (10.96).

Jewish Jealousy

A third Lukan theme is that riots about Christians are also caused by Jews. Luke's dominant emphasis in Acts is that because pagans accepted Christianity after the Jews refused it, Jews opposed gentile conversions out of "jealousy." But first, on "the Jews" in general, here is an example of how Lukan fiction must be distinguished from Pauline fact even about the same incident. Both Paul and Luke record his somewhat ignominious departure from Damascus.

Paul's Version (2 Cor. 11:32–33)	*Luke's Version (Acts 9:23–25)*
In Damascus, the governor under King Aretas guarded the city of Damascus in order to seize me, but I was let down in a basket through a window in the wall, and escaped from his hands.	After some time had passed, the Jews plotted to kill him, but their plot became known to Saul. They were watching the gates day and night so that they might kill him; but his disciples took him by night and let him down through an opening in the wall, lowering him in a basket.

The striking similarity between the two accounts certifies that Luke knows precise Pauline details, but there is also a significant difference. In Paul's version the danger arose when the Nabatean ruler Aretas IV held the city between 37 and 39 C.E., and that, by the way, furnishes the only Paul-derived date for his biography. In Luke it arose from the Jews, no date is therefore possible, and such a scenario is all but impossible in an Arab-controlled city. Furthermore, if Luke knows the fact but changes or creates the enemy, we will have to watch very carefully what he says elsewhere about "the Jews" in opposition to Paul. For example, was there lethal or only nonlethal opposition from other Jews to Paul, and in either case what exactly was the reason for any such opposition? Luke can, for example, explain their refusal to believe Christianity as simple human "jealousy" over pagan acceptance. In

Acts 13:45, "when the Jews saw the crowds, they were filled with jealousy; and blaspheming, they contradicted what was spoken by Paul." And in Acts 17:5, "the Jews became jealous and with the help of some ruffians in the marketplaces they formed a mob and set the city in an uproar." Furthermore, Luke even goes back to the Old Testament for a prophetic model: "The patriarchs, jealous of Joseph, sold him into Egypt; but God was with him" (Acts 7:9).

One footnote in preparation for the next section. Notice the blur at the heart of Luke's claim that Paul always goes first to preach to his fellow Jews in the synagogues on the Sabbath. Does he then turn to pagans because those fellow Jews reject him or do they reject him because he has turned to pagans? Is Jewish rejection cause or effect of pagan conversion? That is never clear in Luke because, as we shall argue below, Paul did not preach first to full Jews or to pure pagans, but to an in-between group of semi-Jewish, semipagan synagogue associates, sympathizers, the so-called God-fearers or God-worshipers. In summary, with that Damascus case as a paradigmatic warning, be careful to distinguish between Luke's *information* about Paul and Luke's *interpretation* of Paul, and be very careful to discern where Luke's *interpretation* becomes Luke's *information* about Paul.

Roman Reaction

A final major theme in Luke's Acts is Roman reaction to Paul. Every Roman or Romanizing authority that Paul encounters declares him formally and explicitly to be innocent. In the theater in Ephesus, the town clerk declared that Paul's companions were "neither temple robbers nor blasphemers of our goddess" Diana and so "he dismissed the assembly" (19:37, 41). Claudius Lysias, the tribune at Jerusalem, wrote to the governor, Felix, at Caesarea that Paul "was accused concerning questions of their [Jewish] law, but was charged with nothing deserving death or imprisonment" (23:29). Two years later, the new governor, Festus, told Paul's case to the Jewish king Agrippa II and his sister Bernice and commented that "they did not charge him with any of the crimes that I was expecting" and "that he had done nothing deserving death" (25:18, 25). After Paul's speech, all three agree, "This man is doing nothing to deserve death or imprisonment" (26:31).

Finally, Luke ends not with Paul's trial or execution, but with this sentence: "He lived there two whole years at his own expense and welcomed all who came to him, proclaiming the kingdom of God and teaching about the Lord Jesus Christ with all boldness and without hindrance" (28:30–31). There you have it, concludes Luke with a Roman audience in mind; we Christians are completely innocent. All troubles come from pagan greed or Jewish jealousy. And the first Jewish war against Rome in 66–70 C.E. should not be held against Christians. To allow Christianity "without hindrance" should be Roman policy. Jesus, Paul, and Christianity are encased by Luke in apologetic garments. It was quite possible, however, as the Roman authorities knew full well, to be an ideological danger without ever being a violent threat.

As we have just seen, Roman officials repeatedly declare Paul innocent of any crime against Rome, but Paul can only be repeatedly declared innocent by being repeatedly accused before those same officials. In other words, Luke both reveals and conceals, admits and denies, that there were constant troubles between Paul and Rome. Take, then, as example and summary, the case of Paul before the proconsul Gallio at Corinth in Acts 18:12–17, which, whether literal fact or metaphorical fiction, is the perfect example of Luke's defense of Christianity in general and of Paul in particular. Look, therefore, at that judicial *bēma,* or tribunal, in Corinth (Figure 14) and see it as the symbolic heart of Lukan rapprochement between Christ and Caesar, between the Christian church and the Roman Empire.

FIGURE 14. *Bēma,* or judicial platform, at Corinth, where Acts of the Apostles says Paul was on trial before the Roman proconsul Gallio.

We are certain Paul was in Corinth, and, in fact, more than once. We are certain Gallio was in Corinth for the summer and early fall of either 51 or 52 C.E. But what about these Lukan claims that Paul was at Corinth in 51–52 C.E.; that he was accused before Gallio's tribunal (*bēma*) by "the Jews"; that the proconsul declared, "Since it is a matter of questions about words and names and your own law, see to it yourselves; I do not wish to be a judge of these matters" and that "he dismissed them from the tribunal"; and that "all of them seized Sosthenes, the official of the synagogue, and beat him in front of the tribunal. But Gallio paid no attention to any of these things." All of that is much more likely Lukan parable than Pauline history. It is, indeed, Luke's first and most paradigmatic combination of Jewish accusation, Pauline innocence, and Roman dismissal. Look, therefore, at our picture of Corinth's *bēma* and see it as a Lukan metaphor for the proper attitude of Rome toward Christianity in general and as a Lukan symbol of the appropriate response of Rome to Paul in particular. Nothing, however, in this book presumes the historical actuality of that encounter with Gallio at Corinth or builds the chronological biography of Paul upon its information.

The Importance of Pagan Sympathizers

When you speak about those *by whom* Paul was sent, Luke and Paul disagree profoundly, as we just saw above. Sent by Jerusalem through Antioch, says Luke. Sent by God through Christ, says Paul. But if you speak of those *to whom* Paul was sent, Luke both obscures and reveals what actually happened.

Luke obscures the *to whom* of Paul's actual mission, because he makes his own theological principle of "first Jews, then pagans" into a historical pattern for Paul. Luke announces this principle in the book of Acts: "It was necessary that the word of God should be spoken first to you [Jews]. Since you reject it and judge yourselves to be unworthy of eternal life, we are now turning to the Gentiles" (13:46). Then, in city after city Luke sends Paul into the synagogue to preach Jesus on the Sabbath to his fellow Jews. That happens at Pisidian Antioch in 13:14, Iconium in 14:1, Thessalonica in 17:1, Beroea in 17:10, Athens in 17:17, Corinth in 18:4, and Ephesus in 18:19 and 19:8. But that raises two intractable problems.

First, Paul himself always insisted that he was called by God as an apostle to the *pagans*: "God . . . was pleased to reveal his Son to me, so that I might proclaim him among the Gentiles" (Gal. 1:15–16). So why, as Luke claimed, was he preaching to fellow Jews against that divine vocation? Second, at Jerusalem Paul had accepted a separation of missionary focus: God "who worked through Peter making him an apostle to the circumcised also worked through me in sending me to the Gentiles," so that all agreed "we should go to the Gentiles and they to the circumcised" (Gal. 2:8–9). So why, as Luke claimed, was he preaching to fellow Jews in the synagogue against that formal agreement?

The answer must be that Paul was doing no such thing. We do not accept that Paul always went first to the synagogue and tried to convert Jews to Jesus as the Messiah. But we do accept something Acts tells us in that very same context, because it is neither derived from nor congruent with Luke's own Jew/Gentile dichotomy. And, as you read the texts that follow, from Philo, Josephus, and Luke, keep constantly in mind those Aphrodisian God-worshipers whose names we now have carved on stone.

Synagogue Situations

The synagogue was a publicly visible place serving as the religious, political, legal, social, and economic center of Jewish life in the pagan cities of the diaspora. Speaking of the theological benefits of such interaction, the first-century Jewish philosopher Philo in *The Special Laws* notes,

> On the seventh day there are spread before the people in every city innumerable lessons of prudence, and temperance, and courage, and justice, and all other virtues. . . . And there are, as we may say, two most especially important heads of all the innumerable particular lessons and doctrines; the regulating of one's conduct toward God by the rules of piety and holiness, and of one's conduct toward men by the rules of humanity and justice; each of which is subdivided into a great number of subordinate ideas, all praiseworthy. (2.15.62–63)

Speaking of the economic benefits, the first-century Jewish historian Josephus in *Jewish Antiquities* says, "No one need wonder that there was so much wealth in our temple, for all the Jews throughout the habitable world, and worshipers of God, even those from Asia and Europe, had been contributing to it for a very long time" (14.110). And, in his *Jewish War*, he also exemplifies that interaction in Syrian Antioch by mentioning how the Jews "were constantly attracting to their religious ceremonies multitudes of Greeks, and these they had in some measure incorporated with themselves"

(7.45). Carry over to the next section two items from those Josephan quotations. In the first one that term "worshipers" uses the Greek verb *sebomai,* and in the second one "in some measure incorporated" refers to something in between nonconversion and full conversion.

Devout Greeks

Throughout Acts, Luke not only speaks of "Jews" and "pagan Gentiles," but also of a third group, an in-between group who are both/and rather than either/or. He calls those ambiguous individuals or groups "those fearing God" or "God-fearers" four times in Acts (10:2, 22, 35; 13:16; with the Greek verb *phobeō*). He also calls them "those worshiping" or "worshipers" four times (13:43, 50; 17:4, 17), and, more fully, "those worshiping God" or "God-worshipers" twice (16:14; 18:17; with the Greek verb *sebomai*). They are clearly distinguished from Jews, for example, in these phrases: "Israelites, and others who fear God" (13:16), "Jews and devout converts" (13:43), "Jews incited the devout women" (13:50), "Jews . . . devout Greeks (17:1, 4), or "Jews and the devout persons" (17:17). And, just as consistently as Luke has Paul in synagogues speaking to fellow Jews, he also has those "God-fearers" or "God-worshipers" in the audience. Indeed, even without either of those terms being used, Luke must have considered as an in-between Jew/pagan that "Ethiopian eunuch, a court official of the Candace, queen of the Ethiopians, in charge of her entire treasury," who, according to Acts 8:27, "had come to Jerusalem to worship" (with the Greek verb *proskyneō*). By whatever name they are called, who are those devout pro-Jewish pagan sympathizers?

Those various terms designate that third path between Judaism and paganism seen at Aphrodisias, that intermediate way in which people retained the culture of paganism but accepted the faith of Judaism, a middle option for those who believed in Jewish monotheism and its moral law, but did not submit to all of its ritual law or socioreligious markers. They are emphatically not "converts," even though the Greek of Acts 13:43 uses the combination "devout converts" and the English translation adds "to Judaism."

If you think of a Jewish diaspora community as an island of Judaism in a sea of sometimes inimical paganism, you can understand how important such a buffer zone of sympathizers would be. They would offer not only economic assistance but also political protection. Think, in other words, of three concentric rings: an inner ring of Jews, whether born Jewish or converted; an intermediate ring of pagan sympathizers, whether ordinary or wealthy; and an outer ring of pagans, whether friendly or unfriendly. That mention of wealthy sympathizers raises the third and final point.

Leading Women

Luke's Acts often notes that the sympathizers were of high standing in their communities and that they involved both women and men. At Pisidian Antioch, near today's Yalvaç between the mountains and lakes in mid-western Turkey, "the Jews incited the devout women of high standing and the leading men of the city, and stirred up persecution against Paul and Barnabas, and drove them out of their region" (13:50). At Philippi in north-eastern Greece, having crossed the northern Aegean Sea into Europe for the first time, Paul met "a certain woman named Lydia, a worshiper of God, [who] was listening to us; she was from the city of Thyatira and a dealer in purple cloth. The Lord opened her heart to listen eagerly to what was said by Paul" (16:14). Southwest from Philippi at Thessalonica, today's Thessaloniki, Greece's second-largest city, at the head of the Thermaic Gulf, "some of them [the Jews] were persuaded and joined Paul and Silas, as did a great many of the devout Greeks and not a few of the leading women" (17:4). Finally, again to the southwest, at Beroea, today's Veroia at the edge of the Thessalonikan plain, "many of them therefore believed, including not a few Greek women and men of high standing" (17:12).

That term "devout" is always literally "worshiping ones" or "worshipers," from the Greek verb *sebomai,* and means that in-between group of God-fearers, God-worshipers, or Jewish sympathizers, that intermediate class who were neither full Jews nor pure pagans. Male reluctance to consider circumcision because of physical pain, medical infection, and social discrimination did not apply to women, and it would not be surprising to find more women than men among those sympathizers. Also, it was especially wealthy sympathizers who furnished political protection as well as economic assistance for any threatened Jewish minority within those pagan cities.

Here are two examples of such female pagan sympathizers from inscriptional evidence. First, in the 50s or 60s C.E., Julia Severa, a member of a leading aristocratic family with a son in the Senate at Rome, was a pagan priestess of the imperial cult at Acmonia, an important Phrygian city on the ancient east-west road across Asia Minor. A synagogue inscription from the 80s or 90s proclaimed, "This building was erected by Julia Severa." There is no mention of "(God-) worshiper" and she may or may not have been considered one by the Jewish community. But that gift made her a powerful patroness. Second, a third-century-C.E. inscription from the synagogue at Tralles in Caria, today's Aydin, on the northern side of the Meander Valley east of Ephesus, announced, "I, Capitolina, worthy and God-worshiper [*theosebēs*], have made all the platform and the inlaying of the stairs in fulfillment of a vow for myself and my children and my grandchildren. Blessings." Claudia Capitolina was from an aristocratic pagan family as important or maybe even more important than that of Julia Severa, and she is explicitly called a God-worshiper. Of all the Jewish practices that pagan sympathizers adopted, synagogue support and attendance were probably the most theologically acceptable, economically helpful, politically important, and socially evident.

Paul, then, did not go to those diaspora synagogues to convert fellow Jews within them, but to convert those semi-Jews around them. His focus was on those pagan *sympathizers* and, of course, he could only or most easily discover them at the synagogue. He was not failing with full Jews; he was succeeding with half-Jews. Of course there must also have been some full Jews and certainly many pure pagans who became part of Pauline communities, but their core was those sympathizers.

Paul, Luke, and the God-worshipers

Paul, it must be emphasized, never mentions a word about any such God-fearers or God-worshipers. Unlike Luke, he would have considered them worse than pagans because they were lost between worlds. For him God-worshipers were not pagans-plus, but pagans-minus. He would not have accepted a form of semi-Judaism and semipaganism. He understood faith and unfaith, but would never have understood semifaith. As he told the Romans, "Whatever does not proceed from faith is sin" (14:23).

Major Hypothesis

We propose, then, two working hypotheses for this book that will fundamentally explain Paul, Luke, and Luke on Paul. The first and *major* hypothesis is that Paul's pagan or gentile mission focused primarily not on full Jews or pure pagans, but on those in-betweens known as God-fearers, God-worshipers, or, more simply, sympathizers (enemies might use some equivalent nasty terms like hangers-on or fellow travelers). And that explains three basic aspects of Paul's life.

PAUL'S LETTERS. Pick up any letter of Paul's and read a passage at random. How could a pure pagan or a community of pure pagans understand what on earth he was talking about? Even granting prior oral instruction and conversion to Christ, how could they understand those intensively Jewish arguments, those extensively Jewish concerns? But sympathizers, on the other hand, knew quite a bit about the Jewish religion's traditional faith, scriptural basis, and ritual requirements. With a core of sympathizers in his communities, Paul already had with him those who were neither Jew nor Greek or, better, both Jew and Greek at the same time.

What Peter Lampe, in "The Roman Christians of Romans 16," says of the Roman Christians to whom Paul wrote his longest letter is true not only for them, but for the recipients of his other letters as well: "Several times in Romans Paul presumes that the vast majority in the Roman church is Gentile. These clear and direct statements seem to contradict the impression that much of the contents of Romans could be understood only by people who were trained in Jewish culture. The solution of the paradox is at hand if we assume that most people in the Roman church were of Gentile origin but had lived as sympathizers on the margins of the synagogues before they became Christian" (1991: 225). We consider that what he says of Roman Christianity was true elsewhere as well.

> Gentile Christians would have been recruited from the ranks of the *sebomenoi* [God-worshipers], who, on the fringes of the synagogues revered the God of Israel as pagan sympathizers of Jewish monotheism. These folk were the main target of the earliest Gentile Christian mission. . . . The fact that everywhere in the Roman Empire uncircumcised pagans—some more, some less observant of the Jewish Law—worshiped the Jewish God in coexistence with Law-abiding synagogues was a situation that probably encouraged the Law-free Gentile Christian mission significantly. (2003: 69–70)

PAUL'S OPPONENTS. Again, if Paul was simply converting pure pagans to Christianity, even to Christian Judaism, why would Jews care? They could ignore or even deride him. Imagine Paul preaching exclusively or even primarily at Corinth to the pagan longshoremen who hauled ships and carried cargo across the isthmus from the northwestern harbor of Lechaion on the Corinthian Gulf to the southeastern harbor of Cenchreae on the Saronic Gulf. If that were his focus, why, on the one hand, would pure pagans care about their "freedom" from Jewish law or, on the other, why would full Jews care about Paul's activities down there at the docks? But if his focus was on converting a synagogue's sympathizers to Christianity, with the result of stripping from Jews their intermediary buffer of support and protection, that would be socially explosive.

Focusing on sympathizers would not only provoke full Jews against him; it would also annoy pure pagans. Pagans might have disliked the idea of pagan sympathizers with Judaism, but they would have disliked even more the idea of pagan converts to Christianity. Judaism as "superstitious atheistic misanthropy" with an ancient country was bad enough, but Christianity as "superstitious atheistic misanthropy" without any country was surely worse. No wonder, therefore, that Paul was attacked on *both* sides, by both Jews and pagans, and that, as he himself admits, he was officially punished by both Jewish and pagan authorities: "Five times I have received from the Jews the forty lashes minus one. Three times I was beaten [by the Romans] with rods . . . [in] danger from my own people, [in] danger from Gentiles" (2 Cor. 11:24–26).

PAUL'S CONVERTS. The emphasis on God-worshipers as Paul's primary converts makes it unnecessary to postulate opponents following Paul from Galatia to Macedonia as a Christian-Jewish countermovement. In any given city, God-worshipers converted to Christianity would be told correctly by both other God-fearers and Jewish friends that it was theologically wiser and socially safer to convert fully, if such were their wish, but to Judaism rather than to Christianity. It was far better, God-worshiping males would have been told, to be full Jews than full Christians. As Jews they would be recognized, accepted, and protected by Rome, but as Christians they were followers of a leader executed by those same Romans. It is not necessary to have Paul followed by a countermission. His God-worshiping converts would have been inevitably pulled by their newer Pauline community in one direction and by their older synagogal contacts in another.

Minor Hypothesis

The second and *minor* working hypothesis concerns Luke and how to read Luke's Acts on Paul. Luke's emphasis on that sympathizer class may well explain why he himself was at the same time so familiar with Judaism, and yet opposed to it, as well as so conversant with Romanism, and yet reconciled with it. He was, most likely, originally a God-worshiper himself, and that is why he spends almost equal time insisting that Christianity is, on the one hand, the only valid heir and continuation of Judaism and, on the other, in no way a threat to Roman law and order. Luke and his family were typical wealthy sympathizers ripe for conversion from semi-Judaism to full Christianity.

There was actually a hint of Luke's sympathizer identity in the first book of his two-volume gospel. The story of the Capernaum official whose son or servant is healed by Jesus at a distance is told in John 4:46–53, Matthew 8:5–13, and Luke 7:1–10. That official comes himself to ask Jesus directly in both John and Matthew, but Luke, and Luke alone, has the request given indirectly: "When he heard about Jesus, he sent some Jewish elders to him, asking him to come and heal his slave. When they came to Jesus, they appealed to him earnestly, saying, 'He is worthy of having you do this for him, for he loves our people, and it is he who built our synagogue for us'" (7:3–5). That mode of intervention, awkward as it is for the story's flow, allows Luke to state explicitly that the centurion was a pagan (implicit at most in the other versions) who was very supportive of Judaism (completely absent in the other versions).

That theme of the pious centurion is continued in Acts 10–11, where the story of Cornelius establishes the theory and starts the program of the gentile mission. "In Caesarea there was a man named Cornelius, a centurion of the Italian Cohort, as it was called. He was a devout man who feared God with all his household; he gave alms generously to the people and prayed constantly to God" (10:1–2). Later, he is described as "Cornelius, a centurion, an upright and God-fearing man, who is well spoken of by the whole Jewish nation" (10:22). Those centurions, one in each volume of Luke's gospel, are the perfect examples of "God-fearers" or "God-worshipers" for Luke. And, of course, Cornelius is one more example of Roman officialdom finding Christianity not only innocent of crime, but acceptable for conversion. They are the ideal or typical sympathizers. They are, says Luke, somebody just like me.

The Hub of the Aegean World

We began with Aphrodisias because, even though Paul never visited that Carian city, its Roman imperial Sebasteion and Jewish synagogal inscriptions are crucial for our understanding of Paul's theological world. We continue with another ancient site, but now a Greek rather than a Turkish one. Once again, Paul never visited it, but it is where you can best see a microcosm of his entire social world. It is the island of Delos at the heart of the Cyclades in the center of the Aegean Sea (Figure 15). Paul sailed across the eastern Mediterranean and around the Aegean, but he never docked at Delos, just as he never walked through Aphrodisias. We focus on this tiny island because over a century of excavations have yielded a rich array of archaeological finds and epigraphic material that cast light on Paul's time and place. We start there because it illustrates clearly the complexities of that ancient Mediterranean world where politics, religion, and economics intertwined, and where Roman officials ruled pagan Greeks among whom lived diaspora Jews. We start at Delos because we can trace through its port a constant flow of peoples, materials, ideas, and religions from east to west and from west to east.

You come to Delos, as always, from the sea and amid the islands (Figure 16). It is early June of 2003, and there is a stiff northwesterner blowing hard in the wide reaches from Naxos northward to Delos, but it calms considerably as you enter the turquoise blue waters of the narrow passage between the tiny island of Delos and the small island of Rinia. You departed that

FIGURE 15. Map of the Aegean showing the location of Delos in the Cycladic Islands.

morning from Naxos, the largest island in the Cyclades, where Theseus un-gratefully abandoned Ariadne and Dionysos gratefully married her. You are headed for Delos, the birthplace of Apollo, just over an hour's travel due north.

You are on a small tourist boat filled inside with backpacking students and elegantly dressed twenty-something couples, aboard not for Delos but for passage to the beaches and bars of Mikonos farther on. Up on the deck are a few middle-aged French tourists reading *Guide Bleus* and a few Swedish families whose children look over the stern at the splashing spray and flying spume. The members of the small crew sit in the cabin, flirt with the singles, or sleep outside on the benches. Since the wind had cleared the air and re-moved the haze, you are on deck to scan the sharpened horizons in all direc-tions. You can see a sweep of islands: to the southwest, Paros; to the west, Siros; to the north, Tinos; and to the northeast, Mikonos, the jet-setting party island that is the final destination for most of your fellow travelers. You glimpse the Cyclades all around you.

As you return that same evening, sunburned, tired, and thirsty from a day on a desolate island inhabited only by archaeologists and lizards, the wind has died down completely, the sea is serenely calm, and schools of jellyfish drift past on the long swells, while dolphins crisscross at high speed before the bow and, off in a distance, swirls of seagulls compete with fishing caiques for the day's catch. Paul probably never saw Naxos or Delos, but he knew small coasters on good days, large transports on bad days, and always that dark blue sea beneath the light blue sky.

Delos, a two-square-mile, mostly north-to-south, and nearly waterless island, might have been completely ignored, were it not the legendary birth-place of the god Apollo and his twin sister Artemis. Praised in a Homeric hymn, Delos came to house an important sanctuary whose oracle was sec-ond only to Delphi in classical times. For much of its history, control of the island alternated between indigenous Delians and colonial Athenians, but throughout the classical period the sanctuary of Apollo and the initially quadrennial Delian festival and games drew pilgrims from across the Greek islands and also from the mainland. The sacred island and its many temples amassed gifts and offerings from abroad, and, especially after Alexander the Great in the late fourth century B.C.E., Delos also attracted bankers and traders from Egypt, Phoenicia, Syria, Asia Minor, and increasingly southern Italy.

After Rome made its presence felt in the eastern Mediterranean during the second century B.C.E., it handed over the island to Athens but, more im-portant, made it a free port to enhance the business interests of merchant

FIGURE 16. Approach to the ancient harbor of Delos.

bankers from Italy, the so-called *negotiatores*. By supporting Delos, Rome also undermined the commercial dominance of its rival, the much larger island of Rhodes. And when Rome sacked Greek Corinth in 146 B.C.E., many of that city's Italian *negotiatores* fled to Delos, where they were met by merchants from across the East. Protected by Romans and governed by Athenians, Delos became the commercial hub of the Aegean.

The island was a microcosm of the Mediterranean world, and Roman expansionist policy combined with a major pagan sanctuary to make Delos something like an international trade fair. It was the center not only of the Cycladic Islands in the Aegean, but also a pivotal stop on the sea-lanes between Asia Minor and the Greek mainland, between Thrace to the north and Crete to the south, and between the Jewish homeland and Italy. The goods that went through its port included amphorae of Cnidian wine on their way to elite urban households, marble blocks quarried from the nearby island of Paros and destined for Rome's construction projects, exquisite marble statues from Eastern temples no longer standing, Egyptian grain on its way to feed plebian mouths in Rome's grain-dole safety net (safety, of course, for those in power).

Slaves were also bought and sold at Delos's market, slaves acquired through Roman civil wars and imperial expansions, and the ancient geographer Strabo claimed that Delos "could both admit and send away ten thousand slaves on the same day" (14.5.2). Its commercial importance and considerable wealth made it conspicuous, however, and Mithridates IV, king of Pontus and enemy of Rome, sacked the island in 88 B.C.E. while Rome was preoccupied with social wars at home and, according to some written sources, slaughtered twenty thousand of the island's inhabitants. The Roman general Sulla returned to the East with five legions, defeated Mithridates, pacified the area, and included a visit to restore the island of Delos. But it was subsequently raided by pirates in 69 B.C.E. and had to be recovered and again restored by the Romans, who this time walled much of the city. Delos never fully recovered its former luster, even after Augustus rid the seas of pirates, and the island's gradual decline and eventual abandonment left it not just as one more archaeological site, but as an entire and protected archaeological island.

Apollo at the Civic Center

Since 1873, the École Français d'Archéologie in Athens has conducted excavations on the island, unearthing swaths of ruins and amassing a treasure of inscriptions that enable a full and vivid picture of life on this once cosmopolitan island. Along the island's flat western shore and below the northern slope of Mt. Kynthos, archaeologists have discovered many of the city's religious temples, civic buildings, and mercantile facilities (Figure 17).

The sanctuary dedicated to Apollo, next to the harbor in the heart of the city, occupied a good portion of the civic center and has absorbed a great deal of the archaeological energy over the past century. As you move up from the harbor, you enter the sanctuary on a set of stairs worn down by centuries of pilgrimage, and you see three successive temples and their altars, each dedicated to Apollo: one from the sixth century B.C.E., another from the late fifth century B.C.E, and the largest constructed over two centuries and completed in the third century B.C.E. The popularity of the onetime sun god Apollo, later more known for his healing, prophetic, and musical prowess, attracted the attention of Hellenistic kings and city embassies, who competed with each other to renovate, enhance, and elaborate the sanctuary's architecture and ornamentation. The detail and precision of written inventories document the many and varied votive gifts to the sanctuary and underscore the overlap between civic and religious operations on Delos.

The archaeological context of the Delian temples reminds us that, unlike religion in the modern Western world, which tends to be monotheistic

FIGURE 17. Overview of the harbor and excavations at Delos, looking down from Mt. Kynthos.

and primarily concerned with personal beliefs, the pervasive paganism at the time of Paul was polytheistic and primarily concerned with civic cults. The gods and goddesses were not seen as so all-powerful or all-controlling that humans could not anticipate and participate in shaping their own fate. Through consulting the oracles, plying the arts of augury, or interpreting signs in the heavens, flights of birds, or animal livers, priests and experts anticipated a city's or a state's standing with the deities. They then participated in determining their fate by solidifying harmony (*concordia*) with the gods or creating peace with the gods (*pax deorum*) by appeasing them with gifts, vows, and animal sacrifices. Local calendars regulated a series of scheduled festivals that included offerings and sacrifices, but unpredictable events or spontaneous crises demanded added attention and immediate response.

Since a city or state's fate hung in the balance, the priests' primary activity was butchering animals: stunning the creature with a mallet, slitting its throat to spill the blood, cutting up the animal, then burning some for the gods and drizzling it with wine, while setting aside other pieces for themselves or for distribution or even sale to the local community. In some ways, sacrifice was a civic performance with procession, pomp, and song, but it was also a civic feast, an open-air barbecue that for many was a rare chance to eat meat. And it not only bonded community and deity, it also bonded community members together and articulated clearly their social hierarchy. In the vast majority of cases, the priesthood in civic temples was only open to male landowning aristocrats who either purchased priestly offices outright or were elected based on their contributions to civic projects.

Apollo's sanctuary was an integral part of civic life, and religion and politics were intimately interwoven with mutual concerns about the temples' ceremonies, treasuries, and priesthoods. It is not surprising that archaeologists uncovered key political structures inside Apollo's sacred complex: the *prytaneion,* which housed the city hearth's eternal flame and was also a reception and dining hall for visiting dignitaries; the theater-like *bouleuterion,* with semicircular tiered seating, where the *boulē,* or council of civic leaders, met; and the *ekklēsiasterion,* where the entire adult male citizenry joined in an assembly (an *ekklēsia*). That word *ekklēsia* for that somewhat democratic deliberative body of a Greek city is, by the way, the same word that Paul uses in his letters and that we translate as "church." Did Paul model his communities along the lines of the civic and urban *ekklēsia*? Or should we look elsewhere on Delos for his model?

Voluntary Associations and Foreign Gods

Among the thousands of inscriptions discovered by French archaeologists on Delos, many document what scholars call congregational cults or voluntary associations. In the cosmopolitan and mobile Mediterranean world, these voluntary associations (*collegia* in Latin and *thiasoi* or *koina* in Greek) were a widespread phenomenon in urban settings, and they especially attracted merchants and freedmen. The migrations and dislocations of peoples after Alexander the Great severed many from their homelands, cities, tribes, and families, and congregational cults reinforced a sense of identity in new homes or provided unionlike guilds to protect and promote particular economic interests. In their cultic aspect they provided a framework for worship of a particular god or gods and the offering of sacrifices to ensure continual divine patronage, and in their congregational aspect they offered social contacts and protected commercial interests. They also permitted a sense of social mobility within a society whose class distinctions were otherwise rigid and impermeable. Members could rise through the ranks of the voluntary association's hierarchy, take on important-sounding titles, and earn some measure of self-esteem or self-importance.

Over twenty congregational cults are mentioned on Delian inscriptions, and a number of their buildings have been excavated. Down in the civic center, altars and inscriptions testify to the "Hermaistai," a *collegium* of Italian merchants who gathered under the patronage of and sacrificed to the Roman god Mercury, whom the Greeks called Hermes. Another inscription mentions the association called the "Heraclesiastai of Tyre, Merchants and Shippers," a group from the Phoenician coastal city of Tyre who worshiped the ancient Semitic god Melkart, now called Heracles in Greek. Another Phoenician association, the "Poseidoniastai of Berytos, Merchants, Shippers, and Warehousemen," met under the patronage of the sea god Poseidon and sacrificed to him for safe passage.

As you walk from the port toward Mt. Kynthos, there is a complex the excavators call the Terrace of the Foreign Gods, which consists of temples to the Syrian gods and three *Sarapeia*, structures dedicated to the Egyptian god Sarapis and his consort, the goddess Isis. The first Sarapeion gives a good indication of the kinds of activities that went on in these voluntary associations. This Sarapeion A (Figure 18), enclosed by walls and rooms encircling a courtyard that contained a small temple (A), was somewhat sheltered but not quite hidden from public view. That temple housed the deities' images and was built above a subterranean crypt and spring. Outside the temple in the courtyard there was a moneybox for donations (J) and three altars (B, F, H), where oxen, pigs, or birds were once sacrificed, and behind that was a large trapezoidal dining hall with marble benches lining all four walls (E; Figure 19). A lengthy inscription found there proclaims that "seats and eating

FIGURE 18. Plan of Sarapeion A on Delos (A, temple; B, F, H, altars; E, dining and meeting hall; J, moneybox for collections).

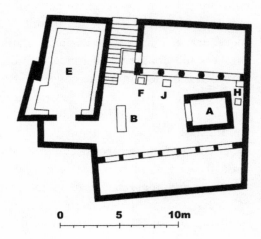

FIGURE 19. The benches of the meeting and dining hall (E) of Sarapeion A.

couches were installed in the dining hall for the feast to which the god invites us," and a now damaged relief portrays the goddess Isis serving Sarapis as he dines at a banquet. The members not only sacrificed but also socialized in the Sarapeion A by eating the meat at sacred meals honoring Sarapis and Isis. Is this little dining hall, which seats some one or two dozen people, the sort of place we should imagine Paul celebrating the Lord's Supper? Or is this sort of place what newcomers expected after Paul invited them to a communal meal? Or did they anticipate a Jewish model instead of a pagan one?

Synagogue Building and Synagogue Inscriptions

During the 1912–13 seasons, the then director André Plassart discovered what he identified as a synagogue—not on the island's western and civic side, but on its eastern and domestic side, amid private residences but near a gymnasium. It was there at the time of Paul, but had two construction phases. The original phase dated to the second century B.C.E., and then it

FIGURE 20. Plan of the
synagogue on Delos (A, main
meeting hall with Seat of
Moses; B, meeting room; C,
portico opening onto the
sea; D, rooms of unknown
purpose; E, cistern opening).

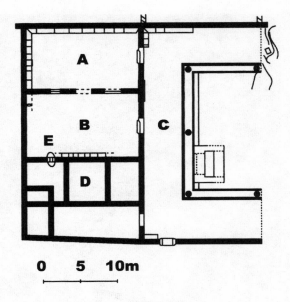

may not have been a synagogue. The renovation phase dated to the mid-first century B.C.E., when pieces of the nearby gymnasium destroyed in 88 B.C.E. were integrated into new walls.

The synagogue faced toward Mikonos and the rising sun, but was so close to the sea that waves erode much of it even today (Figure 20). A stone water basin at the entrance, along with a cistern located in a maze of smaller rooms (D), might have been used for ritual washings, a very common practice in the Jewish homeland. Steps added during renovation led from the seaside eastern portion toward an open portico (C) and a roofed assembly area, which was once a single hall but was then divided into two rooms (A and B). Room A was the main assembly hall and had marble benches on its side walls that could comfortably seat twenty-five people, and another twenty-five or fifty could sit on the floor or on portable benches. A single thronelike seat faced the eastern entrance and was decorated with a palmette on its top and other decorations on its sides (Figure 21). This was possibly "Moses's Seat," the special chair from which the scriptures were read. Matthew 23:2 comments that "the scribes and the Pharisees sit on Moses's seat," and Acts probably imagines Paul preaching to his fellow Jews from such a seat. And we can imagine that twenty-five, fifty, or seventy-five Jews and God-worshipers met there on the Sabbath.

FIGURE 21. The so-called Seat of Moses inside the synagogue at Delos, from which Jewish scriptures were read on the Sabbath.

The design of the building is not much different from that of any other voluntary association, and the main reason for its synagogue identification is not architectural but epigraphic. Four column bases from Rooms A and B were inscribed with *Theos Hypsistos,* Greek for "Highest God" or the "Most High God," titles by which Jews distinguished their one and only God from all other gods within a polytheistic context. The Hebrew Psalms' *El Elyon* was translated *Theos Hypsistos* in the Greek Septuagint translation. In Acts, Stephen says, "The Most High does not dwell in houses made with human hands" (7:48), and a pagan prophetess declares that Paul and Silas are "slaves of the Most High God, who proclaim to you a way of salvation" (16:17). We will meet that term again, by the way, in the Jewish synagogues from the Bosporus kingdom, near the northern Black Sea, in Chapter 4.

The four votive inscriptions were all dedicated by individuals, some of whom had well-known Jewish names:

Lysimachos, on behalf of himself, a thank offering to *Theos Hypsistos*

Laodice to *Theos Hypsistos,* saved by His treatments, a vow

Zosas of Paras to *Theos Hypsistos*

To *Hypsistos,* a vow, Marcia

Another inscription makes the case for a synagogue even more compelling. Found in a nearby house, it announces the generous donation of "Agathocles and Lysimachos to the *proseuchē*." That Greek word is synonymous with "synagogue"; though *proseuchē* literally meant "prayer," Jews customarily used it for "prayer house." That, along with scriptural readings, was one of the primary activities of the synagogue. The Lysimachos who contributed to the *proseuchē*/synagogue is most likely the same Lysimachos who deposited the votive to *Theos Hypsistos* in the very structure he sponsored.

Two marble inscriptions discovered in 1979–80 almost 100 yards to the north of that building further certify its identification as a synagogue, but raise a major question about its owners. Were they Jews or Samaritans?

> The Israelites on Delos, who make offerings on hallowed *Argarizein,* crown with a gold crown Sarapion, son of Jason, of Knossos, for his benefactions toward them.

> The Israelites [on Delos], who make offerings to hallowed, consecrated *Argarizein,* honor Menippos son of Artemidoros, of Herakleion, both himself and his descendants, for having constructed and dedicated at their expense the *proseuchē* of God, the [. . .] and the [. . .] [and they crowned him] with a gold crown and [. . .]

The first inscription testifies to the presence of a Samaritan community on Delos who called themselves "Israelites" and who worshiped (i.e., sacrificed) at the ancient Israelite site of Mt. Gerizim (*Argarizein*). The second inscription makes clear that those Samaritans had a *proseuchē* on Delos, a building "constructed and dedicated" by Menippos son of Artemidoros. But this Menippos is from Herakleion on the island of Crete, his name is pagan, and he funded a *Samaritan,* not a Jewish, synagogue. That first inscription's honoree is from Knossos, also on Crete; his name, Sarapion, is also pagan; and, in fact, he is named after the Egyptian deity worshiped on the other side of the island. Rather than Samaritans who adopted pagan names, these two were likely Cretan pagans now living on Delos who were drawn to the Samaritans' monotheism and morality or perhaps simply associated with them for commercial and social purposes. They may even have been pagan God-worshipers supporting the Samaritan synagogue on Delos, just as other pagan God-worshipers supported the Jewish synagogue at Aphrodisias.

We are left, therefore, with one building but two sets of inscriptions, one set inside the building and another set at some distance from it. Does all that indicate a single Samaritan synagogue? Or were there two separate syna-gogues, a Jewish one already discovered with its inscriptions and a Samaritan one as yet undiscovered for which we have so far only its inscriptions?

We accept that building as a Jewish synagogue and suspect that the Samaritan one still lies buried to the north or else was eroded by the sea. Be that as it may, we stress an important point that is often lost in the scholarly debate over the ambiguity of the archaeological finds: the structure was not radically distinct from its context or clearly identifiable as Jewish. Jews had, to some degree, assimilated architecturally to their diaspora settings, and those on Delos had adopted the more or less common structure of the island's other voluntary associations. Like the members of those other groups, they sat on benches and held banquets; and they inscribed in Greek like their neighbors and not in Hebrew like their ancestors. But unlike their neigh-bors they had no altars and no sacrifices, since, for Jews, sacrificing was only valid in Jerusalem, just as, for Samaritans, it was only valid on Mt. Gerizim. In accordance with the second commandment of Moses, they had no shrines set aside for statues and no images of their deity, even though a few lamps with pagan images were found inside the building. Like many later synagogues, it faced the rising sun, but so did many pagan temples.

In any case, from the outside the building would have looked like the meeting place of a voluntary association or congregational cult to the aver-age person walking Delos's ancient roads. Locals would have known it to be the Jewish synagogue, and they would have been able to identify by dress, look, or personal acquaintance some of the island's Jews. A Jewish traveler, merchant, or official disembarking at Delos's harbor, like Paul did in so many other cities, would have easily located the Jewish community by simply asking for its location.

Jews Among Greeks and Under Romans

How did Jews get to Delos? How did they live? How did they preserve their ancestral traditions? Jews living in the diaspora, like those on Delos and like Paul himself, greatly outnumbered those living in the Jewish homeland of Judea and Galilee. They became expatriates for various reasons after Alexan-der the Great redrew the political map of the Mediterranean and Near East-ern worlds and after the Roman juggernaut crushed any Greek, Semitic, and Egyptian opposition. Some Jews went into the diaspora through war, either as soldiers enslaved abroad on the losing side or mercenaries disbanded abroad on the winning side in some Hellenistic or Hasmonean war. Some were sold into slavery after first Greco-Egyptian, then Greco-Syrian kings, and finally Roman generals like Pompey, Crassus, and Varus stormed though the Jewish homeland. Over time, many Jewish slaves or their children were manumitted, or liberated, but did not return to Judea. Jewish merchants, bankers, or traders were also drawn abroad by economic opportunities, such as those offered by the Delian emporium, and, eventually, many even became Roman citizens.

How would they have related to their homeland and Jerusalem's Temple? Two Jewish scriptures written immediately after the sixth-century-B.C.E. Babylonian deportation capture the alternatives. One option was to yearn for a return to Jerusalem, as found in Psalm 137:1, 4: "By the rivers of Babylon—there we sat down and there we wept when we remembered Zion. . . . How could we sing the Lord's song in a foreign land?" The other option was to settle permanently in the diaspora, as found in the prophet Jeremiah's advice to those same exiles in 29:5–7: "Build houses and live in them; plant gardens and eat what they produce. . . . Seek the welfare of the city where I have sent you into exile, and pray to the Lord on its behalf, for in its welfare you will find your welfare."

Whatever option those initial Babylonian deportees chose, most Jews living in the diaspora under Roman rule, like the Delian Jews, leaned toward Jeremiah's option and "worked for the good" of the cities in which they found themselves. Admittedly, there was a spectrum of responses to diaspora that spanned the extreme poles of outright resistance and complete assimilation. But individual preferences and the dictates of particular local conditions should not obscure the overall pattern for the diaspora in general and for Delos in particular. On the one hand, Jews embraced their traditions and preserved their identity. On the other, they simultaneously accommodated to the realities and accepted the benefits of life outside of Jerusalem and the Jewish homeland.

The synagogue at Delos blended with its context, as did the hundreds of Jewish synagogues that were noticeable but not conspicuous throughout the diaspora. The Jews themselves, however, were not only noticeable, but somewhat conspicuous to their gentile neighbors. According to many comments by pagan authors, Jews distinguished themselves by observing the Sabbath, which often precluded them from military service; by abstaining from pork, which kept them from many civic religious feasts; and by practicing circumcision, which identified their males quite clearly in the nakedness of the public baths. But even if we had never found any synagogue building or inscriptions on Delos, or even if all those discovered there referred to Samaritans and not Jews, we would still know that Jews were on the island from actual texts. The following documents are also very indicative of Jewish life among Greeks and under Romans.

We know from 1 Maccabees 15:17–23 that there was a Jewish community on Delos as early as 139 B.C.E., because it was one of the places to which Rome sent a circular letter proclaiming the Jews as "our friends and allies" within an "ancient friendship and alliance." The letter enjoins a long list of places, with Delos among them in 15:23, not to "seek their [the Jews'] harm or make war against them and their cities and their country, or make alliance with those who war against them."

Like many other cities, states, and peoples who vied for that special relationship with Rome, the Jews of Delos appealed on at least two occasions to that proclaimed friendship. Local communities and groups throughout the provinces eagerly preserved any correspondence with Roman officials relevant to their status and could produce these copies quickly when they felt threatened. In his *Jewish Antiquities,* Josephus preserves a long list of official letters once in the hands of various local Jewish diaspora communities that document Rome's toleration and support of their practices and traditions. Among them are two belonging to the Jews at Delos. In the first one, written in May or June of 49 B.C.E., the Delians proclaim—apparently begrudgingly—that they will obey the Roman legate Marcus Piso by exempting Jewish citizens of Delos from military service:

> Decree of the Delians. "In the archonship of Boeotus, on the twentieth day of the month of Thargelion [May/June], response of the magistrates. The legate Marcus Piso, when resident in our city, having been placed in charge of the recruiting of soldiers, summoned us and a considerable number of citizens, and ordered that if there were any Jews who were Roman citizens, no one should bother them about military service, inasmuch as the consul Lucius Cornelius Lentulus had exempted the Jews from military service in consideration of their religious scruples. We must therefore obey the magistrate." (14.231–32)

Two points merit attention. One is that those "religious scruples" must have included the Sabbath, a day whose rest would have made military service cumbersome. The second point is that, since "Jews who were Roman citizens" were exempt from the military draft, at least some Jews held that valued status and enjoyed its legal advantages.

The second letter preserved by Josephus dates to 46 B.C.E. and is from Julius Caesar himself. He responds to the Jews of Delos who had complained against unfair treatment by civic officials:

> Julius Gaius, Praetor, Consul of the Romans, to the magistrates, council and people of Parium [the nearby island of Paros?], greeting. The Jews in Delos and some of the neighboring Jews, some of your envoys also being present, have appealed to me and declared that you are preventing them by statute from observing their national customs and sacred rites. Now it displeases me that such statutes should be made against our friends and allies and they should be forbidden to live in accordance with their customs and to contribute money to common meals and sacred rites, for this they are not forbidden to do even in Rome. For example, Gaius Caesar, our consular praetor, by edict forbade religious societies to assemble in the city, but these people alone he did not forbid to do so or to collect contributions of money or to hold common meals. Similarly do I forbid other religious societies but permit these people alone to assemble and feast in accordance with their native customs and ordinances. And if you have made any statutes against our friends and allies, you will do well to revoke them because of their worthy deeds on our behalf and their goodwill toward us. (14.213–6)

Two general and two specific observations. Generally, the infringements on the Jews led them to appeal, and successfully at that, to the very highest level of power. And this letter illustrates Rome's tolerant attitude toward foreign religions and their ancestral traditions. Specifically, the letter indicates that as part of their practices, Jews ate together, probably on those very benches, like the ones in Sarapeion A, excavated in their own synagogue. Further, the reference to "collecting contributions . . . for sacred rites," which brings to mind that Sarapeion's collection box and inscriptions commemorating benefaction, might well refer to the Jewish Temple tax, paid by Jews on an annual basis for maintenance of the Temple in Jerusalem. Not unexpectedly, that offering to their homeland Temple led some pagans to suspect Jewish loyalties to their local civic-religious duties.

Although it is not surprising that Delos sought to restrict Jewish customs on some occasions, there was nevertheless no persistent anti-Semitism across the diaspora. There was perhaps more than occasional annoyance with Jews for not participating in the civic-religious cult, and pejorative sneers at Jews are widespread in Greek and Roman texts, but so are derisive jabs at Egyptians, Germans, and a long list of barbarians. Jews were not subject to chronic harassment or ghettoization. Erich Gruen, in his *Diaspora: Jews Amidst Greeks and Romans,* has stressed the remarkable success of Jews in the diaspora, and though they were not subject to chronic persecutions, he captures the common pagan attitude toward Jews: "How could one take seriously a people who adhered to silly superstitions, who would have no social or sexual intercourse with Gentiles, . . . who wasted every seventh day in idleness, . . . who did not eat ham or pork chops, and who mangled their genitals?" (52). Whatever animosity there was, then, tended to result in minor legal restrictions imposed by local populations, but most Jewish communities like those of Delos were quick to appeal to Rome, which intervened favorably. In fact, it was perhaps the success of these appeals and of diaspora Judaism generally under Roman rule that cultivated some of the resentment among local populations competing for Roman favor. Jewish success bred, as suggested earlier, both pagan attraction and thereby pagan resentment.

Religions Mobile and Global

There was, certainly, both a military and an evangelical edge to Roman imperial theology. Whenever Rome took up arms, it first invoked its gods; wherever Rome went, it brought its gods; and whomever Rome conquered, it assimilated their gods into the Roman pantheon. Early on, Italian traders and merchants, like those *negotiatores* who came to Delos, brought their family gods with them. Later, under the Republic, Roman generals campaigning across the Mediterranean settled veterans with their own religious rites in foreign lands. Eventually under and after Augustus, Roman imperial theology was spread, on the one hand, by the imperial cult, which housed deified emperors in temples from Thessalonica to Ephesus, and, on the other, by the cult of luxury, which brought urban amenities in the form of aqueducts, baths, and entertainments to cities from Asia to Syria.

From Rome to the Provinces

VICTORY THROUGH PIETY. Archaeologists can trace the movement of Roman religion in artifact, inscription, and architecture from the center to the periphery across the Mediterranean just as easily as literary scholars can trace Roman awareness of its own greatness across its Latin texts. In 56 B.C.E., for example, Cicero's treatise *On the Soothsayers' Responses* (to questions put them by the Senate) claimed with self-righteous arrogance that Rome's success abroad was due to its morality and religion at home. "We have surpassed all peoples and nations by *pietas* and *religio* and by the one wisdom, i.e., our realization that everything is ruled and governed by the power of the gods." And again, "If we want to compare our affairs with those of others, in regard to other things we will be found to be equal or inferior, but superior in regard to religion, i.e., the worship of the gods" (19). Romans attributed their achievement to divine sanction. The gods were on their side, a fact proven, in albeit circular logic, by their success.

Roman imperial theology was not a crass colonialism accompanied by belligerent fundamentalism. Much evidence, archaeological, epigraphic, and textual, expresses the eagerness with which many conquered peoples believed in and accepted that Roman *euaggelia,* or "good news." Awe for Roman legionary violence aside, Rome's role as peacekeeper, administrator, and builder of civic infrastructure made an impression that should not be underestimated. Many Greeks admired the Romans, especially their religious devotion, and the belief that Roman victory came from piety was widely accepted. In his *Roman Antiquities,* written around the turn of the common era, Dionysius of Halicarnassus, a Greek apologist for all things Roman, noted that the eternal city's mythical founder Romulus "understood that the good government of cities was due . . . first, to the favor of the gods, the enjoyment of which gives success to men's every enterprise" (2.18.1). And, of Rome's origins, he declared, "No one could name any other newly founded city in which so many priests and ministers of the gods were appointed from the beginning" (2.21.2).

Even some Jewish writers adopted this point of view in spite of or maybe because of failed revolts. Josephus's *Jewish War* depicts the legions' destruction of the Jewish Temple as God's cleansing punishment: "God it is then, God himself who with the Romans is bringing the fire to purge his temple and exterminating a city so laden with pollutions" (6.110). And later, in a passage from the Babylonian Talmud's tractate *'Aboda Zara,* a rabbi declares to his fellows only a generation after the war, "Do you not realize that it is Heaven who has ordained this nation [Rome] to rule? For even though they have laid waste his home, burnt down his temple, slain his saints, and persecuted his servants, still their empire is firmly established" (18a).

Eventually even Christian writers felt the same way, so that by the fourth century, the Latin poet and theologian Prudentius could proclaim in his *Reply to the Address of Symmachus,* "God taught the nations everywhere to bow their heads under the same laws and become Romans" (2.602). It was, in effect, this pervasive attitude across the lands and among the peoples conquered by Rome that enabled it to rule successfully for such a long time. Clifford Ando, in his *Imperial Ideology and Provincial Loyalty in the Roman Empire,* has noted how, among the conquered, "belief in divine sanction for Roman conquest inevitably endowed the ideal of an eternal empire with a certain currency" (66). Roman peace in its conquered lands was due in large part to the vanquished acknowledging Rome's divine right to rule.

THE GODDESS ROMA. Belief in Rome's divine right to rule others first finds expression in the ample and widespread archaeological evidence from the provinces beginning as early as the second century B.C.E. There was no Roman-prescribed formula for acknowledging its divine right to rule or for worshiping its imperial power. Instead, without replicating any exact precedence or practice in the city of Rome, communities throughout the eastern Mediterranean adopted the worship of Roman power as part of their local traditions in different ways. Some cities added regular festivals called *Romaia* to their calendars and celebrated them with games and sacrifices, others erected statues and altars to those Roman statesmen who sponsored or governed them, and still others set up cults to the Roman People. But perhaps the most common act of reverence was the public worship of the personification of Rome itself, *Dea Roma,* the goddess Roma.

Many cities that came under Roman rule adopted Roma into their local pantheons. She was usually portrayed with Greek Amazon–like characteristics and one exposed breast. The Amazonian helmet, weapons, and globe captured Rome's militaristic and imperialistic character, while the exposed breast offered a nurturing, merciful, and maybe even erotically seductive aspect. An inscription from the city of Miletus in western Asia Minor details how the priesthood for the Roman People and the goddess Roma was combined, how it could be purchased for a considerable amount by the local elites, and how the games and sacrifices to honor Rome should be performed. Dated to 130 B.C.E., it reads in part,

> With good fortune. The man who buys the priesthood of the Roman People and of Roma shall immediately give to the treasurers and kings

his nomination to the priesthood of a man at least twenty years old. That man nominated . . . shall serve for three years and eight months . . . and shall sacrifice a fully grown victim on the first day of the month of Taureon to the Roman People and to Roma. (Translation from Beard, North, and Price, Vol. 2, 246–7)

There was keen competition among the elites for such expenditures since they led to public honor. The sheer diversity of forms and multiplicity of events indicate that this phenomenon was not imposed by Rome from above, but that it happened, as we saw at Aphrodisias, by acclamation from below. Communities honoring the power of Rome certainly hoped for its favors, whether in the form of marble veneers, aqueducts bringing water to fountains, baths, and sewers, or a wealth of luxury items that peacetime commerce made possible. But perhaps just as important, their responses, as we saw from those galleries at Aphrodisias's Sebasteion, helped people theologize and rationalize their subordination to Rome.

Back to Delos. Epigraphic evidence stored in the French School or littering the site preserves many of the local responses to Roman power. *Romaia* were celebrated according to an inscription from 167/166 B.C.E., and several "managers of the sacred rites" were appointed to administer these festivals. Another inscription, from 140/139 B.C.E., records how the island's Athenian administrators placed a silver crown on a statue of Roma inside the sanctuary of Apollo. And a large but now broken marble table bears a dedication to both Athena Nikē and the People of Rome. Athenians, whom the Romans had restored to power at Delos, paid appropriate homage, but admiration of Rome ran deeply through the social hierarchy and pervasively across the ethnicities on Delos.

In addition to these very prominent civic accolades, Rome was also honored by less public groups. The congregational cult that met at Sarapeion A, for example, set up a marble altar dedicated to Roma. A statue base found in the marketplace records the dedication of a statue to Roma by private initiative. Another votive inscription testifies to a statue of Roma that was placed in a shrine alongside the statue of *Fides,* the personification of faith, that is, of Rome's loyalty and fidelity to its conquered and obedient subjects. The one statue of Roma that excavators have found comes from the house of the Poseidoniasts, and the following inscription accompanied the elegantly draped goddess:

Dedicated to the goddess Roma, our benefactor, by the fellowship (*koinon*) of Poseidoniastai of Berytos, Merchants, Shippers, and Warehousemen, in recognition of her goodwill for the fellowship (*koinon*) and the homeland. Erected when Mnaseas son of Dionysios the benefactor was leader of the association (*thiasos*) for the second time. [Menandros] son of Melas the Athenian made (this sculpture).

But religious interaction cannot be viewed solely in terms of provincial responses to Rome. People were not just attracted to things Roman; Romans were also attracted to things not Roman. Religious movement was not just a one-way process, from Rome to the provinces. It was two-way, with movement in both directions, including from Delos to Rome, Egypt to Rome, and of course Jerusalem to Rome.

From the Provinces to Rome

It is surely the most extraordinary museum in the world. Rome's Museo Centrale Termoellettrica Montemartini is a once abandoned but now converted power plant just beyond the pyramid tomb of the late-first-century-B.C.E. official Gaius Cestius at Porta San Paolo. There, tucked in among cast-iron diesel engines and massive steam turbines from a century ago, is a magnificent collection of statues, both Greek originals and Roman copies.

ATHENA FROM DELOS. Among the museum's statues is an oversized Athena that once adorned the pediment of the temple to Apollo Medicus Sosianus, excavated at the foot of Rome's Capitoline Hill. Apollo, that Delian-born, most Greek of gods, was introduced in Rome perhaps as early as the seventh century B.C.E., and, after a plague in 433 B.C.E., Romans vowed a temple to Apollo Medicus, Apollo "the Healer." That temple was restored and extensively rebuilt in the late first century B.C.E., initiated and funded by Augustus's one-time rival Gaius Sosius, whose name the temple bears. But it was finished by Augustus himself, whose devotion to Apollo also led him to build another temple to Apollo on the Palatine Hill. He even changed Apollo's anniversary on the calendar of festivals to his own birthday, September 23. As part of the temple's restoration, the originally fifth-century Greek Athena was incorporated into the pediment, along with some Amazons and other figures taken from sanctuaries in the Greek East.

During the course of Rome's eastward expansion in the second and first centuries B.C.E., its generals brought many Greek statues, like those of the classical sculptors Polyclitus or Phidias, back to Rome as booty, and for these artifacts high society quickly gained both appreciation and appetite. The Athena that wound up in the pediment of the temple of Apollo Sosianus was shaped from marble quarried on the island of Paros and imitated some features of the great goddess housed in Athens, but was probably originally sculpted for inside the sanctuary of Apollo on Delos. That tiny island, through which so many slaves, merchants, and soldiers moved to find their homes across the Mediterranean, was also the port through which many religious ideas, artifacts, and statues moved. The statue of the goddess Athena made its way from the Delian sanctuary of Apollo to the Roman Temple of Apollo. The statue, once meant to be seen from all sides, had sockets chiseled into its shoulder, and it was stuck up trophylike on a pediment as Roman imperial advertisement.

That statue, from the island of Delos, provides a starting point to assess the complex movement and interaction between Rome and the provinces, the center and the periphery, which, on the surface of it, might seem to be an evangelical conquest by Roman gods and the imprisonment of foreign gods as Roman spoils of war. But a closer look shows there was much more give and take, more religious dialogue than religious monologue.

That Athena is one concrete example of how *Romanitas,* what it meant to be Roman, was being redefined by artifacts, ideas, and communities from across Rome's new provinces. With regard to religion alone, that interchange accelerated from the second century B.C.E. into Paul's lifetime, when foreign religions flourished in Rome. At one level, the movement of religions was a civic phenomenon, as a set of eight mostly Greek inscriptions excavated on Rome's Capitoline Hill makes clear. Individual rulers like the king of Pontus in Asia Minor, Eastern cities including Ephesus and Laodicea, and entire regions like Lycia paraded their allegiance to Rome with public proclamations that included the dedication of statues to the Roman Capitoline Jupiter and offered homage to the People of Rome, as one line puts it, "in recognition of their goodness, benevolence and favor" (*ILLRP* 181).

At another level, above and beyond these public and official proclamations, Roman conquest of the provinces and pacification of the seas, along with the ensuing mobility of soldiers, merchants, and slaves, increased the exchange of religious ideas and the movement of religious communities to an unprecedented level. Once again, tiny Delos exemplifies this phenomenon, and we follow one religion moving through it from east to west, from the provinces to Rome, and from private homes through voluntary associations to public temples closely tied to imperial concerns. Consider, without pleading any one particular Pauline parallel, the movement of the Egyptian goddess Isis from Egypt through Delos to Italy.

ISIS ON DELOS.   Isis came from Egypt to Delos along with other Egyptian divinities early in the Hellenistic era, as demonstrated by a remarkable set of inscriptions uncovered in that above-mentioned Sarapeion A. Commissioned by a priest named Apollonios, Delian by birth but Egyptian by ethnicity, one inscription tells how his grandfather, also a priest, came to Delos in the third century B.C.E. and "brought his god [literally, a statue of his god] with him from Egypt, and continued to worship his god in accordance with tradition." Apollonios's father, along with other devotees, continued to worship Sarapis and Isis in a private home, perhaps Room E of Sarapeion A. Following his death, the son "inherited the sacred images," and the deity requested in a dream that a temple be built. Six months later that sanctuary complex we looked at above was completed, but its expansion beyond the private apartment and into a compound, albeit partially secluded, was not accomplished without resistance. According to the inscription, some "evil men possessed by envy and thrown into a raving madness" litigated to shut down the temple. The suit didn't get far due to a miraculous intervention: "At that time you [Sarapis] and your wife [Isis] aroused great amazement in the people. You paralyzed these wicked-minded men . . . making their tongues incapable of uttering a single word, . . . and the whole community marveled with dread at your miracle on that day and there was great renown for your servant on Delos, the island established by the gods."

Divine intervention notwithstanding, legal opposition continued and the little Sarapeion faced further litigation from some surprising and unexpected plaintiffs—the official priests of Sarapeion C! Like any group threatened by local opposition, Sarapeion A's priests appealed to Rome for a settlement and asked for a so-called *senatus consultum* (an official senatorial decree), which the Senate passed along through its appointed governor in Athens to the local governor on Delos. It was based simply on precedent and local tradition, namely, that the expansion had already occurred. Rome was not eager to infringe upon the religious status quo.

This decision no doubt annoyed the priests of Sarapeion C, who had built their structure in a more monumental and public manner after the

Roman-backed Athenians took control of the island. Sarapeion C (Figure 22) was the most dominant structure on the Terrace of the Foreign Gods, and though some voluntary associations also met there, it was the official civic cult of the Egyptian deities and was managed in coordination with Athenians in power. Its long trapezoidal complex had the look and feel of a civic sanctuary, with two colonnades lining a walkway flanked by alternating altars and little sphinxes that led to a temple whose occupying deity is still uncertain. But on the north end of this complex, a courtyard was surrounded by several temples and shrines, one to Sarapis, one to Isis, and one to the combined Sarapis, Isis, and Anubis. Frequent in the sanctuary is the inscription "Isis the Savior" or in votive dedications "Isis who lends an ear."

Like so much of Delos, Sarapeion C was destroyed by either Mithridates in 88 or the pirates in 69 B.C.E., and its rebuilding focused on Isis's temple, which was repaired with stones from the rest of the Sarapeion and even the nearby sanctuary of the Syrian gods. Worship and sacrifices to Isis resumed and continued well into the second century C.E., apparently at the expense of Sarapis and the other Egyptian gods, whose worship steadily waned. Across the Mediterranean world, Isis was exceeding her husband's popularity, and though originally the "mistress of the house of life" and goddess of maternity and infancy, often shown breast-feeding Horus on her lap, she later took on a more universal character when she moved toward Rome. Isis absorbed a wide array of attributes, becoming the dispenser of life, protector of families, guardian of the fields, and healer and deliverer of those who sought her. She was considered the mistress of the universe who offered salvation by overturning fate, and her multiplicity led to the epithet "Isis in-

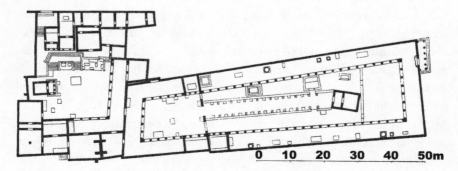

FIGURE 22. Sarapeion C on Delos, with architecture more like a civic sanctuary than the small, houselike Sarapeion A.

voked by innumerable names." She moved from Egypt through Delos at an accelerated rate after the island's destruction in the early first century B.C.E., so that by the time of Paul her worship was firmly established in most of the key cities he visited. There is archaeological evidence of her worship at Thessalonica and Philippi, Ephesus and Corinth. Her shrines and altars are especially common along sea-lanes, whether Mediterranean ports or inland along the river arteries like the Rhine and Danube, and they were located often right where ships docked, as at Corinth's port at Cenchreae. She came, of course and ultimately, to Italy at Puteoli and Cumae, then to Ostia, and finally to Rome itself, the capital of the world.

ISIS IN POMPEII. Pompeii, the city buried by Vesuvius's eruption in 79 C.E., is now a major laboratory for archaeologists as well as a major attraction for tourists. There we see Isis moving from the private sphere to the public realm just as on Delos. Many elements of private homes incorporate Isis imagery in a decorative manner on frescoed walls and in a devotional manner in household shrines. These Egyptian and specifically Isis cultic motifs include metal cans with elongated spouts, metal urns covered with pointed metal leaves, and the sacred Egyptian snake.

Pompeii also has one of Italy's earliest Isis shrines dating to the late second century B.C.E. It was not located in or near the forum like the major civic temples to Apollo, the Capitoline Jupiter, the Concordia Augusta and Pietas, or the later deified emperors. It was constructed in the theater district, an appropriate setting that attracted Greek and other foreign influences. This sanctuary was more secluded, being enclosed by a portico and not visible from the street, so that probably only devotees of Isis used it. But about a century later Isis and her shrine, an *Iseum,* held greater civic importance. The temple was, following the amphitheater, the first building reconstructed after the earthquake of 62 C.E.—unlike the temples in the forum and even the Capitoline temple. The Iseum's restoration is attested on an inscription by the wealthy freedman N. Popidius Ampliatus, whose six-year-old son Celsinus was elected to the city council as a reward. By the 60s C.E. then, Isis had become a cult acceptable to a local Roman municipality (Figure 23).

ISIS AT ROME. By Paul's lifetime, Isis had long since left both her Egyptian home and her husband Sarapis's shadow and had arrived in Rome with a significant following. A rather sizable Iseum was built there during the first half of the first century C.E. and was renovated on a grander scale by the

FIGURE 23. Statue of Isis, the "mistress of the house of life," made of marble with traces of gold plating; from her temple in Pompeii.

emperor Domitian himself toward the end of the first century. Even though Augustus made sure no foreign deities had temples like those of the Roman deities inside the *pomerium,* the religiously sanctioned boundary of the city of Rome, Isis's temple was nevertheless set in a prominent and venerable area in the Campus Martius next to the Saepta Julia, where gladiatorial games were held, and not far from Augustus's Mausoleum and his altar to peace, the *Ara Pacis Augustae.* The Iseum was just as large as Rome's great civic temples. But unlike those, it had two arches to east and west leading into a 230-foot-wide courtyard open to passersby, but flanked to north and south by areas accessible only through narrow gates and probably evident only to devotees. In that southern sanctuary, a colossal statue of Isis was prominently displayed in the semicircular apse's center niche, with smaller niches on either side for Anubis and Sarapis, still Egyptian national deities but now long since eclipsed by Isis's universality.

That architecture might have restricted access, but the characteristics of Isis's priests were clearly recognizable in a way that publicized their devotion. They shaved their heads, wore white robes, and further distinguished themselves by avoiding pork, fish, and wine. And although some rituals took place behind closed doors, devotees of Isis openly paraded statues through the streets of Rome and read aloud their hieroglyph books on festival days; individual initiates also leapt into the nearby Tiber River, an action inexplicable to outsiders. Their activities fostered a kind of faux secrecy, luring the interested and teasing the curious to consider initiation into the "mysteries" of Isis. The architecture and decoration—obelisks, trees, papyrus ornamentations, baboons, and crocodiles—emphasized the temple's exotic character and created Egyptian ambience right in the heart of Rome itself. Though not without some initial hesitancy and even resistance by senators and early emperors, Isis made it onto the official civic-religious calendar by the middle of the first century, and her festival was celebrated each year from October 28 to November 1. Augustus himself had employed Alexandrian artists to decorate his own house with Egyptian vegetal, mythological, and ornamental themes of the sort that also adorned the shrines of Isis. By the end of the first century, she was even wed to the emperor cult, and Domitian refurbished the Iseum after a fire in 80 C.E.

Isis's place on the civic calendar, her temple's prominent location, her official and mostly Egyptian priesthood, and even the adoption of her features into the emperor cult were not the causes of her popularity. They were simply responses to her attraction within ordinary Roman society, and imperial or senatorial acceptance was but an attempt to consolidate their positions by jumping on Isis's bandwagon.

There are Isis-related graffiti from a small group of mostly slaves who met in a modest house on Rome's Aventine Hill. There is epigraphic evidence from devotees who were soldiers and veterans, freedmen and municipal officials, as we saw at Pompeii, and we know that even some members of the imperial family were members of her cult, for example, Poppaeus Habitus, an in-law of Nero, who had depictions of Isis on her family shrine. The initiates included men, women, and children, Romans and Egyptians, foreigners from all the provinces, each of whom found the personal demands of Isis more rewarding than the traditional civic cults. Perhaps also the thrill of foreign rituals and meetings with people from all walks and stations made the cult irresistible to many. That intense personal devotion to Isis, mystical if not ecstatic, is captured in the initiation speech of one devotee, written by the second-century novelist Apuleius in his *Metamorphoses*:

> But my talent is too feeble to speak your praises and my inheritance too meager to bring you sacrifices. The fullness of my voice is inadequate to express what I feel about your majesty; a thousand mouths and as many tongues would not be enough, nor even an endless flow of inexhaustible speech. I shall therefore take care to do the only thing that a devout but poor man can; I shall store your divine countenance and sacred godhead in the secret places of my heart forever guarding it and picturing it to myself. (11.25)

Isis forged ahead in Rome's competitive polytheistic context and faith in her power approached something like monotheism, namely, henotheism, or the belief in one supreme god without denying the existence of others. The attraction was her absorption of many gods' traits, and she thus stood even above Fate, but she never directly challenged pagan polytheism. Devotion to Isis never implied exclusive allegiance, and devotees still participated in civic religion and even had allegiances to other deities. One inscription, for example, made by "Apronianus the civic treasurer," records the dedication of a relief to Mithras in one setting and to Isis in another. Isis captured the spirit of the *oikoumenē,* the Greek term for the inhabited world, and did not directly challenge the Roman imperial theology, whose *peace through victory* constituted the vaunted *Pax Romana.* It is no surprise that not long after Paul's death, Isis and emperor had merged in a marriage made in heaven.

We have chosen, then, to begin at Aphrodisias and on Delos as one particular and one general microcosm of Paul's Roman world. One was an up-and-coming city in Asia Minor where the Sebasteion's sculptural depiction of Roman imperial theology and the Jewish synagogue's inscription containing names of Jews and God-worshipers are constitutive for our understanding of Paul with Jews, among Greeks, and under Romans. The other was a tiny island whose glory days were over, but where we can still see in stone the interaction of gods and goddesses, women and men, Greeks and Romans, Jews, Samaritans, and Egyptians. We can see a world where private and public, religion and society, politics and economics, universality and particularity merged more or less smoothly together. We can see, above all, the Italian warrior goddess Roma moving eastward as an accepted force, but also the Egyptian mother goddess Isis moving westward as an accepted grace. She was not, however, the only Eastern divinity moving westward toward Rome.

2

An Appealing or
Appalling Apostle?

Through visual imagery a new mythology of Rome and, for the emperor, a new ritual of power were created. Built on relatively simple foundations, the myth perpetuated itself and transcended the realities of everyday life to project onto future generations the impression that they lived in the best of all possible worlds in the best of all times. . . . At the same time as his "restoration of the Republic" and the creation of his new political style, Augustus also set in motion a program to "heal" Roman society. The principal themes were renewal of religion and custom, *virtus,* and the honor of the Roman people. Never before had a new ruler implemented such a far-reaching cultural program, so effectively embodied in visual imagery; and it has seldom happened since.

—Paul Zanker, *The Power of Images*
in the Age of Augustus (1990)

Given a history in which the apostle's voice has again and again rung out like iron to enforce the will of slaveholders or to legitimate violence against women, Jews, homosexuals, or pacifists . . . the voice we have learned to accept as Paul's is the voice of the sanctified status quo [so] that continued efforts to reclaim Paul's genuine voice are necessary. For centuries the apostle's legacy has been systematically manipulated by human structures of domination and oppression, from the conservative interpreters of Paul who found their way into the New Testament itself, down to the legitimation of the "New World Order" or the sonorous waves of antifeminist backlash in our own time. . . . [*Liberating Paul*] is written, first of all, for those who have found Paul a stumbling block in their attempt to follow Jesus on the way of justice and peace.

—Neil Elliott, *Liberating Paul* (1994)

∽   ∽   ∽

Two Visions of World Peace

Overture

AUGUSTAN PEACE. It was supposed to have been completed in time for Rome's Jubilee 2000 celebrations. But you are there two years later, on a hot and muggy mid-afternoon in July, and it's still hidden within a canvas and metal cocoon. Jackhammers pound and cranes rotate around a scaffold-clad cube inside the construction zone. Outside it, elegantly dressed Italian women turn the Via di Ripetta into a stylish fashion show while young Italian men weave their Vespas in and out of traffic, up and over curbs, racing toward the Ponte Cavour to cross the Tiber. There are only a few other tourists in sight and, oblivious to the normal near accidents all around them, they stagger through the city's summer heat, looking at clumsily folded maps with hats on and heads down. It's not Rome's most visited area, surrounded as it is by drab concrete buildings from Italy's Fascist 1930s. East of the construction zone is the park around the cypress-crowned ruins of Augustus's Mausoleum, which, long ago stripped of its marble, has become a refuge for homeless people and a place for walking dogs. Still, the new construction hopes to change that decline, and a huge billboard put up by the Commune di Roma announces the restoration's chosen architect, political patrons, and corporate sponsors. There is also an illustration of the new museum for the *Ara Pacis Augustae,* the Altar of Augustan Peace, the magnificent cube of ancient history now hidden behind that protective screen.

That modern billboard does not explain how controversy surrounding the museum's construction and the altar's renovation caused the long delay. The commissioned architect was the American Richard Meier, whose postmodern works have already appeared around the world and include the new J. Paul Getty Museum in Southern California. But many Romans were outraged when he unveiled a plan calling for a long glass and steel museum to encase the *Ara Pacis Augustae,* with a fountained plaza at one end and an auditorium at the other, an elongated jewel box along the bank of the Tiber. Some critics ridiculed it as "Los Angelizing" their city, and the flam-

boyant Italian deputy of culture, Vittorio Sgarbi, derided the piece as an af-
front to Rome's cultural legacy. According to its detractors, Meier's design
lacked adequate continuity with classical Roman styles and thus eroded the
city's distinct heritage with a kind of architectural globalism. Many Romans
preferred a Roman museum for a Roman monument, but the altar of ancient
Roman peace had become an altar of modern Roman strife.

You walk up on the altar's covered west side along the tree-shaded side-
walks of the Lungotevere di Augusto. You watch the muddy brown Tiber
flow sluggishly and deeply below its present embankments, a reminder that
this *Campus Martius* ("Field of Mars"), where the Republic's legions drilled
just north of Rome's ancient center, was once that river's floodplain. It was
on that field of the war god Mars that the Senate decreed in 13 B.C.E. an
Altar of Augustan Peace, which was, according to most art historians, the pin-
nacle of monumental sculpture in Rome, and which copied and adapted, by
the way, a host of foreign elements from Hellenistic and Greek sculpture.
And on that altar's magnificent sculptures is clearly imaged the imperial
order of *Victory and Peace,* or, in the two male and two female panels enclos-
ing the Altar's front and back, the fuller Augustan sequence of *Piety* (Aeneas),
War (Mars), *Victory* (Roma), and *Peace* (Fertility).

FIGURE 24. Benito Mussolini inspects the then newly reconstructed Altar
of Augustan Peace.

The design of the original museum was by the Fascist architect Vittorio Morpurgo, who encased the *Ara Pacis Augustae* within glass and travertine marble when it was first restored, relocated, and realigned to its present position in 1938. Morpurgo had been commissioned by Benito Mussolini, who wanted a prominent location for the altar to indicate the present return of Rome's ancient greatness. The full Latin text of Augustus's political autobiography, the *Res Gestae Divi Augusti* (*res gestae* means "things done," accomplishments, achievements—hence *Acts of the Divine Augustus*), was incised low on the encasement's outer east side and that, by the way, is all that is now left of Morpurgo's structure. The altar's theme and Augustus himself were central to Il Duce's nationalistic and imperialistic rhetoric. There is an extant photograph of Mussolini and his military entourage inside the enclosure beside the altar itself (Figure 24). They are striding past what is now the right side at the place where Augustus himself appears in the frieze above them. All save one officer are looking away from it in another direction. How appropriate. Augustus was no Mussolini, and Mussolini would never be Augustus.

PAULINE PEACE. Modern letters usually have some rather formulaic beginnings ("Hope you are well") and endings ("Best wishes") and so do ancient ones. Later in this chapter, we will separate the seven Pauline letters written by the apostle himself from the six post-Pauline ones written in his name. Here is a medley from the starting ("grace and peace") and finishing phrases ("peace") of those seven genuine Pauline letters (only the starting formula is in Philemon): "Grace to you and peace. . . . May the God of peace himself sanctify you entirely" (1 Thess. 1:1; 5:23); "Grace to you and peace. . . . The God of peace will be with you" (Phil. 1:2; 4:9); "Grace to you and peace" (Philem. 1:3); "Grace to you and peace. . . . Send him on his way in peace" (1 Cor. 1:3; 16:11); "Grace to you and peace. . . . Live in peace, and the God of love and peace will be with you" (2 Cor. 1:2; 13:11); "Grace to you and peace. . . . Peace be upon them, and mercy" (Gal. 1:3; 6:16); "Grace to you and peace. . . . The God of peace will shortly crush Satan under your feet. The grace of our Lord Jesus Christ be with you" (Rom. 1:7; 16:20).

First, that "grace and peace" summarizes the core of Paul's message and mission, faith and theology. The usual salutation in a Greek letter was *chaire* or "greetings," but in a novel, clever, and profound wordplay, Paul switches that to the similar-sounding but theologically more significant term *charis*, "grace" or "free gift." Think, for example, of the air all around us. It is there as *charis,* or gift. You do not earn it, deserve it, or gain it by any personal or even communal effort. But you do have to accept it and cooperate with it by breathing. You could also, of course, refuse it and die by suffocation. To *charis,* or "grace," he adds the traditional and also more theologically significant Jewish greeting, "peace," *shalom* in Hebrew or *irenē* in Greek. And that sequence is important. It is as a free gift that God offers peace to everyone, everywhere. That, actually, puts his whole letter to the Romans in a single terse phrase. And, of course, Paul writes all of that in the common Greek of the diaspora Jews and the Mediterranean world.

Further, that "grace and peace" sequence is such an obvious Pauline opener that the post-Pauline letters had no difficulty in using it to copy his style. Here is the medley of such starts from those later letters: "Grace to you and peace" (2 Thess. 1:2); "Grace to you and peace" (Col. 1:2); "Grace to you and peace" (Eph. 1:2); "Grace, mercy, and peace" (1 Tim. 1:2); "Grace, mercy, and peace" (2 Tim. 1:2); "Grace and peace" (Titus 1:4).

Next, that "grace and peace" is usually specified as "from God our Father and the Lord Jesus Christ." And, finally, that triad of God, the Lord Jesus Christ, and peace appears at other times as well. For example, Paul hopes that "the peace of God, which surpasses all understanding, will guard your hearts and your minds in Christ Jesus" (Phil. 4:7), and he declares, "Since we are justified by faith, we have peace with God through our Lord Jesus Christ" (Rom. 5:1).

It will not do, however, within this chapter or throughout this book, to put Rome's "victory and peace" against Paul's "grace and peace" as if that solved anything, let alone everything. On the one hand, Paul too can speak of victory (but only once), replacing that peace triad just seen with a victory triad: "Thanks be to God, who gives us the victory through our Lord Jesus Christ" (1 Cor. 15:57). On the other, any Roman imperial theologian would have told Paul that "victory" *was* "grace," was a free gift from the gods and especially from Jupiter, Mars, or Venus. Again, if Paul spoke of accepting the "faith of Jesus Christ," as in Galatians 2:16 or Philippians 3:9, a Roman opponent would have reminded him that the *Acts of the Divine Augustus* spoke of accepting the "faith of the Roman people" (32.3). All the good words, the better terms, and the best expressions were available alike for both sides.

The basic questions, therefore, are about means and not just ends, about methods and not just slogans, about the specific content of vision and the precise content of program. What was the difference in content between the free gift of divine grace as seen by the emperor of the Romans and as seen by the apostle to the Gentiles? How exactly did the peace of Rome differ from the peace of God? How exactly did the peace of the Lord Caesar Augustus, divine and Son of God, differ from the peace of the Lord Jesus Christ, also divine and also Son of God?

Overview

This entire book is about the clash between those alternative visions of world peace. One is Augustus's vision, following civilization's normalcy, of *peace through victory*. The other is Paul's vision, following Jesus's radicality, of *peace through justice*. In this chapter we begin that comparison by focusing on one crucial element in each visionary program—on *hierarchy* within the scenario of global victory and on *equality* within that of global justice. We begin in Rome with the two greatest monuments of the Augustan revolution, the clearest, fullest, and finest images there are of Roman imperial theology: First, the Forum of Augustus with its Temple of Mars *Ultor* celebrating the war god as "avenger" of the assassinated and then divinized Julius Caesar. Second, the Altar of Augustan Peace celebrating the *Pax Romana* as *Pax Augustea* with four major panels displaying the full theological narrative sequence of *Piety* with Aeneas, *War* with Mars, *Victory* with Roma, and *Peace* with Fertility.

In both structures there are male and female personifications of gods and goddesses, but after that it is exclusively male in the forum's porticoes, primarily male on the altar's reliefs, and absolutely aristocratic in and on both structures. *SPQR—Senatus Populusque Romanus* ("The Senate and the People of Rome")—was the empire's solemn chant, but that *populus* was nowhere evident on the imperial imagery or statuary of those monuments. There was, of course, plenty of surrounding room for the *populus* to walk and look, admire and learn, be educated, entertained, and indoctrinated.

Then we turn from Roman imperial theology to Pauline Christian theology and confront immediately the objection that Paul is just as chauvinistic, misogynistic, patriarchal, and hierarchical as Augustus except on a much smaller scale, as apostle, not emperor, and in text, not on edifice. In basic rebuttal we distinguish the earlier and authentic Pauline letters from the later and nonauthentic pseudo-Pauline (maybe even anti-Pauline) ones—but all attributed to him within the present New Testament.

We focus on two examples in Paul, slavery and patriarchy, to match those two examples of Augustus, forum and altar. Our argument is that the historical Paul insisted on equality *among Christians* over against the hierarchical normalcy of Roman society. First, a *Christian* mistress or master should not and could not have a *Christian* slave. Second, *Christian* women and *Christian* men were *as such* equal in marriage, assembly, and apostolate. How could one be equal and unequal at the same time, since *in Christ* all were equal before God?

We next look at the later pseudo-Pauline inserts or texts asserting inequality for women in marriage, assembly, and apostolate. Those changes deliberately muted the radicality of Paul's Christian equality back to inequality for women in marriage, assembly, and apostolate. Finally, we explain why the presence of leaders like Thecla, who were female, celibate, and ascetic, developed an opposition whose leaders had to be male, married, and fertile. It was all done in Paul's name, but it negated Paul's example and silenced Paul's challenge.

Marble Monuments as Imperial Metaphors

We know nothing from archaeology about Paul's communities, their architecture, artwork, symbols, inscriptions, or even graffiti. Nothing survives, or perhaps more telling, nothing was ever made, but we know about his activities and those early Christian communities from his many letters. But the Augustan era survives for us in both literary texts and archaeological artifacts. In fact, even without any of those many Augustan authors or Roman historians we could still sketch a portrait of his rule from the many visual images that survived. Since very, very few of the ancients could read and not many more would hear the poetry of Virgil, Horace, or Ovid, images were widespread and of absolute importance for popular consumption. The images of Roman imperial theology appear on the smallest to the largest surfaces, on coins, cameos, and cups, on statues, altars, and forums. They even had an ancient version of streaming video. In the modern version, you stand still and the images stream past you. In the ancient equivalent, the images stood still and you streamed past them. Imagine, once again, a walk along Aphrodisias's Sebasteion from Chapter 1, and think of moving messages as you look below first at the Forum of Augustus with its Temple of Mars and then at the Altar of Augustan Peace. Their messages come only from all the images put together as an interactive streaming unity.

Consider what follows as probes into the Roman landscape of that Augustan era as we inspect in detail the streaming-image messages on two very important artifacts, one a temple's forum as large as a city block and the other an altar's enclosure as small as a room. The Forum of Augustus and the Altar of Augustan Peace illustrate the characteristics of the Augustan revolution that reverberated in space from Rome across the empire and in time from Augustus's reign throughout the first century. Paul was born about two generations after Augustus's birth; spent much of his life in Eastern cities like Damascus, Jerusalem, and Antioch; spread his message in cities of Greece and Asia Minor like Thessalonica, Corinth, and Ephesus; and never went to Rome until he was imprisoned and executed there at the end of his life. We look at Augustan Rome not simply to view the city as Paul would have seen it, but to understand it as essential background or, better, as confrontational foreground, for Paul's mission and message. From Rome there emanated a far-reaching political, cultural, and religious transformation utterly apparent in the art, architecture, and literature of the Mediterranean world. Against all of that Paul advocated an alternative transformation oriented more toward Jerusalem than to Rome, more toward the Jewish God and the Jewish Messiah than to the Roman gods and the Roman Augustus. Two visions of cosmic peace, then, two programs for global kingdom, and two faiths in two different gods clashed profoundly in that first century—and still do as we start the twenty-first.

The Forum of Augustus, whose Temple to Mars the Avenger was vowed by Octavian at Philippi in 42 but not completed until 2 B.C.E., and the Altar of Augustan Peace, decreed by the Senate in 13 and dedicated in 9 B.C.E., embody three themes that resonate in the ancient Augustan texts that describe them. These three themes are characteristic of Augustus's rule and revolution, and he might well have stated them with the terseness of his adoptive father, Julius Caesar: *I restored, I expanded, I consolidated.* First, Augustus restored the Republic and the *pax deorum,* or peace with the gods, and led a return to traditional Roman piety. Second, Augustus expanded the forum, the city, and the empire. And third, Augustus consolidated into a single worldwide empire both those Romans defeated in the civil wars and those nations and peoples conquered in imperial wars. He expanded Roman rule across the Latin *orbem terrarum,* the entire world, and made Rome the capital of the civilized world, the Greek *oikoumenē.*

A Temple to War in the Forum of Augustus

I built the temple of Mars the Avenger and the Forum Augustum on private ground from the proceeds of booty. . . . I excelled all in authority, although I possessed no more official power than others.

—*Acts of the Divine Augustus* (21.1; 34.3)

The modern boulevard between Rome's Piazza Venezia and the Colosseum, the Via dei Fori Imperiali, or "Street of the Imperial Forums"—renamed from the originally Fascist Via dell' Impero, or "Street of the Empire"—runs at a slight angle right over the ancient Forum of Augustus (Figure 25). That street's fast and furious traffic is banned on Sundays and replaced by pedestrians, horse carriages, baby strollers, and bikes. But even slow pedestrians catch only a hint of the Augustan Forum's onetime greatness and get only a glimpse of that most remarkable temple to Mars *Ultor*, Mars the Avenger. At its far end, a 115-foot-high wall of gray tufa stone still stands, built by Augustus's architects into the slope of the Viminal Hill as a fire wall protecting forum and temple from the densely inhabited and highly flammable tenements on its other side. Still visible high up on that wall is the faded imprint of the temple's pediment and its flanking portico roofs,

FIGURE 25. Ruins of the Augustan Forum; the steps in the center once led to the now destroyed Temple of Mars *Ultor*.

which, along with three 60-foot-high Corinthian columns still in position, give an impression of its past magnitude and lost splendor.

To see the dignity of that ancient complex, you have to look past its dilapidated and weed-infested ruins, its rusty iron clamps holding ancient columns in place, and those modern steps and rails that crisscross the site. You have to search Rome for marble inscriptions and sculpture fragments carted off over the centuries, like those two maiden-shaped columns and that shield with bearded deity now in the offices of the Knights of St. John of Jerusalem right behind the Imperial Forum (Figure 32). You have to rely, above all, on more than a century's archaeological work and architectural analysis to reconstruct the Augustan Forum and the Temple of Mars the Avenger that it encased.

In design and detail the Augustan Forum and the Mars Temple were at the same time traditional and innovative, as Augustus ushered in the new by appealing to the past. The plan drew upon a conventional Italian scheme for civic space, widespread inside Rome since the Late Republic, wherein a long rectangular plaza—the forum itself—led to a temple on a high podium approachable by steep stairs (Figures 26 and 27). The forum plaza, lower in elevation, was in a sense the stage for key aspects of civic life. Victorious generals sacrificed here, provincial governors were commissioned here, and the Senate met here to consider war. But all these ceremonies were like pageants enacted below the higher temple, by whose divinity they were consecrated and sanctioned.

It can hardly be emphasized enough that temples in antiquity were not elite museums cordoned off from the masses. They were vibrant public facilities where priests burned incense, killed animals, and placed entrails on smoldering coals; where a chorus might one day process, sing, or dance; and where on most days courts met under the shaded colonnades to select jurors and dispense justice. We should imagine, then, in addition to the cries of animals, the chants or songs of worshipers and the pleas or appeals of the condemned along with the murmur of curious crowds or even the shouts of unruly mobs. In *The Deified Claudius* the second-century Roman historian Suetonius alerts us to that composite reality with an anecdote about that later emperor who "was eager for food and drink at all times and in all places." As the story goes, when Claudius was "holding court in the forum of Augustus and had caught the savour of a meal which was being prepared for the Salii in the Temple of Mars nearby, he left the tribunal, went up where the priests were, and took his place at their table" (33.1). The gods and the laws, divinity and justice, were inextricably entwined in that Augustan Forum under the watchful eyes of the war god Mars from his temple built by the divine Caesar Augustus.

Although the Forum of Augustus had a similar civic function and axial plan as the earlier Forum of Julius Caesar, which it abutted at right angles, Augustus's incorporated into one harmonious whole an unprecedented number of Greek-inspired innovations. The temple pediment's pitch was lower, as on Greek temples, and Augustus used Corinthian columns and capitals in a way that recalled Greek models. More strikingly, the materials used departed dramatically from traditional Italian ones like drab volcanic tufa stone, wooden roof beams, and terra-cotta roof tiles and decorations. Instead, forum and temple were clad in brilliant, colorful marble. He also included an abundance of sculptural elements and a profusion of statues.

We consider first the whole complex, then the parts, the elements, the details. Imagine you are a Greek aristocrat from Hierapolis on your first visit to Rome in the middle of the first century and you are standing at the entrance to the Forum of Augustus. An unofficial but imperious guide insists you listen as he recites from memory an excerpt from Ovid's *Fasti* describing what you are about to see. His literacy is inadequate to the poetic rhythm, but then so is yours to the Latin language. You listen patiently, glad of the temporary shade:

> Mars Ultor drops from heaven to view his honours and temple in the Augustan Forum. Both the god and the work are massive. Mars deserved no other dwelling in his son's city. ["The son is Romulus," says the guide, as if you are a complete idiot.] This temple merits trophies won from the Giants. Here Gradivus ["That's Mars the Marcher," says your informant.] aptly starts feral wars, whether impious foes provoke us from the East, or if any from the West must be tamed. The Lord of Arms views the gables of the towering work, likes the unconquered goddesses at the top. He views weapons of different shapes on the doors, and the earth's arms defeated by his troops. Here he sees Aeneas bearing his burden of love with many noble Julian ancestors. There he sees the Ilian ["That means Trojan," the guide says, as if you had never been tutored on Homer.] lugging a general's arms and glorious deeds under rows of men. He gazes at the temple fringed with Augustus's name, and thinks the work greater when *Caesar*'s read. (5.551–568)

He finishes with a flourish, accepts his fee, and mercifully disappears in search of another customer.

In front of you is a huge rectangular plaza with columned porticoes on each side leading to, at the far end, two semicircular exedrae, or recesses. Between those exedrae is the elevated Mars Temple with steps leading up to its doors. As you walk along the plaza, you find those side porticoes filled with statues and inscriptions recording Rome's famous leaders and conquered peoples, presenting you with a swift course in Roman history. In the very center of the plaza Augustus stood in a *quadriga,* a four-horse chariot, and was proclaimed as *Pater Patriae,* or "Father of the Fatherland."

You walk toward the exedra on the left side. It contains visuals of one of the two great myths of Roman and Julian origins, the story of how Aeneas, son of the love goddess Venus and the Trojan Anchises, had escaped from that doomed city and established a new race on Italian soil. You find that story matched on the opposite exedra by the other myth of Roman and Julian origins, the story of how Romulus (forget murdered Remus), son of the war god Mars and Rhea Silva (a descendant of Aeneas), was suckled and saved by the She-wolf. Myth, legend, and history flow more or less smoothly together under those porticoes and within their terminal exedrae. You approach the temple itself, pass the altar on the steps, and look up at its pediment. From left to right on its triangular frame appear Romulus, Venus, Mars, Fortuna, and Roma. And you know that inside the temple stand its three cult statues, Venus, Mars, and Divus Julius Caesar, from left to right.

FIGURE 26. Reconstruction of the Augustan Forum, looking toward the Temple of Mars *Ultor.*

Congratulations traveler, say Augustus's designers, architects, and sculptors, you have just completed a basic course in Roman imperial theology.

Even though the forum and temple probably contained only one sculpture of Augustus, it was in that four-horse chariot in the very middle of the plaza. That position made him the visual focus of all the heroes and generals, the gods and goddesses that surrounded him. It made it clear that he was the one who *restored* the Republic, who *expanded* Rome's territory to its greatest limits, and who *consolidated* the whole world into one empire under himself. He was the center of that world.

RESTORATION. Augustus vowed a temple to Mars before the battle of Philippi in 42, and when he finally dedicated it in 2 B.C.E., he gave the war god a powerful new title, *Ultor,* the "Avenger," the god who had helped him avenge the murder of his adoptive father, Julius Caesar. But Augustus never portrayed Philippi as an act of revenge to settle a personal score. To avoid a new round of civil wars, he described his fight against his father's opponents as lawful punishment of wrongdoers. He opened the *Acts of the Divine*

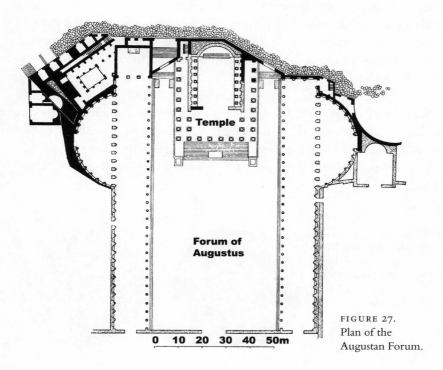

FIGURE 27.
Plan of the
Augustan Forum.

Augustus with this statement: "At the age of nineteen on my own responsibility and at my own expense I raised an army, with which I successfully championed the liberty of the republic when it was oppressed by the tyranny of a faction" (1.1). And again, "I drove into exile the murderers of my father, avenging their crime through tribunals established by law; and afterwards, when they made war on the republic, I twice defeated them in battle" (2). His stated goal was nothing less than the restoration of the Republic.

The *Acts of the Divine Augustus* records the assassins' punishment in a judicial-political tone, and the sculptural program of the Augustan Forum and the Mars Temple accentuates that with a moral-religious note. Augustus avenged Caesar at Philippi and exemplified the socioreligious virtue of *pietas,* "piety," and particularly filial piety, with which he linked himself to Aeneas, who had saved his father from burning Troy. That hero's filial piety was a set-piece scene on lamps, tombstones, and frescos throughout Italy (Figures 28 and 29). Aeneas is usually shown with his aged father, Anchises, on his shoulder and holding his own son, Julus, by the hand. Anchises holds the box containing the family gods (the *penates*) until, as Virgil's *Aeneid* says, "He should build a city and bring his gods to Latium" (1.5–6). A coin minted nearly a century later depicts schematically the configuration of the Temple of Mars *Ultor:* Augustus is below in the center of the forum in his chariot, atop the pediment to right is Aeneas with father on shoulder, and to left is Romulus with trophy in hand.

This iconography made Augustus the heir of Roman history if not the (re)founder of Rome itself. He represents true *Romanitas* and the imagery in the Augustan Forum and the Mars Temple is a microcosm of the broader Augustan program of restoring *pietas* and Roman religion. Most temples had become dilapidated and were in disrepair during the late Republic. Their

FIGURE 28. Coin of Julius Caesar promoting filial piety; on the reverse Aeneas carries his father, Anchises, from Troy, and on the obverse is Caesar's progenitor Venus (47–46 B.C.E.).

FIGURE 29. Tombstone with Aeneas carrying his father, Anchises, and leading his son, Julus, from Troy.

physical condition was seen as a symptom of the neglect of piety and religious ritual, which, in turn, was taken as the root cause of Roman civil war and Republican collapse. In his *Odes* the poet Horace rebukes the Romans for their apostasy: "Your fathers' sins, O Roman, you, though guiltless, shall expiate, till you restore the crumbling temples and shrines of the gods and their statues soiled with grimy smoke" (3.6.1–4).

Augustus revived traditional piety, reactivated ancient Roman rites, and reinstated lapsed priestly offices as a means of restoring the *pax deorum,* or peace with the gods, and he himself took the leading role in this religious renewal. According to his *Acts,* Augustus "restored eighty-two temples of the gods in the city, . . . neglecting none that needed restoration at that time" (20.4). He also enrolled in various priestly colleges, had himself elected to several key priestly offices, and became *pontifex maximus,* or chief priest, in 12 B.C.E. The recently opened marble quarries at Carrara let Augustus coat Rome's temples with a new marble sheeting, front them with marble Corinthian columns, and add a wealth of sculptural detail.

In those actions, as in the Augustan Forum, the restoration of tradition was often a guise for innovation. Conquering generals returned to Rome and traditionally erected temples like the several Republican victory temples excavated and now exposed along the present Largo Argentino in Rome. But after 33 B.C.E., only Augustus and the imperial family were allowed to build temples in Rome. Augustus cultivated and monopolized a special relationship between the gods and the Julio-Claudians, one that was obviously rife with political implications.

In addition to the above-mentioned eighty-two temples, Augustus and his family built or fully restored at least fourteen others, each with explicit imperial connections. One was consecrated to *divus Julius* and one to the *divus Augustus.* Two were constructed for the imperial virtues of *Concordia* (Harmony) and *Iustitia* (Justice). Another was erected to Jupiter *Tonans* (Thunderer) after a lightning bolt narrowly missed Augustus in Spain in 26 B.C.E. Three more were vowed during Augustan military victories: one to his favorite Apollo at Actium, one to the sea god Neptune at nearby Nicopolis, and of course one to the war god Mars *Ultor* at Philippi. As Ovid's *Fasti* tells it, some temples had already "tumbled down . . . with the long lapse of time" and "all the rest had in like sort gone to wrack and ruin, had it not been for the far-seeing care of our sacred chief, under whom the shrines felt not the touch of old; and not content with doing favors to mankind he does them to the gods. O saintly soul, who doest build and rebuild the temples, I pray the powers above may take such care of you as you of them! May the celestials grant you the length of years which you bestow on them, and may they stand on guard before your house" (2.58–66).

EXPANSION. The Temple of Mars the Avenger illustrates the first theme of the Augustan revolution, restoring *pietas* and the *pax deorum* as the basis of the Republic. But the second and closely related theme is epitomized by what Augustus put inside that temple and alongside the cult statues of his progenitors Mars, Venus, and the deified Julius Caesar. Next to their images he placed the legionary standards that had been captured by the Parthians and then recovered as Augustus expanded Rome's territorial control eastward to Armenia. Those standards, taken from Crassus in 53 B.C.E. during one of Rome's most shameful military defeats, had been a Roman obsession for decades. Julius Caesar's plan to avenge it was cut short by his assassina-

FIGURE 30. Augustus's silver denarius with a humbled Parthian kneeling and returning the legionary standards; the obverse depicts Honos, the personification of honor.

tion, and Mark Antony suffered further embarrassing losses in a later attempt. But in 20 B.C.E., Augustus was able—albeit through diplomatic threat of force rather than military use of it—to settle the matter and retrieve the standards. According to his *Acts,* "I compelled the Parthians to restore to me the spoils and standards of three Roman armies. . . . Those standards I deposited in the innermost shrine of the Temple of Mars the Avenger" (29.2).

The standards' restoration played an important role in Augustus's pictorial program, since it symbolized how *piety* resulted in *victory* and how victory led to a vastly expanded empire, a growth that not only confirmed Augustus's stature as *princeps,* "leading citizen," but also justified his program of religious revival. The topic can be seen, among other places, on Roman denarii struck in 19 B.C.E.: a kneeling Parthian bows and returns the standards (Figure 30). In one of his *Epistles,* the poet Horace describes how the Parthian monarch "Phraates, on humbled knees, has accepted Caesar's imperial sway" (1.12.27). It is also exquisitely represented on the cuirass of Augustus's statue found in his wife Livia's villa at Prima Porta (Figure 31). That breastplate's centerpiece features the standards' restoration, in which the Parthian king hands over the eagle-bearing battle insignia to the personified Mars *Ultor* clad like a Roman legionary with a wolf at his heels. But, as Paul Zanker says in his book *The Power of Images in the Age of Augustus,*

> This perfectly straightforward, historical event is, however, only the centerpiece of an image encompassing heaven and earth . . . [as] the victory over the Parthians is celebrated as the culmination of a perfect world order . . . the prerequisite and the consequence of the *saeculum aureum* [Golden Age]. The unique historical event is turned into a paradigm of salvation, in which the gods and the heavens act as guarantors, but need not intervene directly. (189, 192)

At the very top and bottom are canopied Heaven and peaceful Earth. Just beneath Heaven, Moon with her torch disappears behind Dawn with her dew vase as she moves ahead of Sun with his chariot. Just above Earth are Apollo with his griffin and Diana with her hind. All of time and space rotate around that central and cosmic victory event. Factual history is utopian theology.

That scene is echoed in the Augustan Forum, where a statue group in the eastern exedra was dedicated to the hero of the other Roman myth of origins, Romulus, son of Mars, reared by the She-wolf. We know from the representation of the Mars Temple's pediment on a coin as well as many contemporary representations of Romulus that his iconographic emblem was

FIGURE 31. Close-up of the cuirass on the Prima Porta statue of Augustus, with the Parthian king handing over the standards to Mars *Ultor.*

a trophy raised on a pole. That trophy is the *spolia opima,* the spoils due those who killed an enemy leader in single combat, as, according to legend, Romulus did in a duel. Augustus could hardly be more intimately tied to Romulus in this regard, as both defeated their adversaries and both carried the spoils back to Rome. But although Romulus bore the trophy of one enemy, Caesar Augustus put on display in the Augustan Forum "weapons of different shapes" and "the earth's arms defeated by his troops," to repeat Ovid's earlier-quoted *Fasti* passage (5.561–62).

Augustus multiplied victories and added to the territorial expansion begun by Romulus. He defeated the Illyrians, incorporated Egypt into the *imperium,* the empire, and subdued the Cantebarri in northwestern Spain and the Raetians in the Alps. He then moved into Noricum, Pannonia, Germania, and Moesia, while he also colonized Galatia and brought Judea into his orbit with the client-king Herod the Great. The culmination of Rome's expansion under Augustus was underscored by all those famous Romans in the colonnades leading up to Romulus's exedra. As Suetonius says in *The Deified Augustus,* "Next to the immortal Gods he honoured the memory of the leaders who had raised the estate of the Roman people from obscurity to greatness" (31.5).

The expansion of the Roman Empire was the forum's least subtle visual theme. The statues of victorious leaders and vanquished peoples were complemented in daily life by the many military ceremonies and foreign policy debates that took place in the Augustan Forum. Those, as a whole, reinforced the grandeur of the empire and placed Augustus atop the entire *oikoumenē,* or inhabited world. The international or cosmopolitan character of the *imperium* was also achieved in the Augustan Forum by the many allusions to that first divinized world conqueror, Alexander the Great. He had vanquished the eastern Persians on his ascent to world domination. Augustus had subjugated the eastern Parthians (more or less) and was on his way to even greater world domination. The forum, therefore, suggested Augustus's divinity by several references to Alexander.

According to a popular legend, Zeus Ammon had acknowledged his divine paternity of Alexander at the Egyptian oracle in the Siwa Oasis. The upper story of the forum's porticoes was adorned with huge shields depicting the face of that same deity in Roman form, Jupiter Ammon (Figure 32). Augustus's connection to Alexander was made forcefully, according to one source, by his dedicating the forum on August 1, the anniversary of Augustus's capture of Alexandria and conquest of Cleopatra and the beginning of the newly named month of August. Finally, there was a shrine in the forum with a colossal statue of Alexander, and, according to Pliny, two prominent paintings of Alexander on canvas hung in one of the arcades, copies of those by the renowned Greek artist Apelles. Decades later Claudius made the connection with Alexander clumsily obvious when, according to Pliny the

FIGURE 32. Two surviving Caryatids from the Augustan Forum, flanking a shield depicting Jupiter Ammon.

Elder's *Natural History,* "He thought it more advisable to cut out the face of Alexander from both works and substitute portraits of Augustus" (35.94). But the connection was always obvious from the beginning—Augustus was the new divine ruler of the new world order.

CONSOLIDATION. Augustus restored and expanded the empire, but the element of his revolution that more than any other transcended his own life is that he effectively consolidated into one empire both defeated enemies at home and conquered peoples abroad, aspects that are visible in the architecture of the Augustan Forum and the Mars Temple.

First, with regard to internal political enemies. Octavian ruthlessly avenged his father's murderers, pursued Antony and Cleopatra to suicide, and executed Caesarion, son of Cleopatra and Julius Caesar and therefore a competing *divi filius.* But he also repeatedly stressed the Roman virtue of *clementia,* "clemency," in his dealings with defeated civil-war opponents. That clemency was not to be confused with one-sided forgiveness, but entailed a reciprocal relationship that obligated the powerful to leniency and the powerless to loyalty. This explains why, in his forum's gallery of great Romans, Augustus included not only his own family and allies, but some of his own and his father's civil-war opponents. Pompey, who had once been Julius Caesar's greatest threat, was there, but honored for his eastern campaigns in Anatolia and Syria, which took him into the Jewish Temple of Jerusalem in Judea. Augustus, as *Pater Patriae,* or "Father of the Fatherland," sought to integrate the great Roman houses into one Roman family especially by changing animosity directed internally into enmity directed externally. That Mars Temple had been originally vowed to avenge the murder of Julius Caesar, but, by the time it was dedicated forty years later, emphasis on those recovered standards transferred the residual hostilities resulting from Rome's civil wars to Rome's foreign enemies. The temple's symbols managed, contained, and consolidated intra-Roman competition and turned it against extra-Roman opposition.

Next, with regard to external imperial enemies. The forum suggests that Augustus extended the same *clementia* to the peoples conquered by Rome. Architectural styles and materials from the conquered world were combined with Roman styles and Italian materials to create a unique structure expressive of the *oikoumenē,* the whole inhabited world. The details of the new forum recall Ovid's statement on Augustan architecture and culture in his *Ars Amatoria:* "There was rude simplicity of old, but now golden Rome possesses the vast wealth of the conquered world" (3.113–14). The forum and temple were basically Roman in conception, function, and design, but they included earlier Greek elements and later Hellenistic details. They were also made from marble brought from all over the empire.

Some specific examples. The maiden-shaped columns, or caryatids (Figure 32), on the upper story of the porticoes surrounding the forum, drew upon the classical traditions of the Athenian Acropolis. The south end of Athens's famous Parthenon was lined with the original caryatids that Augustus's architects faithfully copied. Incidentally, the Acropolis epitomizes the negotiated reciprocity of styles and religions that we saw at Delos in Chapter 1. In one direction, the widely admired fifth-century-B.C.E. Athenian originals were copied and placed in the Roman Forum of Augustus. But, in the other direction and around the same time, the Athenians built in front of their Parthenon a new temple to the goddess Roma and the divine Augustus. But the consolidation of the various imperial parts into one integrated whole is nowhere more apparent than in the use of marble in forum and temple. Those combinations might be too garish for modern sensibility, but the ancient message could hardly have been clearer. It was multicolored marble from and for a multipeopled empire.

The pavement of the Mars Temple was a rectangular pattern of purple marble from Phrygia (*pavonazzetto,* brought overland some three hundred miles from the Turkish highlands to the sea), pinkish-purple marble from Teos in Asia Minor (*africano,* sometimes called Lucullan red after the general who first brought it to Rome in 74 B.C.E.), and yellow marble (*giallo antico*) from Numidia or modern-day Tunisia. To those colors the rest of the forum added, often in different patterns, a greenish gray marble (*cipollino*) from the Greek island of Euboea and an ocher brown alabaster from the Egyptian quarries along the Nile. Although the floors and lower levels of the Augustan Forum and the Mars Temple were in vibrant colors from around the conquered world, the upper stories and side walls were made from traditional Italian materials. This included volcanic tufa blocks quarried in the Alban Hills and around Gabii; hard limestone travertine, the common material of the late Republic, from quarries between Rome and Tivoli; and finally the dull white and gray Carrara marble, brought to Rome from Luna near Pisa. And the temple, exedrae, and porticoes were roofed with locally made, rustic terra-cotta tiles. In that sense, Italian and Roman materials were the glue that held the complex together; the durable and functional Roman materials enclosed and protected a set of ornate Greek decorations and an array of highly diverse materials, all consolidated into a complex judged in the elder Pliny's *Natural History* as one of the most beautiful in the world (36.24.2).

One final footnote. Vitruvius dedicated his manual *On Architecture* to Augustus, and it would teach engineers and architects for centuries that the goal of public architecture was to enhance empire. In his address to Augustus, Vitruvius praises him: "The state was not only made greater through you by its new provinces, but the majesty of the empire also was expressed through the eminent dignity of its public buildings." The empire reached its greatest territorial expanse under Augustus and, as Vitruvius hoped, it also reached its architectural apex in the Augustan Forum and Mars Temple. He concluded his dedication to Augustus with the hope "with respect to the public and private buildings, that they will correspond to the grandeur of our history, and will be a memorial to future ages" (1.2). They certainly were.

An Altar of Peace on the Field of War

On my return from Spain and Gaul in the consulship of Tiberius Nero and Publius Quintilius [13 B.C.E.] after successfully arranging affairs in those provinces, the senate resolved that an altar of the Augustan Peace should be consecrated next to the Campus Martius in honor of my return, and ordered that the magistrates and priests and Vestal Virgins should perform an annual sacrifice there. . . . By new laws passed on my proposal I brought back into use many exemplary practices of our ancestors which were disappearing in our time, and in many ways I myself transmitted exemplary practices to posterity for their imitation.

—*Acts of the Divine Augustus* (2.2; 8.5)

If the Augustan Forum is the high point of first-century Roman architecture, the *Ara Pacis Augustae,* or Altar of Augustan Peace, is the high point of its sculpture. The 20-by-24-foot altar stood 10 feet tall and was surrounded by a slightly larger enclosure wall. Today the complex has been reassembled from fragments and casts, relocated about 500 yards northward near Augustus's Mausoleum, and realigned from its original east-west axis to its present north-south axis. The first ten Carrara marble fragments were discovered by chance in 1568, and seventeen more were found in 1859. The first scientific excavations in 1903 identified the altar's original location on the Campus Martius and added another fifty-three fragments, but only archaeological work in 1937–38 allowed a full reconstruction of the altar's design. It was then reassembled by combining all available fragments, but even today a cast serves for one panel still in the Louvre Museum in Paris.

The original altar was formally consecrated at the end of the month of Janus, the month of that gatekeeper god whose temple doors were shut whenever Rome was at peace. As Augustus recorded in his *Acts,* those doors were shut three times while he was Rome's *princeps* (13). This new monument also emphasized Pax, or Peace, a goddess already important to Augustus, as can be seen from the beautiful silver denarii he minted in two series of three coin-types apiece to pay his victorious troops after Actium in 31 B.C.E. One series has his head on the obverse and a goddess's figure on the reverse (Figure 33); the other series has a goddess's head on the obverse and his figure on the reverse (Figure 34). And, on every coin, the inscription DIVI F proclaims him *divi filius,* Son of the Divine One [Julius Caesar].

FIGURE 33. One of the two series of silver denarii minted by Octavian for the battle of Actium; the one on the left shows the goddess Pax holding an olive branch and cornucopia; the one in the middle depicts Venus holding helmet, scepter, and shield of Mars; and in the one on the right a winged Victory stands on a globe holding out a wreath.

FIGURE 34. The third coin in the other series minted by Ocatavian for the battle of Actium with Victory on the obverse and a divine nude Octavian with foot on a globe on the reverse.

The proper sequence of those three goddesses is clearest in one series, but only its last coin-type is shown here (Figure 34). First, Augustus addresses his troops before the battle on the reverse with the goddess Peace as their goal and purpose on the obverse (war for peace, once again). Next, he orders the attack with the goddess Venus as helper and protector. Finally, he celebrates victory with the goddess Victory as gift and reward. But notice how Victory flies to him upon a globed earth, which then remains under his right foot (Figure 34). Pax has arrived, and the term *Pax Romana* became a shorthand for both the extent and the security of the Roman Empire.

The restored monument sits on a raised platform accessible by nine marble steps that lead through the enclosure wall to the interior, where the U-shaped altar is approached by another flight of stairs (Figure 35). Grooves and slots cut all along the bottom of the enclosure wall once served as drains through which animal blood was flushed away, a reminder that what is now encased within a disputed museum was once an active sacrificial sanctuary. Priests stunned oxen, sheep, and swine with a mallet and then cut their throats as offerings to the goddess Pax, escorted to Rome by Augustus. Centuries of acid baths and neoclassical restorations have eradicated any trace of that blood and the once brilliant colors that enlivened the magnificent sculptural reliefs. But, though that original palette is lost forever, the ancient message imaged on the enclosure's outside wall is clear to this day. It is a

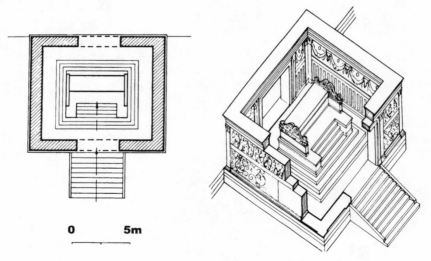

0   5m

FIGURE 35. Plan and axonometric view of the *Ara Pacis Augustae,* the Altar of the Augustan Peace.

message that resonates in the texts of Virgil, Horace, and Ovid, and that we summarize with those same three themes just seen in the Augustan Forum and Mars Temple: *restoration, expansion,* and *consolidation.*

Restoration

During 19–17 B.C.E. Augustus's restoration/revolution finally reached its three-year grand finale—not that everything was done, but everything was at least in place. That climax began with the consecration of the altar in 19, continued with the Augustan laws on (re)marriage and adultery in 18, and was consummated with the Saeculum Games in 17.

THE PEACE ALTAR. No doubt the most impressive and visible parts of the Altar of Augustan Peace were the processions on the upper band of the enclosure's outside wall. These depict, in nearly life-size figures, a religious procession of some forty to fifty people on each side and may even depict the sacrificial procession on the day of the altar's consecration. But it is not an idealized parade of Greek-style heroes or gods. It is a remarkably realistic, relaxed, and even casual depiction of actual and very specific people. But relaxed casualness, too, is a result of Pax.

On the present east side (the original south side), heralds and attendants (now mostly lost) precede Augustus, with head veiled, who stands with a priest known as the *rex sacrorum* and the four *flamines,* priests with spiked headgear representing the major state cults of Mars, Quirinius, the deified Julius Caesar, and Jupiter (Figure 36). After them comes Agrippa, Augustus's admiral, general, and, after he married his daughter, Julia, in 21 B.C.E., son-in-law and heir apparent. His head is also veiled for sacrificial performance. Then come the rest of the imperial family, including several children. The men are dressed in togas and high-laced boots, the women in conservative *stolae* that cover them from head to heel (Figure 37).

On the opposite side of the enclosure wall, the present west side's upper frieze shows a similar full-scale procession of senators and aristocrats. But Augustus, first among equals, is not on that side. He is among the priests and with his dynastic family on the other side. Augustus was chiefly responsible for extending *pax* across the empire, but he understood its basis to be the maintenance of ritual religious duties and the restoration of traditional family values. Those are the themes that occupy the bulk of the altar's sculptural space.

FIGURE 36. The South Frieze of the *Ara Pacis Augustae*, with Augustus (whose body is split in two) leading a procession of priests.

FIGURE 37. The South Frieze of the *Ara Pacis Augustae* continues the procession of the imperial family.

The Augustan plan was to revive the *mos maiorum,* the "way of our ancestors," the habits and customs, the principles and moralities of Rome's idealized and romanticized ancients. He was especially interested in those qualities that transcended law and encapsulated *Romanitas,* with its appropriate virtues for each gender, its proper responsibilities for marriage and family, and its traditional pieties for society and religion.

Think about that for a moment, especially in remote preparation for Paul on law. Horace's *Odes* asked, in lapidary Latin, *Quid leges sine moribus,* "Of what avail are empty laws, if we lack principle?" (3.24.35). In other words, internal morality must precede and generate external law. Augustus wanted to try the reverse and use legislation to generate morality. Paul would have agreed with Horace. But, maybe, law and morality are interactive and dialectical forces? Maybe, for example, a law refused by the morality of one generation might be accepted by the morality of the next?

In any case, Augustus took the moral and legal lead in Roman society. As priests did in preparation for Roman sacrificial rites, he drew his toga over his head in statues (Figure 38) and in the Peace Altar's procession, and his location indicates his role as the presiding official.

Augustus's veiled head, his laureled crown, and his posture closely parallel those of Aeneas just around the corner on the present southeast panel of the altar. Aeneas, with head veiled, is shown sacrificing to those above-mentioned *penates,* the household gods brought piously from Troy and now shown enshrined in their new Italian temple at Lavinium. With him, of course, is his son, Julus, ancestor of the Julian clan.

It is almost as if, visually, the Augustan procession will move around the enclosure's corner to join Aeneas in sacrifice. There is, in fact, no other sacrifice shown ready for them. Past and present, theology and history, piety and empire scroll smoothly before your eyes as you walk around and around that altar. Start anywhere from anything and you will always get everywhere to everything.

FIGURE 38. Statue of a solemn Augustus as a priest with head covered.

THE MARRIAGE LAWS. The altar's processional frieze exemplified Augustus's pro-family and pro-morality stance. The procession included the entire imperial family, complete with children. The expressions, gestures, and postures of both children and elders present a realistic assessment of children's often disruptive behavior. But in spite of that, the sculptures reflect a deep appreciation for Rome's posterity. On the now eastern frieze they squirm and twist, one clings to the folds of his father's toga (Agrippa's, of all people!), one needs to be shushed by an elder, one securely grips two of his patient mother's fingers, and one has his head lovingly patted by a relative in the background. They look at each other or look up at their mothers. But they are emphatically there, out front, almost on display as trophies.

The married women are clad in the *stola,* a draping sleeveless overgarment that became their appropriate Augustan-era matronly dress and replaced the elegant Greek gowns of transparent fabric. The *stola*'s length covered down to the feet, and its shoulder straps protected women "from unwanted attentions," as the erotic poet Ovid later bemoaned, to which he added, in his *Ars Amatoria,* "Away with you, *stola,* trailing down to the feet. I sing of carefree love, of legal thievery" (1.31–34). That kind of poetry, that kind of attitude, and maybe even that kind of indiscretion, got Ovid exiled to the farthest reaches of the empire by Augustus in 8 C.E. Ovid's erotic poetry clashed with the altar's visual program, and Augustus put his full moral and legal authority behind Roman virtue by enacting two sets of laws, the Julian Law on Marriage and the Julian Law on Adultery.

Those two laws took much of what had been in the private realm under the jurisdiction of the *paterfamilias,* the male head of the household, and subjected it to public or civil law, under the *Pater Patriae,* the "Father of the Fatherland." Among the provisions of those laws, for example, was a stipulation that unmarried aristocrats could lose the right to pass on their inheritance. Men between the ages of twenty-six and sixty had to be married or to remarry. Divorced or widowed women between the ages of twenty and fifty had six months to find a new husband. There were incentives to marry at an earlier age and rewards for having multiple children within wedlock— tax breaks, an accelerated climb up the political ladder, and even better seats at the theater. Adultery was now subject to criminal prosecution by the state. The family had become a legitimate concern of the state, since the success of the empire and the presence of *pax* depended on people's adherence to personal morality and sexual decency.

Those moral laws were, however, Augustus's greatest political disaster.

They were vociferously opposed, ignored, and eventually repealed or modified in court, and certainly Augustus's only child, Julia, was an embarrassing poster child for his morality campaign. Augustus banished her from Rome in 2 B.C.E. for her many alleged affairs. Aptly, Augustus's contemporary Livy described the "present time" in the preface to his *History of Rome* as one "when we can endure neither our vices nor their cure" (9).

Augustus himself continually pleaded with the two orders of the Roman nobility to restore family values. Suetonius's *The Lives of the Caesars* records in *The Deified Augustus* how "he even read entire volumes to the senate and called the attention of the people to them by proclamations; for example, the speeches of Quintus Metellus 'On Increasing the Family' " (89.2). Cassius Dio's *Roman History* tells how Augustus "assembled in one part of the Forum the unmarried men of their [the equestrians'] number, and in another those who were married, including those who also had children. Then, perceiving that the latter were much fewer in number than the former, he was filled with grief." The fewer married and fertile ones are first praised because, "we were at first a mere handful, you know, but when we had recourse to marriage and begot us children, we came to surpass all mankind not only in manliness of our citizens but in the size of our population as well" (56.2.2). The more numerous unmarried ones are accused of

> committing murder in not begetting in the first place those who ought to be your descendants; you are committing sacrilege in putting an end to the names and honours of your ancestors; and you are guilty of impiety in that you are abolishing your families. . . . Moreover, you are destroying the state by disobeying its laws, and you are betraying your country by rendering her barren and childless. . . . What you want is complete liberty to lead an undisciplined and promiscuous life. . . . For it is human beings that constitute a city, we are told, not houses or porticoes or marketplaces empty of men. (56.5.1–3)

Remember those speeches when later in this chapter we move to the historical Paul. He would agree against promiscuity, disagree about celibacy, and leave a tradition not exactly in continuity with idealized *Romanitas*. And what then?

All the laws and decrees, all the poems and speeches, and all the art and architecture that promoted the Augustan restoration of marital virtue do not convince one that Romans actually upheld those Augustan standards, as we will see in almost embarrassing detail in Chapter 5. But we do not doubt the

FIGURE 39. A coin of Nero with his bust on one side and the Altar of Augustan Peace on the other, with the inscription ARA PACIS (64–66 C.E.).

sincerity of his efforts, and we take seriously their role in Roman theology as it related to empire and peace. Augustus solicited from the Roman ruling classes the highest moral standards—sexual, marital, social, and religious—so that the goddess Roma could continue to expand their empire and they could continue to enjoy the presence of the goddess Pax. Belief in the moral foundation of the *Pax Romana* continued throughout the Julio-Claudian dynasty and throughout the life of Paul. The very last emperor of that dynasty, Nero, under whom Paul was probably executed, put the Altar of Augustan Peace on his coinage during the years 64 to 66 as a symbol of imperial peace (Figure 39).

THE SAECULUM GAMES. In Virgil's *Aeneid,* the dead Anchises, consort of Venus, father of Aeneas, and grandfather of Julus, prophesies the future to his son on a visit to Hades:

> Hither now turn your two eyes; behold this people, your own Romans. There is Caesar, and all Julus's seed, destined to pass beneath the sky's mighty vault. This, this is he, whom you so often hearest promised to you, Augustus Caesar, son of a god, who shall again set up the Golden Age [*aurea saecula*] amid the fields where Saturn reigned. (6.788–94)

By the end of 19–17 B.C.E. Augustus had led Rome forward into the future by returning it back to the Golden Age. He had restored the *mos maiorum* and thus ushered in a new Golden Age, an occasion that was celebrated with the greatest spectacle of Augustus's reign, the Saeculum Games held in

17 B.C.E. on the Campus Martius. This great celebration involved three days and nights of religious rites and theatrical games, followed by another week of entertainment. It marked the passing of one era, or *saeculum,* and the dawning of a new one. Those games are often called the Secular Games, but it is hard to imagine a less appropriate term for our ears. We prefer to call them the Saeculum Games as the religio-political festival not just for a new *saeculum,* but for the Golden Saeculum come back at last, the Golden Age come round once more.

Augustus commissioned Horace to compose a hymn for the festival heralding this new era. It was to be sung by twenty-seven youths and twenty-seven maidens as themselves the visible results of the marriage fertility it celebrated. Think of that program carved on the Augustan altar as hymned as well in the terse lines of that Augustan poet,

> Rear up our youth, O goddess [of fertility], and bless the Father's edicts concerning wedlock and the marriage law, destined, we pray, to be prolific in new offspring. . . . And what the glorious scion [Augustus] of Anchises and of Venus, with sacrifice of milk-white steers, entreats of you [gods], that may he obtain, triumphant o'er the warring foe, but generous to the fallen. . . . Now Faith and Peace and Honour and old-time Modesty and neglected Virtue have courage to come back, and blessed Plenty with her full horn is seen. (17–20, 49–52, 57–60)

Those specific lines, the rest of the hymn, and Augustan inscriptions and literature generally did not view the inauguration of the new age as an inevitable date on the calendar. This dawning Golden Age had to be sought and maintained by moral and military effort. Vigilance, not indolence, would guarantee in the future "cycles ever new and ages ever better" (66–67), so that the Golden Age was now an ongoing process demanding active Roman participation. The ancient *mos maiorum* was the foundation for peaceful plenitude, and the cornerstone was commitment to marriage and responsibility for family. And note carefully the sequence of events in 19–17 B.C.E. Augustus did not celebrate the Saeculum Games until he had enacted those Julian laws favoring marriage and fertility and forbidding adultery and promiscuity. And Horace brings up those marital decrees immediately as the first thing necessary so that, across the entire world, the "quickening Sun" may not "be able to view aught greater than the city of Rome" (9–12). None ever greater, but only with both marital and military vigilance.

Expansion

Augustus wrote in his *Acts* that "victories had secured peace" (13). Blessed were those who waged war to obtain peace. And Roman *pax* was not a static quality or simply the absence of war, but a dynamic pursuit that demanded constant vigilance and permanent willingness to do battle against the enemy. *Pax* was not just something that was, but something you did. And here, once again, we raise our earlier question. When, within Jewish tradition, Paul spoke of *shalom,* or peace, what precisely was the difference between the divine grace of peace for Augustus and the divine grace of peace for Paul?

This connection between war and peace is clear in the Peace Altar's sculpture and setting. On its present east and west sides, the longest friezes consist of two horizontal bands. We have already seen the upper band's sacrificial processions. But there is also an equally important and equally emphasized lower band of floral and vegetal decorations. Both bands celebrate peace, the upper, as just seen, by pointing to peace's foundations in morality and virtue, the lower by pointing to peace's effects in prosperity and fertility.

The most explicit link between war and peace is made on the outside of the back enclosure wall by a diptych of two seated females, one to left and one to right of the enclosure's back entrance. On the right is the goddess Roma, whom we saw earlier on the island of Delos. On the altar she is

FIGURE 40. Idyllic depiction of the goddess Pax on the Altar of Augustan Peace; note the symbols of abundant fertility, fecundity, and freshwater.

seated atop a pile of defeated weapons and holds, in the most plausible re-construction, a sword in one hand and a scepter or spear in the other. She is accompanied on her right by *Virtus* (Virtue), the personification of bravery and success in battle, and on her left by *Honos* (Honor), the personification of reward and recognition afterward.

On the left side is another female figure variously identified as Ceres, the grain goddess; Venus, the mother of the Julian house; *Tellus,* Mother Earth; or the personification of Italy or even the Roman Empire. But most likely she is Pax herself, for whom artists have created a new iconography by incorporating elements from all those other goddesses and surrounding her with Sky and Sea holding billowing veils to the right and left. She has two children and fruit on her lap, and at her feet are an ox, a sheep, and water bubbling from a tipped-over amphora. All that captures the idyllic abundance brought by peace (Figure 40). Pax appears as fertility and prosperity, but only after and as long as Roma sits on guard atop those conquered arms.

War and peace were intrinsically and intimately linked in the altar's sculptures, the Augustan artistic program, and the Roman mind, a point underscored by the altar's position in the *Campus Martius,* the "Field of Mars." That once marshy but still flood-prone area was transformed by construction and expansion during Augustus's reign. Before his time the plain contained several militaristic monuments like an altar of Mars, a series of victory temples celebrating Roman triumphs, and tombs of famous generals fallen in battle.

Under Augustus there was added a gigantic *horologium,* or sundial, in which a nearly 100-foot obelisk cast a shadow on a large travertine plaza whose markers furnished times for day, month, and season (Figure 41). In the early sixteenth century, a barber discovered part of the obelisk while digging a latrine and the rest was later recovered. The inscription can still be read on the restored and reerected obelisk in the Piazza di Montecitorio:

IMP.CAESAR.DIVI.F.	*Imperator* Caesar, Son of Divine [Julius]
AUGUSTUS	Augustus
PONTIFEX MAXIMUS	Chief Priest
IMP.XII COS XI TRIB. POT XIV	in 10 B.C.E.
AEGUPTO IN POTESTATEM	Egypt under the power of
POPULI ROMANI REDACTA	the Roman People having been brought
SOLI DONUM DEDIT	gave this gift to the Sun

The obelisk was topped with a spiked bronze globe, which cast its shadow on the pavement where the entire religious and civic calendar was articulated. It may even have pointed on September 23, the fall equinox *and* Augustus's birthday, directly at the Altar of Augustan Peace, which was originally situated beside it. Calendar and globe pointed to Augustus as lord of time and world.

A footnote. In the translation above we have retained the title *imperator*, which is usually translated into English as "emperor." But when Augustus's *Acts* proclaim, "I was twenty-one times saluted as *imperator*" (4.1), you realize that "emperor" will not work as a translation. A victorious general was acclaimed by his soldiers as *imperator*, meaning winner, victor, conqueror. Think of victorious legions beating out *im-pe-ra-tor* with sword on shield and understand that something like "world conqueror" is a better translation than "emperor." Once again, first victory, then everything else follows.

Those twenty-one *imperator* acclamations make it clear that the Augustan peace was achieved not just by coercion and violence, but also by acclaim and acceptance. That included not just those aristocratic Roman citizens who benefited most from the *Pax Romana*, those whose attitude was summed up in Horace's *Odes:* "Neither civil strife nor death by violence will I fear, while Caesar holds the earth" (3.14.14–16). It was also shared broadly across the Mediterranean world, as illustrated by an anecdote from Suetonius in *The Deified Augustus*. As Augustus sailed into the gulf at Puteoli near Naples, an incoming Alexandrian ship's crew and passengers dressed in white and burning incense "lavished upon him good wishes and the highest praise, saying that it was through him they lived, through him that they sailed the seas, and through him that they enjoyed their liberty and their fortunes" (98.2).

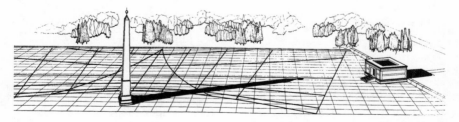

FIGURE 41. Reconstruction of the sundial, or *horologium*, whose obelisk's shadow pointed to the Peace Altar on Augustus's birthday.

Consolidation

The *Ara Pacis Augustae* and its setting in the Campus Martius commemorate how the Roman arts of war spread Augustan plans for peace across the entire world. But the monument and its location also show how that peace brought the entire world to Rome, consolidating both into a single empire. Here are some examples from the altar's setting, shape, and decoration.

The altar stood near the *horologium,* which combined elements from Egypt and Greece. The obelisk that cast the sundial's shadow was brought by Augustus from the Egyptian temple at Heliopolis and was erected on the twentieth anniversary of his conquest of that country. In 1979–80, German archaeologists found a fragmentary inscription that linked the zodiac to the seasons. The writing was in Greek, the language of ancient science, and it tells when "summer begins" and when the "Etesians [the northerly winds] cease" (Figure 42).

The style and workmanship of the altar itself blend Hellenistic and Italian traditions, Greek and Roman techniques. The U-shaped stepped altar is more akin to the older Hellenistic than the contemporary rectangular Roman kind. There is even some affinity with the great Zeus Altar from Pergamum in Asia Minor (now in Berlin), but an even closer stylistic and geographical parallel are the sixth-century-B.C.E. altars from the Latin sanctuary at Lavinium, some twenty miles south of Rome. Lavinium's significance was

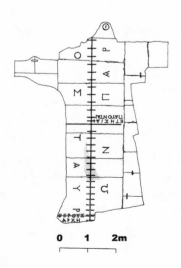

FIGURE 42. Fragment of the pavement of Augustus's giant sundial; the meridian line indicated the times and seasons.

revived at the time of Augustus as the city founded by his Roman ancestor Aeneas and those legendary Trojan refugees. Archaeologists have uncovered near the sanctuary's altars a seventh-century-B.C.E. burial restructured into a fourth-century-B.C.E. monumental tomb, a *heroon,* or hero's sepulcher. This was identified—in ancient myth even if not in actual history—as the resting place of Aeneas. It was the Aeneas story and the Lavinium location that justified to those later Romans the (albeit selective) acceptance of Greek cultural features on Roman soil and the incorporation of Hellenistic characteristics into what became the eventual ideal of *Romanitas* under Augustus and the later Julio-Claudian emperors.

With regard to decoration, David Castriota's detailed analysis of the lower band's floral friezes, in his book on the Peace Altar, compares them to sculptural ornamentation from western Asia Minor, the Aegean islands, and Ptolemaic Egypt. He shows how Augustus's artists did not slavishly copy any single precedent, but rather usurped "centuries of Greek efforts to formulate an imagery of pacific, divinely sanctioned abundance" and subsumed those elements under the Augustan ideology of *pax* (56).

In *The Artists of the Ara Pacis,* Diane Conlin carefully examines the mechanics of the altar's sculptors, "the technical signatures left by chisels, drills, and other tools," and shows that the sculptors were actually locally trained masons who were working within traditional Italian methods developed for indigenous tufa and travertine stone, but who had adopted and experimented with Greek approaches and innovations developed for marble. Their work, entirely hewn in marble from the recently discovered quarries at Carrara in northern Italy, was a synthesis of techniques. They approached their subject with an "eclectic combination of Italian, Greek, and Egyptianizing figural, drapery, and compositional styles" (106).

The Altar of Augustan Peace, then, consolidated an array of styles and traditions into a harmonious whole, revitalizing them in the process and creating the very apex of Roman imperial art. It was a microcosm of the Roman Empire at the time of Paul, which, beginning with Augustus, was consolidating a vast array of peoples and traditions into one homogenous whole and was organizing the *oikoumenē,* or inhabited world, into one global empire—into, that is, one type and method, one vision and program for a unification of the world. There was also, however, another first-century proposal for a restoration, expansion, and consolidation of the earth. It came not from paganism, but from Judaism, not from Augustus and the Julio-Claudians, but from Jesus, Paul, and first Christians.

The Framing of the Apostle Paul

We now follow those two preceding archaeological probes on Roman ground by two exegetical ones on Pauline text. These textual probes concern slavery and patriarchy, one an inequality based on class, the other an inequality based on gender. Where did Paul stand on those twin instances of human injustice and violence? Divergent answers to that question find Paul either absolutely appealing or else utterly appalling.

Our argument starts from the more general problem of the framing (in both senses) of the apostle Paul. In Chapter 1 we saw how, in the New Testament's present sequence, you meet the Lukan Paul of the Acts of the Apostles before you meet the Pauline or historical Paul of his own letters. In other words, Paul gets colored Lukan, sometimes for better, sometimes for worse. But that is only the first half of the framing process from Chapter 1 and is, in fact, the far milder one. The second half of that process is the subject of this chapter.

The New Testament begins with the four gospels, and the next fourteen books are given in this order (note numbers for exact sequence).

(1) Acts of the Apostles	(2) Romans	(6) Ephesians	
	(3) 1 Corinthians	(8) Colossians	
	(4) 2 Corinthians	(10) 2 Thessalonians	
	(5) Galatians	(11) 1 Timothy	
	(7) Philippians	(12) 2 Timothy	
	(9) 1 Thessalonians	(13) Titus	
	(14) Philemon		

Our point is that the non-Pauline columns to the left and right "frame" the Pauline column in the middle.

First, we have seen in Chapter 1 how carefully you must decide what Lukan information may or may not be used for understanding Paul. It cannot be done simply according to one's own likes and dislikes, but must be done according to whether Luke disagrees with Paul (omit it), whether Luke adds to Paul but within his own rather than Paul's theology (bracket it), and whether Luke adds to Paul but within Paul's rather than Luke's own theology (keep it). We shall see many more cases in the course of this book.

Second, scholars generally agree that, although certain of the letters attributed to Paul are authentically Pauline, several others are post-Pauline

and pseudo-Pauline, that is, they were not written *by* him but were attributed *to* him by later writers. The technical term for such fictional attribu-
tions to a historical author is *pseudepigraphs,* and they are not the same as
forgeries (the distinction is one of authorial intention). The seven letters accepted as authentic are given in that middle column, and the six disputed as
inauthentic are given in that right column.

There is a scholarly consensus on the authenticity of those seven letters in
the middle column. But the letters in the right column are quite distinct
from the seven authentic ones in style, tone, vocabulary, and content. Those
differences are cumulatively too much to be the result of using different
secretaries, changing dictation methods, or simply getting old, tired, conservative, or fearful. In this book we accept, therefore, the general scholarly
consensus that the following six letters are inauthentic and post-Pauline:
1–2 Timothy and Titus (very strong consensus), Ephesians (strong consensus), Colossians (less strong consensus), and 2 Thessalonians (weak consensus).

The problem is not just pseudepigraphical writing, an accepted process
within ancient Jewish tradition in which texts were attributed to venerable
ancient figures. New revelations, oracles, testaments, and books were attributed, for example, to Adam, Shem, Enoch, Abraham, the twelve patriarchs,
Moses, Elijah, Ezekiel, Zephaniah, Ezra, Baruch, and Job, to mention just a
few creative inventions. The problem is whether that pseudo-Pauline history and theology is in valid continuity with Paul himself or is, as we will
argue, an attempt to sanitize a social subversive, to domesticate a dissident
apostle, and to make Christianity and Rome safe for one another. Put another way, are those inauthentic Pauline letters just pseudo-Pauline, post-
Pauline, or para-Pauline, or are they actually and deliberately anti-Pauline?
We ask, therefore, who Paul actually was, because only when that is established *from his undoubtedly authentic letters* can you decide to find him likable
or unlikable, see him as agreeable or disagreeable, and, especially, discover
what the precise difference is between Roman imperial theology and Pauline
Christian theology.

Our basic argument is that the New Testament content and sequence has
literally and figuratively *framed* Paul by locating those seven authentic
Pauline letters after Luke's Acts of the Apostles, which corrects Paul's story
before we read him, and among or before those inauthentic letters, which
correct Paul's theology *after* we have read him. We concentrate on the seven
authentic ones rather than the six inauthentic letters to ask this one question: What was the *historical* Paul's position on slavery and patriarchy?

Paul and Slavery

The argument in this section on slavery opposes the authentic, or Pauline, *position* of the historical Paul to the inauthentic, or post-Pauline, *tradition* of the canonical Paul. The main text for discussion is an entire letter about a single, specific slave and the focus is on manumission, the formal process of freeing a slave under Roman law and custom.

"My Child Onesimus, My Own Heart"

Only one of Paul's authentic letters is addressed to an individual person rather than a collective assembly. But that letter to Philemon concerns precisely our present subject. It concerns Philemon's slave Onesimus, who fled to Paul for refuge, and Paul's advice to Philemon on what to do in that situation. It is not, therefore, an abstract treatise on slavery in general, but a practical response to one slave in particular. Paul himself is in prison, but he is still able to write to his convert Philemon about the slave Onesimus. What is absolutely important, here and hereafter, is the Christian principle presumed by Paul in asking for or even demanding the slave's freedom.

ONESIMUS. What exactly was Onesimus's status? Was he a *fugitive* seeking freedom or a *supplicant* seeking asylum? If he were a runaway slave intending never to return, a terrible punishment would have followed his capture—flogging or branding, the mines or the galleys, the arena or the cross. If he were such a fugitive, it would have been suicidally dangerous to have gone anywhere near official Roman authority, let alone a Roman prisoner like Paul. Such an act would have endangered them both. It is much more likely that he was a supplicant seeking not permanent escape, but temporary asylum. There were two accepted options within that rubric, and in both cases the slave's *intention* was crucial under Roman law.

One option was *flight to a god's temple*. Writing *On Mercy* in the mid-50s C.E. to the new emperor Nero at around the same time that Paul was writing to Philemon on love, Seneca the Younger noted that "slaves have the right to seek refuge at a god's statue." They could be seeking a temporary cooling-off period from an angry owner or absolute repossession from a clearly unjust one. It is in that context that he mentioned the notorious Vedius Pollio "for fattening his lampreys with human blood and ordering those who offended him to be cast into his fishpond—or should I say, his snake pit?" (1.18.2).

Another option was *flight to an owner's friend*. The classical example here is the anecdote about Augustus and his friend, that just-mentioned Vedius Pollio. The story is clearly an extreme case of mercy against cruelty, moral authority against physical power, might and right against might and wrong. It was told by that same Seneca the Younger in the late 40s and repeated by the historian Cassius Dio in the early 200s. Here is the incident from Seneca's *On Anger*, an essay dedicated to his elder brother Novatus, better known to us as the Gallio of Acts 18:12–17, where Luke claims that Paul was tried before him. Later, of course, Seneca, Gallio, and Paul would all die at Nero's command. The anecdote concerns what "our deified Augustus did when dining with Vedius Pollio."

> One of the servants had broken a crystal cup. Vedius ordered him to be seized and executed in an unusual way—he was to be thrown to the giant lampreys which were kept in a pool (not for their owner's self-indulgence, as you might think, but to sate his savagery). The boy struggled free and fled to Caesar's feet, asking only for some other form of death, just not to be eaten. Shocked by the unprecedented cruelty, Caesar had him released, ordering all the crystal to be broken in front of him and the pool to be filled in. For Caesar it was right to reprove a friend in this way. He made good use of his power. (3.40.2–4)

Note, as Seneca does, that the slave fled upward, fled to one who was his owner's friend but who could also operate "from a position of superiority."

That was most likely what Onesimus did, and he too fled "upward," fled to the man who had converted his master to Christ. He had, one way or another, deeply angered his owner, feared very serious punishment, and fled, as Roman law allowed, to his master's friend (*amicus domini*) for help. According to the early-first-century-C.E. jurist Proculus, as cited in Peter Lampe, a slave is not a fugitive "who, having in mind that his master wished physically to chastise him, betook himself to a friend (*ad amicum*) whom he induced to plead on his behalf" (1985: 135).

PHILEMON. The poor owner does not stand a chance. Paul pulls out all the rhetorical stops in persuading him about Onesimus's future. How can Philemon possibly refuse him? Here are just a few examples. He emphasizes that he is a prisoner chained for Jesus Christ's gospel. He is also "an old man" (9). He could, he tells Philemon, "command you to do your duty" but prefers to "appeal to you on the basis of love" (8–9). He does not ask for himself but for "my child, Onesimus . . . my own heart," converted to Christ by Paul in prison (10, 12). He announces that he is coming to visit Philemon very soon: "Prepare a guest room for me" (22). He suggests that Onesimus's flight may have happened "so that you might have him back forever, no longer as a slave but more than a slave, a beloved brother—especially to me but how much more to you, *both in the flesh and in the Lord*" (15–16, italics added). He offers to indemnify Philemon himself for whatever losses Onesimus may have caused (19a). He says, ingenuously, "I will say nothing about your owing me even your own self" (19b). Finally, all of this is conducted not privately, but publicly. At the letter's start, Paul writes not just to Philemon alone, but to "Philemon our dear friend and co-worker, to Apphia our sister, to Archippus our fellow soldier, and to the church in your house" (1–2). At the end, he sends greetings not just from himself, but from "Epaphras, my fellow prisoner in Christ Jesus, . . . Mark, Aristarchus, Demas, and Luke, my fellow workers" (23–24). Everyone, hints Paul, is watching you, Philemon.

The letter lacks a single word about the due obedience of Onesimus as slave to Philemon as master, but contains multiple hints about the due obedience of Philemon as convert to Paul as apostle. Delicately and carefully, but relentlessly and implacably Paul presses home his point. Philemon should free Onesimus and should do so voluntarily (14). They are already brothers in the Lord. They are now to be brothers in the flesh as well. There is hardly any other way of understanding that duality "both in the flesh and in the Lord." In every possible way and flirting regularly with manipulation, Paul tries to get Philemon to free Onesimus and to do so willingly. We draw two important conclusions about the Pauline theology that underlies that short, indirect, and oblique communication.

First, we have just caught a first glimpse of something absolutely fundamental for Paul. What is done by external demand or legal command is not enough, never will be enough, and never could be enough. Even if obeyed rather than resisted, decrees mandating conscience come from the outside inward rather than the inside outward. Even with obedience, performance is always reluctant, inadequate, and belated. If Paul commanded and Philemon obeyed, that might not change him definitively for the future. But if, on the other hand, Philemon internalized Paul's attitude toward the oxymoron "Christian owner of a Christian slave," he would know how to handle, not only the present situation, but all future ones as well. And he would do so freely so that, as Paul says, any "good deed might be voluntary and not something forced" (14). On that, we hold one question for the future. Did Paul ever consider that outward and inward, command and relationship, or law and covenant might be necessarily reciprocal, dialectical, and interactive? And, if not, should he have done so?

Second, it is quite clear that Philemon should free Onesimus because Paul wants it. But why should Paul want it? He could have asked for Onesimus in permanent service to himself. He could have demanded forgiveness, not freedom, exoneration, not manumission. He could have said: "Philemon, treat your slave justly and fairly, stop threatening him, for you also have a master in heaven, and with him there is no partiality" (see Col. 4:1 = Eph. 6:9). Why does he demand liberty? Paul sees an impossible or intolerable opposition between a *Christian* master owning a *Christian* slave. How can they be equal in Christ, but unequal in society? How can they be equal and unequal at the same time? He does not and would never accept the idea that they could be equal spiritually, internally, in the assembly, but unequal physically, externally, in the world. Both are Christians, and they must be equal "both in the flesh and in the Lord" (16).

Paul speaks explicitly of only one single case, but his implicit principle extends across all of Christianity. Under God and in Christ, the firstborn Son of the Father, all Christians are equal with one another as children in that divine family. But, says our modern sensibility, that's only about Christians, not about pagans, not about the world at large, not about abstract and universal principles of freedom and democracy. Right. Exactly.

Paul says nothing about equal creation or inalienable rights, but imagine this conversation: Do you think, Paul, that all people should be Christians? *Yes, of course.* Do you think, Paul, that all Christians should be equal with one another? *Yes, of course.* Then do you think, Paul, that it is God's will for all people to be equal with one another? *Well, let me think about that one for a while and, in the meantime, you think about equality in Christ.*

Paul and Patriarchy

That basic Pauline principle of equality among Christians applies not just to slavery, but to patriarchy as well. In Paul's theology, Christian gender inequality can no more exist than can Christian class inequality. Females and males are therefore equal in family, assembly, and apostolate within Christianity. In this section we look first at the position of the authentic Pauline letters on those three points and then at the contrary position of the inauthentic post-Pauline letters on that same threesome. Indeed, the historical Paul opposes *any* superiority, inferiority, or inequality within Christianity, and that wider question will arise more fully in Chapter 6.

Equal in the Family

When he was in Ephesus in the mid-50s, Paul received a set of questions from the Christian assembly he had founded at Corinth. They were clearly matters not just of curiosity but of controversy within a seriously divided assembly. For example, some were asserting or asking whether complete sexual separation and total ascetic abstention were mandatory for Christians, whether such celibate abstention was the normal form of Christian life. Was it not better, they asked, for a man not even to touch a woman?

In 1 Corinthians 7 Paul takes up their question, and insists that, yes, marriage and intercourse are *permissible* but, still, ascetic abstention is *preferable*. "I wish that all were as I myself am," says Paul. "But each has a particular gift from God, one having one kind and another a different kind" (7:7) and, whether marriage or celibacy, "let each of you lead the life that the Lord has assigned, to which God called you" (7:17). The reason, of course, is his presumption of Christ's imminent return: "The appointed time has grown short. . . . For the present form of this world is passing away" (7:29, 31). That is quite clear. Paul distinguishes permissible marriage (you *could*) from preferable celibacy (you *should*), but accepts the latter himself rather than holding both options as equally good, equally holy, equally possible Christian states of life. We emphasize that Paul's preference is about celibacy over marriage and not about inequality over equality for both women and men within either status.

There is a consistent equality of female with male or male with female throughout Paul's discussion in 1 Corinthians 7. It is so explicitly done, so clearly exaggerated, that it is obviously intentional. Whatever he says of one spouse, he then says of the other: the wife does this, the husband does the same; the husband does that, the wife does the same. Watch the persistence of this mutuality as equality over four subtopics: on intercourse (7:3–5), on divorce (7:10–16), on virginity (7:25–28), and on worries and anxieties (7:33–34).

In summary, therefore, and on every subtopic concerning celibacy and marriage, Paul speaks deliberately and overtly in terms not just of mutuality, but of equality. He was not writing a theoretical theological treatise, but rather a practical pastoral letter. And the subject was not equality or inequality, but marriage or celibacy. You must judge his vision by watching his advice and, as far as we can see from 1 Corinthians 7, Paul ultradeliberately and overemphatically treats female and male alike: as for female, so for male; as for male, so for female; what is right for one is right for the other; what is wrong for one is wrong for the other. Sometimes on matters of discrimination and oppression, practice can be even more important than theory since, although you cannot have practice without theory, you can certainly have theory without practice.

Equal in the Assembly

There is, however, one section in 1 Corinthians that seems to silence women within the Christian assembly, which would certainly exalt men over women with regard to their ecclesiastical status. That, of course, would be a strange dichotomy, given what Paul says in Galatians 3:28, that there is neither male nor female in Christ. How, therefore, are we to understand 1 Corinthians 11:3–16?

> I want you to understand that Christ is the head of every man, and the husband is the head of his wife, and God is the head of Christ. Any man who prays or prophesies with something on his head disgraces his head, but any woman who prays or prophesies with her head unveiled disgraces her head—it is one and the same thing as having her head shaved. For if a woman will not veil herself, then she should cut off her hair; but if it is disgraceful for a woman to have her hair cut off or to be shaved, she should wear a veil. For a man ought not to have his head veiled, since he is the image and reflection of God; but woman is the reflection of man. Indeed, man was not made from woman, but woman from man. Neither was man created for the sake of woman, but woman for the sake of man. For this reason a woman ought to have a symbol of authority on her head, because of the angels. Nevertheless, in the Lord woman is not independent of man or man independent of woman. For just as woman came from man, so man comes through woman; but all things come from God. Judge for yourselves: is it proper for a woman to pray to God with her head unveiled? Does not nature itself teach you that if a man wears long hair, it is degrading to him, but if a woman has long hair, it is her glory? For her hair

is given to her for a covering. But if anyone is disposed to be contentious—we have no such custom, nor do the churches of God.

We note immediately that the argumentation is so tortuous that there is no scholarly consensus on either the problem submitted to Paul *by* the Corinthians or the solution returned by Paul *to* the Corinthians. That makes this 1 Corinthians 11 very different from the preceding 1 Corinthians 7 on both those counts.

On the one hand, if you focus only on the women, it is plausible to argue that Paul is subordinating them to men (based on scriptural text, social dress, and church custom). On the other, if you focus only on the men and realize that Roman males normally covered their heads for worship, as with the statue of Augustus as a priest at sacrifice (Figures 43 and 44; and recall Aeneas, Augustus, and Agrippa on the *Ara Pacis Augustae* above), it is plausible to argue that Paul is opposing pagan religious practice. If, however, you notice how the text oscillates constantly between women and men, men and women, you would have to take both sexes into any correct explanation.

Paul takes for granted that both women and men pray and prophesy in liturgical assembly. That is not the problem of this text. Its problem concerns the proper head covering for each of them in that situation. But why was that so important an issue? At Corinth, presumably as a defiant challenge to inequality and a dramatic statement of equality, men and women had *reversed* modes of head covering in prayer, so that men worshiped with covered heads and women with uncovered heads. In other words, *Paul was confronted with a negation not just of gender hierarchy, but of gender difference, and he stutters almost incoherently in trying to argue against it.* Of course, women and men were equal "in the Lord" and "from God," but there should be no denial of ordinary

FIGURE 43. Augustus as priest with head covered.

FIGURE 44. Roman priestess with hair up and head covered.

dress codes or standard head coverings. The *difference* between women and men, however that was customarily and socially signified, must be maintained, even while *hierarchy* or subordination was negated. The passage in 1 Corinthians 11:3–16 is the best Paul can do on that subject. But the text is emphatically not about hierarchical inequality, but about differential equality. Paul presumes equality between women and men in the assembly, but absolutely demands that they follow the socially accepted dress codes of their time and place. Difference, yes. Hierarchy, no. That interpretation of a very difficult passage is strongly confirmed by the next section for, if women are silenced in the assembly, how can they be prominent in the apostolate?

Equal (and More) in the Apostolate

In the mid-50s Paul wrote to groups of Christians, some known by personal contact and others only by report, in a city he soon hoped to visit for the first time. His letter to the Romans concludes in 16:1–15 with mention of twenty-nine named individuals. Of those persons two are pagan householders *some* of whose present or freed slaves are Christians and greeted as "those in the Lord who belong to the family" of Aristobulus and Narcissus (16:10–11). That leaves twenty-seven named Christians. In what follows, watch the statistics, the details, and the names, especially which names are female and which are male.

First, and above all, it is a woman who carries Paul's letter from Corinth's eastern port to the Christian groups at Rome. "I commend to you our sister Phoebe, a deacon of the church at Cenchreae, so that you may welcome her in the Lord as is fitting for the saints, and help her in whatever she may require from you, for she has been a benefactor (*prostatēs*) of many and of myself as well" (16:1–2). Recall, by the way, that Jael, the leading and only female God-fearer in the Aphrodisias inscription in Chapter 1, was also called a protector, patron, or benefactor (*prostatēs*). A Pauline letter carrier would also have to circulate, read, and explain it among the Christian communities at Rome.

Second, two presumably married couples are singled out for rather extraordinary praise. "Greet Prisca and Aquila, who work with me in Christ Jesus, and who risked their necks for my life, to whom not only I give thanks, but also all the churches of the Gentiles" (16:3–4) and "Greet Andronicus and Junia, my relatives [fellow Jews] who were in prison with me; they are prominent among the apostles, and they were in Christ before I was" (16:7). Notice, that Prisc[ill]a is mentioned first in that designation.

Third, in the total of twenty-seven individual Christians in the above list, ten are women (Phoebe, Prisc[ill]a, Mary, Junia, Tryphaena, Tryphosa, Persis, an unnamed mother, Julia, and an unnamed sister) and the other seventeen are men (Aquila, Epaenetus, Andronicus, Ampliatus, Urbanus, Stachys, Apelles, Herodion, Rufus, Asyncritus, Phlegon, Hermes, Patrobas, Hermas, Philologus, Nereus, and Olympas). Conversely, however, five women (Mary, Tryphaena, Tryphosa, Persis, and that unnamed mother) and six men (Epaenetus, Ampliatus, Urbanus, Stachys, Apelles, and Rufus) are singled out for special praise.

Fourth, it may be unfair to assess which gender gets the highest praise among those accolades or epithets, but one point should be noted. Paul's Greek root for special apostolic activity is *kopiaō*, meaning "worked hard." He uses it of himself twice, in Galatians 4:11 and 1 Corinthians 15:10, but four times in Romans and exclusively for women, for Mary, Tryphaena, Tryphosa, and Persis.

Fifth, in one way or another everyone Paul knows personally gets some sort of comment. Herodion, for example, is "my kinsman" (i.e., fellow Jew). But it is interesting to compare in terms of gender the first seventeen individuals known to Paul by personal contact with the last ten known only by hearsay report. Of the ten people indirectly known to Paul, only two are woman and eight are men, but of the seventeen people directly known, nine are men and eight are women. In other words, those known to Paul by direct contact are about evenly divided between women and men.

Finally, there is Junia, a case that would be funny to ridiculous if it were not sad to tragic. For the first twelve hundred years of Christianity, commentators had no trouble identifying her name as female, presumably the wife of Andronicus (16:7), like Prisca is of Aquila (16:3–4). In Greek, by the way, her name appears in the accusative case as *Junian*. Then the name started to be identified as male—*Junian* was alleged to be the accusative case of the male name Junia(nu)s. Unfortunately, however, there are over 250 known cases of a female Junia in antiquity and not a single one ever discovered for the male abbreviation of Junianus to Junias. The problem, of course, was with Paul's supreme accolade for both members of that married couple and specifically for the female Junia. It was even suggested, as a backup position, that if Junia were female, Paul's compliment should read "prominent *to* the apostles" rather than "prominent *among* the apostles." Clearly, then, the only reason for suggesting a masculine meaning is to avoid a major *female apostle.*

Unequal in the Family

After those three authentic Pauline texts establishing female and male equality within Christianity in family, assembly, and apostolate, we turn to three inauthentic post-Pauline ones moving in exactly the opposite direction.

Greco-Roman moral thought developed codes for the ethical running of households, which were, then as now, the heart of society's health. Those household codes concerned the proper moral relationship between all members of the extended family, husbands and wives, parents and children, slaves and masters. We look now at two post-Pauline examples of such moral instructions, first in Colossians 3:18–4:1 and then in Ephesians 5:22–6:9, the latter a development of the former commandments. Notice that there is a hierarchy both vertically (spouses, parents, owners) and horizontally (husband/wife, parent/child, owner/slave) in these lists.

COLOSSIANS 3:18–4:1. First, wives must "be subject to your husbands, as is fitting in the Lord," and husbands must "love your wives and never treat them harshly." Next, children must "obey your parents in everything, for this is your acceptable duty in the Lord," and fathers (not mothers) must "not provoke your children, or they may lose heart" Finally, slaves get a very long admonition to "obey your earthly masters in everything, not only while being watched and in order to please them, but wholeheartedly, fearing the Lord. Whatever your task, put yourselves into it, as done for the Lord and not for your masters, since you know that from the Lord you will receive the inheritance as your reward; you serve the Lord Christ. For the wrongdoer will be paid back for whatever wrong has been done, and there is no partiality." And, correspondingly, masters (not mistresses) must "treat your slaves justly and fairly, for you know that you also have a Master in heaven."

EPHESIANS 5:22–6:9. First, on husbands and wives, the text seems much less worried about wives obeying husbands than about husbands loving wives. It is the latter that receives most space.

Wives, be subject to your husbands as you are to the Lord. For the husband is the head of the wife just as Christ is the head of the church, the body of which he is the Savior. Just as the church is subject to Christ, so also wives ought to be, in everything, to their husbands.

Husbands, love your wives, just as Christ loved the church and gave himself up for her, in order to make her holy by cleansing her with the washing of water by the word, so as to present the church to himself in splendor, without a spot or wrinkle or anything of the kind—yes, so that she may be holy and without blemish. In the same way, husbands should love their wives as they do their own bodies. He who loves his wife loves himself. For no one ever hates his own body, but he nourishes and tenderly cares for it, just as Christ does for the church, because we are members of his body. "For this reason a man will leave his father and mother and be joined to his wife, and the two will become one flesh." This is a great mystery, and I am applying it to Christ and the church. Each of you, however, should love his wife as himself, and a wife should respect her husband.

Despite the clear lack of equality between wives and husbands, it seems easier to be a wife "subject" to a husband like church to Christ than a husband "loving" a wife like Christ to church. Self-sacrifice, be it noted, is demanded of husband, not wife. It is surely terribly and sadly ironic that Christian tradition demanded subjection from wives and then, rather than demanding self-sacrifice from husbands, transferred that to wives as well.

Next, children must "obey your parents in the Lord, for this is right. 'Honor your father and mother'—this is the first commandment with a promise: 'so that it may be well with you and you may live long on the earth.' And once again, only fathers are warned, "Do not provoke your children to anger, but bring them up in the discipline and instruction of the Lord."

Finally, and without expansion over its Colossians source, slaves must "obey your earthly masters with fear and trembling, in singleness of heart, as you obey Christ; not only while being watched, and in order to please them, but as slaves of Christ, doing the will of God from the heart. Render service with enthusiasm, as to the Lord and not to men and women, knowing that whatever good we do, we will receive the same again from the Lord, whether we are slaves or free." Conversely, masters must "do the same to them. Stop threatening them, for you know that both of you have the same Master in heaven, and with him there is no partiality."

What is most striking about those texts, however, is that, if you bracket their explicit Christian motivation, they emphasize general family values that would be quite acceptable across contemporary Roman social theory and practice. Augustus, were he still alive, would have been extremely pleased. It seems most likely, therefore, that their purpose was to insist that Christian families were not at all socially subversive, but were as good as, if not better than, the best of those around them. For our present argument, these texts represent a first step in collating Christian and Roman household ethics.

Unequal in the Assembly

Paul's authentic letters were written to communities and not to individuals, with the exception of Philemon. The letters to Timothy and Titus are three inauthentic post-Pauline letters to individuals, to Timothy imagined as left by Paul in charge of Ephesus and to Titus imagined as left by Paul in charge of Crete. There is, by the way, not the slightest hint in his authentic seven letters that Paul ever left anyone in charge of the communities he founded—that is why he always writes to the Thessalonians, Corinthians, Galatians, Philippians, Romans, but never to a presiding elder or overseer as representative of the community. Note, for example, this specific sequence: "Paul and Timothy, servants of Christ Jesus, to all the saints in Christ Jesus who are in Philippi, with the bishops and deacons" (Phil. 1:1). The subject of female leadership within the Christian assembly arises in the post-Pauline 1 Timothy, but also as an insertion within the Pauline 1 Corinthians.

1 TIMOTHY 2:8–15. In this text female leadership is absolutely forbidden by this pseudo-Pauline author. Women are not allowed to teach or instruct men. Women are to remain silent.

> I desire, then, that in every place the men should pray, lifting up holy hands without anger or argument; also that the women should dress themselves modestly and decently in suitable clothing, not with their hair braided, or with gold, pearls, or expensive clothes, but with good works, as is proper for women who profess reverence for God. Let a woman learn in silence with full submission. I permit no woman to teach or to have authority over a man; she is to keep silent. For Adam was formed first, then Eve; and Adam was not deceived, but the

woman was deceived and became a transgressor. Yet she will be saved through childbearing, provided they continue in faith and love and holiness, with modesty.

Clearly, of course, pseudo-Paul would not bother to forbid what never happened. That prohibition therefore tells us that women were praying and teaching within the community's catechetical practice and liturgical worship. But this text dismisses women from those functions and relegates them to home, silence, and childbearing. Augustus, you will recall, would have been particularly pleased with those injunctions.

1 CORINTHIANS 14:33b–36. The problem here is not with an inauthentic Pauline letter like 1 or 2 Timothy or Titus, but with an insertion from that later tradition into an original, earlier authentic letter of Paul. In the New Revised Standard Version of the Bible this unit appears in parentheses:

> (As in all the churches of the saints, women should be silent in the churches. For they are not permitted to speak, but should be subordinate, as the law also says. If there is anything they desire to know, let them ask their husbands at home. For it is shameful for a woman to speak in church. Or did the word of God originate with you? Or are you the only ones it has reached?)

Those parentheses emphasize manuscript problems in the earliest textual transmission. First, the passage is not at its present location but at the end of the chapter in some manuscripts. Second, those verses are given as a separate paragraph in all Greek manuscripts. Third, that section was deemed problematic very early, and this is the most important argument for its later insertion into Paul's original text.

Unequal in the Apostolate

We saw, from 1 Timothy 2:8–15 in a post-Pauline letter and 1 Corinthians 14:33b–36 as a post-Pauline insertion, that female leadership was crudely denigrated in order to establish exclusive male control of the Christian assemblies. It is no surprise, therefore, to find male status as an absolute condition for Christian leaders. But that is only one of the three conditions mentioned. Leaders had to be male, that is, nonfemale; married, that is noncelibate; and fertile, that is, nonascetic. What is the point of those latter two conditions?

In 1 Timothy 3:1–13 and Titus 1:5–9 the requirements for an elder or bishop and for a deacon, the two male leadership roles discussed are what any Greco-Roman moralist would expect for public office of any type. But two items stand out as somewhat unusual or surprising—marriage is presumed and so is fertility.

1 Timothy 3:2, 4	1 Timothy 3:12	Titus 1:6
Now [an elder or bishop] must be above reproach, married only once. . . . He must manage his own household well, keeping his children submissive and respectful in every way.	Let deacons be married only once, and let them manage their children and their households well.	[An elder or bishop is] someone who is blameless, married only once, whose children are believers, not accused of debauchery and not rebellious.

In that triple requirement of male, married, children, the first element is standard patriarchy, but why are those other two emphasized?

Two hints are given elsewhere. One is from 1 Timothy 4:3–5, which warns solemnly against those who "forbid marriage and demand abstinence from foods, which God created to be received with thanksgiving by those who believe and know the truth." Another is from 1 Timothy 5:23, where pseudo-Paul tells Timothy, "No longer drink only water, but take a little wine for the sake of your stomach and your frequent ailments." That ultraconservative and pseudo-Pauline position on women is due, in other words, not just to general patriarchy, although it is definitely grounded in it, but also to something else as well. We can see that something else most clearly in the various extracanonical *Acts* of the apostles and most especially in the *Acts of Thecla* within the present *Acts of Paul*. You will, of course, remember Thecla from our cover and Preface.

Feminism in the Arena

In the mid-second-century *Acts of Paul* the apostle gives a sermon composed of thirteen beatitudes that emphasize cumulatively that the only blessed ones are "the pure in heart, who have kept the flesh pure, who have re-nounced the world, who have wives as if they had them not, who have kept their baptism secure, who have departed from the form of this world." The climactic beatitude says, "Blessed are the bodies of the virgins." The imme-diate pagan accusation against Paul is, quite correctly, that "he deprives young men of wives and maidens of husbands, saying: 'Otherwise there is no resurrection for you, except you remain chaste and do not defile the flesh but keep it pure'" (11). That is certainly clear: bodily resurrection is for celibates only (and, preferably, for virgins). But, once again, within patri-archy, that ideal creates different problems for the male Paul and the female Thecla.

Thecla's would-be husband, Thamyris, persuades the governor to scourge and expel Paul but to condemn Thecla to being burned alive. She is saved in the arena by a rainstorm and catches up with Paul on the road. "And Thecla said to Paul, 'I will cut my hair short and follow you wherever you go.' But he said, 'The season is unfavorable, and you are comely. May no other temptation come upon you, worse than the first, and you endure not and play the coward'" (25). No comment is necessary on that interchange, but it gets worse. To Alexander, another would-be husband, Paul denies Thecla in words reminiscent of Peter's betrayal of Jesus. Paul says, 'I do not know the woman of whom you speak, nor is she mine'" (26). Thecla rejects Alexan-der and shames him for his forceful public advances by ripping his cloak and knocking the crown from his head. She is condemned to the beasts in the arena. But here miracles far greater than a rainstorm intervene.

First of all, the ensuing division is not between Christians and pagans, but between women and men or, better, between females and males. Here are the steps. "The women were panic-stricken, and cried out before the judg-ment seat: 'An evil judgment! A godless judgment'" (27). Next, Thecla, who had been abandoned by her birth mother, Theoclaia, receives an adop-tive mother, Tryphaena, who is powerful enough to protect her purity in prison (27, 31). Then, when they bind Thecla to a fierce lioness, "the li-oness licked her feet.' And, once again, "the women and their children cried out from above, saying, 'O God, an impious judgment is come to pass in this city!'" (28). That continues with "a shouting of the people and the women who sat together, some saying, 'Bring in the sacrilegious one!' but others, 'May the city perish for this lawlessness! Slay us all, proconsul. A bitter sight, an evil judgment'" (32). The climax of this theme is this extraordinary de-scription in which the conflict is female against male not only among humans but even among animals:

Lions and bears were set upon her, and a fierce lioness ran to her and lay down at her feet. And the crowd of the women raised a great shout. And a bear ran upon her, but the lioness ran and met it, and tore the bear asunder. And again a lion trained against men, which belonged to Alexander, ran upon her; and the lioness grappled with the lion, and perished with it. And the women mourned the more, since the lioness which helped her was dead. (33)

Second, Thecla sees in the arena a pit of water and, having been earlier refused baptism by the apostle Paul, she proceeds to baptize herself. Lightning protects her from the animals in the water. When other animals are sent in against Thecla "the women cried aloud" and threw so much of their perfume into the arena that the animals "were overpowered as if by sleep" (34). Third, after Tryphaena faints, the governor releases Thecla, "the women cried out with a loud voice, and as with one mouth gave praise to God," and Tryphaena's "maidservants also believed" (38–39). Finally, Thecla dresses herself in a male cloak and goes to meet Paul, who, this time and rather belatedly, tells her, "Go and teach the word of God" (41).

Scholars have suggested that stories like those about Thecla were created by women for women and circulated orally among them before being written down and collected into the *Acts of Paul*. That is certainly possible, but can hardly be proved or disproved. But it is not anachronistic to term them early Christian feminism because of that division not just between women and men, but between females and males. Other scholars have proposed that letters such as those to Timothy and Titus were written specifically against those Thecla-type stories. That is also quite possible but, again, can hardly be proved or disproved.

We have yet to see much more about the historical Paul throughout the rest of this book. But we have already seen that two absolutely divergent traditions claimed the name of that apostle after his death. One moved him into an ultraconservative position of male-over-female superiority, the other into an ultraradical one of necessary male and female celibacy. The ultraconservative option is not just patriarchal misogyny. It demands male leadership, to be sure, but one that is noncelibate and nonascetic. Its leaders must be male, married, and fertile—in short, socially conventional. Just like any decent Roman paterfamilias. The ultraradical option has both female and male leadership, but Thecla outdoes Paul in every way possible. The leadership there is female, unmarried, celibate, and virginal. And each claims to be Pauline and the only true Christianity. If, however, Roman authority thought that the ultraradical option was Christianity itself, it would probably have declared it an illicit religion. The ultraconservative option was one major step on the road from Christ to Constantine. It is sad, however, that the Christian tradition did not adopt a firm both/and rather than a strict either/or; that is, Christian life and leadership could be equally female or male, married or celibate, conventional or ascetic. That, certainly and regardless of his personal preferences for himself, was the authentic Pauline position for Christian converts and assemblies.

3

The Golden Age,
or As Golden as It Gets

The Augustan age is often called the Golden Age, *aurea aetas* or *saeculum aureum*. . . . We are dealing, once more, with a notion that was evolving during this period. It was based, as always, on previous traditions that led to new adaptations and departures. . . . One of the most significant changes in the Golden Age concept at Augustus' time is that the Golden Age comes to connote a social order rather than a paradisiac state of indolence. . . . The Secular [i.e., *Saeculum*] Games of 17 B.C. . . . did not celebrate the advent of millennial, passive bliss but took place only after one of the cornerstones of the Augustan program, the legislation on marriage and morals, had been passed in 18 B.C. . . . The notion of the Golden Age or *saeculum* at Augustus' time was distinctive and specific in the sense that it involved ongoing labor and moral effort rather than being a celebration of easy fulfillment. . . . Tranquility is made possible only through war, victory, and dominance. . . . No specific iconography exists that would point to a "Golden Age" of easy bliss. The reason is simple enough: there was no intention to convey such an impression.

—Karl Galinsky, *Augustan Culture:
An Interpretive Introduction* (1966)

Seneca's essay *On Clemency* . . . is the first work to articulate the Golden Age ideology systematically as a whole. The essay was written early in Nero's reign [mid-50s C.E.], at a time of renewed interest in the Golden Age theme. . . . Given Seneca's position as the emperor's mentor, it may in some sense be taken as an expression of the "official line.". . . Seneca assumes the basic sinfulness of mankind, its *scelus*. . . . Secondly, the presence of the emperor provides the only possible hope of escape. . . . Thirdly, however, for the emperor to succeed as saviour he must practice clemency. . . . Fourthly, Nero has already demonstrated his natural predisposition towards mercy by his unwillingness to execute criminals; the preconditions are thus fulfilled for the Golden Age to return. . . . In Pauline Christianity . . . it is Christ, not the emperor, who acts as the mediator between heaven and sinful mankind. It is Christ not the emperor who has the power to undo *scelus,* sin, by his grace or *clementia,* forgiveness. It is faith, allegiance, voluntary submission to Christ that will bring about or make ready for the return of Paradise, original innocence.

—Andrew Wallace-Hadrill, "The Golden Age
and Sin in Augustan Ideology" (1982)

⁕ ⁕ ⁕

The Divinity of a World Conqueror

Overture

It is dawn in Paul's Thessalonica, today's Thessaloniki, then the Roman provincial capital of Macedonia, now the second-largest city in Greece, but then as now named for the sister of Alexander the Great and then as now climbing from the northeast corner of the Thermaic Gulf up the circling slopes of Mt. Khortiatis.

You are on a two-week Pauline tour around the Aegean, this is the first full day after a transatlantic flight through Munich, and you have no idea how tired you are or how much more tired you yet will be. The plan is that, as at home, you will get up each morning at dawn to jog for an hour before breakfast, and today you are right on schedule for this trip's first—and last—run. Your hotel is just west of the old city and a block or so in from the bay. You cross the negligible Saturday morning traffic toward the main commercial port to run east along the seafront. It is the first week of May in 2000, the air is crisp to cool, the wind is slight to nonexistent, and only a few waiting freighters break the surface of the bay to your right.

But jogging is for thinking, and this is the question. Where in this metropolis of a million can you glimpse anything from the first century, from the world that Paul knew, from the city that Paul visited in the early 50s C.E.? The Roman port is completely obliterated, the extant forum dates from around 200, and the triumphal arch of Galerius dates from around 300 C.E. So what about the year 50? You pass the fifteenth-century White Tower, where workers are setting up platforms under surrounding trees for tomorrow's folk festival. But the Christian antiquities in the tower's Byzantine Museum start a few centuries after Paul's time. Nothing first-century there.

The esplanade is wider now and ahead are the shrubs and trees surrounding the marble and bronze of the Alexander monument. On a raised platform, a large marble-sheathed pedestal holds a statue of the twenty-something general astride Bucephalos rearing toward the east. Alexander rides bareback (stirrups had not yet been invented), his left hand reins the warhorse's head slightly to the left, and his right hand holds a short sword. Two lines of small uninflected Greek letters identify him as *Alexandros/o Megas,* or Alexander the Great (*megas,* by the way, is the first Greek root in "megalomania").

At the left front of the platform, as if in a linked column following Alexander, stands the technological core of his killing machine. Five tall pikes stand upright in marble sockets with five round shields attached about one-third of the way up from the bottom. Greek hoplites had long used massed shoulder-to-shoulder attacks, but with larger shields and much shorter spears. Alexander perfected his father's invention of phalanxes using 18-foot pikes extending 12 feet in front of each soldier. Those *sarissai* were so heavy that they required two hands for steady horizontal thrusting but, with shields suspended from their necks, those in the first five rows of the phalanx could all extend their lethal iron points into the killing zone.

Slightly behind and extending to the right of those five symbolic pikes is a long marble-framed and marble-supported bronze frieze. The scene is a classically stylized version of the battle of Issus mosaic from Pompeii's House of the Faun, now in the National Archaeological Museum in Naples (Figure 45). In both scenes, the left half shows Alexander attacking, and the right half shows Darius fleeing. One half is the West and the future. The other is the East and the past. In May of 2000 you have not yet heard the words, but you already know the concepts. It was not shock *and* awe. It was shock *against* awe. It was shock *over* awe. Shock from the vastly fewer number of massed Macedonian phalangists (the anvil), their flanking aristocratic cavalry (the hammer), and a forward-charging leader protected only if his companions could keep up with him. Awe from the vastly greater number of dispersed Persian troops, their scythed chariots and war elephants, and a leader well protected by elite bodyguards to the rear. Shock destroys awe, as always in the Western way of war, whenever the enemy marches out to death and destruction in the proper and expected manner.

Alexander was brave, brilliant, and a military genius. He was also savage, brutal, and a paranoid alcoholic. In theory, he went east to liberate the Ionian Greeks, to avenge earlier Persian invasions, and to civilize a unified

FIGURE 45. Mosaic from Pompeii showing the Persian king Darius fleeing Alexander the Great at the battle of Issus.

world. In actuality, he slaughtered his way from the Granicus to the Indus, died young, and left his surviving generals a terrible war machine to turn against one another. It was not democracy replacing autocracy, but simply one autocracy displacing another. But even when the short, two-edged steel stabbing swords of the Roman legions made obsolete the long pikes of the Hellenistic phalanxes, Greek held as a common language. And without that *lingua franca* Paul could not have reached his converts or written his letters. But that grace came at a ghastly price, whisper the ghosts of Tyre and Gaza. You leave the seafront, turn north past the Archaeological Museum and the grounds of the International Trade Fair toward the campus of Aristotle University, and then head west along the Egnatia Odos, which recalls the name but does not trace the route of Rome's ancient Via Egnatia. You finish the run from Egnatia into Monastiriou Street and the Capsis Hotel.

"It was not until the reign of Augustus," writes Victor Davis Hanson in *The Wars of the Ancient Greeks and Their Invention of Western Military Culture,* "that Alexander—the propagandistic potentialities of his hero worship for any would-be world conqueror were obvious—was seen in his now familiar role of Alexander Magnus" (174). Recall, for example, from Chapter 2 that Alexander was portrayed at the Forum of Augustus as the prototypical human-become-divine by world conquest. Macedonian globalization in the fourth century B.C.E. was a prototype for Roman globalization in the first century C.E. Augustus followed Alexander into divinity by world conquest.

Outline

From Alexander to Augustus, the world conqueror establishes cosmic peace through global victory. And that both necessitates and confirms a transcendental birth from a human mother, but a divine father. Such origins and such triumphs promise not just universal peace, but utopian or eschatological peace in a world transfigured by farms that do not fail, animals that do not attack, and humans who do not kill.

This chapter starts as Roman civil wars created Mediterranean chaos and threatened the empire's very survival. We counterpoint Virgil's poetic suggestion of an imminent utopia for a rejuvenated Rome with Horace's equally poetic proposal of an imminent departure from an abandoned Rome. But, more pointedly, we contrast visions of *utopia* (Greek, "beyond this place") or *eschaton* (Greek, "beyond this time") in the Roman tradition's emphasis on peace and bodily prosperity with the Jewish tradition's on justice and bodily resurrection.

Rome's Golden Age had brought to Thessalonica "peace and security." But, says Paul in 1 Thessalonians 5:3, it was all delusion. It was God's Golden Age that had begun, and it would be climaxed *soon* by the arrival (Greek *parousia*) not of a divine Claudius, but of a divine Christ. But what, asked his new Thessalonian converts, about those who had died there under Roman persecution? Just as the honored dead in their stately tombs would first greet an emperor arriving along the main road into the city even before the living dignitaries met him at the gate, so would the martyred dead be first to greet the arriving Christ. Their death would not disadvantage but advantage them at that *parousia*.

Christ's advent would be sudden and unexpected, like a nighttime thief's arrival. Still, Christians need not worry because they were no longer living in present night but were already living in future daylight by the love with which they shared together what little they had in a community of mutual support and reciprocity. We, Paul writes to the Thessalonians, "are all children of light and children of the day" and "we belong to the day" (1 Thess. 5:4–8).

We have, however, some final questions for Paul. The *parousia* of Christ was not as soon as he expected. He was off by two thousand years and counting. Was he wrong only about the time or also about the fact? Can we say that his "soon" meant not in the first, but the twenty-first century, or that any biblical "soon" means simply whenever? Could it be that there was only one coming of Christ, that it was more than enough if believers would accept it, and that insistence on a second coming is but the positive face of a refusal to do so?

The Hope of an Ideal World

If you are left profoundly hopeless by your present world of time and place you can go, at least in imagination, to some ecstatically ideal place or to some rhapsodically perfect time. The verbal options are *utopia* ("no place"), putting the emphasis on ending present place, or *eschaton* ("last thing"), putting the emphasis on ending present time. And, of course, you can mix and match to your heart's content or your mind's limit. If somebody receives a special divine revelation about the precise place or imminent advent of this Golden World, the message is termed an *apocalyptic* (Greek, "revelatory") utopia or eschaton.

Paul stood astride the line between Judaism and paganism, between Jewish covenantal eschatology and Roman imperial eschatology, between Christian and Augustan utopian visions, each announcing not just the imminent advent of the Golden Age, but proclaiming that it had already begun. It is pointless and inaccurate to exalt Jewish utopianism in its most ideal form against Roman utopianism in its most brutal practice. On the one hand, each tradition can imagine human or divine savagery in establishing that Golden Age. On the other, although they agree closely in imagining the *physical* and *animal* world brought to final perfection, they differ profoundly in imagining the *social* world in its eschatological consummation. That is not a difference between the bad Romans and the good Jews, but between the conquering Romans and the conquered Jews. It is fair to say that, as we saw in Chapter 2, the Roman eschaton was peace through victory while the Jewish utopia was peace through justice. A *shalom* from the heart of the Jewish tradition opposed a *pax* from the core of the Roman Empire. Here are two examples from each tradition intended not only to lay out options but also to assess alternatives.

Paradise Gained or Paradise Lost

AN ESCHATOLOGICAL BIRTH. Virgil's *Eclogue* 4 is the voice of ecstatic hope written in the glow of October 40 B.C.E., when Antony married Octavian's sister Octavia and permanent peace seemed possible. It imagines their soon-to-be-born child (male, of course) growing to adulthood even as the wheel of time brought round once more the Golden Age to Italy and all the world.

> And in your consulship, Pollio, yes, yours, shall this glorious age begin, and the mighty months commence their march; under your sway any lingering traces of our guilt shall become void and release the earth from its continual dread. He shall have the gift of divine life, shall see heroes mingled with gods, and shall himself be seen by them, and shall rule the world to which his father's prowess brought peace. (11–17)

Virgil then addresses this once and future boy directly. In your childhood, there will be no lack of fertility in field or farm and no danger from wild animals or lethal poisons. "Unbidden, the goats will bring home their udders swollen with milk, and the cattle will not fear huge lions. The serpent, too, will perish, and perish will the plant that hides its poison; Assyrian spice will spring up on every soil" (21–25). In your youth, "a few traces of old-time sin will still live on," so that hard labor and foreign war will again appear. In your adulthood, however, laborless fertility will be total as "every land will bear all fruits. . . . No more will wool be taught to put on varied hues, but of himself the ram in the meadows will change his fleece, now to sweetly blushing purple, now to a saffron yellow; and scarlet shall clothe the grazing lambs at will" (42–45). This is not just an Italian or Roman vision, but a global and cosmic one: "See how the world bows with its massive dome" as "earth and expanse of sea and heaven's depth" and "all things rejoice in the age that is at hand" (50–52).

But notice the primary emphasis in that rhapsodic prophecy. It is about the earth's unworked prosperity, the world's unlabored fertility. Certainly war between humans or strife between animals is fleetingly noted, but it is workless wealth that is underlined. A magnificent vision of divine change, to be sure, but not exactly a social, let alone a political, program for human participation in that new creation. Still, all this is soon to happen here upon this Roman earth. But that is not exactly how Horace saw things at exactly that same time. Virgilian point begot Horatian counterpoint.

A UTOPIAN FLIGHT. As the 40s became the 30s B.C.E., the first round of Roman civil war left Pompey defeated and Caesar victorious, the second round left Caesar murdered, and the third round left his assassins, Brutus and Cassius, defeated at Philippi by his avengers, Antony and Octavian, the not yet Augustus. By then, most Romans anticipated round four and could do the math: One warlord equals regal tyranny, two warlords equals civil war, and three warlords equals social anarchy. All equations seemed equally hopeless.

In his *Epode* 7 Horace asked, "Does some blind frenzy drive us on, or some stronger power, or guilt?" (13–14). Does continuing civil war indicate that "a bitter fate pursues the Romans, and the crime of a brother's murder, ever since blameless Remus's blood was spilt upon the ground, to be a curse upon posterity"? (17–20). Had the inaugural and fratricidal murder of Remus by Romulus (think of the biblical parallel of Abel by Cain) placed upon Rome a fateful destiny of civil war?

In *Epode* 16, as if in reply to *Epode* 7's terrible question, Horace offers an equally terrible answer, since "a second generation is being ground to pieces by civil war, and Rome through her own strength is tottering" (1–2). This city that no one else could conquer, "this selfsame city we ourselves shall ruin, we, an impious generation, of stock accurst," and wild animals and wilder barbarians will soon track through "the ashes of our city" (9–12). And the solution? Abandon Rome immediately and take ship westward vowing never to return. But the vow must be absolute, never to return until, *per impossibile,* rocks float, the Apennines become peninsulas, and "the trustful herd fear not the tawny lion."

> Having vowed these solemn pledges and whatever can prevent our sweet return, let us go forth, the State entire, or the portion better than the ignorant herd! . . . Us the encompassing Ocean awaits. Let us seek the Fields, the Happy Fields, and the Islands of the Blest. . . . Jupiter set apart these shores for a righteous folk, ever since with bronze he dimmed the luster of the Golden Age. (35–37, 41–42, 63–64)

Horace describes the Golden Age on those mythical isles as Virgil did in his *Eclogue* 4 or Isaiah in the quotation below. It is the standard dream of feral harmony and unlabored fertility: "There the goats come unbidden to the milking-pail; and the willing flock brings swelling udders home; nor does the bear at eventide growl 'round the sheepfold, nor the ground swell high with vipers" (49–52).

For Horace, at that stage, the Golden Age was not imminent in historical time and present place, but only in mythical time and distant place for those who would abandon Rome. The early 30s B.C.E. were Virgil's paradise gained, but Horace's paradise lost.

A Question of Divine Justice

COSMIC TRANSFORMATION. In Jerusalem by the 730s B.C.E., the prophet-priest Isaiah had already imagined a perfect world where animals and humans lived together in harmony, peace, and nonviolence:

> The wolf shall live with the lamb,
>   the leopard shall lie down with the kid,
> the calf and the lion and the fatling together,
>   and a little child shall lead them.
> The cow and the bear shall graze,
>   their young shall lie down together;
>   and the lion shall eat straw like the ox.
> The nursing child shall play over the hole of the asp,
>   and the weaned child shall put its hand on the adder's den.
> They will not hurt or destroy
>   on all my holy mountain;
> for the earth will be full of the knowledge of the Lord
>   as the waters cover the sea. (11:6–9)

That is not only far earlier than Virgil's *Eclogue* 4; it may well be its indirect source. But Isaiah's animal-to-animal and animal-to-human serenity is prefaced by human-to-human peace. Those preceding verses are but the second half of a prophetic hope whose first half in 11:1–5 imagines a perfect ruler even before that perfect world in 11:6–9. This king will be both ideal ruler and Davidic heir, because "with righteousness he shall judge the poor, and decide with equity for the meek of the earth" (11:4). An ideal world demands an ideal ruler.

The utopian dream of a perfect earth had three standard and intertwined components: a *physical* or pastoral world of unlabored fertility, a *feral* or animal world of vegetarian harmony, and a *social* or human world of warless peace. Only those last two elements are present in Isaiah 11:1–9, but all three are present, for example, in *Sibylline Oracles* 3, from Egyptian Judaism between 163 and 145 B.C.E. First, "the all-bearing earth will give the most excellent unlimited fruit to mortals, of grain, wine, and oil" (744–45). Next, based on the above Isaian vision, "wolves and lambs will eat grass together in the mountains" as God "will make the beasts on earth harmless" and "serpents and asps will sleep with babies and will not harm them, for the hand of God will be upon them" (788, 793–95). Finally,

> There will be no sword on earth or din of battle, and the earth will no longer be shaken, groaning deeply. There will no longer be war . . . but there will be great peace throughout the whole earth. . . . Prophets of the great God will take away the sword for they themselves are judges of men and righteous kings. There will also be just wealth among men, for this is the judgment and dominion of the great God. (751–55, 781–84)

Furthermore, Israel's utopian eschatology could be articulated with or without an *apocalypsis,* or revelation, of its permanent content in heaven or its imminent advent on earth and with or without a messianic protagonist, a transcendental figure through whom the Golden Age would arrive. But here the alternatives multiply. God could also do it without any such help; God alone could do it directly and immediately. And, if there were such a Messiah, it could be an angel or a human, and, if human, it could be a king, a priest, or a prophet. Or some combination of those preceding options. There were even Jews, within Judaism's long and varied tradition, who could proclaim pagan rulers as God's Messiah: the Persian monarch Cyrus, by Isaiah (44:28a; 45:1, 13) in 539–530 B.C.E.; the Egyptian pharaoh Neos Philometor, by the Jewish *Sibylline Oracles* (3:652–56) in 163–145 B.C.E.; or even the Roman emperor Vespasian, by Josephus in his *Jewish War* (6:312–13) in the 70s C.E.

BODILY RESURRECTION. No doubt the Roman conquerors and the Jewish conquered would never quite agree on the specifics of utopia, but both could at least imagine, even if differently, a transformed world and an idealized leader. There was, however, one special theme within Jewish apocalyptic eschatology that would have struck Greco-Roman paganism as utterly alien and totally absurd, namely, the general bodily resurrection. Where did that come from and why? It came from one very general background and one very specific foreground.

First, the general background. Jewish covenantal faith believed that the world was created in goodness by a God who was just. It must therefore be administered fairly and equitably for itself, for its animals, and for its humans. But the world is normally unjust (say the conquered) so, someday, God must make it just once again. That divine righteousness, or making right, was to be effected here below upon this good earth among embodied humans and not in heaven among disembodied spirits. In other words, a transformed world, whether with Isaiah's vegetarian lions or Virgil's multicolored lambs, whether with animal-animal, animal-human, or human-human peaceful coexistence, would demand transformed bodies. If, therefore, you imagine a this-earthly utopia or a this-worldly eschaton, you have to think about transfigured bodies and not just about disembodied spirits or immortal souls. But all of that was but a very general focus on world, earth, and body.

Second, the specific foreground. In the 160s B.C.E., the Syrian monarch Antiochus IV Epiphanes launched a religious persecution against those Jews who resisted his enforced hellenization and urbanization of the Jewish homeland. Where, many Jewish writers asked, was God's justice when martyrs were being brutalized, tortured, and murdered? There would have to be, some Jewish writers answered, a day of global reckoning, a tribunal of cosmic justice, a general bodily resurrection in which those who had suffered in the flesh could be openly, publicly, and officially declared vindicated by the just God for whom they had died. In other words, the general bodily resurrection was not about the survival of individuals, but about the justice of God. The chant was this: God will overcome someday. And soon!

The eschaton involved for Pharisaic but not for Sadducean Jews both the *bodily* transformation of world and the *bodily* vindication of martyrdom. Daniel 12:2–3 is the classic text: "Many of those who sleep in the dust of the earth shall awake, some to everlasting life, and some to shame and everlasting contempt. Those who are wise shall shine like the brightness of the sky, and those who lead many to righteousness, like the stars forever and ever."

There are even clearer texts in 2 Maccabees as the martyrs insist that their tortured bodies will be returned to them by God's future justice:

And when he was at his last breath, he said, "You accursed wretch, you dismiss us from this present life, but the King of the universe will raise us up to an everlasting renewal of life, because we have died for his laws." . . . He quickly put out his tongue and courageously stretched forth his hands, and said nobly, "I got these from Heaven, and because of his laws I disdain them, and from him I hope to get them back again." (7:9–11)

Finally, "a certain Razis, one of the elders of Jerusalem" manages to out-Cato even the Roman Cato's noble and suicidal death by falling on his sword, and "with his blood now completely drained from him, he tore out his entrails, took them in both hands and hurled them at the crowd, calling upon the Lord of life and spirit to give them back to him again" (14:37, 46). Biologically crude but theologically clear.

For that popular first-century Pharisaic Judaism, therefore, any future world of divine justice and righteousness demanded at its inception a general bodily resurrection in which the just, especially the martyrs, would be vindicated and the unjust, especially the persecutors, would be punished. Cosmic transformation, yes, but bodily resurrection also. It was a matter of divine justice.

Augustan Eschaton as Golden Age

COSMIC SAVIOR. After the battle of Actium and as the 30s ended, everything Roman had changed utterly. But so had the very idea of the Golden Age. It was now accomplished and accompanied by a divine savior here below upon this earth. That would become more important even than the Golden Age itself or, better, that would become its equivalent institution. And for the vast Mediterranean population that was completely credible in context.

In the 20s, after Octavian had become Augustus, Horace's *Ode* 1.2 mourned that, in the slaughter of Rome's decades-long civil wars, "our children" had been "made fewer by their parents' sins" and asked, "To whom shall Jupiter assign the task of atoning for our guilt?" (21, 29–30). He suggested various divine candidates, but ended with the present actuality of Augustus as a god incarnate:

> You, winged son [Hermes-Mercury] of benign Maia, if changing your form, you assume on earth the guise of man, right ready to be called the avenger of [Julius] Caesar; late may you return to the skies and long may you be pleased to dwell amid Quirinus's [Roman] folk; and may no untimely gale waft you from us angered at our sins. Here rather may you love glorious triumphs, the name of "Father" (*Pater*) and "Chief" (*Princeps*); nor suffer the Medes to ride on their raids unpunished; while you are our leader, O Caesar. (41–52)

Augustus as divinity incarnate is both atonement for Rome's past sins and protector of Rome's present borders.

He hints in *Ode* 3.5, another poem from the same period, that maybe a god on earth known through victory is better than a god in heaven known through thunder. "We believe that Jove is king in heaven because we hear his thunders peal; Augustus shall be deemed a god on earth (*praesens divus*) for adding to our empire the Britons and dread Parthians" (1–4). Whether that rather ambiguous "for" means "if," "when," "since," or "because," present divine incarnation on earth has immediately practical benefits over absent divine rule in heaven.

In *Epistle* 2.1, an open letter to Augustus written about a decade later and possibly his very last work, Horace noted that earlier Roman and Greek heroes like Romulus, Liber, Hercules, or Castor and Pollux had, despite all their great benefactions for humanity, been accorded divinity only *after* death. It seems, he continued, that "envy is quelled only by death that comes at last," especially since one "scorches with his brilliance who outweighs merits lowlier than his own, yet he too will win affection when his light is quenched." But Augustus is different from all those preceding posthumous divinities, because "upon you, however, while still among us, we bestow honours already, set up altars to swear by in your name, and confess that nothing like you will hereafter arise or has arisen before now" (12–17). Dead divinity is standard, but live divinity is unique in past, present, and future. Augustus controls time as well as space.

Those texts from Horace articulate clearly the core of Augustus's personal, dynastic, and imperial theology. But very few people across the Roman Empire could read, hear, or understand the lyric Latin of that magnificent poet. How was that theology popularized among ordinary people? Think not texts, but images, images, images.

HIS FATHER'S STAR. The young Octavian grasped one astrological phenomenon early in his life and stressed its cosmic significance ever afterward. Immediately after Julius Caesar's assassination on the Ides of March in 44 B.C.E., the eighteen-year-old Octavian brushed aside senatorial opposition and celebrated games honoring the slain Caesar's victory that July. That proved to be impeccable timing. When a comet appeared in the sky, Octavian urgently promoted and the people willingly accepted it as the apotheosis of Julius Caesar, now divine and taking his place among the heavenly gods. That moving star's interpretation was endorsed by an *haruspex* named Vulcanius, one of those archaic Etruscan interpreters of heavenly thunderbolts, animal entrails, and celestial portents whose role in Rome had lapsed for some time. He explained that the comet signaled the new age, and a poem allegedly from the prophetic Sibyl of Cumae near Naples combined Greek and Etruscan eschatological doctrines to interpret the sign as the end of the ninth and the beginning of the tenth and final age, the age of the sun god Sol, whose metal emblem was gold.

Octavian displayed that star everywhere as he vied for power with Antony. It is engraved on ring gemstones and pressed into clay seals and cheap glass beads, but it is found especially on coins whose legends made the logical conclusion that, if Julius Caesar was now divine, his adopted son Octavian was therefore "son of a divine one" or "son of god." The title is variously abbreviated from DIVI FILIUS as DI FI, DIVI F, or DIVI FI. Whatever opposing senators might have thought, Octavian was the self-proclaimed and popularly acclaimed divine son, and when Roman sacred law deified Julius Caesar in 42 B.C.E., Augustus's status had legal sanction.

WRITTEN IN HEAVEN. But the message of Augustus as divine son was not limited to small artifacts like coins. Recall that great Augustan sundial on the Campus Martius mentioned in Chapter 2, and now take a closer look at its cosmic implications. Consider the point its designers intended with that plaza-sized artifact as well as the range of impressions left on those ancient pedestrians strolling in its parklike atmosphere. Some may have only intuited subtle hints, but others certainly recognized the detailed articulation of Augustus's cosmic position: earth and sun, monument and shadow lined up to point out his epochal importance. This was obvious in the very use of sun and calendar, obelisk and orb. But it was spelled out in the layout's details, according to the German archaeologist Edmund Buchner. He has creatively if not convincingly argued that, on the fall equinox of September 23, which was also Augustus's birthday, the sundial's shadow pointed right into the *Ara Pacis Augustae* and further that, on the winter solstice in December, it pointed toward the day of Augustus's conception when the zodiac moved into Capricorn, another sign featured prominently in Augustan iconography. In other words, Augustus's destiny was written in the stars.

Suetonius's *The Lives of the Caesars* tells in *The Deified Augustus* how the Greek astrologer Theogenes from Apollonia on the Via Egnatia predicted "an incredible career" for Augustus, but then when Augustus revealed his birth-date and the astrologer calculated the configuration of the heavens at that time, he "sprang up and threw himself at his feet. . . . From that time on Augustus had such faith in his destiny, that he made his horoscope public and issued a silver coin stamped with the sign of the constellation Capricornus, under which he was born" (94.12).

Astrological phenomena then appear frequently on Augustan coinage from Rome. A gold aureus minted by Octavian in 36 B.C.E. depicts the Temple of the Divine Julius with the star as comet of his apotheosis in its pediment. A bronze denarius minted by the senator L. Lentulus in 12 B.C.E. shows a larger Augustus placing the comet on the smaller Julius Caesar (Figure 46). Across the empire and on their own initiative, mints eagerly spread that good news. In the west, a series of Spanish denarii between 17 and 15 B.C.E. show Augustus's zodiac sign, Capricorn, with a globe under its feet and a cornucopia, or horn of plenty, above its back. In the east, an Ephesian denarius and cistophorus show Capricorn and a cornucopia accompanied by the legend AUGUSTUS, encircled by Apollo's laurel wreath (Figure 47).

SON OF APOLLO. The cistophorus's laurel wreath points to another component of Augustus's cosmic significance. Octavian adopted the sun god Apollo, with his laurel and lyre, prophecy and discipline, in very early opposition to rival Antony's preferred wine god Dionysos, with his ivy and vine, ecstasy and luxury. It pitted new-dawn against late-night imagery. After Octavian became securely Augustus, that contrast faded and Augustus consolidated Dionysiac elements into the later iconography of the *Ara Pacis Augustae*. But the ancient Greek sun god born on the island of Delos served another, even more important function in Augustan propaganda.

Apollo lent Augustus a cosmic significance and so was prominent in Augustan art, architecture, and theology. A few examples. First, as illustrated in Chapter 2, Apollo and his iconographic griffin were seen to center right on the cuirass of Augustus's very important Prima Porta statue (Figure 31). Second, a lyre-playing Apollo can be seen on a fragmentary wall painting from

FIGURE 46. Denarius of Augustus minted in Rome, with Augustus placing the star upon Julius Caesar.

FIGURE 47. Denarius and cistophorus of Augustus, with his zodiac sign, Capricorn, and horn of plenty.

Augustus's own Palatine palace. Third, right next to and connected with that palace, Augustus built a new temple for Apollo in a prominent place on the Palatine Hill. Augustus later transferred the Greek *Sibylline Oracles* from the Capitoline temple of Jupiter to that new Palatine temple of Apollo. The antiquity and ambiguity of those cryptic Greek prophecies accommodated favorable Augustan interpretations and included predictions of his Golden Age. But before he moved them next door to his house, he purged and edited them to clarify and accentuate how they pointed to him and his era. Finally and above all, Suetonius's *The Lives of the Caesars* tells in *The Deified Augustus* how he was conceived of a human mother, Atia, but a divine father, Apollo (94.4). Apollo was the god of medicine and music, but also the god of prophecy in his great oracular shrines at Delphi in Greece, Didyma in Turkey, and Delos in the Cyclades. Conception by a god of prophecy guaranteed your future, guaranteed that you *were* the future, more than any spoken oracle or written text could ever establish.

NEW GOLDEN AGE. Recall once again that Saeculum Hymn sponsored by Augustus, composed by Horace, and sung chorally by twenty-seven girls and twenty-seven boys at the great New Golden Age celebrations on and around the Campus Martius in 17 B.C.E. The hymn's invocation opened the Saeculum Games and appeals to Apollo both indirectly and directly: "O quickening Sun, that in your shining carriage ushers in the day and hides it, and are reborn another and yet the same, never may you be able to view any greater than the city of Rome. . . . Do you, Apollo, gracious and benign, put aside your weapon and give ear to your suppliant sons" (9–12, 33–34).

Nearly two millennia after that celebration and almost on Augustus's birthday, an accidental discovery on September 20, 1890, in the western end of the Campus Martius provided remarkable details about those eschatological games that celebrated the dawning Golden Age. Workmen were constructing a sewer along the Tiber at Piazza P. Paoli just before the Corso Vittorio Emanuele crosses the Tiber on a bridge of that same name. They discovered a medieval wall constructed of random bits of earlier material from the surrounding ruins. By day's end when that wall was disassembled, the crew turned over to officials over one hundred inscribed fragments, seven of which, with an eighth added later, were in minuscule script from the Augustan period. They once belonged to a nearly 10-foot-high plaque attached to an even larger square pillar, erected to record the ritual proceedings of the Saeculum Games.

The inscription preserves a terse and methodical register of the three-day celebration that counterbalances Horace's poetic and choral script, and it reveals Augustus's pronounced and personal role in the games' rituals. The preparations for the celebrations included ritual bathing and purification of the people, and once they began, women in mourning were to set aside any sign of grief and courts were to suspend the administration of justice. But Augustus himself was clearly orchestrating and presiding over the rites, as one paragraph describing the sacrifice to the Fates illustrates:

On the following night, on the Campus Martius, next to the Tiber, [the Imperator Caesar Augustus sacrificed] according to Greek rite [nine female lambs to the divine Fates] as whole burnt offerings; and by the same [rite he sacrificed nine female goats as whole burnt offerings and spoke the following prayer:] "Fates. As it is [prescribed for] you in those books . . . [I beg you and pray that] you may increase [the power and majesty of the Roman people] . . . in war and peace; [. . . and that you may grant eternal safety,] victory and health [to the Roman people, . . . and the legions of the Roman people]; [and that you may keep safe and expand] the state of the Roman people, [. . . and that you may be] favorable and propitious [to the Roman people], . . .

[to me, to my house, to my household] . . ." (*CIL* 6.32323, translation from Beard, North, and Price, Vol. 2, 140–44)

"Those books," of course, are the Greek *Sibylline Oracles*. That same prayer and similar sacrifices were repeated to the major Roman deities by day and night all over the city and included Apollo. With the prophet-god Apollo, Augustus controlled the future, and with the *Sibylline Oracles* under wraps, he also controlled past predictions of the present. The Golden Age was tightly managed.

INTERACTIVE ESCHATON. The Golden Age involved, as that divine savior himself insisted, not feral serenity, unlabored fertility, and passive indolence, but activity, involvement, and participation. It demanded security abroad and piety at home, martial vigor and marital fidelity, military and moral rearmament, the rebuilding of temples and the restoring of families. Listen again, for one last time, to the choral voices of Horace's hymn for those Seculum Games of 17 B.C.E. There is nothing in that public chant about golden indolence. Golden Age, yes. Golden Laziness, no.

First, of course, comes morality, as you recall from Chapter 2. "Rear up our youth, O goddess, and bless the Fathers' edicts concerning wedlock and the marriage-law, destined, we pray, to be prolific in new offspring" (17–20). Next, comes fertility, but it is the normal abundance allowed by peace. "Bountiful in crops and cattle, may Mother Earth deck Ceres with a crown of corn; and may Jove's wholesome rains and breezes give increase to the harvest" (29–32). Then, Augustus appears as a new Aeneas with a thousand-year-old divine pedigree, descendant of the Trojan Anchises and the goddess Venus. "And what the glorious scion of Anchises and of Venus, with sacrifices of milk-white steers, entreats that may he obtain, triumphant o'er the warring foe, but generous to the fallen!" (49–52). With the Parthians, Indians, and Scythians subdued, Faith, Peace, Honor, Modesty, Virtue, and Plenty have returned. Finally, may Apollo, "prolong the Roman power and Latium's prosperity to cycles ever new and ages ever better" (66–68).

Augustus's program was an active utopia, an interactive eschaton. It was not just hope for the future, but promise for the present. And anyone who wished to counter it would have to offer not just hope for a possible future, but promise for the visible present. Enter Paul, then, a generation later and from a background in Jewish apocalyptic eschatology, which he pointed straight at the heart of that Roman imperial eschatology so relentlessly emphasized by Augustus's successors. It was a cosmic clash of gods, lords, and saviors, a global struggle not just between future possibilities, but between present actualities, a debate in which exactly the same words had absolutely different meanings.

A Divine Dynasty for a Golden Age

The East's widespread enthusiasm for the emperor exceeded that of the Roman people and certainly that of the Roman Senate. One might suggest, cynically, that divine worship there was primarily to solicit benefits and benefactions from Rome. But one must remember that the stability and security provided by imperial rule had already led to those blessings, and such global grace or cosmic peace surely had to come from a god, right? Rather than a secular, cynical approach to such imperial feasts, rituals, and honors, we take a religio-political approach that assumes a considerable degree of sincerity on behalf of most provincials, and we stress that the pervasiveness of Roman imperial theology's emperor cult across the Mediterranean was one of the key features of Paul's world. It consolidated the various parts of empire into a single whole and was the glue that held the *oikoumenē,* or civilized world, together. Cyclical festivals and communal rituals, the persistence of images carved in marble and inscribed on stone, and the prayers and priesthoods of imperial temples were the most important factors in holding people subject to Rome together, people who over time would come to consider themselves as fully Roman.

We do not assume that "*the* emperor cult" or "*the* imperial cult" ever existed as a monolithic entity, since the archaeological, epigraphic, and literary evidence reveals a striking diversity of forms for honoring and worshiping the contemporary supreme and divine Roman. The phenomenon was not regulated by any Roman priestly hierarchy or unified under a set of Latin doctrines. Instead, local initiatives to honor the Julio-Claudian emperors, based on local political conditions and local religious traditions, created a broad range of "imperial cults," and cities or even provinces outdid each other with lavish and creative tributes to the emperor. And within cities across the empire, the rich competed for expensive services to the emperor and priestly offices in his cult, and they sponsored buildings, games, and even lotteries for his sake.

The cult might have meant different things to different participants and spectators, but it was the most recognizable feature to travelers like Paul in the thousands of cities that dotted the Mediterranean. For the urban poor, participation in the cult's seductive festivals was hard to resist, and any reticence appeared unreasonable, since the imperial cult always accommodated local gods and regional traditions. For freed slaves and urban artisans, there were, in the name of Augustus, Tiberius, Caligula, or Claudius, philanthropic benefits like free theatrical shows or gladiatorial games as well as public feasts that distributed sacrificial meat and even complimentary drinks to lubricate the social graces. For the elite, the imperial cult provided, in the words of Stephen Mitchell's *Anatolia,* "a context, even a language, in which they could express their ambitions, impress their communities, and achieve positions of power and authority" (117). In short, the imperial cult created an urban civic life that, in one direction, demanded loyalty to emperor and stability of empire and obtained, in the other, economic and political benefit, but perhaps most important, social recognition and communal honor at the local level.

It is no surprise then that the surface of the lost Roman Empire is littered with faces of dead emperors on coins, and the ground is filled with their heads on statues and their names on stones. Artifacts, from the smallest coins through the largest temples to whole cities, give an absolutely clear archaeological picture of Caesar's centrality to the empire's inhabitants. In any city that Paul visited, evidence of emperor worship appears repeatedly in present excavations. Archaeologists find inscriptions for the imperial cult, usually. They find statues of the imperial family, usually. They find emperors on coins, always.

The Julio-Claudian emperors included Julian descendants of Augustus's sister Octavia or daughter, Julia, along with Claudian descendants of his second wife, Livia. Caligula and Nero came from the former line, Tiberius and Claudius from the latter. The Claudians certainly produced better imperial stock and yet Augustus's divine charisma flowed on through all his successors until it was renewed once again in the next, Flavian dynasty. It was no longer personal or even dynastic; it was imperial. Here are some examples across the entire Julio-Claudian dynasty. Read them against the background of our opening epigraphs on the Golden Age with Augustus and with Nero.

Augustus

Michael Pfanner has examined the ancient techniques available for mass production and compared the numbers from Napoleonic France to estimate that there were between twenty-five and fifty thousand portraits of Augustus across the empire, not including those of his successors and the imperial family. Certainly then, his programmatically copied facial features and hair locks made him the most recognizable person in the world. His statues stood deity-like in temples, his busts represented imperial justice in law courts, and his images were paraded through imperial cities on various anniversaries, a tradition that continued for later emperors.

That image was accompanied by an equally programmatic theology or cosmology. One inscription from Egypt, cited in Ethelbert Stauffer's *Christ and the Caesars,* calls Augustus's conquest liberation and the emperor himself heaven's shining star. He is described in cosmological terms as the "ruler of oceans and continents, the divine father among men, who bears the same name as his heavenly father—Liberator, the marvelous star of the Greek world, shining with the brilliance of the great heavenly Saviour" (99). Another inscription, dated March 17, 24 B.C.E., from Socnopaei Nesus in the Egyptian Fayyum, cited in Deissmann's *Light from the Ancient East,* show how malleable and adaptable the Roman imperial theology actually was. Augustus is called "god of god," applying the ancient title of divine Horus, child of divine Isis and divine Osiris, to the Roman emperor (345).

Tiberius

Augustus himself had only one child, Julia, and he married her off repeatedly in hopes of a blood heir, but none of her heir-apparent sons lived to full maturity. Reluctantly, then, Augustus accepted Tiberius, his stepson from Livia's previous marriage to Claudius, as adopted son and heir apparent. With Augustus finally dead and senatorially divinized, Tiberius was *divi filius,* Son of God, and emperor for the next two decades. Tiberius did not dare rely only on his predecessor's divine charisma, but initially depended heavily on his own very successful military career. That conjunction of victory and divinity, with both flowing from Augustus to Tiberius, is beautifully illustrated on two sardonyx cameos, one 7 by 9 inches and now in the Kunsthistorisches Museum in Vienna, the other 10 by 12 inches and now in the Bibliothèque Nationale de France in Paris.

The former cameo, known as the *Gemma Augustea,* contains two almost equal registers (Figure 48). On the bottom section, to the left, four Roman soldiers erect a trophy with two barbarian captives, one female and one male, ready to be tied to it. To the right, two Roman allies drag two other

FIGURE 48. The *Gemma Augustea,* with Augustus seated Jupiter-like amid his court in the upper register, and Roman soldiers with defeated barbarians in the lower register.

captives, again one female and one male, toward it by their hair. On the larger top section, at the left, the toga-clad Tiberius descends from his chariot led by the goddess Victory. His nephew, the young militarily clad Germanicus, stands between him and Roma. In the center, the goddess Roma and Augustus divinized as Jupiter recline on a double throne with conquered arms beneath their feet. She looks, as do all other upper-register eyes, at Augustus, who looks past her toward Tiberius. She, by the way, is seated at his right and not vice versa. Below the seminude and divine Augustus is Jupiter's symbolic eagle and it too looks upward at him. Above him is Capricorn, his zodiacal birth sign. In his right hand he holds the augur's short staff and in his left the tall imperial scepter. To the right, the *Oikoumenē,* or Inhabited World, crowns him with an oak wreath. Beside her, Ocean (male) is standing and Earth (female) is seated with the children and cornucopia of safety and fertility. The occasion imaged is the triumph of the victorious Tiberius on October 23, 12 C.E. The message is very clear: Augustan divinity sits atop Roman victory and, from both, fertile peace extends over sea, land, and all the inhabited earth.

The latter cameo, known as the *Grande Camée de France*, has not two but three registers (Figure 49). The bottom section is filled with defeated men, women, and children. In the much larger middle section, on the far left is Kleio with her scroll, ready to record history. In front of her is the young Caligula. To the right of them is Germanicus with his wife Agrippina behind

FIGURE 49. The *Grande Camée de France,* with the divine Augustus looking down on his wife Livia and his successor, Tiberius.

him. In that section's precise center, Tiberius sits on a throne in almost exact duplication of Augustus on that other cameo. He is seminude, wreathed, with an augur's *lituus* in his right hand and the tall spear-staff in his left. To the right of him on a lower throne is Livia, his mother and wife of the dead Augustus. Conquered Armenia, with head bowed, is seated in front of her. To right of her, Germanicus's son, the younger Drusus, points upward to the top register's heaven. And, finally, at the extreme right, his wife, Aemiia Lepida, looks upward along his pointing arm.

The top register shows, again from left to right, eminent dead members of the Julio-Claudian dynasty now in heaven. At the left is the elder Drusus, brother of Tiberius; in the center is a wreathed Augustus with aegis and scepter; and at the right is a mounted Marcellus. A small Eros, child of Mars and Venus, brings Marcellus to Augustus. In front of Augustus, Aeneas, the divine Trojan ancestor of the Julio-Claudian line, carries upward a large globe. The occasion imaged is the return of Germanicus from the north and his departure to the east (and death) in 17 C.E. Once again the message is clear: The divine Augustus protects his dynasty from heaven, but now war dominates exclusively over peace.

There still exists, from the Peloponnesian city of Gytheum near Sparta, a detailed account of celebrations for the imperial family from the reign of Tiberius in 15 C.E. Note, as you read, that this inscription was not simply a record put up on a wall, but a prescription for a large and repeated citywide festival:

> The *agoranomos* [marketplace overseer] shall celebrate the first day of the god Caesar Augustus, son of the god, our Savior and Deliverer; the second day for the emperor [Ti]berius Caesar Augustus, father of the fatherland; the third day for Julia Augusta [Livia], the Fortune of our nation and city; the fourth day (of Victory) for Germanicus Caesar; the fifth day (of Aphrodite) for Drusus Caesar; and the sixth day for Titus Quinctius Flaminius; the *agoranomos* shall be responsible for the good order of the contestants. . . . When the *agoranomos* is holding the thymelic [i.e., musical and theatrical] games, he shall conduct a procession from the temple of Asklepios and Health, including the . . . young men and the other citizens, wearing bay-leaf garlands and white clothes. Also in the procession will be the sacred maidens and the women in sacred clothes. When the procession reaches the Caesareion, [they] shall sacrifice a bull on behalf of the safety of our rulers and gods and the eternal continuance of their rule. After their sacrifice,

they will bid the common diners and the magistrates to sacrifice in the agora. [And the] priest of the god Augustus Caesar shall deliver three painted images of the god Augustus and of Julia Augusta and of Tiberius Caesar Augustus, also for the theater. . . . And they shall put up a stone column with this sacred law inscribed on it and they shall deposit a copy of this sacred law in the public archives, so that this law may, displayed for all to see in a public place and in the open air, prove the gratitude of the People of Gytheum towards the rulers. . . . (*SEG* 11.923; translation from Beard, North, and Price, Vol. 2, 254–55)

In another inscription from Gytheum Tiberius replied that he was pleased with divine honors for his father Augustus, but was content himself to have honors "suitable for mortal men" (*SEG* 11.922). But like it or not, the festival and rites went on unchanged, and Tiberius was honored like a god by having a bull offered to him by the people "on behalf of the safety of our rulers and gods." Like so many similar rituals from around the Mediterranean, the festival at Gytheum gave the very wealthy a chance to associate themselves with the emperor, gave the youth of the city a familiarity with the imperial family, and, after a highly visible procession, gave banquets to the people in honor of the emperor.

Caligula

Gaius Julius Caesar Germanicus was affectionately nicknamed Caligula, or "Little Boot," by soldiers stationed on the Rhine under his father Germanicus. He survived the accidents, assassinations, and poisonings under Tiberius and his power-hungry adviser Sejanus to become emperor in 37 C.E. His appetite for sexual pathology and immediate divinity is well known, if not exaggerated, and he was finally assassinated after only four years of rule.

Even in his short reign, Caligula was able to establish some cosmic significance and divine honor abroad. A statue of him was placed in the temple of Apollo on the island of Calymnus, and an accompanying inscription suggests that the temple was dedicated to them both (*IGR* 6.1022). An oath of loyalty to Caligula survives in inscription from the city of Assos in Turkey, sworn by both Romans and Greeks, but note its full cosmic or, better, apocalyptic and even messianic, imagery:

Since the announcement of the coronation of Gaius Caesar Germanicus Augustus, which all mankind had hoped and prayed for, the world has found no measure for its joy, but every city and people has eagerly hastened to view the god as if the happiest age for mankind had now arrived: It seemed good to the council and to the Roman businessmen here among us, and to the people of Assos, to appoint a delegation made up of the noblest and most eminent of the Romans and also of the Greeks, to visit him and offer their best wishes and to implore him to remember the city and take care of it, even as he promised our city upon his first visit to the province in the company of his father Germanicus. (*SIG* 3.797)

But unlike Tiberius, Caligula drew heavily upon his bloodline from Augustus and very shortly proclaimed himself divine. A silver sestertius from very early in his reign depicts a draped and veiled representation of *Pietas,* that is, religious piety but especially filial piety, that recalls his great-grandfather Augustus. It is surrounded by the abbreviated legend "Gaius Caesar, great-grandson of Divine Augustus, Augustus, *pontifex maximus,* with tribunician power for the third time, father of the country." The reverse shows Caligula, togate and veiled like a priest, sacrificing a bull in the Temple of the Divine Augustus, a structure begun and nearly completed by Tiberius, but dedicated by Caligula in his very first year as Caesar (Figure 50).

A slightly later coin of Caligula is even more obvious in his reliance for divinity on Augustus as progenitor rather than on himself as *imperator* on the battlefield. One side portrays the divine Augustus crowned with the rays of the sun god Sol or maybe Apollo, and the other side has Caligula crowned with Apollo's laurel wreath and sporting facial features and hair curls remarkably similar to his great-grandfather's (Figure 51). The accompanying legend simply states that Gaius Caesar was *pontifex maximus,* the title that Augustus had so desired and patiently awaited and was quickly snatched up by Caligula. He was a priest without piety and a savior without benefaction,

FIGURE 50. Coin of Caligula veiled as a priest sacrificing a bull at the Temple of the Divine Augustus.

and it only took four years of taking without giving until the legions took charge of his removal.

Claudius

After the army assassinated Caligula and most other possible heirs, the club-footed and stuttering Claudius was found hiding behind a curtain and was crowned emperor by the army. That was primarily to avoid the return of the Republic and with it the bloody civil wars that pitted the legions against each other. Claudius was able to restore some dignity to the imperial line and, like Augustus before him, he actually introduced new practices in the guise of old ones. He meticulously observed rituals, carefully recited prayers, and was fond of antiquarian aspects of Roman history. For example, citing an ancient (and certainly forgotten) custom that those who expanded the empire could also extend the city's sacred boundaries, he increased both after his conquest of Britain. He also revived the ancient Etruscan art of the *haruspices,* probably in part to curtail foreign superstitions in Rome from Celtic druids or Eastern astrologers. But, perhaps most important, and again like Augustus before him, he celebrated the Saeculum Games on the Campus Martius in 47 C.E. A cadre of scholars and astronomers creatively calculated their next date using a 100-year rather than a 110-year cycle, and, after favorably determining that the games should fall on the eight hundredth anniversary of the founding of Rome, it was happily discovered that that dawning of a new age fell exactly six years into Claudius's reign.

Claudius was also able to have the Senate vote his posthumous deification, a decision that was not without initial opposition and later ridicule. A first-century parody, probably written by Seneca, the tutor and then adviser of Claudius's successor, Nero, has the Olympian gods bitterly contest the issue, with the god Augustus himself pleading against deification. But Nero

FIGURE 52. Coin of Claudius announcing the "Hope of Augustus."

later forced Seneca to commit suicide, possibly for not taking imperial deification seriously enough, and Claudius remained a god. From a thousand miles away and two centuries later, the dry Syrian Desert at Dura-Europos has preserved a standard military calendar whose papyrus text lists August 1 as the birthday of the god Claudius (*divus Claudius*) and as a major feast day on which an ox was to be sacrificed to him, Jupiter, and Augustus.

In 41 c.e. Claudius minted a coin with the female personification of *Spes* (Hope), advancing and holding a flower, accompanied by the legend *Spes Augusta,* the "Hope of Augustus" (Figure 52). Perhaps this was to announce his dynastic hopes for his newborn son, Brittanicus, or more likely it simply sought to confirm the eschatological continuity of the Golden Age from Augustus to Claudius. He, after all, was born on August 1, the feast day of *Spes,* and he intended to exploit the cosmic significance of that event. We will have more about Claudius on coin and statue below in Thessalonica.

Nero

Nero became Caesar after Claudius's death, but he was the last of the Julio-Claudian dynasty. A monument found in excavations during the early 1990s on the northeastern slope of the Palatine Hill reveals how Augustus, the onetime *princeps,* had in fact begun a dynastic rule that would bring the imperial cult even into Rome itself. A previously unknown temple that served the imperial cult was discovered with an accompanying monument to the divine Julio-Claudian dynasty. Two sets of inscriptions were found. One is on a bronze sheath that covered a wood and concrete statue base. The other is on a set of marble plaques nearly 15 feet long that attached to another base for imperial statues, presumably also bronze, but that are yet to be found.

The monument was dedicated by a group of brass musicians (bronze, actually), the *aenatores,* who played trumpet, clarion, and bugle at military events and sacred ceremonies. The first inscription was for the then future emperor Tiberius from sometime prior to his adoption by Augustus in 4 C.E. Tiberius's inscription and statue were the fixtures around which Claudius later built a dynastic monument when he restored the temple and added statues of Augustus, himself, and his wife, Agrippina, the mother of Nero. Those inscriptions are still preserved on the marble base. They immortalize the emperor Augustus as son of the divine Caesar and chief priest (IMP CAE-SARI DIVI F AUGUSTO PONTIFICI MAXIMO . . .), identify Claudius also as the chief priest (PONTIFICI MAXIMO), and describe Julia Agrippina, the doting mother of Nero, as the wife of the god Claudius (DIVI CLAUDI). Caligula was never present, having been subject to *damnatio memoriae,* posthumous erasure from all inscriptions or statues. But later a statue of Nero was added with the longest inscription, identifying him in various ways, including chief priest, the son of the divine Claudius, and great-great-grandson of the divine Augustus.

Rome had embraced Augustus's founding of a dynasty that passed on divinity and chief-priesthood, including the title of *pontifex maximus,* the supreme bridge builder between heaven and earth, and it continued all the way to Nero. That dynastic temple was destroyed in the great fire of Rome in 64, its inscription was fragmented, and the area covered in to accommodate Nero's new and extravagant Golden House. Very shortly, however, the monument was no longer necessary, as the dynasty ended in 68 C.E. when Nero was forced to commit suicide.

The Via Egnatia Across the Balkans

To Thessaloniki Now

You are speeding along an empty four-lane divided highway through Greece in a little red and rented Citroen doing well over the legal 120 and more like 170 kilometers per hour. Because there was absolutely no one else on the road, no one at all, for at least an hour. That morning you started from Dodoni, Zeus's most ancient oracular site, visited by Homer's Odysseus and maybe not many others since, and were heading toward the north-western corner of Greece just south of the Albanian border inland from the island of Kerkira, or Corfu. You were driving on what the map shows as little yellow squiggly lines indicating single lanes with, at best, tractors and, at worst, goats to slow your pace. Occasionally those yellow squiggly lines turned into white squiggly lines indicating all the above, but on dirt roads with potholes. Then you stumbled unexpectedly upon an on-ramp to the big pink-highlighted and black-dotted streak that your map says is still under construction. But it was clearly finished that mid-June morning in 2003, and you take it as fast as you can toward the Adriatic Sea and the modern town of Igoumenítsa, first port for the car ferries from Brindisi on the heel of the Italian mainland. From there you will turn south inland and then go along the coast to the site of Octavian and Agrippa's victory over Antony and Cleopatra off Cape Actium on the southern promontory of the Ambracian Gulf.

The motorway stops as suddenly as it began, with an end-of-freeway sign at a massive construction site for a suspension bridge over a river and a tunnel through a hill (Figure 53). But before you return to the little yellow and white lines on the map, you pause to read the big blue and gold sign in Greek and English, put up by the European Union, that announces the new Egnatia Odos, the new Via Egnatia. The sign emphasizes that half the cost of those cranes, bulldozers, and cement mixers in front of you is being paid by the European Union's Community Support Framework and much of the rest is funded by the European Investment Bank. You learn later that the total cost is estimated at 1.15 trillion Greek drachmas, a currency made obsolete by

FIGURE 53. Construction of the new Egnatian Way, cutting through central Greece.

the Euro but calculated in 2003 at about 300 to the dollar. You also learn later that, after the Egnatia Odos Motorway is completed and its terminal ends linked up, its 425 miles will include 1650 bridges with a combined length of 25 miles and 76 tunnels with a combined length of 30 miles.

Construction along that 1100-yard-wide swath of land has unearthed 270 historical and archaeological sites, which have slowed the project down and required the contractors to pay over 2.5 billion drachmas for salvage excavations at over 40 sites. That, of course, is a reminder of ancient geopolitics along the original Via Egnatia, which had much the same purpose, to link Rome and Italy with Asia Minor and the East. But that ancient project, built by the Roman proconsul Gnaeus Egnatius between 146 and 120 B.C.E., was much more pressing, since travel by air was not available and travel by sea all but impossible for six months of the year. The only way to send the legions eastward and bring booty westward was to construct, on an unprecedented scale, an all-weather road with solid pavement, bridges, leveled grades, water stations, and milestones.

The new Odos will cut the travel time from Igoumenítsa on the Adriatic to Thessaloniki on the Aegean from five to two and a half hours, and from Igoumenítsa to the Turkish border from twelve to six hours. Greece will then effectively link west to east, Italy to Turkey, and Europe to Asia. As you relinquish your small strip of the new Egnatia Odos that summer morning, you ponder the obvious parallels with the original one. Is it still about empire for the few or about justice for the many? Here is a simple test. By the time that new Egnatian motorway is completed, will Turkey be a full member of the European Union; will Turkey be the first non-European and non-Christian country to join that alliance? If not, if its 65 million inhabitants are excluded, we will then know that the new motorway is, like its ancient predecessor, again about empire, still about empire, always about empire. But above all else, as you get off that road's new western end at the start of the twenty-first century, you think about Paul getting on its old eastern end near Philippi in the middle of the first century (Figure 54).

To Thessalonica Then

The floodplains of four rivers flow into the Thermaic Gulf from encircling mountains and give Thessalonica a rich hinterland but, as so often around the Aegean Sea, frequent earthquakes and alluvial deposits increased the land even as they silted up the harbor. To the northwest, for instance,

FIGURE 54. The Via Egnatia at Philippi, with deep ruts etched from traffic on the pavement.

Pella, birthplace of Alexander the Great and first capital of Macedonia, was once navigable to the sea, but is now 12 miles inland. Macedonian glories echo in Thessalonica's name, but when Paul arrived in their city to form a faithful Christian community around the year 50 C.E. under Claudius, the Thessalonians had already been a loyal Roman community for two hundred years and were enjoying unprecedented prosperity and diversity. Macedonia became a Roman province in 146 B.C.E., and Thessalonica became its capital since it was situated on a small bay and also on that paved, all-weather road from the Adriatic to the Aegean. City and citizens were well set for an important future, for, that is, an important *Roman* future.

At the time of Paul, Thessalonica had a population of around forty thousand from all around the Mediterranean. It was one of the smaller provincial capitals, much smaller than Achaian Corinth, Asian Ephesus, Syrian Antioch, or Egyptian Alexandria. But its location, not its size, was what counted. Again, the city's location on the Via Egnatia and the Aegean, with access to tributaries of the Danube, made it the obvious seat of Roman power but also an attractive site throughout later history, so that Thessalonica was continually inhabited from Paul's time through the Byzantine and Ottoman eras right up to the present, leaving archaeologists little opportunity for wholesale excavations. There is an ongoing dig at the ancient Roman forum, a site that occupies nearly a city block in the downtown area, but many of its structures date from the second and third centuries C.E.;

most first-century artifacts come from in and around modern construction projects and are small or fragmentary.

GREEKS. From bits and pieces that have been accidentally unearthed, we know much about the ancient city's commercial and cosmopolitan character from the third century B.C.E. During rebuilding projects in 1920 and 1939, an entire sacred complex dedicated to the Egyptian gods Sarapis and Isis was discovered, but it has since been covered up, sealed, and built upon. Established as early as the third century B.C.E. most likely by Egyptian traders, the sacred area continued to thrive well into the first century C.E., when a temple for Osiris, a baptismal-like basin, and several altars for Isis *Lochia,* or Child-bearing Isis, were erected. A bilingual Latin and Greek inscription from the Augustan period honors a donor for building a new porch (*pronaos*) and repairing the temple of Isis, showing that by this time others were supporters and adherents of those foreign gods. Alongside Egyptians, who lived among a population of Greek, Macedonian, and Thracian descent, there is also evidence for Italian traders from an early period. Those were the *negotiatores* that we saw on the island of Delos in Chapter 1 and they were attracted to Thessalonica by the commercial opportunities along the Via Egnatia.

ROMANS. There were also, of course, high-born Romans in the city who administered the province. They were organized in their own association, the "union of Romans" (*IG* X 2, 1 nr. 32, 33), but they mingled with others in the cosmopolitan and polytheistic city. The Roman Publius Salarius Pamphilos, for example, is named a priest of Isis and Sarapis on one inscription (*IG* X 2, 1 nr. 83). There is also a marble stele listing members who met and ate in honor of the Egyptian dog-headed god Anubis, and nine of the fourteen names are Roman. That stele was erected in honor of the Roman who had established the group's house (*oikos*), where they met and ate (Edson 181 f, Inventory # 1254). In spite of the number of Romans in the city and their prominent political role, the vast majority of inscriptions found at Thessalonica were in Greek, as the Romans remained political masters but willingly immersed themselves in the cultural world of the Hellenistic East.

An almost totally destroyed inscription, for example, *may* refer to Antony and Octavian as "benefactors and saviors." Thessalonica, having sided with Antony and Octavian, was promised by Brutus and Cassius to their legions for rape, plunder, and booty. After the victories of the Caesarian forces at

Philippi, Thessalonica was saved from that threatened fate and gained some measure of independence for its loyalty. The citizens even started to count time by the "years of Antony," although that would turn out to be a rather short era. Next, the goddess Roma was emphasized as the link between the city's older Greek divinities and its newer Roman sponsors.

Then, after the battle of Actium, in the early 20s, the city minted coins with the head of Julius Caesar on the obverse and that of Octavian on the reverse. Julius was named as "god" (*theos*), but Augustus was not called the usual "son of god" (*theou hyios*), although the juxtaposition of both heads may have intended that point. Eventually, as extant inscriptions testify, a "temple of [Juliu]s Caesar" was erected and a "priest and agonothete of Imperator Caesar son of god" was appointed in the first half of the first century. That person, thereafter always mentioned in first place among priestly listings, was in charge of sacrificial cult and temple upkeep as *priest* and in charge of athletic contests and other sacred games as *agonothete*. That combination of a temple for Julius and a priest and agonothete for Augustus was probably how Thessalonica honored "Caesar" as a general name for the Julio-Claudian dynasty. There is, in general, a striking transformation in the epigraphic record at the beginning of the imperial period. In earlier times, city assemblies or local priesthoods proclaimed written civic announcements, but, after Augustus, such local institutions, priesthoods, and deities waned and inscriptions appealed instead to Roma, Roman benefactors, and especially the imperial family.

JEWS. We must assume that a fair number of Jews had found their way to Thessalonica in spite of the meager archaeological evidence. Philo's *On the Embassy to Gaius* mentions Jews in "Macedonia" (36 or 281) and, of course, Luke's Acts speaks of them in Philippi and Thessalonica, although his account, as we see below, must be read very carefully not so much for their presence as for their actions and motives. Archaeological evidence for Judaism in Thessalonica at the time of Paul remains to be discovered, though there are some Jewish names and menorahs on burials and sarcophagi from much later periods, a fourth-century Hebrew-Greek bilingual inscription of the Samaritan but not Jewish community, a third-century sarcophagus of Marcus Aurelius Jacob, a Jew who became a Roman citizen, and his wife, Anna Asyncritus, that mentions synagogues, as well as scattered dedications to "the Most High God" (*theos hypsistos*), the common but not exclusive divine epithet used by Jews.

CHRISTIANS. Paul and his community would have been hard pressed to avoid Roman imperial theology in Thessalonica during the reign of Claudius. Thessalonica's mints produced coinage for the entire province and that city accepted dynastic divinity for the emperors Augustus through Claudius. One coin's side was struck with Augustus and the Greek legend *theos sebastos,* "the god Augustus." On the other side is Claudius. The point is clear enough. The divinity of Augustus continued through his dynasty to Claudius.

An even more striking index of that divine continuity from Augustus to Claudius across time and from Rome to Thessalonica across space is in Thessaloniki's Archaeological Museum, the building you passed at the early morning start of this chapter. It houses two almost identical statues. That "almost" comes less from any difference between them than from the head-

FIGURE 55. Statue of Augustus in divine pose, found at Thessaloniki.

FIGURE 56. Headless statue of Claudius in divine pose and imitating Augustus, found at Thessaloniki.

less condition of the second one. The first or fuller statue is of Augustus poised in imperial address and divine undress (Figure 55). The voluminous robe wraps around him from lower waist to upper knee with its surplus draped over his left forearm. He strides forward on his right foot with the left bent slightly behind it. His right arm is raised with closed fist and index finger pointed upward. The second or broken statue is identical from the neck down. But the head is missing and so is the raised right arm. The second statue is usually considered to represent Claudius (Figure 56).

Both are similar to that most famous statue of Augustus that was already mentioned in Chapter 2 (Figure 57). It is a marble copy of the bronze original and was found in 1863 at Prima Porta on the Via Flaminia in the villa of his wife Livia. Today it is in the New Wing of the Vatican's Chiaramonti

FIGURE 57. Prima Porta statue of Augustus; note his bare feet alongside Cupid, the son of Venus, indicating his deified status.

Museum. If you compare the Roman and Thessalonian Augustus, one difference is immediately obvious, but so are the even more striking similarities. In Rome, he is dressed in military uniform, probably so that the cuirass can depict the cosmic implications of his Parthian "victory." But in both statues, the raised right arm, extended index finger, straight right leg, bent left leg, and large mantle draped around the lower body and over the left forearm are identical. In Rome, even with cuirass and spear, he is divinely barefoot, and a small Cupid, child of Venus, rides a dolphin to support his right leg. But, maybe more than all else, it is the hairstyle that iconographically establishes both identity and continuity. The hair is combed forward over the forehead, and in the center a single pointed lock curves rightward toward two others curving leftward.

It is unfortunately now impossible to compare the facial features and hairstyles of those two statues in Thessaloniki. But the common seminudity and body pose emphasize one very important point. Augustus, of course, was four ways divine, by ancestral descent from Venus and Anchises, by miraculous conception from Apollo and Atia, by paternal adoption from the divine Julius Caesar, and by official decree from the Roman Senate. But all that divinity was not just personal and individual charisma. It flowed from him and continued after him, first as a dynastic privilege, and then as an imperial prerogative. Within the Julio-Claudian line, it survived Caligula and Nero. Then, after a year of renewed civil war, it continued into the Flavian dynasty of Vespasian and Titus, surviving even that dynasty's disastrous Domitian. The Augustan revolution held firm, and the similarity of those two Thessalonian statutes emphasized their continuity across time from before to during (and, of course, after) Paul's life. Imperial divinity was, quite simply, the ideology that held the Roman Empire together and the theology that allowed Greek pride and tradition gracefully to accept Roman law and order. In any case, that divine charisma was still relatively fresh when Paul reached Thessalonica under the emperor Claudius.

"In Spite of Great Opposition"

Paul went from Asia to Europe across the northern Aegean, earlier Homer's wine-dark sea, later Yeats's dolphin-torn and gong-tormented sea. On his way from Philippi to Thessalonica, he "passed through Amphipolis and Apollonia" according to Acts 17:1. (A footnote. There is an inscription in

Amphipolis's museum dedicated to "Imperator Caesar, God, Son of God, Augustus, Savior, and Builder of the City"). Those two places were the regular overnight stops for a traveler making almost 30 miles per day on the Via Egnatia, a fast pace in good weather on a great road. The scenery was beautiful; past Mt. Pangaion to the Strymon River at Amphipolis and then on to the Chalkidike peninsula's northern lakes at Apollonia. But our text of 1 Thessalonians indicates that Paul's mind was probably not on vista, but on violence along that three-day journey. As he recalls to the Thessalonians later, "Though we had already suffered and been shamefully mistreated at Philippi, as you know, we had courage in our God to declare to you the gospel of God in spite of great opposition" (1 Thess. 2:2).

But what happened at Philippi was repeated at Thessalonica. Paul and his colleagues were finally forced to flee Macedonia and take refuge to the south in the adjoining Roman province of Achaia. Notice that such a flight across provincial boundaries suggests opposition primarily from Roman authority. From there he sent Timothy back to the Thessalonian community for news of its situation, and, as he recalls to them later, the news was very good.

> Therefore when we could bear it no longer, we decided to be left alone in Athens; and we sent Timothy, our brother and co-worker for God in proclaiming the gospel of Christ, to strengthen and encourage you for the sake of your faith, so that no one would be shaken by these persecutions. Indeed, you yourselves know that this is what we are destined for. In fact, when we were with you, we told you beforehand that we were to suffer persecution; so it turned out, as you know. . . . But Timothy has just now come to us from you, and has brought us the good news of your faith and love. He has told us also that you always remember us kindly and long to see us—just as we long to see you. For this reason, brothers and sisters, during all our distress and persecution we have been encouraged about you through your faith. (1 Thess. 3:1–4, 6–7).

That is a good example of Paul operating as the center of a network of co-workers. Timothy is "brother and co-worker *for God,*" not just *for Paul,* and he is sent to "strengthen and encourage you for the sake of your faith" and not just to see and report back.

Their fidelity continued and Paul extols their continual faith even under persecution as now a model for *both* provinces:

You became imitators of us and of the Lord, for in spite of persecution you received the word with joy inspired by the Holy Spirit, so that you became an example to all the believers in Macedonia and in Achaia. For the word of the Lord has sounded forth from you not only in Macedonia and Achaia, but in every place your faith in God has become known, so that we have no need to speak about it. (1 Thess. 1:6–8)

Earlier worry about their perseverance gave way to later enthusiasm for their strength. Recall, by the way, that Paul's program concentrated especially on Roman provincial capitals as bases from which he and his co-workers could operate most widely, travel most swiftly, and influence the surroundings most effectively. Philippi and then Thessalonica. Athens and then Corinth.

Persecution by Whom?

We return once more to that basic problem of the Lukan Paul versus the Pauline Paul discussed in Chapter 1. As we saw there, Paul explained his Damascus flight as an escape from Nabatean civil power, but Luke detailed it as an escape from Jewish religious power. Our method is to accept Luke when he agrees with Paul, to omit Luke when he disagrees with Paul, to bracket Luke when he adds independent data that is theologically and tendentiously Lukan, but to accept such data cautiously and carefully when no such biases or prejudices are evident. And we have here a classic case where Luke's Acts is both profoundly right and profoundly wrong at the same time. This is his account of Paul at Thessalonica:

> [At] Thessalonica . . . there was a synagogue of the Jews. And Paul went in, as was his custom, and on three sabbath days argued with them from the scriptures, explaining and proving that it was necessary for the Messiah to suffer and to rise from the dead, and saying, "This is the Messiah, Jesus whom I am proclaiming to you." Some of them were persuaded and joined Paul and Silas, as did a great many of the devout Greeks and not a few of the leading women. But the Jews became jealous, and with the help of some ruffians in the marketplaces they formed a mob and set the city in an uproar. (Acts 17:1–5)

We focus first on "the Jews" in that account and leave aside for the moment the "great many of the devout Greeks and not a few of the leading women."

JEWS. Luke's theological theme develops the following historical pattern: Paul always goes first to the Jews; some accept him and others reject him; but when non-Jews then accept him, the Jews are jealous and cause a riot. But that makes little sense as theology and even less as history. What happens to those Jews who accept him? And why should those Jews who reject him care about pagan acceptance? Luke, however, continues with that theme. Paul flees Thessalonica for Beroea, today's Veroia, on the southwestern edge of the Thessalonian plain, and "when the Jews of Thessalonica learned that the word of God had been proclaimed by Paul in Beroea as well, they came there too, to stir up and incite the crowds" (Acts 17:13). Finally, Paul must flee again, this time "to the coast" for a boat "as far as Athens" (17:14–15). But, as noted above, fleeing Macedonia for Achaia (as earlier to flee Damascus for Jerusalem) was much more likely to have been to avoid Roman civil authority than to escape Jewish religious authority.

There is, however, another passage in 1 Thessalonians that, while confirming the primary danger as Roman, also exposes the anti-Jewish tendency of Luke's account. It also returns us to another topic from Chapter 1, namely, later interpolations within our present authentic Pauline letters. Paul tells the persecuted Thessalonians,

> You, brothers and sisters, became imitators of the churches of God in Christ Jesus that are in Judea, for you suffered the same things from your own compatriots as they did from the Jews, who killed both the Lord Jesus and the prophets, and drove us out; they displease God and oppose everyone by hindering us from speaking to the Gentiles so that they may be saved. Thus they have constantly been filling up the measure of their sins; but God's wrath has overtaken them at last. (2:14–16)

We agree with New Testament scholar Birger Pearson that this passage is probably a post-Pauline insertion that assumes the destruction of the Jerusalem Temple in 70 C.E. and a definitive split between Christian assembly and Jewish synagogue in both Thessalonica and in Judea. Note how "the Jews" are viciously blamed for their execution of Christ and the prophets, their expulsion of the apostles, and their opposition to gentile salvation. It seems forgotten that Jesus, Paul, and the apostles were all themselves Jews. After 70 C.E. "Jews" had become "the other" for Christians and were almost a theological concept rather than a historical people. "God's wrath has overtaken them at last" refers to the destruction of Jerusalem and its Temple in 70 C.E.

as a punishment from God. But even that interpolation admits that, at Thessalonica, it was "your own compatriots" and not the city's Jews who caused their suffering.

SYMPATHIZERS. We return now to that key phrase from Acts 17:4 above, "a great many of the devout Greeks and not a few of the leading women." This is where Luke got it exactly right, because that is a piece of information not at all required by his overall scenario of Jews first and then Gentiles. It is possible that his emphasis on "leading" might be a Lukan upgrade, but that mention of "women" is probably accurate. Those "devout Greeks" are, of course, the "God-fearers" or "God-worshipers." Our proposal is that Paul went to the synagogue not for the Jews, but for those pagan sympathizers, and it is precisely his focus on those semipagan or semi-Jewish sponsors, protectors, and patrons that would obviously have infuriated Jewish synagogue members. Put bluntly, Paul was poaching on dangerous territory, dangerous not just in very abstract theology, but in very practical politics. That could certainly cause serious trouble between Paul and loyal synagogue Jews or even between pro-Pauline and anti-Pauline God-worshipers.

Even though Paul himself never uses the term "God-fearers" or "God-worshipers," he does make it clear in 1 Thessalonians that those converts had "turned to God from idols, to serve a living and true God" (1:9), that, in other words, they were originally pagans. They might have "feared" or "worshiped" the Jewish God, but they did not accept that God fully or follow that God completely. You, Paul would have said to them, are neither Jew nor Greek, and your only salvation now is God in Christ. Because, he would have said to them, you cannot have pagan gods at meals, baths, and festivals six days a week and the one true God at the synagogue on the Sabbath. Torah is all or nothing.

ROMAN(IZER)S. Although Paul would certainly have generated Jewish opposition by converting sympathizers, it was only provincial Roman and Rome-appointed authorities that could force a flight from Macedonia into Achaia. The public accusation against Paul was not just that he was causing or provoking a riot among Jews and sympathizers. Here is how Luke continues with what happened next at Thessalonica:

> While they were searching for Paul and Silas to bring them out to the assembly, they attacked Jason's house. When they could not find them,

they dragged Jason and some believers before the city authorities, shouting, "These people who have been turning the world upside down
have come here also, and Jason has entertained them as guests. They
are all acting contrary to the decrees of the emperor, saying that there
is another king named Jesus." The people and the city officials were
disturbed when they heard this, and after they had taken bail from
Jason and the others, they let them go. (Acts 17:5–7)

As seen in Chapter 1, Luke prefers to explain Jewish antagonism to
Christians as mere jealousy and pagan antagonism as mere greed. That is
what all the fuss is about, he maintains, as he downplays anything anti-
Roman about Christianity. But at Philippi in Acts 16:21, the accusation is
about "advocating customs that are not lawful for us as Romans to adopt or
observe," and at Thessalonica in 17:7, the indictment is about "acting contrary to the decrees of the emperor, saying that there is another king named
Jesus." In other words, Luke has Paul's opponents charge Christians with
anti-Romanism, charges that he himself never actually refutes. We therefore
take them very seriously, especially because those charges ring true as we
read Paul's 1 Thessalonians.

Persecution for What?

Recall what has already been said about Roman imperial theology, the
emperor cult, and especially Thessalonica under Claudius as Paul arrived at
that city for the first time. Piety engendered Victory, and she engendered
Peace in both Roman theology and Thessalonian history. Against that background, one of the most striking aspects of 1 Thessalonians is the number of
Pauline terms that were religio-political in a world where those two aspects
of power were never separated at any depth. We often hear those words
today in English as distinctively novel or even uniquely Christian, but first-
century ears would have heard them very differently in their original Greek.
They were expressions absolutely guaranteed to prick up Romanized ears
and raise Romanized eyebrows. And, when they were heard, they would
have engendered serious suspicion about Pauline intentions.

That opening, "Paul, Silvanus, and Timothy, to the church (*ekklēsia*) of
the Thessalonians in God the Father and the Lord Jesus Christ: Grace to you
and peace," was much more subversive than we imagine. The standard Pauline
term for a Christian community is *ekklēsia,* a Greek word today usually
translated "church." But the word originally meant the citizens of a free

Greek city officially assembled for self-governmental decisions. Maybe that
was perfectly innocent, but also maybe not. And anyone familiar with Judaism would have heard in his "peace" the content of the Jewish *shalom* of
justice and not that of the Latin *pax* of victory.

Next, Paul believes absolutely that "Jesus" or the "Messiah/Christ" or the
"Lord" all refer to the same person. Paul can speak of the Lord Jesus Christ
or of the Lord Jesus or, most simply, of the Lord. On the one hand, "lord"
was a polite term usable by slave to master or disciple to teacher. On the
other, "the Lord" meant the emperor himself. What we see here is what
Gustav Adolf Deissmann described, almost a hundred years ago, as "the
early establishment of a polemical parallelism between the cult of Christ and
the cult of Caesar in the application of the term *kyrios,* 'lord'" (1965: 349).
Or, if you prefer, polemical parallelism as high treason.

Further, Paul speaks about "God, who calls you into his kingdom and
glory" (2:12). But, elites would have said that the kingdom, power, and
glory to which we all are called belong to Rome. Paul writes about "the
gospel of God" (2:2, 8, 9) or "the gospel of Christ" (3:2) or, more simply, of
"the gospel" (1:5; 2:4). What do you mean, the city's leaders might have
asked, by talking about one single, unique gospel (*euaggelion*) over against
the plural "good news" (*euaggelia*) about dynastic successions and imperial

FIGURE 58. Front and back of an altar from Praeneste, honoring the sacred Augustan *pax*
and *securitas,* "peace and security."

victories from Rome? And finally there is this one most inflammatory phrase. "When they say, 'There is peace and security,'" writes Paul in 5:3, "then sudden destruction will come upon them, as labor pains come upon a pregnant woman, and there will be no escape!" But the mantric slogan of "peace and security," seen, for example, on an altar from Italian Praeneste (Figure 58), was precisely what Rome promised and delivered to its conquered provinces. There is, Paul says, an imminent catastrophic threat to that Julio-Claudian serenity, and he openly mocks its imperial complacency. Then, there is this next example, maybe the most significant in the entire letter.

"We Will Be with the Lord Forever"

The Greek word *parousia* can have the ordinary meaning of "arrival" or "return." Paul, for example, can rejoice in the *parousia* of absent friends and co-workers such as Stephanas, Fortunatus, and Achaicus in 1 Corinthians 16:17 or Titus in 2 Corinthians 7:6–7. But he can also speak of his own *parousia* to one of his Christian communities, for example, in 2 Corinthians 10:10 or Philippians 1:26 and 2:12. In those latter cases there may be a deliberate hint of this next meaning where it is almost a technical term.

In its ancient context *parousia* meant the arrival at a city of a conquering general, an important official, an imperial emissary, or, above all, the emperor himself. Whether that advent was good or bad news for the citizens depended absolutely on their prior relationship with the arriving one. It is probably necessary in those cases to translate *parousia* not just as "visit," but as "visitation." Here is a classic example that shows how the result of such a visitation (*parousia*) depends absolutely on the nature of its reception (*apantēsis*).

In November of 333 B.C.E., Alexander the Great defeated and humiliated Darius of Persia at Issus in northwestern Syria, as we saw at the start of this chapter on that bronze monument at Thessaloniki's seafront. He then marched inexorably southward toward Egypt. The Jewish high-priest Jaddus remained unwisely loyal to Darius and repulsed Alexander's initial demand for submission, according to Josephus's *Jewish Antiquities* (11.327–28). After devastating sieges at Tyre and Gaza, Alexander finally turned against Jerusalem. Jaddus was afraid, "not knowing how he could meet (*apantēsai*) the Macedonians," so he sacrificed for deliverance and "God spoke oracularly to him in his sleep, telling him to take courage and adorn the city with wreaths and open the gates and go out to meet them (literally, make the *hypantēsin*), and that the people should be in white garments. . . . And, after doing all the things that he had been told to do, [he] awaited the coming (*parousian*) of the king." It was a moment for trepidation certainly and celebration possibly. (Note, once again, those technical Greek terms for the "coming" and the "reception.")

A visitation from the emperor was a very special occasion for any given city and quite possibly a once-in-a-lifetime event. In times of war it was of course a threatening advent, as in the above story, but under the *Pax Romana,* an imperial visitation would usually be a happy occasion. It demanded tremendous preparation for civic sacrifice, aristocratic festivity, and popular celebration, but especially a formal greeting by elites and people at the submissively opened gates of the city. Notice Paul's use of those technical terms for visitation and reception. He uses *parousia* for "our Lord Jesus at his *coming*" in 1 Thessalonians 2:19, "the *coming* of our Lord Jesus with all his saints" in 3:13, "the *coming* of the Lord" in 4:15, and "the *coming* of our Lord Jesus Christ" in 5:23. He uses *apantēsis* for when the Thessalonian Christians will "*meet* the Lord in the air" at his *parousia* in 4:17. That metaphor controls the entire discussion.

"The Dead in Christ Will Rise First"

The Thessalonian question concerns the relative status of those dead and those alive at the Lord's *parousia,* or coming from heaven to earth. The Thessalonians were worried that those who had already died might somehow be disadvantaged at the *parousia.* Had those Thessalonians died natural deaths or had they been martyred during that persecution because of Paul? The latter alternative seems most likely for two reasons. One is that Paul is extremely defensive about himself in this letter, for example, "You are witnesses, and God also, how pure, upright, and blameless our conduct was toward you believers" (1 Thess. 2:10). That tone would be very understandable if he had escaped Thessalonica by flight while others had died there as martyrs. Another is that it may have been martyrdom that made them "an example to all the believers in Macedonia and in Achaia," so that "not only in Macedonia and Achaia, but in every place your faith in God has become known, so that we have no need to speak about it" (1:7–8).

In any case, that same question was asked about fifty years later, in a Jewish apocalypse written after the destruction of Jerusalem and its Temple but attributed fictionally to Ezra. He asks, "Yet, O Lord, you have charge of those who are alive at the end, but what will those do who were before me, or we, ourselves, or those who come after us?" And the Lord answers, "I shall liken my judgment to a circle; just as for those who are last there is no slowness, so for those who are first there is no haste" (4 Ezra 5:41–42). It is not clear whether that did or did not help Ezra, but it is the obvious answer: All will arise at the same time just as a circle is all there simultaneously. But that is not Paul's answer:

> For this we declare to you by the word of the Lord, that we who are alive, who are left until the coming (*parousian*) of the Lord, will by no means precede those who have died. For the Lord himself, with a cry of command, with the archangel's call and with the sound of God's trumpet, will descend from heaven, and the dead in Christ will rise first. Then we who are alive, who are left, will be caught up in the clouds together with them to meet (*apantēsin*) the Lord in the air; and so we will be with the Lord forever. (4:15–17)

Notice two details in contrasting Paul's response with God's reply in 4 Ezra. Ezra does not presume that his generation will be alive when that great moment arrives, and the answer asserts simultaneity rather than precedence. But Paul presumes that he and his generation will still be alive ("we") at the Lord's *parousia,* and he affirms that the dead will rise first and the living will go "with them" to greet Christ. What is Paul's source for that claim? It is, quite bluntly, neither faith nor hope, neither tradition nor theology, but an absolutely magnificent act of consolation based on a brilliant use of metaphor.

The Parousia of the Lord

First of all, the metaphor of formal urban visitation gives Paul a powerful visual answer to the question of the Thessalonians. Any important visitor coming along the major road to an ancient city would first meet the dead before they were greeted by the living. Take for example the city of Hierapolis above the white travertine basins of Pamukkale at the eastern end of the great Meander Valley. If you walk out along the northern road, for example, you find yourself today in an absolute jumble of broken sarcophagi, shattered tombs, and wrecked mausoleums (Figure 59). But if you put that destroyed and quarried necropolis back in its original format, you can easily imagine an imperial visitor meeting first the elite dead before any meeting with the elite living. And, of course, says Paul, dancing fast and fancy on his

FIGURE 59. Mausoleums and sarcophagi of the dead lining the road leading into Hierapolis, Turkey.

theological feet, that is how things will be at the *parousia* of Christ. We will not all go up together, but first the dead, then the living.

Second, the *parousia* metaphor means that Christians do not ascend to stay with Christ in heaven, but to return with him to this transformed world. Paul says nothing about an eschatological world or utopian earth here below, but simply that all believers "will be caught up in the clouds . . . to meet the Lord in the air; and so we will be with the Lord forever." The metaphor of *parousia* as state visit would presume that those going out to greet the approaching ruler would return with him for festive rejoicing within their city. So also with Christ. Paul probably took it for granted that all together would then descend to dwell upon a purified earth. The *parousia* of the Lord was not about destruction of earth and relocation to heaven, but about a world in which violence and injustice are transformed into purity and holiness. And, of course, as mentioned above, a transformed *world* would demand not just spiritual souls, but renewed *bodies*.

Third, we translate *parousia* as the "return" or "second coming" of Christ. It is perfectly correct that Paul is not just talking about one more visitation among many from Christ. It is the great final eschatological visitation. But nobody ever thought that the emperor was only present at a visitation. He was always present on coins, in statues, through altars, temples, and forums. So also with Christ. It is better not to use translations for *parousia* that in any way imply a prior absence.

Finally, when those terms of visitation and reception are used of Christ, does it mean that his visitation is just like that of the emperor, is greater than that of the emperor, or is the replacement for that of the emperor? Are those terms, in other words, a calculated anti-*parousia*? Is that choice of metaphor both consolation and confrontation?

"Like a Thief in the Night"

Paul is also wise enough to assuage fear without promoting fantasy. No further details are given, no other specifics are supplied. Nothing is said about afterward and even less about beforehand. There is nothing about signs, hints, and indications telling one that the *parousia* is imminent. It will come absolutely without warning, "like a thief in the night" (1 Thess. 5:2, 4) and when one hears the cry of command, the archangel's call, and the sound of God's trumpet (4:16) it will already be too late. Those are concomitant events and not preceding indicators. Paul's metaphor of a nighttime thief precludes any computation of preceding steps or warning signs and their presence in 2 Thessalonians is one of the indications that it is a post-Pauline letter. In that text pseudo-Paul denies that the *parousia* or "day of the Lord is already here" because

> that day will not come unless the rebellion comes first and the lawless one is revealed, the one destined for destruction. He opposes and exalts himself above every so-called god or object of worship, so that he takes his seat in the temple of God, declaring himself to be God. . . . And you know what is now restraining him, so that he may be revealed when his time comes . . . whom the Lord Jesus will destroy with the breath of his mouth, annihilating him by the manifestation of his coming (*parousia*). The coming (*parousia*) of the lawless one is apparent in the working of Satan, who uses all power, signs, lying wonders, and every kind of wicked deception for those who are perishing, because they refused to love the truth and so be saved. (2 Thess. 2:3–10)

On the one hand, that is like saying that the night thief will not come unless there is first the sound of breaking windows and smashing doors. One is therefore safe until after that happens, so that the metaphor of unpredictability breaks down. On the other, those absolutely enigmatic events seem to indicate a continuation, intensification, and specification of the persecution mentioned in 1 Thessalonians. In both letters, it is Satan who is the main opponent. But now Satan works though a "lawless one" who claims to be the one true God. Regardless of the details, it is probably the theology of Roman imperialism and the ideology of emperor worship that, one way or another, lies behind that description. Who or what, in that first-century Thessalonian context, "opposes and exalts himself above every so-called god or object of worship, so that he takes his seat in the temple of God, declaring himself to be God"? But that, as pseudo-Paul admits, was already there in present time and not just an advent in future time. In any case, Paul's own *parousia* metaphor is profoundly qualified by that thief-in-the-night metaphor. They are almost, in effect, two contradictory images, for the fact and time of a ruler's *parousia* are always known in advance, but that of a night thief's arrival are unknown. That latter image even undermines Paul's expectation that Christ's *parousia* would happen in his own lifetime or at least in the lifetime of his own generation. It also negates all attempts to establish warning signs and imminent hints despite our human lust for such security and certainty. If not the hour, then the day; if not the day, then the year; if not the year, then the century, the millennium, the whenever.

"We Belong to the Day"

There is, however, one vitally important concomitant to the Pauline emphasis on the impending *parousia* of the Lord in 1 Thessalonians. After that thief-in-the-night image of Christ's advent in 5:2, Paul says,

> You, beloved, are not in darkness, for that day to surprise you like a thief; for you are all children of light and children of the day; we are not of the night or of darkness. So then let us not fall asleep as others do, but let us keep awake and be sober; for those who sleep sleep at night, and those who are drunk get drunk at night. But since we belong to the day, let us be sober, and put on the breastplate of faith and love, and for a helmet the hope of salvation. (5:4–8)

Paul insists that Christians are not simply awake at night or merely alert in darkness against that thief-in-the-night advent of Christ. They are already children of light and children of the day who belong to the morning and its light.

Paul touches here, even if only in passing, on something absolutely basic to his theology. It is presumed most emphatically in his letters and, therefore, in our subsequent chapters. It is discussed most explicitly in 1 Corinthians 15. It is asserted most clearly in 2 Corinthians 3:17–18: "Now the Lord is the Spirit, and where the Spirit of the Lord is, there is freedom. And all of us, with unveiled faces, seeing the glory of the Lord as though reflected in a mirror, are being transformed into the same image from one degree of glory to another; for this comes from the Lord, the Spirit." That does not say that Christians *have been* transformed or *will be* transformed but that they *are being* transformed. Transformation is a process arching from past, through present, into future consummation.

There is clearly causality and continuity between the bodily resurrection of Jesus in the past and the bodily resurrection of the Thessalonian Christians in the future: "Since we believe that Jesus died and rose again, even so, through Jesus, God will bring with him those who have died" (4:14). Furthermore, in between those past and future moments, the present Thessalonian Christians are not just waiting for "the day of the Lord" (5:2), not just ready "for the day" (5:4), but are actually already in it, with it, and belonging to its light (5:5, 8). In other words, resurrectional transformation is process, not instant, period, not moment. *But that is something absolutely and creatively new within Pharisaic Judaism's theology of the general bodily resurrection.*

There are, in any faith or religion, state or empire, moments of powerful swerve, moments of change, alteration, transmutation, metamorphosis, moments that could never have been foretold in prospect but that almost seem inevitable in retrospect. And there were quite a few such magnificent swerves around the Mediterranean in that first century C.E. There was the transmutation of Greek heroic divinization and regional divinity into the Roman imperial theology, the transformation of local divinity into a divine savior for all the world. There was also the transmutation of Temple Judaism into Pharisaic and then rabbinic Judaism. There was the metamorphosis of general messianic expectation into a single coming of two messiahs in Essene Judaism and a double coming of one messiah in Christian Judaism. *But the great and unnerving transmutation of Pharisaic Judaism into Christian Judaism was the proclamation that the general resurrection had already begun when God raised Jesus of Nazareth from the dead.*

Recall what we said above about bodily resurrection and its attendant judgment as the last act or grand finale by which God finally justifies (that is, makes just) this unjust earth. Imagine if somebody mocked a Pharisee by asking how long that would take—would it take months or even years for God to raise everyone, restore their bodies, reward the good, and punish the wicked, all in a public trial? Surely the answer would be something like this: God created this good earth in six days and will restore it to its original goodness in three. But nobody had ever thought that it would be a period rather than an instant, a process rather than a moment. Within this swerve of faith, everything had now to be rethought, renewed, reimagined. Maybe, it was easier for Paul, who thought that eschatological resurrection as a period and that utopian transformation as a process would be just a few years long, ending within his own or at least his generation's lifetime. Still, the crucial point is that his proclamation was not exclusively about the imminent or even distant future, but was emphatically about a past-present-future continuum. And that had one very important result. The past is history, the future is prophecy, but the present is experience. *To claim that God has already begun to transform this earth into a place of divine justice and peace demands that you can show something of that transformative activity here and now. To which Paul would have replied unabashedly: To see God's transformation in process, come and see how we live.*

The Meaning of Love

Paul asks the Thessalonians to "remember our labor and toil, brothers and sisters; we worked night and day, so that we might not burden any of you while we proclaimed to you the gospel of God" (1 Thess. 2:9). Later, writing to the Philippians, he mentions, "Even when I was in Thessalonica, you sent me help for my needs more than once" (Phil. 4:16). Thessalonica had not subsidized Paul. Rather, Philippi had subsidized Thessalonica. Next, he admonished the Thessalonians "to work with your hands, as we directed you" (1 Thess. 4:11) and "to admonish the idlers" (5:14). Finally, writing to the Corinthians later, he recalls "the grace of God that has been granted to the churches of Macedonia; for during a severe ordeal of affliction, their abundant joy and their extreme poverty have overflowed in a wealth of generosity on their part. For, as I can testify, they voluntarily gave according to their means, and even beyond their means" (2 Cor. 8:1–3). What social status are we imagining for those Thessalonians?

At the start of his letter Paul recalls their "work of faith and labor of love and steadfastness of hope in our Lord Jesus Christ" (1 Thess. 1:3). And, again at the end, he encourages them to "put on the breastplate of faith and love, and for a helmet the hope of salvation" (5:8). What does Paul mean by love? To *love* meant to *share,* a love assembly was a share-assembly, a love meal was a share-meal. That is already clear in this present letter. "So deeply do we care for you that we are determined to share with you not only the gospel of God but also our own selves, because you have become very dear to us" (2:8).

Put together, then, the class status of the Thessalonian assembly with that loving as sharing; clearly the sharing was from want to want rather than from plenty to plenty. And do not think of it as humanly extensive charity, a free giving of *our* stuff, but as divinely distributive justice, a necessary sharing of *God's* stuff. For Paul, a Christian assembly of sisters and brothers was one that had committed itself to sharing together just as in an ordinary human family because it actually was a divine family, the family of God. This commonality was basic to Pauline Christianity, and it explains the emphasis on working in this letter. The specter of the lazy freeloader already shadowed the theology of creation behind Christian sharing, and it continued into the post-Pauline letter we call 2 Thessalonians.

> Now we command you, beloved, in the name of our Lord Jesus Christ, to keep away from believers who are living in idleness and not according to the tradition that they received from us. For you yourselves know how you ought to imitate us; we were not idle when we were with you, and we did not eat anyone's bread without paying for it; but with toil and labor we worked night and day, so that we might not burden any of you. This was not because we do not have that right, but in order to give you an example to imitate. For even when we were with you, we gave you this command: Anyone unwilling to work should not eat. For we hear that some of you are living in idleness, mere busybodies, not doing any work. Now such persons we command and exhort in the Lord Jesus Christ to do their work quietly and to earn their own living. (2 Thess 3:6–12)

Loving as a fair and equitable sharing of a world that belongs to a just God is what gives content to Paul's assertion to the Galatians that "a new creation is everything" (Gal. 6:15) and to Paul's claim to the Corinthians that "if anyone is in Christ, there is a new creation: everything old has passed away; see, everything has become new" (2 Cor. 5:17). *What better deserves the title of a new creation than the abnormalcy of a share-world replacing the normalcy of a greed-world?*

Two Thousand Years and Counting

When he wrote to the Thessalonians, Paul expected the coming of the Lord within his own lifetime. He said, "We who are alive . . . will be caught up in the clouds . . . to meet the Lord in the air" (1 Thess. 4:17). Later, after and probably because of his near execution at Ephesus, he could write to the Philippians, "My desire is to depart and be with Christ" (Phil. 1:23). By then he could imagine dying before the *parousia* of Christ, but he still presumed that it would occur within his own generation's lifetime or at least very, very soon. Even after that remark to the Philippians, he could write in 1 Corinthians of "the impending crisis," since "the appointed time has grown short" and "the present form of this world is passing away" (1 Cor. 7:26–31). And still, as late as to the Romans, he could write, "Salvation is nearer to us now than when we became believers; the night is far gone, the day is near" (Rom. 13:11–12).

On that question of time, Paul was completely wrong—wrong by two thousand years and counting. It is disingenuous to claim that by "soon" he meant not soon for him in the first century, but soon for us in the twenty-first century or for any Christians in any other century. Paul was wrong, just as every other hope, expectation, proclamation, or prophecy of imminent apocalyptic consummation has been consistently wrong throughout all of human history—at least so far. But Paul, like Jesus before him, did not simply proclaim the imminent end of evil, injustice, and violence here below upon this earth. They proclaimed it had already begun (first surprise!) and that believers were called to participate cooperatively with God (second surprise!!) in what was now a process in human time and not just a flash of divine light (third surprise!!!). Whatever Jesus and Paul said about the length of that process was flatly wrong, and anything they said about the details of its conclusion may also be flatly wrong. But the first and fundamental challenge they offer to Christian faith is this: Do you believe the process of making the world a just place has begun and what are you doing about joining the program? We conclude by imagining another conversation with Paul.

Question to Paul: "You expected that the visitation of Christ would occur in your own lifetime. We know now that you were wrong about that. You were off by two thousand years and counting. Does that mistake bother you, Paul?"

Answer from Paul: "No, not really, but please allow me to quote something I once said: 'I am convinced that neither death, nor life, nor angels, nor rulers, nor things present, nor things to come, nor powers, nor height, nor depth, nor anything else in all creation, will be able to separate us from the love of God in Christ Jesus our Lord' (Rom. 8:38–39). I always knew the difference between faith, which is a life's commitment, and theology, which is a mind's speculation. I never thought that believing what God would do meant knowing how or even when it would happen. Besides, it is my experience that whatever details we give about the human future are *usually* wrong, but whatever details we give about the divine future are *always* wrong. Have you noticed that?"

Blessings for All the Earth

Rome did not rely on the inertia or the awe of her subjects to compel their quietude; her guardians instead defined, distributed, and ultimately decorated the landscape of their *imperium* [empire], while their images stood in every square, their names marked every road, and their coins jingled in every market in the empire.

—Clifford Ando, *Imperial Ideology and Provincial
Loyalty in the Roman Empire* (2000)

Just as the Romans planted colonies of retired solders about the world, which were really little bits of Rome set down on foreign soil, so the Jewish colonies in the various big cities might be compared to little bits of Jerusalem in a foreign country.

—Henry Vollem Morton, *In the Steps of St. Paul* (1936)

Only three Roman cities in central Anatolia outside the province of Asia have yet been excavated on a substantial scale: Ancyra, Pessinus, and Pisidian Antioch. In each case the central feature of these excavations has been a temple dedicated to the imperial cult, built in the time of Augustus or Tiberius. . . . Emperor worship was not a political subterfuge, designed to elicit the loyalty of untutored provincials, but was one of the ways in which Romans themselves and provincials alongside them defined their own relationships with a new political phenomenon, an emperor whose powers and charisma were so transcendent that he appeared to them as both man and god. . . . The third major Julio-Claudian temple found in Galatia [after Ancyra and Pessinus] is the Corinthian podium temple at Pisidian Antioch. . . . A copy of the *Res Gestae* [*Acts of the Divine Augustus*] adorned the area around the propylon.

—Stephen Mitchell, *Anatolia:
Land, Men, and Gods in Asia Minor* (1993)

❦ ❦ ❦

Two Letters to the Galatians

Overture

Tourists flock today to Turkey's seaside resorts and turquoise beaches or Istanbul's covered bazaars, historic palaces, and magnificent mosques. But although around fifty tourist buses wait at the exit from Ephesus, none usually waits at the gate of Pisidian Antioch, and if one drives through the country town of Yalvaç, it is usually on its way to somewhere else.

You make the three-hour drive north from the coastal city of Antalya, Paul's Attalia, and its adjacent ancient Perge, inland along the route of the Augustan Via Sebaste through the western Taurus Mountains, the rough terrain of Isparta, the lakeside town of Eğirdir, to the ruins of Pisidian Antioch about half a mile up a slope from modern Yalvaç. The great Pauline scholar Sir William Ramsay said after a visit to that onetime Roman city in 1905, "The situation of Antioch is very fine, but the locality is now deserted, forlorn, and devoid of ruins that possess any interest or beauty." Today, the situation is as fine as ever, the locality is not exactly deserted, and the ruins may not as such possess much beauty, but surely their interest is a very different matter.

In spite of on-and-off excavations before and after World War I, the latter with the aid of Francis W. Kelsey of the University of Michigan and under the direction of David M. Robinson of Johns Hopkins University, not much seems to have changed except for some scattered yellow rusting signs in German and Turkish. Tall brown weeds and charcoal gray dirt engulf the few protruding stones and surround the few excavated areas, but, on this sunny August day in 2002, you are privileged to have the young and energetic Ünal Demirer, newly appointed director of the Yalvaç Museum, as your very special guide. You walk past the site's gate, guards, and the inevitable kiosk selling books, trinkets, and sodas. You stay carefully clear of a bulldozer hoisting a newly cut limestone block to reconstruct the Roman city gate and, it is hoped, bring more tourists to the site. Ünal leads you along a wire fence to one church and then up the hill to another. The first one's outlines are clearly visible. It is a large fourth-century basilica with some damaged mosaics near which was found a font inscribed with the words "Saint Paul." The second church is a much smaller one, but there is no evidence for the speculation that it was built atop the synagogue where Paul preached in Acts 13. "Maybe Paul's synagogue is under this small church," Ünal says, shrugging his shoulders. "Who knows?" In any case, you are not there for what Christianity later made of Paul, but for what Augustus earlier made of Galatia through cities like Pisidian Antioch, and for what Paul confronted in that world with his gospel of Christ.

To Ünal's surprise you drift away from the churches and move farther up the hill along a plaza once named after Tiberius and toward a temple once dedicated to Augustus (Figure 60). It is hard to imagine the ancient temple from its present remains, and it looks much worse than in excavation photographs from Ramsay in 1912–14 and Robinson in 1924. Only worn courses of gray limestone blocks survive in the front, and crags from the badly eroded bedrock foundation remain in the back. But still very striking is the cavernous imprint of the plaza's massive apse that had been shaped by cutting away an enormous volume of earth and rock from the hillside. The fluted columns, decorated blocks, colored marbles, and terra-cotta tiles that once composed the temple's two-storied portico backdrop have long since been stripped away, but the overall site remains very impressive. And, of course, it was built on the highest point in the city.

Later you take a little yellow Fiat taxi about half a mile down to Ünal's museum in Yalvaç, but that short ride covers two thousand years in a few

FIGURE 60. The Tiberia Plateia in Pisidian Antioch, photographed by the University of Michigan in 1924; the front steps lead to the colonnade and the Temple of Augustus.

minutes. You leave the quiet of those ancient ruins above the bustling modern town. You leave the site of the ancient sanctuary of the mother goddess Men and later temple of Augustus's imperial divinity. You careen through a roundabout surrounded by European cube-shaped multistoried and multicolored apartments. You turn hard past a state-of-the-art football stadium with deep green grass and turquoise plastic seats. You turn yet again and then you hit the main road clogged with pedestrians there for the market. Yours is the only car, and your driver eases gently through the crowd without using his horn. Women veiled in traditional garb display linen bolts and cotton weavings; stands are filled with pots, pans, and pistachio nuts; and farmers lead horse-drawn carriages filled with onions and garlic down the street. And fruit, fruit everywhere. Then and now, Antioch and Yalvaç are both towns on a well-watered and fertile steppe ringed closely to east and distantly to west by mountains, then and now cereals and fruits abound, and then as now the River Anthius streams down from the Sultan Daglari massif to the serenity of mountain-ringed Lake Eğirdir. Geography is continuity.

Inside the cream-colored museum the displays are sleek, elegant, and well lit. Outside, Ünal strides along the north side of the walled garden surrounding the museum. On your right you pass dozens of small Latin fragments of the *Acts of the Divine Augustus* set in cement within metal frames attached to the side wall of the museum. You continue on past two much larger fragments of the Greek *Acts of the Divine Augustus* sitting on the cemented ground. The Latin texts come from Pisidian Antioch, the Greek ones from Apollonia, now Uluborlu, nearby to the southwest but on the other side of Lake Eğirdir. "Terrible conservation. We must redo it properly," comments Ünal.

He then shows you, to the left at the end of the garden pathway, the one artifact he is sure you came to see. It is the Sergius Paullus inscription (Figure 61). According to many scholars, this mostly broken inscription but with that name still preserved verifies the historical accuracy of Luke's Acts of the Apostles. On the island of Cyprus, it was "the proconsul, Sergius Paulus, an intelligent man, who summoned Barnabas and Saul and wanted to hear the word of God," in Acts 13:7. Then, in spite of competition from a Jewish magician named Elymas, the governor "believed, for he was astonished at the teaching about the Lord," in Acts 13:12.

From other inscriptions we know the career of Sergius Paullus culminated with a consulship at Rome in 70 C.E. and that his family was well connected with other highborn Roman colonists in his native Pisidian Antioch.

Maybe, some speculate, Sergius Paullus recommended Paul to his friends and family in Pisidian Antioch, which was the very next stop on his itinerary after Cyprus? "Paul and his companions set sail from Paphos and came to Perga in Pamphylia," according to Acts 13:13–14, "but they went on from Perga and came to Antioch in Pisidia." Maybe, some further speculate, Paul even changed his name from the Hebrew Saul to the Latin Paul[lus] after that encounter on Paphos? That Antioch inscription is certainly tangible evidence for the existence of that historical figure mentioned in Acts. But was he actually one of Paul's first gentile converts or is that story only further proof of Luke's familiarity with historical individuals of political importance in the time and place of Paul?

It is certainly valid to debate, in particular, the historicity of Sergius Paullus as an early and aristocratic pagan convert to Christianity and even, in general, the historicity of Luke's Acts on all such pro-Pauline Roman defenders. But there is also an even more important question to be debated, and Yalvaç's Museum is a good place to think about it. That one place now holds both the Sergius Paullus inscription and both Latin and Greek fragments of Augustus's political autobiography, the *Acts of the Divine Augustus,* whose relatively full Latin version and Greek paraphrase is on the Ankara

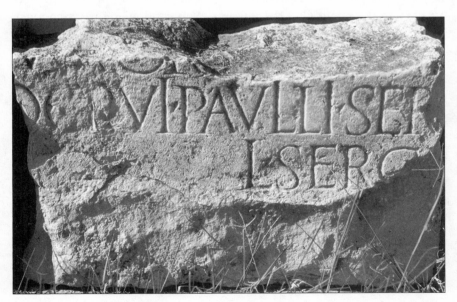

FIGURE 61. Fragmentary inscription found at Pisidian Antioch with the name Sergius Paullus, mentioned in Acts 13.

temple to be seen in the Epilogue. You think about the coincidental proximity of the Sergius Paullus and Augustus fragments in that same town's small museum. That latter text says, "I was given the title of Augustus by decree of the Senate . . . and a golden shield was placed in the Curia Julia . . . in recognition of my valour, my clemency, my justice, and my piety" (34). How, you wonder, could a convert of Paul be both a disciple of Christ and an official of Caesar? Who can serve two masters? Jesus asked in Luke's gospel, but Luke seems to have forgotten that warning in his Acts of the Apostles.

Augustus's autobiographical and religio-political *Acts* is about twenty-seven hundred words long in its original Latin. It was primarily addressed to Rome itself, but also applied, of course, to all those provinces fully or partially Romanized. Our extant copies, however, come from that single province of Galatia. As just seen, two large Greek chunks from Pisidian Apollonia and multiple tiny Latin fragments from Pisidian Antioch are now in the garden of Yalvaç's museum, but the fullest copies of both versions are still on the walls of Ancyra's Temple of Rome and Augustus in Old Ankara (more on that in our Epilogue). Maybe that is all accidental coincidence or maybe its distribution was specifically focused on that province? In any case we imagine, as it were, the *Res Gestae Divi Augusti* as that emperor's "letter" to the Galatians, earlier than the *Res Gestae Divi Christi,* Paul's later and alternative letter to those same Galatians. Paul, of course, announced a different savior for a different world, a different salvation for a different earth, a different God and Son of God for a different creation. He proclaimed Jewish covenantal *shalom* against Roman imperial *pax*.

Outline

Augustus's program for Romanizing all the Galatians and Paul's program for Christianizing at least some of them, the former based on Roman imperial theology's peace through victory, the latter based on Jewish covenantal theology's peace through justice, come together in this chapter with a focus on the province of Galatia. We will hear two messages in two "letters" as triumphant marble confronts fragile papyrus.

We start with generalities about Romanization. Its two foundations were the creation of cities, especially those for disbanded soldiers (*coloniae*), and their adornment by the good works (*euergetism*) of local aristocrats, legionary veterans, and foreign immigrants. Its three successive constructional stages were roads and ports, temples and statues, aqueducts and baths, and those are exemplified by four urban examples in Italy, Greece, Syria, and Judea. Next, we make the threefold process specific for Anatolia with the imperial cities of Ancyra (Ankara), Pessinus, and Pisidian Antioch.

Then, before turning from total Romanization to initial Christianization, we have an interlude on the Jewish diaspora synagogue, but use, perforce, an example from the northern coast of the Black Sea. We chose it to recall those God-worshipers first seen *materially* in that early-third-century Aphrodisian inscription from Chapter 1. In the present case, first- and second-century Jewish inscriptions emphasize the religio-political and socioeconomic significance of the synagogue as the urban interface between paganism and Judaism in one specific site, but also underline the volatile implications of Paul's convert poaching among pagan synagogue sympathizers anywhere.

Finally, we turn to Paul himself and to his Galatian letter about the controversy between his vision of Christianity and the opposition to it from synagogue loyalists, especially from God-worshipers now torn between *two* visions of the Jewish world that had already won their admiration. We do not presume that only his fellow Jews would oppose Paul's intrusive activities. Pagan God-worshipers would also have split over loyalty to the Jewish synagogue versus allegiance to the Pauline gospel. We look at the basic and extremely powerful argument of the opponents against Paul's position and study the five arguments—historical, experiential, exegetical, baptismal, and emotional—Paul used against it. We also wonder, who prevailed in Galatia? It may not have been Paul because, in promising blessings for all the earth, there were potent competing options in Galatia from imperial Romanism, traditional Judaism, and Pauline Christianity.

The Blessings of a Roman World

Armies pacified Rome's opponents, but cities integrated them into its empire, and urban amenities seduced them into complicity. Rome's military success at expanding its territories was second only to its organizational success at retaining those territories; as a reminder, the Latin word for "city," *civitas,* is now philologically but was then ideologically the very root of what we call "civilization."

Before we focus on Roman Galatia in particular, we look first at Romanization as a general interactive process between imperial authority and provincial locality. We focus on two devices, three stages, and four examples of that imperial transformation. And, of course, as the blessings of Rome flowed eastward along legionary roads to consolidate the world into one empire (*imperium*), Paul was coming westward along those same legionary roads with the alternative blessings of Abraham to convert the world into one very different assembly (*ekklēsia*). Whose are the blessings, then, and whose is the world?

Two Devices for Romanization

COLONIAE. In modern usage a colony is any foreign territory conquered and controlled by an empire. But in Roman usage a *colonia* was a city and its rural hinterland founded or refounded for legionary veterans or disbanded soldiers, and that is our meaning here. Julius Caesar had founded a series of *coloniae,* or colonies, abroad, but Augustus more intensively and more intentionally urbanized those recently conquered territories. Tiberius continued that process—Caligula's short reign and self-obsession stalled the process—but his successors, Claudius and Nero, more than made up for him. They all pursued what Michael Mann, whose work is cited as an epigraph in this book's Prologue, has called a *territorial* empire, an empire that functionally integrated and operationally unified all of its acquired territories. Their policy was to consolidate the provinces into a single cohesive whole, and to do so the Julio-Claudians either founded new colonies or refounded existing cities by giving them new constitutions, adding buildings, and, very often, renaming them in honor of the emperor or members of the imperial family.

Across all areas under Roman control, from Italy through Greece and Turkey into Syria and Egypt, the political ideals of autonomy and independence that had defined the classical Greek *polis* (or city-state, which, by the way, had been severely degraded under Hellenistic kingship) were replaced in the Roman *civitas* by two aims that were both functional and ideological. One was to use cities as administrative centers for supervising the production and distribution of local and regional resources. That also, of course, meant taxation flowing back to Rome. The other one was to build communities by creating for the empire's urban populations a common form of civic life, a common set of civic buildings, and a common Roman culture. That also, of course, meant loyalty flowing back to Rome. In spite of an empire that encompassed a multicultural mix of peoples and traditions, Roman urbanization enveloped that diversity with a unifying monoculture that shared an aesthetic with regard to urban design, offered universal expectations with regard to its structural components, and fostered an ethos of keen competition between cities for local achievement and urban prestige.

EUERGETISM. Local aristocrats bore the chief responsibility for civic life's urban structures, and within each city they competed among themselves to construct and renovate, enhance and enlarge, their cities through *euergetism* (literally, from the Greek, "good works") or benefactions. Competition to sponsor civic projects was fierce, and some of the well-to-do were willing to deplete their own private resources for the sake of public works. But, not surprisingly, they were also the chief beneficiaries of the blessings of Roman urbanization and received the first fruits of the *Pax Romana*. In each city, local aristocrats along with Roman expatriates like provincial administrators, retired soldiers, and Italian traders received their due rewards for these civic benefactions. If they could get their city or group of cities (a *koinon*) to submit suitably humble requests to the emperor, accompanied by due honors like putting his face on coins, naming months after him, or even renaming the city, they would receive in turn tax relief or even material, technical, or staff support for additional building projects. Key sponsors of such legislation were appointed to legislative bodies, civic offices, or priestly duties; those offices engendered further and more intimate services to imperial interests; and those services, in turn, obtained imperial land grants, tax relief, or business licenses. The urban structures were built through the flattery of emperors and the sycophancy of aristocrats, but that system of exchange had a sincerity that was very real, its financial rewards were very tangible, and its social rewards were very envied among those who could afford to play the game.

The blessings of urbanization extended beyond the few powerful landowners to include the urban lower classes as well. These received their share of the blessings in the form of city life's amenities. They were often the recipients of aristocratic benefaction in the form of entertainment—the well-to-do might sponsor games or shows in the venues they had constructed or pay for handouts like a grain dole, cash distribution, or lottery. City life even afforded some possibility for upward mobility. Freedmen, for example, could join various associations and by pooling their resources sponsor some benefaction to garner honor and status. This whole system, rooted at the local level and open to the considerable latitude of regional creativity, provided a remarkably cohesive urban life across the Roman Empire.

Three Stages in Romanization

ROADS AND PORTS. The first wave of Roman roads and ports were at once practical and ideological. The roads were built by and for the legions. They were first and foremost military routes that only afterward served as trade and communication arteries between the empire's cities and its capital at Rome. Across the empire, Roman engineers built roads suited to the local climate and adapted to readily available materials. Legionaries first surveyed the land and cut two ditches anywhere between 18 and 25 feet apart for the curbs, to be made of locally available stone blocks. Then, with the help of forced or coerced local labor, they dug foundation ditches between 3 and 8 feet deep, filled them with stones of descending size, put gravel and sand at the top, and typically capped it all with massive pavers fitted snugly together. This system, which cost according to some late Republican inscriptions around 100,000 sesterces per mile to repair, was sturdy, reliable, and spectacular. At that time, by the way, an unskilled laborer made from 2 to 4 sesterces a day.

That spectacular nature had an ideological impact. The Roman roads expressed the Roman outlook on the world. They did not meander along the contours of geography, but often cut across or bridged over natural obstacles, displaying the emperor's ability even to subdue topography and dominate nature, not unlike what was implied with *centuriation,* the rigidly orthogonal division of land and distribution to veterans. The roads were expansionist, designed for Roman troop movement to the periphery, and built without fear of enemies from beyond that periphery daring to use them against Rome (though, ironically, Paul did). As most roads entered cities, they led under triumphal arches commemorating imperial victories. They were marked with milestones that along with distances and dates always proclaimed IMP. CAESAR DIVI F., "Imperator Caesar, Son of God." They also served as reference points in Roman spatial imagination. In 20 B.C.E. Augustus set up in the Roman Forum beside Saturn's temple the Golden Milestone (*milliarium aureum*), which was the starting point of all the imperial roads and recorded distances from all the empire's great cities. That milestone made Rome the center of the world, whatever Greeks might say about Delphi or Jews might think about Jerusalem.

The expanding road system linked up with ports, many of which were constructed or renovated with the newly invented hydraulic concrete. Made from a volcanic sand mixture, it could be poured into casings, floated out to sea in sections, and submerged with remarkable speed. Ports and their break-waters went up, and Rome was no longer reliant on the natural harbors and the great coastal cities of old, but could redraw the Mediterranean map with nodal centers serving Roman interests, chiefly legionary paths to the periphery and the importation of luxury items and spices from the East and corn from Egypt.

STATUES AND TEMPLES. The second wave of Romanization was not just the peculiarity of the emperor cult, but the panoply of Roman imperial theology. The emperor cult, again? By now you may be tired of that whole subject. It has come up, one way or another, in every section of this book, and it will do so until the very end. If we have overwhelmed you somewhat, we have achieved no more than the cumulative effect of all those imperial images and institutions on city dwellers across the Roman Empire. We do insist, however, that the term "emperor cult" is much too narrow. That was, certainly, the core of Roman imperial theology, but, for example, you could hardly take Christian medieval theology and call it a "Christ cult." It was that, of course, but only as the center of an entire world of meaning. What we stress throughout this book is not the isolated peculiarity of emperor worship, but the integrated universality of imperial theology.

On a daily basis, then, those ports and roads funneled local, regional, and imperial travelers to city centers, where the emperor's statue or temple was located. It could be a Sebasteion, an Augusteum, or part of some local cult where elites sponsored festivals, games, and sacrifices for Caesar. This wave of Roman urbanization, perhaps the most pervasive one in the archaeological record, was the physical and visible expression of local gratitude for the blessings of the *Pax Romana* or, alternatively, the demand for imperial allegiance. It was repetitive and redundant, but ultimately accepted.

AQUEDUCTS AND BATHS. The third wave of Roman urbanization discernible in the archaeological record was the spread of facilities for entertainment and leisure, most particularly the intensification of public bathing across the hellenized East and its introduction in more remote areas. Large-scale and luxurious urban bathhouses were not explicitly promoted by Augustus, as they would have conflicted with his austere program of piety and morality. But those luxuries developed intensively under the later Julio-Claudians and reached their apex in the early second century. The trend took advantage of new Roman technology using mortar and domed roofs,

FIGURE 62. Roman aqueduct at Caesarea Maritima, first built by Herod the Great and then rebuilt by the Roman legions.

and hypocaust tiles enabled underground heating systems with circulation through clay pipes in the walls. For centuries, the Greek world had attached tub-and-basin baths to the gymnasium, where wealthy male youths competed in athletics as part of a broad education. But, under Rome, the athletic aspect became a mere appendage to the centrality of bathing. In fact, as a whole, the role of athletics in building individual character was replaced by the spectacles and blood sports of the arena.

The baths were affordable and served public hygiene. Their hot, warm, and cold pools, their libraries, lecture halls, massage and weight rooms, their barbers and body-hair pluckers made the baths the most treasured institution in urban areas. On a daily basis, men would congregate in the afternoon and some stay late into the evening; women eagerly awaited their allotted times, though some places permitted mixed bathing; and closure of the public baths was a feared censure that kept communities in line. The imperial cult was more visible, but bathing made the cult of luxury and Romanization every bit as seductive.

New technology made some constructions possible, but it was ultimately the *Pax Romana* that enabled the extension of that new technology's arch and mortar outside the walled cities. Aqueducts enabled urban communities to tap into water supplies from great distances far outside their defensive walls (Figure 62). And that peace and ensuing prosperity made affordable the enormous cost of those aqueducts and large and luxuriously decorated public baths. Baths and aqueducts, running water and sewage removal, became the most pervasive and certainly the most appreciated blessings of Roman rule. Over time, they made urbanites think of themselves as Roman, and to a great extent they shaped what it meant to be Roman.

Four Examples of Romanization

We choose four cities to highlight the effects of Romanization: Pompeii in Italy, Nicopolis in Greece, Antioch in Syria, and Caesarea Maritima in Judea (Figure 63). That sweep from west to east serves as background for the Galatian cities in its middle.

POMPEII ON THE CAMPANIAN COAST. Under Augustus a set of alterations undertaken by local initiative and private expense transformed the urban landscape of Pompeii and imitated the Augustan revolution's emphasis on piety and virtue. Almost all of the Pompeian aristocrats who sponsored public structures also copied Augustus by enrolling in priestly offices. Not surprisingly, then, temples were the most important and visible buildings they built. Two examples will suffice.

The first is a temple to *Fortuna Augusta* (Augustan Good Fortune) built on private land and paid for by one M. Tullius from his private funds. On a

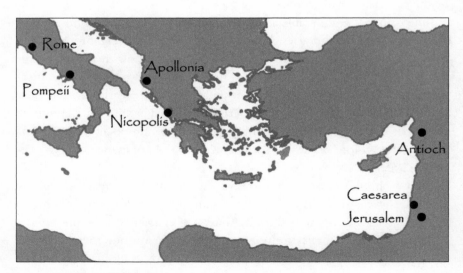

FIGURE 63. Map of Romanization.

FIGURE 64 *(above)*. Entrance to the Eumachia
building in Pompeii, with styles similar to the
Ara Pacis Augustae. FIGURE 65 *(right)*. Statue
from the Eumachia building with a veiled head
as a sign of piety and with features akin to
those of Livia and Concordia.

little plot at a well-traveled intersection, it mimicked Augustus's new lavishly marbled temples in Rome, but on a smaller scale. Accompanying
the statues of the imperial family was a toga-clad male priest, very likely
M. Tullius himself, who in promoting Augustus also promoted his own association with the *princeps.*

The second example is that enormous community building dedicated
later in Augustus's reign by the widow Eumachia, who as a civic priestess
sponsored the building in part to support her son's election to civic office.
The large structure stood in the middle of the eastern side of the forum and
was dedicated to *Concordia et Pietas Augusta* (Augustan Harmony and Piety).
It echoes several themes and styles from the Augustan Forum and the *Ara
Pacis Augustae,* by a gallery of Roman and Pompeian heroes in its portico, by
inscriptions to Aeneas and Romulus, and by "luxuriant vines" that, as Paul
Zanker says, "look as if they could have come from the same workshop

FIGURE 66. Plan of
Pompeii's forum
prior to its
transformation
under Augustus.

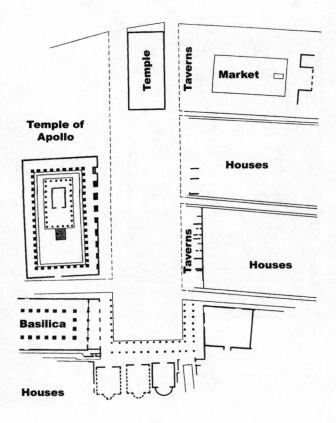

responsible for the Ara Pacis" in Rome (320; Figure 64). To flatter the imperial family, Eumachia had the statue of the goddess Concordia carved with
the features of Augustus's wife Livia, but to flatter herself, she had her own
statue imitate both Concordia and Livia, with head veiled as a sign of piety
and as a symbol of her priestly status (Figure 65). Her building on the east
side of the forum, two other imperial structures to its north, and an altar in
the center of the forum reoriented the area's north-south axis to an east-
west axis (Figures 66 and 67).

But even more significant for the daily lives of ordinary people was the
new and abundant flow of water that came with Julio-Claudian rule. Earlier
Pompeians relied on a set of rainwater cisterns and deep wells, but by the
end of Augustus's rule the city had tapped into the nearby imperial aqueduct
that supplied the Roman fleet in the Bay of Naples. Paid for by Pompeians
but permitted by and credited to Augustus, the new system distributed run-

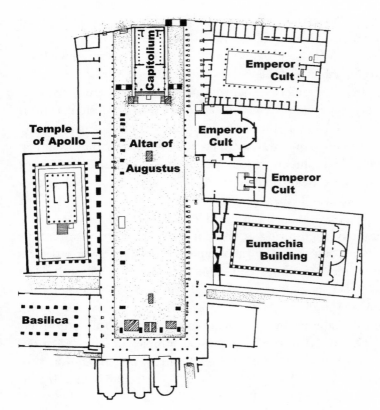

FIGURE 67. Plan of Pompeii's forum after Augustus; note the various structures associated with him and the imperial cult.

ning water to wealthy private houses, public fountains, and very, very luxurious baths.

NICOPOLIS ON THE AMBRACIAN GULF. Octavian founded Nicopolis, the "Victory City," in northwestern Greece immediately after his triumph over Antony and Cleopatra off Cape Actium. It commemorated that victory, provided a place to settle veterans from both Roman armies, and secured the Greek mainland at this very close point to the heel of the Italian peninsula. It facilitated trans-Mediterranean trade and travel, reinvigorated the area's devastated economy, integrated indigenous Greeks and colonial Romans, and was all paid for from the spoils of battle along with generous (forced?) donations from people like Herod the Great, who had earlier been a friend of the defeated Antony. It even became a museum-like site in Augustus's own lifetime.

Augustus made Nicopolis the chief regional center by moving there the locally popular Actian Games and elevating them to equal prestige with the Olympian Games. That gave the Victory City a double meaning: It attracted the greatest athletes of the world against the backdrop of the greatest victory of all time. Reminders of that victory were everywhere. The prows from Antony's defeated ships were fastened into a memorial, similar to the Rostra in Rome's forum, and it became part of an open-air sanctuary to Augustus's patron deity, Apollo. Built on the hill overlooking the city and its two ports, the battle trophies were jointly dedicated to the sea god Neptune and the war god Mars. Below in the city, Augustus and his imperial descendants were worshiped as divine.

Augustus's new city was fed by an aqueduct that was itself a major technical feat of legionary engineering. It brought abundant freshwater from the source of the river Louros along an almost imperceptible slope whose descent was a mere 250 feet over 30 miles with channels cut through hills and arched bridges over both ravines and rivers. Though, other than the small theater (odeon; Figure 68), little inside the city has been fully excavated (much more is promised), baths fed by the aqueduct are among the ruins still visible aboveground. One of them is an Augustan-era complex in the sacred grove between the Apollo sanctuary and the city, the area where the quadrennial Actian Games were held. That bath was a world-class facility with its barrel-

FIGURE 68. The odeon at Nicopolis, Augustus's new "Victory City."

vaulted ceilings and domed roofs. The imprints from marble panel inlays on the floor and the peg holes for marble wall sheeting are still visible, along with remnants from mosaic floors. In those pools and baths world–class competitors bathed every four years, including much later in 66 C.E., when the emperor Nero won (or, probably more accurately, was allowed to win) the laurel wreath in the chariot race. In the years in between, the leading citizens, their guests, and maybe even a good deal of the citizenry bathed there in regal style.

ANTIOCH ON THE SYRIAN ORONTES. Antioch on the Orontes River, third–largest city in the empire, was the capital of Syria, a strategic province directly under Augustus's control. Today it is Antakya-Hatay, but after a 1939 plebiscite it is in mid–southern Turkey rather than northwestern Syria. Antioch was already large in Hellenistic times and connected to important Eastern caravan routes with a port on the Orontes at coastal Seleucia. Coins give it the name "metropolis," often bear the image of Apollo, and frequently date to Octavian's accession. He visited the city twice, once right after the battle of Actium and again in 20 B.C.E. It is likely that, for that second visit, an official *adventus* or *parousia* (recall that term from Chapter 3), Herod the Great paved and colonnaded the main street, whose outlines are still visible in the modern city and whose remnants could still be seen until quite recently. This was one of the very first colonnaded streets in the empire; large–scale columns had previously been used only for temples and sanctuaries. Herod's construction lent the city and Augustus's visit there a civic-religious tone that was accentuated even more a few years later when the city council put up in the main intersection a statue of Tiberius in gratitude for his benefaction.

A citizen of Antioch named John Malalas, or John the Orator, focused on bathhouses in his sixth–century account of the city's expanded construction under the Julio-Claudians. He relates how Julius Caesar constructed an aqueduct for the purpose of supplying a new bathhouse on the upper slope of the city, how Augustus's then probable heir Agrippa built two bathhouses, naming one after himself, and how Tiberius put up another at the spring where Alexander the Great had once created a fountain. That excessive luxuriousness and licentiousness in bathing was the exactly what Juvenal in his *Satires* criticized at the start of the second century C.E., when he lamented how the moral sewage "of the Syrian Orontes has long since poured into the Tiber" (3.63–65). It is ironic, though, that Rome first promoted bathing and the cult of luxury to consolidate cities like Antioch into its urban monoculture, only later to condemn aspects of them as Eastern decadence.

In modern Antakya-Hatay a mounted statue of Atatürk stands in the center of a roundabout just west of the major bridge over the muddy brown Orontes. Immediately south of that statue is the Archaeological Museum, with an entrance you could miss if you were not looking for it. But that museum is where the lost glory of Antioch still shimmers in magnificent mosaics from the luxurious villas in the southern suburbs of Daphne, whose groves and waterfalls are still beautiful but also tawdry with littered garbage. In that small but well-presented museum is one of the finest collections of Roman mosaics in the world. Most of them are post-Pauline from the second or third centuries, but you can at least imagine backward from them to the luxury of aristocratic Antioch in Pauline times.

CAESAREA ON THE MEDITERRANEAN SEA. Herod the Great created Caesarea in honor of his new patron and political savior Augustus (hence *Caesarea*). He built it from nothing in the middle of his Mediterranean coastline (hence today we add *Maritima* to distinguish it from many other Caesareas). Its massive and ultramodern port was named *Sebastos,* Greek for the Latin *Augustus.* With that great all-weather harbor Herod the Great oriented his kingdom toward Rome, and with those names he told Rome what it wanted to hear. Like those three cities just mentioned, it had a modern port to link it with Roman-controlled sea-lanes, imperial temples that encouraged allegiance, and flowing water for urban amenities.

The harbor facilities were built with new Roman technology, Italian *pozzalana* cement, and massive breakwaters extending some 800 feet into the open sea to enclose a harbor of nearly 40 acres. But no well-built Roman road system was constructed to reach most of inland Palestine until the second century C.E., after the two Jewish revolts and with the permanent stationing of legions inside the country.

The city's great Temple to Roma and Augustus has been badly destroyed and extensively built upon over the centuries. But with the help of Josephus's eyewitness account and bits and pieces of columns and capitals, an estimate of the temple's onetime grandeur can still be established. It rose to a height between 80 and 110 feet. It stood at the center of the city, in a plaza to which both thoroughfares led, but it was slightly off grid so that its glistening façade greeted sailors turning into the port. A life-sized cuirassed torso of the emperor Trajan (98–117 C.E.) and a seated but headless Hadrian (117–

FIGURE 69. Inscription from Caesarea Maritima, telling of a building by Pontius Pilate in honor of Tiberius.

38 C.E.) survive and testify to the continued worship of the emperor in that temple. But Josephus tells us that Herod had originally installed there massive statues of the goddess Roma dressed as Hera Argos and of Caesar Augustus as Zeus Olympios. An important inscription found in 1962 on a stone, turned upside down and reused in the theater's renovation, refers to a *Tiberium* dedicated to the emperor Tiberius, a structure Pontius Pilate erected to honor that emperor (Figure 69). Herod the Great obeyed Torah in Jerusalem by rebuilding Zion's Temple without images or icons. But in nearby coastal Caesarea he was one of the very first to bestow divine honors on Augustus in a temple, a tradition then spreading all across the Mediterranean and that continued at Caesarea for many emperors to come.

Finally, after port and temple, came water. Since Caesarea had no freshwater source, an aqueduct, still partially visible to this day north of the ruins, brought water from springs some 10 miles away (Figure 62).

Pacifying Celts in Roman Galatia

We turn now from Roman urbanization in general to that process for Galatia in particular. In 25 B.C.E., Octavian, just become Augustus, established the new Roman province of Galatia from disparate geographical regions and peoples. What was to become Galatia in central Anatolia had been a relative backwater inhabited in the west by Phrygians caricatured in Rome for their exotic and ecstatic worship of the mother goddess Cybele, in the south by the least hellenized of the fiercely independent Pisidians, and in the center mostly by the warlike Celtic tribes who had wandered there from Gaul in the third century B.C.E. Note, of course, the linguistic linkage between Celts and Galatians: C-L-T becomes G-L-T. Those warrior Celts are well known from the famous statue *The Dying Gaul* in Rome's Capitoline Museum (Figure 70). It is actually a Roman copy of the original bronze statue at Pergamum celebrating, not a first-century-C.E. Roman, but a third-century-B.C.E. Greek victory over the invading Celts. For the most part, those peoples lived in small towns, retained a tribal organization, were largely untouched by hellenization, and preserved their own language, customs, and religion.

Augustus's Galatia stretched in a northeast-to-southwest swath across the central Anatolian plateau from the Pontic to the Taurus mountains. In its south he founded Roman colonies populated with many legionary veterans, such as Derbe, Lystra, Iconium in Lycaonia, and Antioch in Pisidia. In

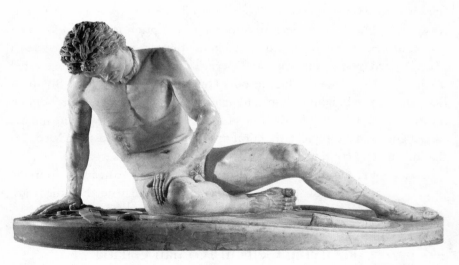

FIGURE 70. *The Dying Gaul,* Roman marble copy of a Greek original depicting a Celt defeated in battle in Anatolia.

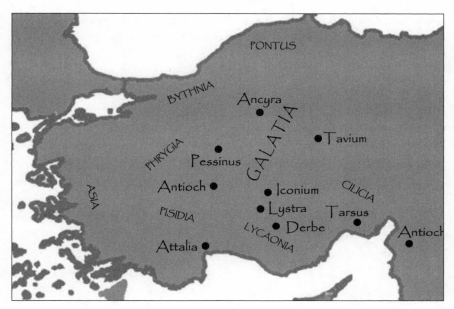

FIGURE 71. Map of Galatia.

its north he created new cities for the three Celtic tribes to be urbanized and Romanized. For the westernmost Tolistobogii tribe, within the eastward bend of the river Sangarius, he created the city of Pessinus. For the easternmost Trocmi, within the westward bend of the river Halys, he established the city of Tavium. In the center, between those two rivers, he organized Ancyra for the Tectosages and made it the capital of the entire province (Figure 71).

Scholars have long debated whether Paul wrote his letter to those northern and ethnic Celts called Galatians (not mentioned in Luke's Acts) *or* to those southern inhabitants, not ethnic Celts or Galatians, who were living in the province named Galatia (mentioned in Acts). Was Paul using a tribal name for the north *or* a political name for the south? Was he addressing those northern cities founded as new cities for Romanized Celtic tribes *or* those southern cities (re)founded as Roman colonies mostly for discharged veterans? Or was he writing a circular letter to cover a vast area of both north and south?

Luke states in Acts 13–14 that Paul, along with and under Barnabas, visited those southern cities in his second mission. But, afterward, and as we see in more detail below, there was an irrevocable break between Paul and Barnabas at Syrian Antioch on the Orontes. Because of that parting of the ways, then, we doubt that Paul ever again visited or even wrote to those southern assemblies that "belonged," as it were, to Barnabas. By inference, then, we suppose that by "Galatians" Paul probably intended communities in those northern cities like Pessinus, Ancyra, or Tavium rather than southern ones like Pisidian Antioch, Iconium, Lystra, or Derbe.

In any case, both north and south were undergoing the steady process of Romanization and urbanization in the middle of that first century. In both places, Celt and Latin, indigene and expatriate, were forming a culture we will call Roman and with which Paul had to deal. In that regard, both north and south were becoming Roman in the same three-step process that we saw earlier from Pompeii to Judea. It was always about imperial roads, temples, and amenities.

Imperial Roads

The Roman-built Via Egnatia ended at the Bosporus, but on its other side in Anatolia there was an already well-traveled Persian road system dating to before Alexander the Great. It had two main eastward arteries that the Romans used and later upgraded to their all-weather military standards. A northern, Pontic route went south of the Black Sea to Armenia and Adiabene, whose queen and prince were converted to Judaism in the first century C.E. A southern route began at Pergamum on the Aegean coast, swung south through Ephesus, cut inland to avoid high mountains, and then crossed the Anatolian plateau to the Cilician Gates at Tarsus, gateway to Syria and the eastern frontier. Both routes were crucial to supply the Roman legions guarding Syria against the Parthian Empire farther east. For a century before Augustus, both roads were vulnerable to attacks from those unhellenized, unurbanized, and uncivilized peoples in what was to become the province of Galatia.

Pacifying that Anatolian area was crucial for defensive success against the Parthians as a linchpin of Rome's global strategy. Augustus established those Galatian colonies and cities, connecting them with sturdy and reliable roads. The first main route, named after himself as the Via Sebaste, began at the sea in the south-central Anatolian port of Perge and ascended over a steep pass through the highlands of Pisidia to the colony of Pisidian Antioch. From there it extended east along an old Persian road to the colonies of Iconium and Lystra, the very path that Acts says Paul took on his missionary journey. Surviving excavated sections show it was 20 to 26 feet wide and built for the heavy wheeled traffic that accompanied the legions.

The Roman roads of Galatia implicitly symbolized but also explicitly articulated Rome's and specifically the emperor's domination. For example, a milestone in Galatia announces "Imperator Caesar Son of God Pontifex Maximus, . . . made the Via Sebaste under the care of his legate Cornuto Aquila . . ." (*CIL* 3.6974). In Pisidia near the Galatian border with Asia Minor, an altar dedicated to Augustus in 5/4 B.C.E. was erected near the Via Sebaste by the local Mylians along with Roman and Thracian immigrants.

But the new roads were much more than a symbol of Roman authority; they brought Roman power, swiftly and violently, into remote regions. Milestones tell us that the Via Sebaste was completed in 6 B.C.E., exactly the date when Augustus sent P. Sulpicius Quirinius and his Seventh Legion on the final significant military operations in the region. Moving along that road against the rebellious Homonadeis tribe in the remote mountain valleys of southeast Galatia between 6 B.C.E. and 4 C.E., those forces systematically razed fortresses and villages and sold the surviving men and captured women into slavery. The roads efficiently moved the Roman legions along their track of violent enforcement, and they were also a permanent reminder of their swift avenging access. The success of that road system and urban network is best illustrated by the fact that the Seventh Legion stationed in Pisidian Antioch by Augustus was removed in 7 C.E. and never replaced. By the time Paul traveled those Galatian roads, there was little sign of a military presence, since by then the locals had been pacified and were included among the once conquered but now Roman people.

Imperial Temples

The final epigraph at the start of this chapter was from Stephen Mitchell's exhaustive study of the Galatian province and its surrounding regions. "Emperor worship was from the first an institution of great importance to the provincial communities," he emphasizes, "and one that had, quite literally, a central role to play in the development of the new cities" (100). Although very little archaeological work has been undertaken in the part of Turkey once encompassed by Galatia, those sites that have to some degree been excavated, like Ancyra, Pessinus, and Pisidian Antioch, reveal the centrality of the imperial cult to Roman urbanization. From Ancyra-Ankara to Pessinus-Balhisar and from there to Antioch-Yalvaç is about equal distance on a curving southwestern trajectory.

ANCYRA. Ancyra's imperial temple to Roma and Augustus, begun under Augustus and completed under Tiberius in 19/20 C.E., was made of marble and, with its imposing size, it was the most visible monument of the city. We return to it once more in our Epilogue. In design and style, it blended several traditions. Although approached by steep stairs and fronted by eight Corinthian columns, both typically Roman, the overall plan was more in the Greek peristyle tradition, in which external columns created a covered walkway around the temple walls (Figure 72). The closest parallel is the great Hellenistic temple of Athena at Priene in Asia Minor, many of whose elements it appears to mimic and which was rededicated to Athena and Augustus. Architecturally, the temple expressed the new Roman monoculture as a blend of East and West, regional and imperial elements. It is therefore no surprise that a Greek paraphrase of the *Acts of the Divine Augustus* was put on the south and more publicly visible side (Figure 73), while the original Latin, reserved for the atrium's internal walls, was only visible upon entry into the temple. With its roughly east-west orientation, it opened not, as is

FIGURE 72. Reconstruction of imperial Temple of Rome and Augustus in Ancyra, combining local and Roman architectural traditions.

FIGURE 73. Greek text of the *Res Gestae* inscription from the imperial Temple of Rome and Augustus in Ancyra.

customary, to the east and rising sun, but to the west and Rome. That subtle and suggestive message was complemented, of course, by the massive temple's expensive materials and prominent position, which, like the emperor himself, dominated the city's landscape.

Local Galatian participation in the imperial cult is attested by a remarkable inscription from Ancyra dating to Tiberius's reign that lists the chief priests of the divine Augustus and the goddess Roma as well as their benefactions to the local population. Celtic-Galatian names predominate in that list, but some have already adopted Greek and even Latin names. Apart from the obvious inclusion of sacrifices, other benefactions drew upon various regional customs. In the Greek tradition, those priests supplied olive oil for the populace: "Castor son of King Brigatus, . . . olive oil for four months" in 20–21 C.E. They sponsored games in the Roman tradition, namely, blood-sport spectacles rather than athletic competitions in the Greek tradition: "Pylaemenes son of King Amyntas, . . . gladiatorial spectacles . . . bull-fighting" in 22–23 C.E. and "bull wrestling; fifty pairs of gladiators; . . . wild-beast fight" in 30–31 C.E. But, also, in the Celtic tradition, they hosted banquets for tribal delegates or entire tribes: "Albiorix son of Ateporix . . . public banquet; set up statues of [Tiberius] Caesar and Iulia Augusta" in 23–24 C.E. Competition was fierce; the tendency was for later priests to

outdo their predecessors. Honors and status were tied to the level of aristocratic generosity, and those also led to greater and greater rewards for the
common citizens, all associated with worshiping the emperor.

PESSINUS. A short time after the temple of Augustus was built in Ancyra, another was built in Pessinus, capital of the westernmost Tolistobogii
tribe of Celts and formerly a Phrygian holy site. The Pessinus temple had
six Roman-style Corinthian columns on the front, but was surrounded by a
Greek-style row of columns. Its most interesting aspect is that the temple
was fronted by a monumental stairway of around thirty steps that cut right
through the middle of a theater-like orchestra dating to the Tiberian or
maybe even the Claudian era. That theater-like seating was not just ornamental, but was used for games or spectacles in honor of the emperor and as
part of the imperial cult. Recall the blood sports and imperial statues from
those just-mentioned Ancyra inscriptions. There are also fragments from
the temple at Pessinus that mention the "imperial priests of the Pessinian
Tolistobogii."

PISIDIAN ANTIOCH. According to the Acts of the Apostles, Paul was in
Pisidian Antioch twice (13:14; 14:21). That colony was in many ways a
Rome in miniature and would have shown him clearly what the capital was
like in microcosm. The colony adopted and replicated aspects of Rome in
its construction and constitution. Like the mother city, it was laid out with a
sacred city limit, or *pomerium,* its neighborhoods were divided according
to Roman tribal names, and it had a set of similarly named priesthoods.
Pisidian Antioch's imperial temple, at the city's highest point and visible
from miles around, was more in the Roman architectural tradition than either of those at Ancyra and Pessinus. In its design, detail, and setting at the
east end of a long plaza that was surrounded by a two-storied colonnade and
portico, it was similar to the Mars Temple in Rome's Augustan Forum. Like
the other Galatian imperial temples, it faced Rome and was approached
from the west along the plazalike Tiberia Plateia, the main Tiberian Boulevard, through a major triple-arched gate that focused all attention on the
temple's façade. Those entering through that monumental gate into the imperial temple's plaza, whether for civic business, legal dispute, imperial celebration, or official banquet, were met by a large inscription set in bronze
letters, since stripped but decipherable from the many peg holes that held
the letters in place (Figure 74). It begins: IMP. CAES[ARI DI]VI F. AUGUSTO.

FIGURE 74. Circular inscription along the Tiberia Plateia leading to the Temple of Augustus; the bronze letters have since been stripped, but the text is decipherable.

PONFI[F]ICI M[AXIM]O, "For the Imperator Caesar Augustus, son of god, *pontifex maximus.*"

In addition to this inscription, the University of Michigan excavations found bits and pieces of the gate's iconographic and epigraphic scheme. This included scenes from Augustus's defeat of the hostile Pisidians (similar in many ways to the friezes at Aphrodisias), his birth sign, Capricorn, and those many small fragments from the Latin text of the *Acts of the Divine Augustus* seen earlier in the Yalvaç Museum. The colony of Pisidian Antioch was initially and primarily settled by Romans, as the names in the predominantly Latin inscriptions make clear, but there were surely intermarriages, and local Celts and Pisidians as well as nearby Isaurians and Lycians who had been conscripted into legionary or auxiliary service also retired in Antioch and the other Galatian colonies. They were consolidated with Romans into a single city, which served as a nodal point to collect and transmit taxes as well as to stabilize and pacify the region.

The imperial cult was not restricted to these three urban sites or limited to the time of Augustus. It spread across Galatia and intensified in subsequent decades. It covered that very large province with extraordinary speed. In the north, right after Paphlagonia's annexation to Galatia in 6/5 B.C.E., those inhabitants took an oath to the divine Augustus, according to an inscription found in 1900 by Franz Cumont and dating to 3 B.C.E. The nearly 6-foot stele, broken in two by late antiquity, stood near ancient Phazimon on the main highway from Ancyra toward the Black Sea. Sworn by all the people of the region, local or Roman, in cities and countryside, at "the command of Caesar Augustus, the son of god," the covenant reads,

> I swear by Zeus, the Earth, the Sun, and by all the gods and goddesses including Augustus himself, to be favorable to Caesar Augustus, his sons and his descendants forever, in speech, in actions, and in thoughts, considering as friends those he considers so, and regarding as enemies those he judges so, and to defend their interests I will spare neither body, nor soul, nor life, nor my children. . . .

Later the text specifies that those who break the covenant's stipulations will suffer with their "body, soul, and life." Treason against the emperor was a capital crime. The text further says that the oath could be sworn at any number of the local center's Sebasteia and their altars to Augustus, or at the nearby city formerly called Phazimon but now renamed Neapolis and, even later, *Neoclaudiopolis,* the "New City of Claudius." Only three years after its incorporation into the Galatian province, the area was filled with imperial cult sites.

That process continued in the Galatian province well after Augustus, so that by Paul's time there are no signs of fervent imperial flattery dying down. All across Galatia, a host of cities adopted Claudius's name in the middle of the first century as a way to honor him and acquire his benefaction. In addition to that Phazimon, which became Neoclaudiopolis, in the north, we find in the south Claudiopolis, Claudioderbe, Claudiconium, Claudiolaodicea, Claudiocaesarea Mistae, and Claudioseleuceia. Local civic councils were eager to renew the covenant and its cycle of allegiance and benefaction.

Imperial Amenities

As always, many of the benefits that came from allegiance to Caesar were in the form of urban amenities. City life, so to speak, was the blessing of that covenant, which included entertainments, spectacles, and, above all, abundant water flowing securely through aqueducts for public bathing. Pessinus's temple-theater was the venue for gladiatorial combats funded by the imperial chief priests. In 31–32 C.E., for example, "M. Lollius [sponsored a] public banquet in Pessinus; 25 pairs of gladiators and 10 pairs in Pessinus; olive oil for the 2 tribes for the whole year; erected a divine statue in Pessinus" (Mitchell, 108). Just east of Ancyra's imperial temple, across a stream and cut

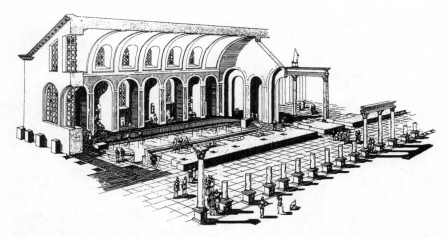

FIGURE 75. Reconstruction of the Roman baths at Ancyra; though over a century after Paul and more elaborate than those of his time, they indicate the trajectory on which Romanization was heading.

into a slope, was a theater that surely witnessed blood spectacles, pantomimes, and farces in the Italian style during the first century. And though dating almost two centuries after Paul, the only other Roman structure to survive Ancyra's twentieth-century urbanization under Atatürk was a gigantic bathhouse east of the imperial temple. At around 450 by 600 feet, it was one of the largest and certainly most spectacular baths in the Roman world, and it underlines the trajectory of Roman urbanization in the first century (Figure 75).

We know much more about Pisidian Antioch, whose ruins still lie scattered on the sloping outskirts of the modern town of Yalvaç. Apart from those initial excavations in the 1920s, the site has again been subject to recent probes and surveys. A badly overgrown horseshoe-shaped stadium lies unexcavated on the outskirts of the city, and there is also an excavated theater whose present sign indicates it as the setting for Thecla's trials in the *Acts of Paul and Thecla* mentioned in Chapter 2. An inscription also mentions the construction of a temporary theater for gladiatorial games.

The aqueduct at Pisidian Antioch was built sometime during the early part of the first century, and it brought ice-cold water from springs 7 miles away at a higher elevation of about 1,000 feet (Figure 76). The route curved a bit along the contours of the land, but to reach the city, it had to tunnel through hills and cross gullies and valleys with arched bridges. The underground

FIGURE 76. At the source of the aqueduct leading to Pisidian Antioch, taken in 1924 with one of the original University of Michigan excavators on top.

vaulted channels were made of rough stone and mortar and accessible through regularly spaced manholes that had ladderlike footholds cut into their shafts, so that workers could climb down and clear obstructions or repair leaks. The bridges and raised sections of the aqueduct were uniformly spaced, shaped arches were elevated with appropriately sized piers, and some of them stand to this day 30 feet above the ground.

Once inside the city, the water was put to various uses. Although as yet unexcavated, we can presume that, as at Pompeii, drinking water was fed to elite houses and neighborhood fountains, with excess water flushing sewage through belowground channels. A U-shaped *nymphaeum,* or fountain complex dedicated to the nymphs or river goddesses and pure-water guardians, is visible today where the water entered the city. Aesthetically it was an oasis-like structure at the end of a long street with bronze statuary, colored marble sheeting, and dedicatory inscriptions that proclaimed the city's wealth and abundance. At Pisidian Antioch's other side, just inside the main city gate, water cascaded down decorated waterfalls into a semicircular fountain. It greeted visitors with a soothing sound, but also established an aura of abundance. Its shade and marble walls functioned like an air conditioner on those hot summer days atop the western Anatolian plateau. All that water was controlled, of course, by the city's urban elites, who managed its distribution as they saw fit—it was taken from the countryside to the city, and there used primarily for bathing and beautification, as the blessings of Roman rule spread to Galatia.

Interlude: The Diaspora Synagogue

Before turning from the Romanization of all the Galatians by Augustus to the Christianization of some Galatians by Paul, we pause to look at the importance of the Jewish diaspora synagogue. Our theory has been that Paul went to those diaspora synagogues not to convert his fellow Jews, but to convert their pagan God-worshipers to Christianity. This section emphasizes the religio-political and socioeconomic importance of those synagogues as the interface of paganism and Judaism by taking one fascinating example. It is probably an example we might never have imagined unless we had inscriptional evidence for its existence.

Synagogue Manumissions

Inscriptions from the Roman client-kingdom of Bosporus, a territory now split between eastern Ukraine and southern Russia, indicate one somewhat surprising synagogue function. They also supply archaeological evidence extending from the early first to the early third century C.E. for the presence of those pagan sympathizers or God-worshipers first seen from that early-third-century Aphrodisian inscription in Chapter 1. In other words, they push the *inscriptional* existence for pagan sympathizers back to as early as 16 C.E. in a Jewish area on the fringes of the classical world. We cite them here in the translations by Irina Levinskaya.

The Bosporus kingdom included both sides of the strait connecting the Sea of Azov with the Black Sea on a north-south axis and separating the tip of the Caucasus Mountains from the jut of the Crimean Peninsula on an east-west axis. The main cities were the capital, Panticapaeum, now Kerch, on the European side, and Phanagoria and Gorgippia, now Anapa, on the Asian side of the Kerch Strait and its central Taman Gulf. Those inscriptions record how a synagogue was the setting, guarantor, and medium for manumitting, or granting freedom to, slaves. They also detail certain post-manumission legal obligations the freed slaves had to perform. That process was quite customary at pagan temples—there are about thirteen hundred extant from Apollo's great temple at Delphi in Greece (including three Jewish ones). Manumission meant freedom and did not mean that the individuals were being given to or bought by the temple to remain there as its slaves. In the actual process, however, the slaves to be freed gave the purchase price to the temple, which used it to "buy" their freedom for them and thereby guarantee it before the god or goddess. The slaves were thus fictionally "dedicated" to the temple.

About one-third of those Delphi inscriptions contain an ongoing obligation to "remain with" (the Greek verb is *paramenein*) the master, mistress, or family for some stated length of time. Thus, for example, although Kleon made Histiaios "free and inviolable by anyone for his entire life, doing as he pleases" (*SGDI* 1738), Krato made Sosikrates "remain with Krato doing all that is asked for as long as Krato lives. And if he does not remain exactly as written, let the [fictional] sale be invalid and incomplete" (*SGDI* 1721). Similar restrictive obligations also appear in the Jewish Bosporus texts. One owner, for example, stipulates that manumission is "on condition that they remain with me till the end of my life" (*CIRB* 73). But there are also special obligations *to honor* and *to attend* the synagogue after manumission. The question is whether those latter obligations entailed economic or religious duties. Was it a case of part-time economic service or full-time religious attendance? And, if the latter was demanded as a condition for freedom, would they have rendered those freed slaves the functional equivalent of "God-worshipers," with or without that name?

Sixteen synagogue-associated manumission texts were discovered in those three Bosporus areas from the first three centuries C.E., but here and now we focus on the five earliest examples explicitly and precisely dated to 16, 41, 51, 59, and 81 C.E.. None of the five was found in its original position; the middle one is a light yellow marble block now in Moscow, and the other four are white marble slabs now in the Hermitage Museum in St. Petersburg. There are also two main formulas evident across those five examples, and in reading them and other similar ones, recall that the term "prayer house" (*proseuchē*) indicates the Jewish meeting hall as place or building, while "synagogue" (*synagōgē*) emphasizes the group or gathering that met there.

ABOVE: View from Philippi, where history changed; there Octavian and Antony's imperial army defeated the Republican forces, and there Paul later took on imperial forces.
BELOW: Alleged place in Philippi where Paul was imprisoned by Rome.

LEFT: Claudius, divinely nude and cloud-cloaked, rules all Land and Sea, receiving cornucopia to left and rudder to right, from the Sebasteion at Aphrodisias. ABOVE: Augustus, divinely nude but cloaked, and the winged Victory to right, set up an arms-trophy above a barbarian prisoner, from the Sebasteion at Aphrodisias.

ABOVE: The emperor Claudius over the female personification of Britannia, poised to pierce her, from the Sebasteion at Aphrodisias. RIGHT: The emperor Nero over the female personification of Armenia, from the Sebasteion at Aphrodisias.

ABOVE, LEFT: Statue of the goddess Roma, erected on the island of Delos by a group of merchants and shippers to honor Rome. ABOVE, RIGHT: Statue of a phallus at the Temple of Dionysos on Delos. BELOW: Approaching the port of Delos, where ancient sources speak of 10,000 slaves being shipped through on a daily basis.

ABOVE: King Darius fleeing the battle of Issus, where Alexander's Greek troops crushed the Persians. BELOW: Only scant excavations are possible around and under the modern city of Thessaloniki, where Paul established an early Christian assembly.

ABOVE, LEFT: Statue of Augustus found at Thessaloniki, in divine pose.
ABOVE, RIGHT: Statue of Claudius found at Thessaloniki, in divine pose.
BELOW: Model of ancient Thessalonica's Roman Forum.

ABOVE: Ruins of the Temple of Augustus at the Roman colony of Pisidian Antioch, in the province of Galatia. BELOW: Fragments of the *Res Gestae,* or "Acts of the Divine Augustus," found at Pisidian Antioch.

ABOVE: Inscription mentioning Sergius Paullus, whose family was from Pisidian Antioch and who met Paul on Cyprus according to Acts.
BELOW: Dying Gaul; the earlier Celts in Anatolia would later be integrated into the Roman province of Galatia.

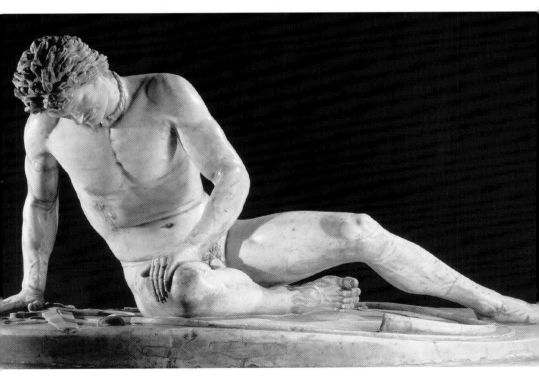

ABOVE: Fresco in the Grotto of St. Paul at Ephesus; to the right, Thecla's eyes have been etched out and her hand has been scratched off and burned by later visitors. BELOW: Excavations of the Artemision by the Austrian Archaeological Institute, dedicated to the patron-goddess of Ephesus.

ABOVE: Inscription at Ephesus proclaiming Caesar Augustus a Son of God (DIVI F) and high priest (PONTIFICI MAXIMO). BELOW: The great theater at Ephesus, where according to Acts, Paul's activities instigated a riot.

ABOVE: Pompeiian Forum in the shadow of Mt. Vesuvius, whose eruption in 79 C.E. froze in time urban life in the first century. BELOW: House of the Bicentenary in Herculaneum; lining the street are shops like those in which Paul worked and worshiped.

ABOVE, LEFT: Bas-relief of an erotic scene found at Pompeii.
ABOVE, RIGHT: "Herein dwells happiness" reads this inscription from Pompeii,
with the phallus serving as a kind of good luck charm. BELOW: A tavern or
bar from Pompeii, with an altar in the background.

ABOVE: Overview of the isthmus that separates the Greek mainland from the Peloponnese; Corinth had two harbors at this strategic site. BELOW: Overview of the excavations by the American School of Classical Studies at Corinth.

ABOVE: Inscription from Corinth naming the treasurer Erastus, whom Paul mentions in Romans 16:23; still readable even though the bronze letters have long since been removed. BELOW: The so-called *bēma* at Corinth, where according to Acts Paul stood trial before Gallio.

ABOVE: Arch of Titus in Rome, honoring the emperor who earlier, as general, had destroyed the Jewish Temple in Jerusalem in 70 C.E. BELOW: Sacking of Jerusalem and carrying off the spoils from the Temple, on the Arch of Titus in Rome.

ABOVE: What's left of Emperor Nero's Golden House, the largest and most ostentatious home built in ancient Rome. BELOW: Catacombs of Priscilla in Rome; members of Rome's Christian community buried their dead in niches.

ABOVE: Temple Mount in Jerusalem, expanded by Herod the Great and visited by Paul just prior to his final arrest. BELOW: Remains of the artificial harbor at Caesarea Maritima, built by Herod the Great; from here, Paul sailed on to Rome for his trial and execution.

"TO THE MOST HIGH." One formula has an opening invocation whose full form is specifically Jewish and whose content indicates that Jewish prayer houses served the same purpose for manumissions as did those pagan temples. Here is an example from Gorgippia in 41 C.E.:

> To the Most High God, Almighty, blessed, in the reign of the king Mithridates, the friend of ? and the friend of the fatherland, in the year 338, in the month Deios, Pothos, the son of Strabo, dedicated to the prayer house in accordance with the vow his house-bred slave-woman, whose name is Chrysa, on condition that she should be unharmed and unmolested by any of his heirs under Zeus, Ge, Helios. (*CIRB* 1123)

Similar examples can only be dated more imprecisely between 68 and 92 C.E. (*CIRB* 1126) or 93 and 124 C.E. (*CIRB* 1125).

First, the threefold opening formula of God as Highest, Almighty, and Blessed, especially that final epithet, is distinctively Jewish. Second, "dedicated to the prayer house" does not mean that the slave was actually sold to the synagogue, but was freed by having it pay to the owner the fee he or she had first given to it. The point of that fictional sale was to involve the synagogue as sacred witness, guarantor, and medium of the entire process. The synagogue operated, in other words, as a sacred place, just like (or instead of?) a pagan temple. Third, the terminal mention of the pagan gods Zeus, Ge, and Helios does not indicate non-Jewish ownership, Jewish idolatry, or even syncretism. The formula was the local legal formula for those gods as witnesses and was simply accepted as such.

HONOR AND ATTENDANCE. Another formula appears in inscriptions from Phanagoria in 16 C.E. (*CIRB* 985) and 51 C.E. (*SEG* 43.510) and from Panticapaeum in 81 C.E. (*CIRB* 70):

> In the reign of the king Aspurgus, the friend of the Romans, in the year 313, on the 7th of the month Daisios, Phodacos, the son of Pothon, dedicates his house-bred slave Dionysios, who is also (called) Longion (?) in the prayer house (?) . . . on condition that he honours [the prayer house] and is conscientious in his attendance there. (*CIRB* 985)

> In the reign of the king Cotys, on the 1st day of the month Xandikos, Psycharion and his sons Sogos and Anos. Karsandanos and Karagos and Metroteimos are set free for (in?) the prayer house without let or

hindrance on condition that they are conscientious in their attendance to prayer house and honour it and they become free also under the joint guardianship of the Jewish community (*tēs synagōgēs tōn Ioudaiōn*). (*SEG* 43.510)

In the reign of the King Tiberius Julius Rhescuporis, friend of the Emperor and friend of the Romans, pious, in the year 377, on the 12th of Pereitios, I, Chreste, formerly the wife of Drusus, set free in the prayer house, my house-bred slave Heraclas once and for all in fulfillment of a vow to move without let or hindrance from any of my heirs wherever he wants unimpededly, in accordance with my vow, on condition that he honours the prayer house and is conscientious in his attendance there, with the agreement of my heirs Heraclides and Heliconias and also under the joint guardianship of the Jewish community (*tēs synagōgēs tōn Ioudaiōn*). (*CIRB* 70)

Those second examples also indicate the Jewish prayer house as a medium for manumission. But just as there were often restrictive obligations in temple manumissions, so also here, and under the "synagogue of the Jews" as witnesses. The owners, whether full Jews or themselves God-worshipers, demand "honor for" (*thōpeia*) and "attendance at" (*proskarterēsis*) the Jewish prayer house as a condition of manumission. Those twin obligations appear in all three of the above manumissions and also in *CIRB* 73, dated more generally to the first half of the first century. And, for future reference, note that duality. But, once again, we repeat those earlier questions. Are those obligations economic service or religious attendance? Are those freed slaves to continue as or become God-worshipers? Are those twin terms the Bosporus words for that pagan-sympathizing status?

Scholarship is divided on that question, but we accept the emphasis on religious attendance rather than simple economic service. For this latter obligation, one term would have been quite sufficient: attend *or* serve. Take, for example, this parallel from pagan temple manumissions. We already saw those familial obligations "to remain" in both pagan temple and Jewish synagogue manumissions. But there could also be a sacral obligation to remain with the temple itself. E. Leigh Gibson, in *The Jewish Manumission Inscriptions of the Bosporus Kingdom*, cites second-century manumissions from the temple of the goddess Ma in Macedonian Beroea that combine both familial and sacral restrictions. Popios Aelios Amatokos frees Neikon "to serve after my death and that of my wife on festival days during every celebration" and Agathon frees Epagathos to "serve me throughout the time of my life staying with the goddess on festival days" (48). But for a Jewish obligation of religious and not just economic attendance both sincerity and presence are required. The freed Jewish slave must accept the obligation both internally *to honor* and externally *to attend*. We think, in other words, that the twin terms are the local equivalent of the term "God-worshiper" elsewhere. But, of course, synagogue attendance is here an unfree legal condition rather than a free social association as at Aphrodisias.

GOD-WORSHIPERS? There is one other inscription that seems both to confirm that understanding of *honor and attend* as religious (with or without) economic obligation and to indicate that the formula is the local equivalent of "God-worshiper" status elsewhere. There is only one case where that specific term is present in those Bosporus manumission texts, in a first-century inscription found at Panticapaeum in 1928, published in 1935, but now reported as missing from the Kerch Museum (*CIRB* 71, cited in Levinskaya, 74).

> I free in the prayer house Elpias, my household slave, so that he will be undisturbed and unassailable by any of my heirs, on condition that he attends (*proskarterein*) the prayer house under the guardianship of the Jewish community, and worships God (*kai theon sebōn*).

That agrees in general with the second formula seen above from Panticapaeum and Phanagoria, but it is that last expression that is of immediate interest. On the one hand, it is syntactically strange in English as in Greek, because, if it modifies the freed slave, you would expect it earlier after "attends the prayer house." On the other, *attend and worship* may be but a different formulation of the twofold legal obligation seen earlier as *honor and attend* the prayer house.

Some scholars have proposed to emend the Greek text from three to two words by omitting the *n* and running the last two words together. Instead of *kai theon sebōn,* meaning "and worships God," we would then have *kai theo[n]sebōn,* meaning "and of God-worshipers." In other words, the synagogue would be identified as that "of the Jews and God-worshipers." To omit the *n* and combine those two words is surely possible, but first, as you can see from those three other second-formula examples, there are usually two conditions: *to honor* (not the same verb as to *worship,* by the way) and *to attend* the synagogue. That emendation loses that duality in this text. Second, no mention of "God-worshipers" has even been found in any other Bosporus text.

If the emendation is not accepted, then the freed slave is legally obligated to remain or become a "God-worshiper." Since this text did not have the standard double obligation of *honor* and *attend,* but only that latter word *attend* earlier in the text, that final obligation of *worship* was considered necessary as well. In other words, therefore, whether it is emended to refer to "the synagogue of the Jews and God-worshipers" or unemended to refer to the freed slave's religious obligation, we have evidence of the term "God-worshiper" in one first-century Jewish manumission text from Bosporus. And that of course confirms the double obligation of *honoring* and *attending* the prayer house as the local designation of what elsewhere is termed a "God-worshiper."

Finally, there is one very fragmentary inscription from the first half of the second century found at Gorgippia but now lost (*CIRB* 1127). It was, most likely, one of the "Most High God" texts seen with that first formula above. It has only these sentences:

> whose name is . . . on condition that she should be unharmed and unmolested both by me and by any of my heirs, remaining attached (*prosmenousa*) to the prayer house.

The double obligation of *honor and attend* or *attend and worship* appears here as a single obligation using the classical "remain with" expression.

None of those difficulties or debates should obscure this very major point. On the borders of the classical world in the early first century, Jewish communities and buildings were fully integrated into local civil and religious life. Were they not, those manumission texts would be socially irrelevant, if not legally invalid. And, in very many cases, we cannot even tell if the slave owners were full Jews, proselytes, or themselves God-worshipers. But at least the freed slaves were to remain or become the latter, to honor and attend the synagogue without becoming full Jews.

When you think, therefore, of Paul's convert poaching in diaspora synagogues, never underestimate the combined opposition, both Jewish and pagan, he would have experienced. And do not presume pagan God-worshipers would all or always have been on his side.

The Rhetoric of Religious Polemics

We turn now to Paul's alternative vision for the future of Galatia and emphasize immediately a preliminary point concerning religious polemics (and probably any other type of rhetorical strife) in this and the other letters of Paul. The purpose of polemics is not to conduct a fair, accurate, and objective debate, but to demolish opponents by impugning their motives, ridiculing their arguments, and caricaturing their views. That is the nature of all polemics, but maybe especially of religious polemics, yesterday, today, and tomorrow. "When Paul denounces people," writes Francis Watson in *The Romans Debate,* "he does not do so with scrupulous fairness; the idea that one should be fair to one's opponents was not widespread in antiquity" (212). Or in modernity, we would add. Furthermore, Paul's opponents do not get to answer back (probably with equal polemics) in his letters. We only hear Paul's arguments and, unanswered, he always wins. Finally, we have therefore to imagine what opponents would have responded and whether the letter's recipients would have been persuaded by Paul or by his adversaries. Above all else, we have to decide in any given case what exactly was at stake for each side and whether there might have been better alternatives to either position.

Paul's letter to the Galatians is at once apologetic and polemical with a tone both bitterly reproaching and emotionally pleading, a text as cold as the Taurus heights in winter and as warm as the Anatolian plateau in summer. As far as we can understand the situation from Paul's response to it, opponents had told his Galatian converts that his gospel was all wrong, that their males must still be circumcised, that Paul was nothing but a subordinate missionary (not even an apostle), and that, moreover, he was living and teaching in disagreement with his superiors at Jerusalem and Antioch. That attack explains Paul's opening sentence, which is less a statement of identity than a manifesto. The counterattack begins, as it were, on the outside of the envelope. "Paul an apostle—sent neither by human commission nor from human authorities, but through Jesus Christ and God the Father, who raised him from the dead" (1:1). That is also why we get Paul's vocation story so soon after that opening (1:11–17). He received, says Paul, a divine call at Damascus and not a human job at Jerusalem.

After that opening challenge, Paul uses five main counterarguments—historical, experiential, exegetical, baptismal, and emotional—some weak, some strong, but possibly persuasive enough cumulatively to hold those Galatians to Paul's "gospel of Christ." But we do not know what happened at Galatia after this letter was received. This, however, may be indicative. At the end of the first century John of Patmos wrote to seven cities in the province of Asia, and Clement of Rome wrote to Corinth in Achaia. At the start of the second century Ignatius of Antioch wrote to six cities of Asia and a few decades later Polycarp of Smyrna wrote to Philippi in Macedonia. Those mention only three of the four main Pauline provinces, Asia, Macedonia, and Achaia, but not Galatia. What happened to Galatia?

History: Agreement and Disagreement

Paul's first argument is historical, and the background is given in Galatians 1–2 and Acts 15. This is also a case where you can see most clearly how drastically Luke retells Paul. Acts 15 says that all was harmonious agreement between Paul and the other apostles at both Jerusalem and Antioch. Paul has two points to make against his opponents in this first response. He says that there was important agreement at Jerusalem (Gal. 2:1–10), but equally important disagreement at Antioch (2:11–14). He argues that he is not a messenger sent by Jerusalem through Antioch, but an apostle sent by God through Christ.

Paul at Jerusalem

After their mission together to Cyprus and southern Anatolia in Acts 13–14, Barnabas and Paul went to Jerusalem because "false believers secretly brought in . . . slipped in to spy on the freedom we have in Christ Jesus, so that they might enslave us" (2:4). Some Christian Jews demanded circumcision for any pagan males converted to Christianity. But Paul reports that James and Peter agreed with Barnabas and himself in refusing that demand. They agreed to establish two missions: one led by Peter to convert Jews and the other led by Barnabas and Paul to convert pagans. "When James and Cephas and John, who were acknowledged pillars, recognized the grace that had been given to me, they gave to Barnabas and me the right hand of fellowship, agreeing that we should go to the Gentiles and they to the circumcised" (2:9). Notice, by the way, that Barnabas is still mentioned ahead of Paul at this stage. Had Jerusalem decided otherwise, male pagan converts to Christianity would have been even less common than similar ones to

Judaism. For Paul, the circumcision of male pagan converts was not nego-
tiable, as it contradicted his Damascus mandate from God. In fact, of course,
and despite whatever his Galatian opponents said, the other apostles all
agreed with him on this exemption. We will return in Chapter 7 to this very
important final point: "They asked only one thing, that we remember the
poor, which was actually what I was eager to do" (2:10). But all of that raises
two vitally important questions.

FIRST QUESTION. How on earth could a fervent Christian Jew like
James of Jerusalem, James the Just, James the brother of the Lord Jesus, have
ever allowed such a dispensation for pagan converts?

First, Jewish tradition had long announced a future day when God would
end the evil, injustice, and violence that relentlessly destroyed God's world
and oppressed God's people. There would then be, here below upon this
earth, a magnificently utopian (end-of-this-place) or eschatological (end-
of-this-time) world. There would be, they believed and hoped, a restored,
transformed, and transfigured world. God would overcome, someday. We
have already seen that fervent hope in the preceding chapter.

Second, as Paula Fredriksen emphasizes, that sacred tradition imagined
two utterly divergent divine solutions concerning the nations, the Gentiles,
the great conquering empires who caused so much havoc and destruction.
One was *extermination,* the Great Final War at Mt. Megiddo (Armageddon)
when, according to Revelation 14:20, the blood of the slain would be "as
high as a horse's bridle, for a distance of about two hundred miles." The
other was *conversion,* the Great Final Banquet on Mt. Zion, when, according
to Isaiah 25:6–8,

> The Lord of hosts will make for all peoples a feast of rich food, a feast
> of well-aged wines, of rich food filled with marrow, of well-aged
> wines strained clear. And he will destroy on this mountain the shroud
> that is cast over all peoples, the sheet that is spread over all nations; he
> will swallow up death forever. Then the Lord God will wipe away the
> tears from all faces, and the disgrace of his people he will take away
> from all the earth.

Nothing is said about male circumcision before that Great Final Banquet;
neither is anything said about that banquet's menu being kosher. Those si-
lences would, of course, allow arguments in either direction. Either those
requirements are not mentioned because they are no longer operative, or

they are not mentioned because they are always operative and assumed. *Remember that point and counterpoint throughout this chapter.*

Similarly, in the magnificent vision repeated verbatim in Micah 4:1–4 and Isaiah 2:2–4,

> In days to come the mountain of the Lord's house shall be established as the highest of the mountains, and shall be raised up above the hills. Peoples shall stream to it, and many nations shall come and say: "Come, let us go up to the mountain of the Lord, to the house of the God of Jacob; that he may teach us his ways and that we may walk in his paths." For out of Zion shall go forth instruction, and the word of the Lord from Jerusalem. He shall judge between many peoples, and shall arbitrate between strong nations far away; they shall beat their swords into plowshares, and their spears into pruning hooks; nation shall not lift up sword against nation, neither shall they learn war any more; but they shall all sit under their own vines and under their own fig trees, and no one shall make them afraid; for the mouth of the Lord of hosts has spoken.

That conversion, it must be emphasized, is not to Judaism (with circumcision for males and kosher rules for all), but to Judaism's God. There will be only one God, but that will be a God of justice, peace, and nonviolence.

Third, many of Jesus's earliest companions moved from Galilee to Jerusalem almost immediately after his execution, and that transfer derived most likely from imminent apocalyptic expectation. The great day when God would finally clean up the world's injustice had already started, any day now Jesus would return in triumph, and where else would they meet him if not in Jerusalem?

Finally, then, James and all the others decided that, following the *conversion* option, male pagan converts did not need to be circumcised in this climactic eschatological moment.

SECOND QUESTION. You could accept all of the above and not think that anyone was supposed to go out and bring in those Gentiles, that anyone was supposed to participate with God in any way beyond hope, prayer, and holiness. How did Paul know that humanity and divinity were to collaborate in this eschatological instant-become-era? That is why Paul's vocation was so important. It is not simply a conversion from Pharisaic Judaism to Christian Judaism or from persecutor to apostle. It is not even a special vocational call to something quite ordinary and traditional. It was, instead, a stunning correlative to the novelty of eschatological climax as extended time span. It established, for Paul, the divine program not just of passive expectation, but of interactive participation in that climactic process. God was not doing it all directly, but had called Paul (especially Paul) to lead the way.

It is not possible to overemphasize the novelty and profundity of those two creative steps. First, the eschatological climax was to be an age and not just an instant, a process in time and not just an end of time. Second, in this new epoch the human and the divine were to cooperate with one another.

Paul at Antioch

If all was settled at Jerusalem, what exactly was the issue at Antioch? Understand, by the way, all those new questions that would inevitably arise from this Christian Jewish mutation, from trying to live faithfully and participate actively in an eschatological climax that involved an era rather than an instant, a process occurring over human time (even if expected to be short) rather than a flash of divine light. Two missions, one led by Peter to convert Jews, and another led by Barnabas and Paul to convert pagans, sounded like a magnificent compromise at Jerusalem. But the Gentiles were not clearly separated geographically from the Jews, and, besides, all those first apostles were themselves Jews. How exactly would that work out in practice as distinct from theory and in diaspora cities as distinct from Jerusalem? What happened at Antioch was therefore inevitable. It was only a matter of time.

Here is the Antioch problem. When a Christian Jewish assembly and a Christian gentile assembly existed in the same city and wanted to eat together in celebration of the Lord's Supper, were kosher restrictions necessary for everyone or unnecessary for anyone? Should the Gentiles change and accept kosher or the Jews change and avoid kosher? The custom at Antioch was the latter option—kosher was not observed by anyone at joint meals. But James commanded them to change and follow the former option—kosher was to be observed by everyone at joint meals. All agreed to do so, except Paul, who accused Peter of hypocrisy (he uses the word twice). "I said to Cephas before them all, 'If you, though a Jew, live like a Gentile and not like a Jew, how can you compel the Gentiles to live like Jews?' " (2:14). Simon, by the way, was his ordinary name; Peter and Cephas were bilingual nicknames, the former in Greek and Latin, the latter in Hebrew and Aramaic.

Like everyone else, Peter had first gone along with the no-kosher-for-anyone option at joint meals, but he now wanted Gentiles to submit to the kosher-for-everyone alternative. We do not have Peter's reply, but undoubtedly he would have said something like this: "It is not hypocrisy, Paul. It is simple courtesy." Paul admits to the Galatians that everyone, even Barnabas, opposed him at Antioch, and although he does not say so, we think he broke with them all and went west never to return except for one final, fatal visit to Jerusalem. But the question is, was his position the most advisable one at Antioch?

The question is not about religious, theological, or moral options, but about strategic, tactical, and rhetorical alternatives. We do not intend to second-guess Paul's decision from a safe distance and a much later time. We ask that question because later, writing in 1 Corinthians 8 with regard to sacrificial meats and in Romans 14–15 with regard to precisely this same kosher-for-all or kosher-for-none debate in that city's Christian Jewish and Christian pagan community, Paul himself gives a very different solution. In those two cases, as we see in Chapters 6 and 7, Paul admits a general freedom but advises a specific restraint. Why not refrain, he says in those two later places, from eating pagan sacrificial meat or Jewish nonkosher food to avoid scandal for others and to maintain community with them?

In any case, after citing that attack on Peter, Paul continues with a sentence that repeats all of its key words thrice ("justify," "law-works," "faith," "Jesus Christ") and pounds its point home in drumbeat rhythm (2:16):

> A person is justified
>> not by the works of [the] law
>>> but through faith in Jesus Christ.
>>>> And we have come to believe in Christ Jesus,
>>> so that we might be justified by faith in Christ,
>> and not by doing the works of [the] law
> because no one will be justified by the works of [the] law.

That passage sets up an absolute disjunction between two modes of justification, that is, between two ways of becoming just, righteous, and holy in union with a just, righteous, and holy God. That bifurcation may or may not have applied to his Galatian converts, but Paul surely knew it did not apply to James, Peter, or Barnabas, or any other Christian at Antioch. It is rhetorical and polemical overkill. We will leave any further discussion of Paul on law in general and on Torah in particular until Chapter 7, where Paul returns to that theme in writing to the Romans.

But notice one point for future reference. The Greek phrase is literally "works of law" or, better, in English, "law-works." It is not a clash between *faith* and *works,* but between *faith-works* and *law-works.* In Galatians 2:16, as just seen, Paul speaks negatively about "*works* of law," but in 5:6 he says positively, "The only thing that counts is faith *working* through love." He tells the Thessalonians, "God's word . . . is also *at work* in you believers" (1 Thess. 2:13) and admonishes the Philippians to "*work* out your own salvation with fear and trembling; for it is God who is at *work* in you, enabling you both to *will* and to *work* for his good pleasure" (Phil. 2:12–13). Please read that last admonition seven times, as it is one of those places where you can see all of Pauline theology in two verses. The ultimate clash, therefore, is not between *works* and *faith* but between *law-works* and *faith-works.*

But why exactly was Paul so obdurate on this point at Antioch? Why not accept kosher-for-all as a simple courtesy extended by gentile converts to Jewish converts within common meals for the unity of Christian Judaism? Why not the same conclusion at Antioch as later at Corinth and Rome? There is certainly a value to freedom, but often an even greater value to unity. Paul must have been still in serious shock from his Jerusalem experience with those who advocated circumcision for male gentile converts. Had their view prevailed, it would have destroyed his own message, mission, and mandate from God. At Antioch, therefore, he may have overreacted by refusing to give at all, even on kosher requirements, and thereby broke irrevocably with all the other apostles.

Experience: "God Has Sent the Spirit"

Paul's second argument is experiential and it is a powerful argument, as it presumes something that was a regular feature of the Pauline assemblies. It is exactly the same argument that Peter used in Acts, and Luke tells the whole story twice—first as it happens in Caesarea and then as Peter reports it in Jerusalem. He argues that you cannot demand circumcision tradition or kosher regulation for gentile converts who had already received the Holy Spirit before and without them.

> *Event:* While Peter was still speaking, the Holy Spirit fell upon all who heard the word. The circumcised believers who had come with Peter were astounded that the gift of the Holy Spirit had been poured out even on the Gentiles, for they heard them speaking in tongues and extolling God. Then Peter said, "Can anyone withhold the water for

baptizing these people who have received the Holy Spirit just as we
have?" So he ordered them to be baptized in the name of Jesus Christ.
(Acts 10:44–48)

Report: "And as I began to speak, the Holy Spirit fell upon them just as
it had upon us at the beginning. . . . If then God gave them the same
gift that he gave us when we believed in the Lord Jesus Christ, who
was I that I could hinder God?" When they heard this, they were silenced. And they praised God, saying, "Then God has given even to
the Gentiles the repentance that leads to life." (Acts 11:15–18)

Clearly, then, the advent of the Holy Spirit was externally and visibly manifested by signs and wonders. That is how Peter and the others were empiri-
cally sure of its presence. This was also the experience of Paul and his
converts, and we will discuss it further in Chapter 5. But for now, Paul chal-
lenges his wavering Galatians with this argument:

The only thing I want to learn from you is this: Did you receive the
Spirit by doing the works of the law or by believing what you heard?
Are you so foolish? Having started with the Spirit, are you now ending
with the flesh? Did you experience so much for nothing?—if it really
was for nothing. Well then, does God supply you with the Spirit and
work miracles among you by your doing the works of the law, or by
your believing what you heard? (Gal. 3:2–5)

Paul picks up this experiential argument again later when he mentions
that they are now God's adopted children "and because you are children,
God has sent the Spirit of his Son into our hearts, crying, 'Abba! Father!'"
(4:6; notice that transition from "you" to "our"). That "Abba" is not just a
statement of faith, but a cry of ecstasy. That is a forceful, powerful, and experiential argument that opponents could only rebut by claiming those ecstatic experiences were demonic and not divine, were from hell and not
from heaven.

Exegesis: "A Sign of the Covenant"

Paul's third and central argument is exegetical. And if, in reading it and trying to follow its logic, your head begins to spin, you are getting the right effect. It does not seem that Paul's male converts had already accepted

circumcision—"*if* you let yourselves be circumcised," he says in 5:2. They probably wrote to him asking about its necessity and letting him know the arguments of his opponents, about whom Paul says nastily, "I wish those who unsettle you would castrate themselves" (5:12). Apart from disputing Paul's integrity and authority, what precise *biblical* argument did the opponents use to make his male converts even consider circumcision? They must have argued from Abraham because, if they had not, Paul's counterargument is inexplicable. They chose to attack Paul's Galatian teachings by appealing to God's covenant with Abraham from Genesis 17 in the first book of Moses's five-book Torah. Genesis gave them two powerful bases from which to argue that male gentile converts had to be circumcised to become full members of God's people.

The Argument Against Paul

First, God made a covenant with Abraham. But a covenantal bond is a two-way relationship with duties, obligations, and commitments on both sides. From God's side that covenant involves the promise of *progeny* and *land*. Read Genesis 17:1–8 and note its drumbeat emphasis on progeny ("exceedingly numerous, . . . multitude of nations, . . . exceedingly fruitful; . . . nations . . . and kings, . . . offspring, . . . offspring, . . . offspring"). But there are also obligations on Abraham's side. He must, of course, "walk blameless before God" (17:1), but there is also this special obligation:

> God said to Abraham, "As for you, you shall keep my covenant, you and your offspring after you throughout their generations. This is my covenant, which you shall keep, between me and you and your offspring after you: Every male among you shall be circumcised. You shall circumcise the flesh of your foreskins, and it shall be a *sign of the covenant* between me and you. Throughout your generations every male among you shall be circumcised when he is eight days old, including the slave born in your house and the one bought with your money from any foreigner who is not of your offspring. Both the slave born in your house and the one bought with your money must be circumcised. So shall my covenant be in your flesh an everlasting covenant. Any uncircumcised male who is not circumcised in the flesh of his foreskin shall be cut off from his people; he has broken my covenant." (Gen. 17:9–14, italics added)

Circumcision is not itself the covenant, but it is the "sign of the covenant." God commands it for Abraham, for all his male progeny, and for all his male slaves. That, said Paul's Galatian opponents to Paul's Galatian converts, is what your God demands and your Paul avoids. That was the first half of the opponents' accusatory argument.

Second, that same Genesis 17 ends by speaking both about Ishmael, the child already born to Abraham from the slave woman Hagar, and about Isaac, the child promised to Abraham from his wife Sarah. Both children must be circumcised, but God states, "As for Ishmael, I have heard you; I will bless him and make him fruitful and exceedingly numerous; he shall be the father of twelve princes, and I will make him a great nation. But my covenant I will establish with Isaac" (17:20–21). Paul's opponents must have emphasized that *all* of Abraham's male progeny were circumcised, whether slave-born through Hagar and Ishmael or freeborn through Sarah and Isaac. Therefore, they must have argued, even Abrahamic descent and circumcision are not enough. That applied alike to Jews, descended from Isaac, and to Arabs, descended from Ishmael. The Abrahamic covenant was specified and fulfilled in the Mosaic covenant at Mt. Sinai. You must, they insisted to Paul's Galatian converts, observe the full Torah to be freeborn heirs of Abraham. You must follow the Jewish calendar, for example, by "observing special days, and months, and seasons, and years," as Paul accuses them of already doing in Galatians 4:10.

Those actually are two irrefutable arguments. In themselves they are unanswerable. The only adequate response is that the Abrahamic covenant of circumcision (and all other succeeding covenants, such as the Mosaic covenant) are here and now totally renewed and radically transformed by the present eschatological covenant, as foretold in the Law, the Prophets, and the Psalms. In Chapter 7 we see Paul himself using this equally irrefutable argument in Romans 15. But here, to the Galatians, Paul is caught. He must argue back as best he can on Abrahamic ground because that is the terrain chosen by the opponents. Paul could not use the biblical texts announcing an eschaton when God would finally justify (i.e., make just) the world by establishing a divine utopia upon earth. At that time, Gentiles would stream to Jerusalem and convert not to Judaism but to God, and there would be no need for male circumcision traditions or universal purity regulations. In any case, his opponents chose the textual battleground of Abraham, from Genesis, in Torah. Paul had to meet them there or lose all credibility with their common audience.

The Counterargument by Paul

First of all, Paul's instinctive and basic response is extremely astute (whether it worked or not is another question). Modern scholarship distinguishes between the Abrahamic covenant as given in the various separate sources now combined into one consecutive account in Genesis 11–25. The opponents used Genesis 17:1–27, from what scholars now call the later Priestly tradition, which certainly emphasizes circumcision and never mentions faith. Paul went immediately to Genesis 15:6, from what scholars now call the earlier Yahwist tradition, which certainly emphasizes faith and never mentions circumcision. It is a brilliant answer, but imagine an ongoing argument. *Paul*: Abraham's faith was the basis of the covenant's acceptance. Therefore, faith without circumcision is what counts. *Opponents*: Of course faith is primary. Who ever said otherwise? But, afterward, circumcision was the external sign of the covenant's abiding inner presence. Not faith *without* circumcision but faith *with* circumcision is what counts.

Second, Paul continues with a linked barrage of seven biblical proof-texts rather than a sustained exegesis of Genesis 15. Paul cites, by the way, from the Greek Septuagint translation and not from the Hebrew text—quite often the argument only works from that source. Here is the sequence of linked proof-texts:

(1) Galatians 3:6 = Genesis 15:6
"[Abraham] believed God, and it was reckoned to him as righteousness."

(2) Galatians 3:8 = Genesis 12:3; 18:18
"All the Gentiles shall be blessed in you."

(3) Galatians 3:10 = Deuteronomy 27:26
"Cursed is everyone who does not observe and obey all the things written in the book of the law."

(4) Galatians 3:11 = Habakkuk 2:4
"The one who is righteous will live by faith."

(5) Galatians 3:12 = Leviticus 18:5
"Whoever does the works of the law will live by them."

(6) Galatians 3:13 = Deuteronomy 21:23
"Cursed is everyone who hangs on a tree."

(7) Galatians 3:16 = Genesis 13:15; 17:8
   "And to your offspring"

The core argument is clear enough. The blessings promised to Abraham are now available to the Gentiles through his offspring Christ. They "live" them through faith-works and not through law-works because, with a jump from "blessed" to "cursed," the law finds the *crucified* Christ cursed and so also are all those "in Christ Jesus." We leave further discussion of faith-works and law-works until Chapter 7. But, for now, why does Paul argue as he does, with a blitz of linked citations rather than with a sustained exegesis of a single text?

First, he must do the best he can against an almost impregnable position. Second, the multiplicity of his texts might have made his position more persuasive, showing that he knew the biblical tradition more fully and completely than did the opponents. Third, argumentation by linking together multiple individual proof-texts was probably the only method Paul could have used. He had to argue on his feet and on the road. He did not have access to biblical scrolls.

Think, for a moment, of the difference between a traveling scholar with access only to past learning in present memory as against a scribal scholar with access to a magnificent library of biblical and other texts. Paul had memorized sequences of citations on key subjects, and he could mix and match orally for any required occasion. His education in the synagogue at Tarsus had prepared this very intelligent youth to be an apologist for Judaism and a polemicist against paganism amid the well-educated Tarsians around him. That earlier on-his-feet education prepared him also for later on-the-road argumentation.

Finally, Paul has to face the second half of the opponents' argument—that the Abrahamic covenant was completed for Jews by the Mosaic covenant. His response uses the same proof-text linkage as earlier, but now in a much shorter two-text version (and again he cites the Greek Septuagint translation):

(1) Galatians 4:27 = Isaiah 54:1
   "Rejoice, you childless one, you who bear no children, burst into song and shout, you who endure no birth pangs; for the children of the desolate woman are more numerous than the children of the one who is married."

(2) Galatians 4:30 = Genesis 21:10
   "Drive out the slave and her child; for the child of the slave will not share the inheritance with the child of the free woman."

But Paul's argument on this second point is even more radical than on that first one. His opponents must have said that the full children of Abraham came from the free woman Sarah through Isaac and not from the slave woman Hagar through Ishmael and that they, not the Ishmaelite Arabs and other Gentiles, had stood before God at Mt. Sinai. They alone had both the Abrahamic and the Mosaic covenant. Paul simply turned that on its head by saying, "Hagar is Mount Sinai in Arabia and corresponds to the present Jerusalem, for she is in slavery with her children" (4:25). That is a little breathtaking in its exegetical impertinence—Mt. Sinai is in Arabia, but Arabia is the home of Hagar, Ishmael, and their descendants; therefore those who, like "the present Jerusalem," stand with Mt. Sinai belong to a tradition of slavery not of freedom. No doubt that made Galatian heads swim and maybe even Galatian minds change. Maybe.

Two footnotes. First, it is almost impossible to imagine pure ex-pagans reading or hearing this letter or that argument. Paul's Galatian assembly must have contained a very large core of God-worshipers. And, of course, that group's males would also be most vulnerable to a demand for circumcision and Torah. Second, it is not necessary to imagine Paul followed everywhere by Jewish Christian countermissionaries demanding circumcision and kosher practices from his converts. That is possible but hardly necessary. If the core of his assemblies were God-worshipers, their former Jewish friends, associates, and colleagues would have tried to bring them back to synagogue loyalty. *If* you want to move beyond God-worshipers and become *full* members of God's people, they would have said with both plausibility and sincerity, you should convert not to Christianity, but to Judaism. That would be theologically better and socially safer—we at least have a country, a tradition, and a history with the Romans. Please, be careful, they would have warned them.

Baptism: "All of You Are One"

Paul's fourth argument is a baptismal one. It is actually a subpoint to the general Abrahamic issue, but it is important enough to emphasize under its own heading. The opponents' emphasis on circumcision from Genesis 17:9–14 established a triple distinction and a triple hierarchy. Circumcision distinguished Jew from Gentile, male from female, and slave from free. Only the first mentioned in each category were to be circumcised since the command applied only to free Jewish males and their slaves. But in Galatians Paul says,

> As many of you as were baptized into *Christ* have clothed yourselves with *Christ.* There is no longer Jew or Greek, there is no longer slave or free, there is no longer male and female; for all of you are one in *Christ* Jesus. And if you belong to *Christ,* then you are Abraham's offspring, heirs according to the promise. (3:27-29, italics added)

Notice, first of all, that double mention of Christ that frames the central negation of those three hierarchies. Paul is not saying that everyone is created equal or that all are equal before the law or even before God. He is not talking about democracy or inalienable God-given rights. His point is that all are equal *in Christ,* that is, what you were before baptism is now irrelevant to your life after baptism. But his focus is on hierarchy and superiority, not on difference or distinction. In Christianity, as we say institutionally, or in Christ, as Paul says mystically, a Jewish Christian is not superior to a gentile Christian, nor a male to a female Christian, nor a free Christian to a Christian slave. And, of course, as we saw for slavery and patriarchy in Chapter 2, that equality extends to all of life for Christians, to life both inside and outside the Christian assembly.

It seems probable that part of the baptismal ceremony was some such declaration of equality in Christ, although it did not have any universally set formula. Paul himself cites it differently in 1 Corinthians 12:13 (italics added): "For *in the one Spirit* we were all baptized into one body—Jews or Greeks, slaves or free—and we were all made to drink *of one Spirit.*" And notice, once again, that such a negation of inequality applies to those "in the one Spirit," which is simply a different way of saying "in Christ."

Paul reminds the Galatians that, at and after their baptism, they had accepted such equality in Christ. Baptism was a ceremony alike for all, whereas, he argues, circumcision established a differential hierarchy between Jew and Greek, slave and free, male and female. We emphasize once again, from the principle established in Chapter 2, that such equality in Christ involved the total life of a Christian, internal and external, religious and social. *It did not concern outsiders, but it did concern the outside of insiders.* The importance of in-Christ equality will reappear later when Paul writes about hierarchy and superiority within their Christian assemblies to the Corinthians and Romans.

Emotion: "Because of a Physical Infirmity"

Paul's final argument is, like his first, an autobiographical one, but the emphasis now is on prior contacts with his Galatian converts rather than on prior relations with the Jerusalem authorities. It also has a highly emotional tone, addressed to "My little children, for whom I am again in the pain of childbirth until Christ is formed in you" (4:19). Since they had accepted him then in such difficult circumstances, how could they abandon him now?

Three Missions in Paul and Luke

You can organize Paul's adult life from his own letters around three great apostolic missions and, in general, they date to the 30s, 40s, and 50s C.E. Acts also gives Paul three great missionary journeys, but they are not the same threesome as in Paul's letters. Further, Paul ends each mission with a Jerusalem visit, but Luke gives him twice as many Jerusalem visits. Here is a summary of those comparisons, with Jerusalem visits in italics:

Mission	In Paul's Letters	In Luke's Acts of the Apostles
I	Nabatean Arabia in Gal. 1:17 *Visit 1* (Gal. 1:18–20)	*Visit 1* in Acts 9:26–30
II	Syria and Cilicia (Gal. 1:21) North Galatia (Gal. 4:13?)	Cyprus and South Galatia in Acts 13:1–14:28
		Visit 2 in Acts 9:26–29 = *Visit 3* in Acts 11:29–30
	Visit 2 (Gal. 2:1; 2 Cor. 12:2–4)	= *Visit 4* in Acts 15; 22:17–21
III	North Galatia, Macedonia, Achaia, Asia (Rom. 15:19)	(1) South and North Galatia, Macedonia, Achaia (Acts 15:36–18:17) *Visit 5* (Acts 18:18–22) (2) Asia (Acts 18:23–21:16)
	Visit 3 (Rom. 15:22–27)	*Visit 6* (Acts 21:17)

Luke, on the one hand, omits Paul's Arabian mission because it does not fit his own programmatic Jerusalem-to-Rome trajectory. Also, in keeping with that outward-from-Jerusalem emphasis, Luke increases Paul's visits there from three to six. But there seems no reason why Luke would invent that entire journey to Cyprus and southern Galatia in Acts 13–14, so, despite Paul's silence on it, we take it as basically historical. Finally, Luke split Paul's third mission in two and left two clues to his division. One is that too swift trip to Jerusalem, Antioch, and back in Acts 18:22–23: "He went up to Jerusalem and greeted the church, and then went down to Antioch. After spending some time there he departed and went from place to place through the region of Galatia and Phrygia, strengthening all the disciples." Another is that double visit to Ephesus before and after it in Acts 18:19 and 19:1.

Paul, on the other hand, omits Luke's Cypriot and South Galatian mission, because it does not fit his own programmatic independent vocation. As Luke tells that story in Acts 13–14 he uses the sequence "Barnabas and Paul" or "Paul and Barnabas" about evenly. But, despite "they said" here and there, Paul is usually the recorded speaker, for example, at Paphos on Cyprus (13:9–10) and at Antioch in Pisidia (13:16–41). Paul is also the one who healed the man crippled from birth at Lystra (14:8–11). But the most revealing moment occurs after that very healing. "When the crowds saw what Paul had done, they shouted in the Lycaonian language, 'The gods have come down to us in human form!' Barnabas they called Zeus, and Paul they called Hermes, because he was the chief speaker" (14:11–12). But, as everyone knew, although Hermes might be chief speaker, Zeus was chief god. In other words, and despite Luke's editorial changes, Barnabas, not Paul, is in charge of that mission.

It is possible to see three divergent strategies behind Paul's three great missions. The first mission, in the 30s C.E., in Arabia, would have been assisted, on the one hand, by the fact that Jews and Arabs had a common ancestor in Abraham and both cultures circumcised their males. But it would have been destroyed, on the other hand, by the war between Herod Antipas and his "divorced" father-in-law, Aretas IV, in 37 C.E. The second mission, in the 40s C.E., under Barnabas as leader, was much more a traveling mission, did not focus on capital cities, and may well have done exactly what Luke described—focused on converting both Jews and God-fearers inside the synagogues. The third mission, in the 50s, with Paul as leader, focused on Roman provincial capitals and on the God-fearers rather than on full Jews or pure pagans. We make no attempt in this book to establish a more precise Pauline chronology, because that can only be done or even attempted by accepted Lukan data, especially about Paul before Gallio at Corinth in 51–52, that is not historical.

"Because of a Physical Infirmity"

Paul's stay in Galatia's northern cities was not part of any planned program of missionary activity. In his final argument, he reminds the Galatians of that "first" visit:

> You know that it was because of a physical infirmity that I first announced the gospel to you; though my condition put you to the test, you did not scorn or despise me, but welcomed me as an angel of God, as Christ Jesus. What has become of the goodwill you felt? For I testify that, had it been possible, you would have torn out your eyes and given them to me. (4:13–15)

We take three points from that appeal. Paul's stay in Galatia was accidental rather than planned. It happened because of some illness that seems to have especially affected his sight. That was a "first" visit, so that there was at least one other later one. Where, when, how, and why did Paul first meet those addressed in the plural as "the assemblies of Galatia" in both Galatians 1:2 and 1 Corinthians 16:1. It is uncertain, by the way, whether that plural means more than one city or more than one community in the same city. Paul speaks of the "assemblies" in Judea (1 Thess. 2:14; Gal. 2:14), in Asia (1 Cor. 16:9), and in Macedonia (2 Cor. 8:1), but only in that last case does he certainly mean two different cities, Philippi and Thessalonica.

Granted that Paul's Galatians were in those northern cities, he must have been going through them to somewhere farther north. Were he simply heading westward, the far easier routes were much farther to the south along the Taurus range and the Meander Valley. In that direction, he would not have been anywhere near those Romano-Celtic cities. The best guess, and it is only that, would be that he was originally heading northward to the Roman province of Bithynia-Pontus along the southern shores of the Black Sea. Illness would then have stopped him more likely at Pessinus, Germa, or Ancyra than at Tavium to the east. Our tentative hypothesis, therefore, is that Paul did not return with (under) Barnabas from southern Galatia as presumed by Acts 14:21–28, but continued northward until he fell ill in upper Galatia. Such independent experience may also have been important later for his own forceful position at Jerusalem and especially at Antioch.

Is Paul's "physical infirmity" in Galatians 4:13 an isolated incident, or is it part of the wider "thorn in the flesh" mentioned in 2 Corinthians 12:7–10? And, further, is there a connection between recurrent illness and ecstatic mysticism in Paul's life? (A connection, we emphasize, is neither a reduction nor an equation.) In telling the Corinthians about a mystical experience in 2 Corinthians 12:1–7a, Paul emphasizes twice that only God knows whether it was "in the body or out of the body." Then, immediately, he balances the "exceptional character of the revelations" with this correlation:

> Therefore, to keep me from being too elated, a thorn was given me in the flesh, a messenger of Satan to torment me, to keep me from being too elated. Three times I appealed to the Lord about this, that it would leave me, but he said to me, "My grace is sufficient for you, for power is made perfect in weakness." So, I will boast all the more gladly of my weaknesses, so that the power of Christ may dwell in me. Therefore I am content with weaknesses, insults, hardships, persecutions, and calamities for the sake of Christ; for whenever I am weak, then I am strong. (12:7b–10)

That text mentions "in the flesh" once and "weakness(es)" or "I am weak" four times. Although it is less apparent in our translation above, those same words reappear in Galatians 4:13–14. The phrase "physical infirmity" is literally "weakness of the flesh," and "my condition" is literally "in my flesh." Hypothetically, therefore, we think that Paul had some recurrent illness that may have precipitated or accompanied mystical revelation. But what was it?

In his justly famous book *St. Paul the Traveler and Roman Citizen* of 1894–95, Sir William Ramsay proposed that Paul's recurring illness was some sort of chronic malaria. He was speaking there about the climate at Perga, where Barnabas and Paul arrived on that joint mission in Acts 13–14. But in his later book, *The Cities of St. Paul,* he suggested that people in low-lying Tarsus would have been just as susceptible to that disease.

> In respect of the danger of malaria the case of Tarsus was similar to that of Perga, and even worse. . . . Wherever this abundant moisture and fertility characterise the sea-plain in this extremely hot country, fever is prevalent and the climate is depressing, while insect pests make human life wretched for a considerable part of the year. The bad effect is exaggerated by neglect and the increase of marshes; but it is unavoidable and only partially curable. (96)

We propose, following Ramsay, that Paul had contracted malaria during his youth at Tarsus from a climate that easily produced the chills and fevers, the uncontrollable shivering and profuse sweating, the severe headache, nausea, and vomiting of chronic malarial fever. He may also have relapsed into it during the joint mission under Barnabas and preferred to go north toward the Black Sea rather than to return, as Acts 14:25 says they did, through low-lying Perga to the Mediterranean. The "thorn/stake in the flesh" may have been Tarsus's most permanent mark on Paul.

Eschatology Here and Equality Now

We saw in Chapter 2 that Paul presumed equality or mutuality and opposed slavery or patriarchy *for those in Christ*. We also saw that presumption summarized in Galatians 3:28, within the specifics of the present Abrahamic argument: "There is no longer Jew or Greek, there is no longer slave or free, there is no longer male and female; for all of you are one in Christ Jesus." That never meant or could have meant for Paul internal as distinct from external, spiritual as distinct from physical, or ecclesiastical as distinct from social realities. But, by now the objection must also be evident. Is not all of this an obvious retrojection of, at best, present democratic ideals or, at worst, present political correctness from the twenty-first back to the first century? Or, conversely, are we claiming that Paul invented all of that as one more claim for Christian superiority over Judaism?

In reply we cite the Jewish *Sibylline Oracles* 2:313–38, a contemporary first-century Jewish text that is peculiarly appropriate for three reasons. In time, it comes from the Augustan age in the generation before Paul. In place, it comes from Phrygia, along whose eastern borders Paul moved northward through Galatia. In genre, it is apocalyptic eschatology and describes the utopian perfection of an earth transformed by divine action. First, "all must pass through the blazing river and the unquenchable fire." Next, "as many as were concerned with justice and noble deeds, and piety and most righteous thoughts" are lifted by angels from out that "blazing river" and placed upon an earth renewed into radical egalitarianism,

> The earth will belong equally to all, undivided by walls or fences. It will then bear more abundant fruits spontaneously. Lives will be in common and wealth will have no division. For there will be no poor man there, no rich, and no tyrant, no slave. Further, no one will be either great or small anymore. No kings, no leaders. All will be on a par together.

Bring together, then, that example of Jewish apocalyptic theology with what we saw about Pauline Christian equality in Chapters 2 and 3. That just-cited apocalyptic rhapsody helps us understand how Paul ever conceived such a program of radical egalitarianism *in Christ*. It was simply his understanding of life in the community of apocalyptic consummation, his interpretation of community in the eschatological instant-become-era, his application of utopian equality to utopia already begun. Apocalypse begun meant equality now—at least *in Christ*. We are not retrojecting global democratic hopes or universal human rights onto an apostle who would never have understood them. When Paul looked at pagan society, he did not say that there should be no slave-owning masters or female-dominating males. He said, more simply, there should be no pagans, only Christians, and that Christians are all equal before God. Still, it may be necessary to repeat and expand a little that dialogue we imagined between ourselves and Paul in Chapter 2.

Do you think, Paul, that all men are created equal and endowed by their Creator with certain inalienable rights? *I am not speaking about all men, but about all Christians.* But do you think, Paul, that all people should be Christians? *Yes, of course.* And do you think, Paul, that all Christians should be equal with one another. *Yes, of course.* Then do you think, Paul, that it is God's will for all people to be equal with one another? *Well, let me think about that one for a while and, in the meantime, you think about equality in Christ.*

5

Goddesses, Gods, and Gospels

In Ephesus, the Roman Empire ruled by means of a primarily Greek elite. This was the general strategy of Rome in the East: to bolster the local elite and form them into a force useful to Rome. . . . In Philippi, the Romans ruled without the medium of any Greeks, and Latin ruled unchallenged until well into the third century. . . . Romans owned almost all the land. Romans had all the political control in the city. Romans largely monopolised wealth and high status. . . . The experience of empire was far more acute for the Greeks of Philippi . . . [who] were almost all economically dependent on Romans. . . . The social context for poor Greeks, or Greeks who subsisted but struggled, was not simply a context in which power went with wealth, as it would in Ephesus, but of power going with wealth which was held by Romans. . . . My estimate for the proportions of Romans and Greeks in the town [of Philippi] is of 40 per cent Romans to 60 per cent Greeks—or, two Romans to every three Greeks. Even after slanting the figures to estimate the composition of the church, we still have 36 per cent Romans to 54 per cent Greeks—or, one Roman to every two Greeks. No other city in which Paul founded a church is likely to have had this many Romans. In none of the other cities was the experience of everyday life so firmly under the control of local, visible Romans.

—Peter Oakes, *Philippians: From People to Letter* (2001)

Political power and legitimacy rest not only in taxes and armies, but also in the perceptions and beliefs of men. The stories told about emperors were part of the mystification which elevated emperors and the political sphere above everyday life. Stories circulated. They were the currency of the political system, just as coins were the currency of the fiscal system. Their truth or untruth is only a secondary problem. . . . The parallelism between the cults of emperor and Christ is striking: the following terms were used frequently of both: god (*theos*), Son of god, god made manifest, lord (*Kurios*), lord of the whole world, lord's day (*Sebaste*—pagan, *Kuriake*—Christian), saviour of the

world, epiphany, imperator, sacred writings. . . . In Latin there was a distinction between *deus* and *divus*.. . . Strictly, *deus* was used for the immortal gods
and *divus* for gods who had been men. . . . In Greek, both were called *theos*
and the Greek equivalent of *divi filius* was *theou huios,* son of god. . . . The
unity of a political system rests not only in shared institutions, taxes and military defences, but in shared symbols, in the minds of men. Emperor cults, and
all that they involved . . . provided the context in which inhabitants of towns
spread for hundreds of miles throughout the empire could celebrate their
membership of a single political order and their own place within it.

—Keith Hopkins, *Conquerors and Slaves* (1978)

∽ひ   ∽ひ   ∽ひ

The Gospel of Caesar Augustus as Lord

Overture

With their green floodplains clearly visible in satellite images from outer
space, the westward-flowing rivers that drain the Anatolian plateau of central Turkey have silted old harbors, created new deltas, and successfully
pushed back the Aegean Sea for the past two millennia—helped significantly, of course, by earthquakes. (Will those eastern Greek islands be western Turkish peninsulas one day?) The ancient river Cayster is today's Little,
or Küçük, Menderes and reaches the coast near the ruins of Ephesus. About
15 miles to the south, the ancient river Meander is today's Great, or Büyük,
Menderes and reaches the coast near the ruins of Priene. The Büyük
Menderes, largest of those westward river systems, still meanders muddily
through cotton fields and fruit orchards until eventually coastal mountains
turn it sharply to the southwest and the sea. There is constant traffic and
constant building along what is, in September of 2002, a two-lane road and
what is, one year later, a four-lane highway along the Meander Valley. But
with fertile land too precious to waste, it becomes a six-lane expressway
northward only at Aydin, beneath the site of ancient Tralles. For past and
present, for then and now, the Meander Valley's floor determines route,
whether for river, rail, or road.

In antiquity the Meander split into two arms near that coastal range, the
westward one passing below Priene's craggy heights, enriching its fertile

fields, and flowing finally into the northwestern corner of Latmikos Bay. You drive today along the coastal road from ancient Miletus, modern Balat, to ancient Priene, modern Güllübahçe, and notice an unexpected but also unimpressive mound beside the road. It is hardly worth a second glance except as a reminder that you are moving across land that once was sea, over a plain that once was entrance to that bay, and that Miletus was then a harbor city on the bay's southwestern promontory. Today, the area's frequent earthquakes and the river's alluvial deposits have so filled in the shoreline that both Miletus and Priene are now far from the sea, what is left of Latmikos Bay is now the still somewhat salty but inland Bafa Lake, and Lade Island is now that white inland hillock you just saw near the road. In Acts 20:15 Luke has Paul sailing into Miletus. He would have serious trouble sailing there today. But even with all those changes of terrain, the mountains still stand to northwest and southeast overlooking that great valley, and the Aegean is still there, even if much farther to the west.

Priene was built on the lower reaches of one of those coastal mountains, then Mt. Mycale, now Samsun Daglari. The on-site plan shows you an ancient city designed as a terraced triumph of grid over terrain, and you can still see its major east-west streets intersected at strict right angles with minor but stepped north-south alleys. But today the classical sites of Turkey can be graded by how many tour buses are there at any one time. Ephesus has a minimum of twenty-five buses at a time. Aphrodisias has a maximum of five. And Priene has no buses most of the time. You come there on a sunny late September day in 2002 by taxi from Kusadasi and have the ruins almost all to yourself.

The towering Masada-like acropolis north of Priene makes the Acrocorinth or even the Acrophilippi look insignificant in comparison. It is warm that afternoon, but even at the site's entrance you are high enough for a good breeze, and it strengthens as you climb higher among the ruins to the Temple of Athena (Figure 77). You ponder insincerely and dismiss eventually any idea of climbing that towering acropolis. The view out over the lower Meander Valley is already spectacular enough, the site already difficult enough, and your purpose already specific enough.

Your focus is on the site where a by then fragmentary inscription from 9 B.C.E. was discovered by German archaeologists at the end of the nineteenth century. Its two parts are now stored in Berlin's Pergamon Museum, and Gustav Adolf Deissmann's book shows their earliest pictures. Its original site is to the immediate north of the agora, or public square. A covered

FIGURE 77. The Athena Temple at Priene, with reconstruction currently under way.

portico, or sacred stoa, long as a football field, once offered some shade from the relentless southern arch of the Mediterranean sun. At its eastern end was the *prytaneion,* the sacred hearth or eternal flame of the city's destiny, and to its immediate west was the *bouleuterion,* the meeting chamber and dining room of the city's council. We are, in other words, in the religio-political heart of the city. And, by the way, retain in mind that entire architectural complex for later comparison with the upper agora, or sacred forum, at Ephesus.

Continuing westward at Priene, the rest of the stoa opened into fifteen small but clearly distinguishable rooms whose walls are still halfway intact. You know that the inscription was originally in the ninth room from the west, the seventh from the east, and that the room had a wider entrance than those around it as well as a seat around the inside walls. It is easy enough to find that room once sacred to Augustus—it now has a rather large tree growing against the middle of its right side wall. The absent inscription is the fullest example of two documents known also from several other provincial cities of the Roman province of Asia. They contain the earliest and most striking instances of the term "gospel" or "good tidings" (*euaggelia*) used for Augustus in Roman imperial theology. And they contain in detail why exactly their content is good news for all creation. The texts given below are composite scholarly reconstructions integrating the Priene version with fragments discovered in four other Asian cities, for example, Apamea, where it was dug out of a garden in the mid-1920s.

The first part records how Paulus Fabius Maximus, Roman governor of Asia, proposed to the Asian League of cities that they change their calendar so that Augustus's birthday would be henceforth New Year's Day (Figure 78). Here are some key lines from his letter:

> [It is a question whether] the birthday of the most divine Caesar is more pleasant or more advantageous, the day which we might justly set on a par with the beginning of everything, in practical terms at least, in that he restored order when everything was disintegrating and falling into chaos and gave a new look to the whole world, a world which would have met destruction with the utmost pleasure if Caesar had not been born as a common blessing to all. For that reason one might justly take this to be the beginning of life and living, the end of regret at one's birth. . . . It is my view that all the communities should have one and the same New Year's Day, the birthday of the most divine Caesar, and that on that day, 23rd September, all should enter their term of office.

The second part records the enthusiastic response and official decree establishing that calendrical change for everyone, but especially for the start of all civic magistracies (Figure 79). You can easily imagine the competitive public celebrations that all those simultaneous inceptions necessitated. Here again are some key lines:

> Since the providence that has divinely ordered our existence has applied her energy and zeal and has brought to life the most perfect good in Augustus, whom she filled with virtues for the benefit of mankind, bestowing him upon us and our descendants as a saviour—he who put an end to war and will order peace, Caesar, who by his epiphany exceeded the hopes of those who prophesied good tidings (*euaggelia*), not only outdoing benefactors of the past, but also allowing no hope of greater benefactions in the future; and since the birthday of the god first brought to the world the good tidings (*euaggelia*) residing in

FIGURE 78. Upper portion of the Priene inscription announcing that Augustus's birthday would henceforth begin the new year.

him. . . . For that reason, with good fortune and safety, the Greeks of Asia have decided that the New Year in all the cities should begin on 23rd September, the birthday of Augustus . . . and that the letter of the proconsul and the decree of Asia should be inscribed on a pillar of white marble, which is to be placed in the sacred precinct of Rome and Augustus. (*SEG* 4.490; translation from Braund, 122)

Apparently as early as 29 B.C.E., that is, immediately after Augustus's victory at the battle of Actium, a golden crown had been decreed in the Roman province of Asia for whoever best honored Augustus, "our god," and, twenty

FIGURE 79. Lower portion of the Priene inscription, describing the *euaggelia* ("good news") of Augustus.

years later, that diadem was given to the governor Paulus Fabius Maximus, who had "discovered a way to honor Augustus that was hitherto unknown among the Greeks, namely, to reckon time from the date of his nativity."

In the Roman province of Asia, to take just those two Priene inscriptions, the divine Augustus was not just lord of empire and earth, but also of calendar and time. Lord of history, therefore, since there never was before nor ever would be again good news or gospel (plural *euaggelia*) surpassing that which announced his birth. In every city of rich Roman Asia there was decreed, for all time past, present, and future, but one overwhelming gospel, the good news of Augustus's advent, epiphany, and presence, the good news of a global Lord, divine Son, and cosmic Savior.

A footnote. Just to the northwest of that sacred room are the ruins of what was once the oldest, largest, most magnificent, and most important of the city's several temples. It stood on an east–west axis atop high terraced support walls along a rocky spur and was visible from anywhere on the plains below. The architrave beam above its entrance now sits broken on the ground, but still proclaims in Greek capitals that "The people [dedicated it] to Athena Polias and to the World-Conqueror Caesar, the Son of God, the God Augustus" (Figure 77).

Overview

This chapter is about the contrast between divine control and divine uncontrol, between the normalcy of *imperial,* or self-glorifying, divinity and the challenge of *kenotic,* or self-emptying, divinity. Caesar and Jesus were both destined for divine Sonship, but although Caesar accepted it as domination, Jesus accepted it as crucifixion. How then, the imprisoned Paul in Ephesus asks the enthroned Caesar in Rome, is your God my God and your people my people? There is, in the continuity from Augustus to Claudius and from Jesus to Paul, a fundamental clash of gospel, a basic divergence in what is good news for all the world.

We begin with Rome's careful control of religion both in a provincial capital and in the imperial capital itself. At Ephesus, for example, the Temple of Artemis-Diana was eventually integrated into the Roman religious establishment. In Rome, however, charismatic religion, especially with an Eastern accent, was authoritatively monitored and controlled at least by aristocratic contempt. Furthermore, imperial control was primarily by males, and the violence of martial conquest intertwined obscenely with that of sexual conquest. Male Nero grips female Britain in an image of conquest as rape.

We turn next to Paul, imprisoned and facing possible execution at Ephesus and writing to the Philippians a letter extraordinary in both tone and theology. We first explain the most probable causes and conditions of his imprisonment, chained to a guard, allowed visits from friends, but under daily threat of execution. We also emphasize the mystical union between Paul and Jesus in their common sufferings under Roman power.

Finally, and above all else, we look at the absolute normalcy of imperial divinity, that is, at how divinity is almost always understood by most people—in charge, in control, above, dominant, and on top. But, as Paul learned under capital charges in prison and hymned in Philippians 2:6–11, Christ received exaltation by crucifixion. How, then, did that change forever the nature of his exaltation? Even more important, what did that say about the very character of God if Jesus was, as Paul said in 2 Corinthians 4:4, the very "image of God"?

Ephesian Goddess and Roman God

At Ephesus, the goddess Artemis was both claim to fame and reason for wealth. Twice in a story from Acts, Luke records the defiant, ritual chant, "Great is Artemis of the Ephesians" (19:28, 34). The oracle of Apollo made Delos rich and famous and, when his twin sister, Artemis, moved to Asia Minor, she made the city of Ephesus wealthy and renowned. As one Ephesian inscription says,

> The deity over our city, Artemis, is honoured not only in her own city which she has made more famous than all other cities through her own divinity, but also by Greeks and foreigners; everywhere shrines and sanctuaries of her have been dedicated, temples founded and altars erected to her because of her vivid manifestations. (*I. Ephesos* 1a.24; Price 130–31)

The first modern explorers and archaeologists came to Ephesus not in search of Paul, but of Artemis. They came to find her Artemision, the great temple of the Ephesian goddess that was counted as one of the seven wonders of the ancient world. It was first located in 1869 by J. T. Wood, a British railway engineer who came to the region in 1863 to build the railroad from Izmir along the Meander Valley to Denizli. He began excavations on behalf of the British Museum, which were continued by D. G. Hogarth in 1904–5. Although many of the underground ruins were below the water table, Wood and Hogarth traced the outlines of a massive complex larger even than a football field. Excavations by the Austrian Archaeological Institute since 1965 have sketched a rather clear picture of the temple's various phases and expansions: first the early-eighth-century temple (Figure 80), next the enormous sanctuary with its surrounding double row of columns built in the sixth century B.C.E. by the tyrant Croesus, and finally the later Hellenistic and Roman renovations and alterations. The archaeologists had also to study the hodgepodge incorporation of the Artemision's building blocks into other structures, first in the nearby St. John Basilica and then in the Isa Bey Mosque. In spite of its past glory, visitors gain little sense of its onetime grandeur as they stand in its present lush-green and marshy surroundings. Massive column drums litter the site, and a single standing column, erected in 1973 from various others and still about thirteen feet shorter than any of the originals, only emphasizes the desolation of the often flooded site.

FIGURE 80.
Excavations by the
Austrian Archaeological
Institute of the eighth-
century Artemision
at Ephesus.

Artemis Inviolate?

Artemis was mythologically known as the virgin huntress. She was revered for protecting women through the transitions from virginity to motherhood and through their child-rearing years, but she also protected young boys and animals. In most of the Greek world, the youthful goddess's iconography included quiver and bow, a loosely fitting tunic and fawn skin, and hunting dogs or a deer at her feet. But at Ephesus she adopted some Eastern attributes, and her cult statues strike a more rigid and matronly pose, with headdress, necklaces, a tight skirt with tile-shaped animal decorations, and, most characteristically, a unique series of breastlike protuberances from bust to waist (Figures 81 and 82). She was not a mother, but was maternal, and probably for that reason her temple was renowned as a place for safely seeking asylum and securely depositing money. Recall, by the way, the discussion in Chapter 2 about slaves fleeing for protection to a deity's shrine or an owner's friend. The inviolability of the virgin Artemis's sanctuary was legendary; stories abound of large financial deposits and numerous runaway slaves, unhappily betrothed daughters, insolvent debtors, or just plain thieves seeking asylum in her sanctuary. The inviolate precinct of Artemis was marked with inscriptions, like the one that announced, "The boundary (*temenos*) of Artemis's asylum. . . . Whoever crosses, he is himself accused" (*I. Ephesos* 5.1520).

Slaves could be manumitted there by their masters, and mistreated slaves who fled there could gain asylum and be handed over to serve the goddess. Some inscriptions show that the priests of the Artemision could even grant Ephesian citizenship as part of a sacred act in which the new citizens made sacrifices to Artemis and then shared the sacrificial meat at a banquet (*SEG 1989* 1165, 1167).

But what happened to Ephesus when Roman power encroached? And especially what happened to the virgin huntress's temple when a new male god called Augustus became dominant at Ephesus? Would it be enough, as at Priene above, to inscribe the main frontal beam of the temple to both Artemis and Augustus? Who would be in control at Ephesus, and would Artemis still remain inviolate?

As Rome took over Asia Minor toward the end of the second century B.C.E., its seizure of the wealth there was so much resented that, at the start of the first Roman war with Mithridates VI of Pontus in 88 B.C.E., the Ephesians hunted down the local Italian population and slaughtered even those who sought asylum by clinging to the altar of Artemis. Rome punished Ephesus

FIGURE 81 *(above).* Excavation of the Ephesian cult statue of Artemis by Austrian archaeologists. FIGURE 82 *(right).* Ephesian Artemis, in matronly pose with breastlike protuberances.

by exacting heavy taxation, gathered by the dreaded *publicani,* who bought five-year rights at auction, by confiscating numerous estates and mines, and by establishing grazing dues, harvest tithes, poll taxes, and custom tolls. Julius Caesar had to stop Pompey twice from shrinking the temple's boundary and impounding its land.

Similarly, Augustus restored to the city and temple objects and funds that Antony confiscated when the city was his headquarters. But, after Actium, Augustus's leniency gave Ephesus both tax breaks and privileges, making it *the* metropolis of Asia. But he was also judicious in his favors. Antony had extended the temple's asylum boundaries but, according to Strabo's *Geography,* "this extension of the refuge proved harmful, and put the city in the power of criminals; and it was therefore nullified by Augustus Caesar" (14.1.23). Among the *Epistles* of the Pythagorean saint and Pauline contemporary Apollonius of Tyana in Cappadocia is one "To the Ephesians in the Artemision" condemning "the people who by night and day share the home of the goddess; otherwise I should not see issuing thence thieves and robbers and kidnappers and every sort of wretch or sacrilegious rascal; for your temple is just a den of robbers" (65). What is emphatically clear is that Roman power now expanded or restricted those asylum boundaries and Roman control now monitored the fugitives who fled there.

Roman Blessings Once Again

Augustan and later Julio-Claudian rule brought to Ephesus those Roman blessings seen in Chapter 4, blessings whose archaeological remains still overwhelm visitors who stroll around the site today. As in Galatia, at Ephesus urban amenities were extensively developed after Augustus's ascendancy. He himself sponsored the construction of a water system that, according to one inscription, was for "the people of Ephesus." At one point the remains of a massive two-storied aqueduct, made mostly of expensive marble blocks, still span the Dervenddere River. The project, sponsored by the Roman expatriate C. Sextilius Pollio, along with his wife and son, was built in honor of Augustus (Figure 83) to feed the cities' many baths. The later phases of three lavish and luxurious baths have also been excavated, along with marble fountains and a sewage system around and under the city. Torrential storms in early September of 2002, by the way, were handled better by those ancient sewers around the ruins of Ephesus than by the modern sewers around the luxury hotels in modern Kusadasi.

FIGURE 83. Aqueduct at Ephesus, paid for by C. Sextilius Pollio and his family, built in honor of Augustus.

But in addition to those amenities, Ephesus's entire urban landscape was transformed under Augustus as its civic space underwent a radical renovation and expansion. The original city was situated between the harbor and the slopes of Mt. Pion, today's Panayir Dag. To its south across a narrow valley was the much larger Mt. Coressos, today's Bülbül Dag. In the first century a new civic center was constructed south of the older agora along that valley on the lower slopes of Mt. Pion. The complex's main components and even their topical relationships parallel those seen earlier at Priene: an agora or forum on an east-west axis, a long stoa (covered portico) to its north, the *bouleuterion* (council chamber) and the *prytaneion* (city hearth) beside one another on the stoa's northern side, and close to them a shrine or temple.

Those large-scale projects were built around what has been variously called the state agora (to distinguish it from the older commercial agora) and the upper square, but maybe sacred forum might not be inappropriate. Toward the west end of this forum was a temple surrounded by columns in Greek style, although its location on an east-west axis in a large empty space was more Roman and akin to what we saw for the Augustan Forum's Temple of Mars in Chapter 2. Since this Ephesian temple was almost completely dismantled in late antiquity, its identity has been vigorously disputed. Some scholars suggest it was first built by Antony and Cleopatra and dedicated in thinly veiled self-allusion to the Greek wine god Dionysos and Egyptian mother goddess Isis. Others think it was a temple to Augustus himself. In any case, it was clearly a monument to Roman power, in a commanding position, and within a large open space. So also was the great sanctuary to the later emperor Domitian built just west of that forum temple several generations later, and of its identification there is not any doubt.

All along the nearly 500 feet of the northern side of the state agora, a set of four steps led up to an open triple-aisled and double-storied imperial portico, or royal stoa. The same C. Sextilius Pollio who built the aqueduct sponsored this royal stoa, which he dedicated jointly to Artemis, Augustus, Tiberius, and the people of Ephesus (*I. Ephesos* 2.404). As a Roman, he strove to unite local and imperial deities, to create a space where both expatriate Romans and indigenous Ephesians could integrate at ease, to consolidate east and west—at least symbolically—in this single structure. Many of the columns' capitals were sculpted in the form of bull heads (Figure 84), recalling the typical animal sacrifices to major deities. The statues in the royal stoa

FIGURE 84. Bull-head capital atop the columns in Ephesus's State Agora; bulls were sacrificed to major deities, and the State Agora was dedicated to Artemis, Augustus, and Tiberius.

are long since looted or destroyed, but two huge seated statues of the imperial couple, Augustus and Livia, crowned its eastern end. They emphasized the piety and fidelity of their matrimony and lent a religious ambience to Ephesus's civic life.

Other artifacts discovered by the Austrian excavators imply a marriage between Augustus and Artemis, Rome and Ephesus. Extending north off the imperial portico was a series of complementary buildings built under Augustus and, later, Tiberius. At the eastern end was a semicircular theater, or *odeion,* used as a *bouleuterion,* or council chamber, for the city. Immediately to its west and on an east-west axis opening eastward was a Rhodian-style temple dedicated to two deities, but once again identification is very unsure. Possibly it was dedicated to the goddess Roma and the deified Julius Caesar, since Cassius Dio's *Roman History* records that Augustus "granted permission that precincts sacred to Rome and to his father Caesar, whom he named the hero Julius, should be dedicated in Ephesus . . . the most important cit[y] in the province of Asia" (51.20.6). More likely, it was dedicated jointly to Artemis and Augustus, since her statue has been found there, as was his portrait head along with part of an inscription that reads "foundation of Augustus and the dedication of the sanctuary" (*I. Ephesos* 3.902).

To this temple's immediate west was the *prytaneion,* the city's sacred hearth or eternal flame. Foreign dignitaries were met and hosted with banquets in that special precinct, and, according to one inscription, a Roman freedman named C. Julius Nikephoros paid for sacrifices there to both Roma and Artemis in 27 B.C.E.. It was a generous gift that earned him a lifelong civic office (*I. Ephesos* 859a). Once again, that temple, located between council chamber and sacred hearth, is clearly imperial but also nuptial, possibly of Rome and Caesar, but certainly of Rome and Ephesus.

The Control of Religion in Rome

As Rome's control expanded eastward over newly conquered areas like Asia in the second century B.C.E. and newly created provinces like Galatia in the first century C.E., people streamed from Rome to the periphery, but also from the periphery to Rome. That flux of people mingled religions, rituals, and beliefs within a single empire. As we saw at Delos in Chapter 1, Apollo moved from the Cyclades to take up residence in Rome, devotees of the goddess Isis moved from Egypt through Delos to Rome, and Jewish communities flourished across the empire, including in its capital. Paul, for example, would eventually proclaim his vision of messianic Judaism to Rome itself. Although quite tolerant in theory, Rome's own imperial religion coped uneasily with this new diversity.

In Rome even more so than in Greece, religion was inextricably interwoven with politics. The various civic priesthoods rotated among the senatorial class, and it was they who performed all public rites and ceremonies. Appointment to the priesthood was dependent on land ownership, that is, on wealth, and was not reliant on charisma or any special knowledge, since sacrifices needed only the proper ritual and decorum in order to preserve the vital *pax deorum,* the peace with the gods. But Roman priesthoods were dependent on gender, that is to say, maleness, with one exception. The Vestal Virgins were priestesses who kept alight the eternal flame of the city's hearth in the Roman Forum and guarded, among other objects, the *fascinum,* the erect phallus that protected the city of Rome. They were selected from girls beyond reproach, born of senatorial families, then manumitted from their fathers, and upon entry to the priesthood they dressed in lengthy *stolae* and matronly headdresses. They were committed to serve a thirty-year term during which they refrained from all sexual activity, and infractions were punished with entombment and slow death by starvation. Those restrictions notwithstanding, they were publicly visible women who performed various ceremonies, and even had the right to make a will, a power no other women shared.

Roman religion was of the state, for the state, and therefore controlled by the state. Cicero's *On the Laws* recites the standard Roman attitude that "no one shall have gods to himself, either new gods or alien gods, unless recognized by the State" (2.19). That is why there were chronic tensions and periodic repressions after foreign religious elements entered Rome. Two examples suffice, the suppression of certain devotions to the Greek Dionysos, the Roman Bacchus, and to the Anatolian mother goddess Cybele, the Magna Mater. Both examples involved women deemed outside proper male senatorial control who contrasted forcibly with those Vestal Virgins fully under male senatorial control.

Ecstasy and Women

The suppression of the Bacchanalia is dated to the early second century B.C.E., but is narrated by Livy's *History of Rome* in the Augustan era, and that latter era's perception is more important to us than the former era's actuality. We are watching, in other words, Roman attitudes around the time of Paul rather than Roman realities from two centuries earlier. As Livy tells the story, a cult of the Greek god Dionysos, the Roman Bacchus, was started by a "nameless Greek" who was "a dabbler in sacrifices and a fortune-teller; nor was he one who, by frankly disclosing his creed and publicly proclaiming both his profession and his system, filled minds with error, but a priest of secret rites performed by night" (39.8). Both senatorial consuls had to investigate these "clandestine meetings" in which, according to Livy, worship was conducted in frenzied orgies that defied traditional social boundaries by mingling rich and poor, city and country, slave and free, and, perhaps most problematic, men and women. He describes their nocturnal activities in some detail:

> To the religious element in them were added the delights of wine and feasts, that the minds of a larger number might be attracted. When wine had inflamed their minds, and night and the mingling of males with females, youth with age, had destroyed every sentiment of modesty, all varieties of corruption first began to be practiced, since each one had at hand the pleasure answering to that to which his nature was more inclined. There was not one form of vice alone, the promiscuous matings of free men and women, but perjured witnesses, forged seals and wills and evidence, all issued from this same workshop: likewise poisonings and secret murders, so that at times not even the bodies were found for burial. Much was ventured by craft, more by violence. This violence was concealed because amid the howlings and the crash of drums and cymbals no cry of the sufferers could be heard as the debauchery and murders proceeded. (39.8)

Although the meetings were initially restricted to women, according to Livy a priestess later initiated men as well, and the meetings quickly degenerated into sexual orgies punctuated with ecstatic prophesies, wild convulsions, and married women running through the city in Bacchic dress with disheveled hair and flaming torches. Those who were less eager to "join in the crimes" were carried away on a machine and sacrificed, and the devotees were so many that they "almost constitut[ed] a second state; among them were certain men and women of high rank" (39.13). The final decree went beyond the case of the Bacchanalia and ordered "that no celebration of the rites should be held in secret" (39.14).

No doubt Livy's account is more story and slander than history and reality, as those charges of mingling classes and sexes, of ritual murders, and of nocturnal debauchery are similar to the later and equally unbelievable charges against the Christians. But Livy's worry about out-of-control religion was real, was widely shared among Rome's ruling elite, and was not fabricated.

There is even some archaeological confirmation that the Bacchanalia was suppressed in the early second century B.C.E. A bronze tablet was found in southern Italy displaying a senatorial decree that strictly controlled even if it did not completely forbid Bacchanalian activities. Adherents had to register any cult with the local authorities under sanction of capital punishment. It further restricted their numbers and the extent to which sexes mixed: "No man . . . shall seek to be present among the female Bacchants unless presented to the urban praetor and he gives permission with a senatorial decree." In addition, "No one shall seek to perform rites in secret," and finally, "No more than five men and women are gathered together, nor shall more than two men or more than three women seek to be present there, except by permission of the urban praetor and the senate" (*ILS* 18.2, 10, 19; translation from Beard, North, and Price, Vol. 2, 290–91).

Another piece of archaeological evidence makes clear that the repression was real. In the Etruscan city of Volsinii, a third-century-B.C.E. grotto has been discovered that was once used for the worship of Dionysos. It was then in a publicly visible area, not concealed as in Livy, but that sanctuary was nevertheless shut down and a terra-cotta throne with Dionysiac features was smashed to pieces in the early second century B.C.E., around the time of that senatorial decree and Livy's story. Rome restricted religious practices as it saw fit, and in particular sought to control women, the mixing of men and women, and the mingling of men and women from different classes. It was never about theological orthodoxy, but always about social control.

Castration and Men

As Hannibal advanced toward Rome during the Second Punic War of 218–202 B.C.E., the *Sibylline Oracles* were said to recommend what the Delphic oracle confirmed, namely that a sanctuary and games for the mother goddess, the Magna Mater, should be established in Rome. Rome was never averse to including foreign deities into its pantheon as a way of adding to its power and incorporating others into its empire, a process that, to stress again, also redefined what it meant to be Roman. An embassy went to Asia Minor's Pergamum, secured the Magna Mater's black meteorite stone from the Phrygian sanctuary at Pessinus, and brought it and its cult to Rome, but that initial attraction soon turned to rejection.

Along with the worship of the mother goddess came that of the youthful and handsome Attis, who, according to the Roman understanding of the myth, had castrated himself in a frenzy brought on by a jealous Magna Mater. He died, but she resurrected him, and he became the model for the *galli,* priests who castrated themselves with a broken potsherd or stone, dressed in bright colors, and wore effeminate hairstyles and bonnets (Figure 85). They were the antithesis of the various Roman priestly colleges, whose *pietas* was always heavily laden with decorous solemnity, or *gravitas.* The *galli* intentionally spilled and splashed blood on themselves during sacrifice, but the Romans meticulously avoided sullying their dress. *Galli* priests danced erratically with tambourines and sang ecstatic songs. Roman priests moved slowly and deliberately with self-control and moderation. The *galli* were shamanlike ecstatics outside civic life—their appointment depended not on a record of civic duty or suitable family lineage, but on personal devotion and what we might call charisma. Roman priests were embedded in political and civic life, were fathers of important families, and were men.

But most despicably in Roman eyes, *galli* priests were neither men nor women. Their self-mutilation was particularly disdainful to Roman authors. In dismissal they slandered them with the charge of performing oral sex with women in spite of being eunuchs. The savage vulgarity of Martial's *Epigrams* emphasizes Roman inability to understand such non-Roman religion:

FIGURE 85. Portrait of a *gallus* on a tomb, with effeminate features and musical instruments (cymbals, tympanum, and double Phrygian flute).

What, *Gallus,* have you to do with a woman's pit?

This tongue of yours ought naturally to lick men's middles.

Why was your prick cut off with a Samian sherd, if a cunt *(cunnus)* was so pleasant to you?

It's your head should be gelded, for though you are a *Gallus* in the groin, still you mock Cybele's rites, in mouth you are a man. (3.81)

Notice, however, both what is taken for granted as normal and what is mocked as abnormal in that text's crude linguistic savagery. The *galli* confused Roman males because, once self-mutilated, they no longer met the basic criterion for male sexual behavior, which was defined as penetration and control. Yet according to Martial's slander they nevertheless stooped so low as to penetrate women with their tongues, commonly considered degrading and anti-masculine by Roman males. The *galli* crossed and therefore confused what Roman male elites considered to be proper sexual roles. Furthermore, they crossed legal categories, as a first-century story in Valerius Maximus's *Memorable Deeds and Sayings* makes clear. A priest of the Magna Mater named Genucius once received an inheritance, but it was disallowed because he was neither a man nor a woman. Like the *galli*'s sexual behavior, Genucius's legal status didn't fit the Roman legal system for inheritance (7.7.6).

Unlike the Bacchanalia, however, the cult of the Magna Mater had been officially invited to Rome, and it benefited from originating near Rome's mythical mother city of Troy. So Rome never banned Cybele outright or returned the stone to Pessinus, but instead attempted to integrate her into civic life. Her sanctuary was even built on the Palatine Hill, where Augustus would eventually be her neighbor (to watch over her?). In his *Antiquities of Rome,* the late-first-century-B.C.E. historian Dionysius of Halicarnassus emphasizes that the mother goddess was carefully controlled and restricted there, as Rome "banished all the fabulous clap-trap" and had "praetors perform sacrifices and celebrate games in her honour every year according to the Roman tradition." But in spite of Rome's tolerating Phrygian priests who acted weird, begged for alms, and dressed oddly, "by a law and decree of the senate, no native Roman walks in procession through the city arrayed in a pari-coloured robe, begging alms or escorted by flute players, or worships the goddess with the Phrygian ceremonies." Dionysius stresses that the Romans "abominate all empty pomp that falls below proper standards of decency" (2.19.3–5).

Patrolling the Unacceptable

How should we characterize the problem that Rome had with the Bacchanalia and the cult of Magna Mater? To the Latin mind they went beyond the bounds of proper *religio* and were therefore *superstitio,* superstition. By *superstitio* the Roman did not mean something magiclike that was beyond belief, but rather an unmoderated excess and uncontrollable devotion to some one single form of the holy. Such *superstitio* was usually seen as intending personal rather than imperial gain. It undermined the father's control over family members and their devotion to the father. It was usually characterized as *hysterical;* that is, it involved too many women and too much emotion and was not easily controlled by wealthy men in the earlier Republic or Caesars in the later empire. What was feared in both those cases was some direct access to the gods through revelation, some unfettered ability to link with supernatural powers.

The kind of behavior that was alarming to Rome is what we usually associate with a shaman, an ecstatic or charismatic holy individual. It subverted the proper Roman control of civic religion. It negated the absolute integration of politics and religion. It threatened Caesar both as ruler, or *imperator,* and as chief priest, or *pontifex maximus* (not to speak of both as divine). Remember that in addition to the many gods and goddesses, the Romans believed very strongly in the paranormal, the mystical, the magical. They used Etruscan *haruspices* to divine the future, read the livers of sacrifices, and explain the flights of birds. They consulted the oral prophecies of Apollo's priestesses and the written prophecies of the *Sibylline Oracles.* Horoscopes and astrology were an integral part of their scientific world. But the ambiguity of those forms made them each malleable to political control, and there was an almost theatrical procedure in incorporating them ceremonially in senatorial debates or imperial political decisions. Mary Beard, in "The Roman and the Foreign" in *Shamanism, History, and the State,* notes that what was perhaps most disturbing to Romans about these two preceding cases was that they threatened the "sole guardians of access to the gods" and "were effectively challenging the wider authority of that elite and the social and cultural norms they [had] long guaranteed" (178).

Another set of stories narrated by both the Jewish historian Josephus and various pagan writers relates Rome's interest in patrolling unacceptable religious behavior and particularly in controlling meetings that were or could be in some ways subversive. We allow, once again, considerable literary license on the historical details as authors tell their tales, but emphasize the very absolute reality of that underlying imperial distrust for meetings and practices hidden from the open civic arena and therefore beyond Caesar's ordinary control. The incidents each show an underlying fear of meetings and a certain amount of xenophobia.

In one case, Josephus's *Jewish Antiquities* relates how the emperor Tiberius crucified some priests of Isis and threw her statue into the Tiber after learning of a plot that tricked a married Roman noblewoman into having sex with a suitor disguised as the dog-headed Egyptian god Anubis in the temple of Isis (18.65–80). Shortly after that incident, Tiberius expelled Jews from inside the city limits and conscripted others to serve in the notoriously harsh climate of Sardinia after hearing about a wealthy Roman woman being defrauded of a small fortune that she intended as a donation to Jerusalem's Temple (18.81–84). Suetonius's *Lives of the Caesars* records those events in *Tiberius,* but in much more general terms, and adds that the emperor "banished the astrologers as well" (36) and that he "forbade anyone to consult soothsayers secretly and without witnesses. Indeed, he even attempted to do away with the oracles near the city" (63.1). In *The Deified Claudius* that emperor "utterly abolished the cruel and inhuman religion of the druids among the Gauls, which under Augustus had merely been prohibited to Roman citizens" (25.5). Cassius Dio's *Roman History* says that Claudius ordered Jews, "while continuing their traditional mode of life, not to hold meetings," and further that he "disbanded the clubs . . . and abolished the taverns (*tabernas*) where they were wont to gather and drink" (60.6.7). In short, any meeting or place where unruly behavior might trigger unrest was prohibited.

All of those accounts are rife with inconsistencies and chronological problems, but all we emphasize here is the consistency of Caesar's interest in patrolling and controlling the religious landscape. We do have one very clear statement from a later emperor, Trajan, emperor from 98 to 117 C.E., when he responds to a question from Pliny the Younger, whom he had sent as a emergency governor of Bithynia-Pontus along the Black Sea's southern coast. Pliny requests permission to organize a *collegium* of around 150 firefighters in the city of Nicodemia. Earlier fires had damaged the temple of Isis and the sanctuary of the goddess Men, and Pliny hoped to gain permission for a fire brigade, assuring Trajan that "it will not be difficult to keep such small numbers under observation" (*Letters* 10.33). But, as recorded in Pliny's *Letters,* Trajan denies the request and stresses his reason:

If people assemble for a common purpose, whatever name we give them and for whatever reason, they soon turn into a political club. It is a better policy then to provide the equipment necessary for dealing with fires, and to instruct property owners to make use of it, calling on the help of the crowds which collect if they find it necessary. (10.34)

Physical fires could threaten property and life, of course, but could not threaten imperial rule's integration of politics and religion into a single smoothly operating power. But there were other fires that could threaten or even subvert that collaboration, and those should not even be risked. Better no firefighters than ones who might get ideas, ask questions, and imagine remedies. The control of fire could be negotiated; the control of empire could not.

Violent Pornography in Sex and War

The emperor controlled the empire's religio-politics first on the supreme level of imperial theology, next on the intermediate level of foreign religions, local cults, and all groups meeting privately for whatever reason, and finally on the individual level of marital morality and sexual privacy. Remember from Chapter 2 how Augustus tried to restore piety and morality in the most private realm of family life, and to extend his control into areas like procreation and sex with the Julian Law on Marriage and the Julian Law on Adultery. Those family values were drawn from Rome's traditionally conservative farmer-warrior society and were later idealized as the *mos maiorum,* "the way of our ancestors." Augustus's legislation was part of the religio-political theology in which success and control abroad depended upon piety and morality at home, in which martial victory depended on sexual purity.

Our present discussion, however, is not about Augustus's moral rearmament on sex and marriage, or about agreement on its potential virtues, or even about agreement on its absolute failure. We leave aside, for here and now, the arguable good or arguable bad points of those Julian Laws to probe instead two much deeper and more deadly levels. Those laws were grounded in the standard presuppositions of broader Mediterranean or even generally universal patriarchy, in which women, as the possession of men, were to be held under male control. In Chapter 2 we spoke of Pauline equality for Christian females and Christian males in family, assembly, and apostolate. We also saw there how the post-Pauline or even anti-Pauline tradition muted that radicality back inside the normalcy of Roman patriarchy. We now look at the implications of that patriarchy in the less public and more private realm of sexuality and family. We emphatically stress that, *then as now,* patriarchal sexuality had and has *less* to do with bodily views or divine imperatives and much *more* to do with male manipulation, paternal control, and imperial power.

There is also, however, an even deeper level beneath patriarchy but caused by it and interacting with it. When you read that vicious epigram from Martial about the *galli,* did you find its language unacceptable in the public realm? Is it impolite, rude, crude, and vulgar? Is it pornographic? And what is the difference between vulgarity and pornography? As we consider several of the texts in this section, those questions will be consistently presumed and implicitly asked. But this is our deepest question: What about the conjunction of sex and war, the collaboration of possession and penetration by phallus and sword, the coincidence of violent pornography by sexual and martial control? Why do we have so many vulgar words for bodily functions that are perfectly human and natural, but no vulgar words for the slaughter of war that is surely inhuman and unnatural? Must we distinguish absolutely between *vulgarity,* which includes words too impolite for public use and acts too private for public display, and *pornography,* which always includes violence, whether ideological, rhetorical, or physical, and applies to both sex and war with a deadly male symbiosis? Should we transfer the use of "obscene" from sex to war, transfer it from what describes our humanity crudely to what destroys our humanity profoundly?

Phallus and Control

For Rome, not unexpectedly, normative sexual behavior was scripted according to power relations based on gender, age, and status, with the adult landowning male as the most powerful. We can already see that patriarchy-power nexus in the frequent depiction of the phallus as a magic-like symbol of power. It was used to ward off the evil eye, to protect houses from intrusion, and to ensure fecundity. On Delos, for example, while Apollo's sanctuary was guarded by a row of lion statues, Dionysos's temple was guarded by two enormous erect phalli (Figure 86), the symbol of uncontrollable pleasure and the sacred object of his mysteries. Other sanctuaries and large villas across the Mediterranean were protected by herms, square bonze or marble pillars with a bust on top and male genitals protruding from the front of the pillar (Figure 87). More modest private

FIGURE 86 *(left)*. Statue of a giant phallus (broken) before the Temple of Dionysos on the island of Delos. FIGURE 87 *(right)*. Herm from the workshop of Boethos, bronze with ivory inlay.

houses in Pompeii often engraved or scratched an erect phallus near the entrance to ward off curses or serve as good-luck charms. Its power was not that clearly distinguished from sensual pleasure, as the ambiguity of one accompanying inscription makes clear: *Hic habitat felicitas,* "Herein dwells happiness," surrounds the phallus (Figure 88).

A common reaction to that display of male genitals is simply to say that the ancient Greeks and Romans, unlike today's Western cultures, shackled by a puritanical past, had a healthier view of the human body. In classical

Greece, the gymnasium (from *gymnos,* "nude") was literally a place of nudity, the idealized young male (*kouros*) was nude, and statues of gods and goddesses, heroes and heroines were regularly sculpted in the nude. The Roman elite eagerly collected or copied those statues for rich villas across the empire. Greco-Roman urbanites were seemingly at ease with the nude human body, which was a commonplace appreciated as an aesthetic ideal. Aside from the body, they seemed more readily conversant in matters of sex and love, as can be seen in the popularity of elegiac poetry written by the likes of Ovid or Tertullus. Even some of Pompeii's graffiti have a romantic and almost eternal quality about them, for example, "Lovers, like bees, lead a honey-sweet life," and "Let him who chastises lovers try to fetter the winds and block the endless flow of water from a spring" (*CIL* 4.8408; 1649). Those walls also preserve an honest assessment of relationships, such as the pain of rejection or spurned love. We read on those same Pompeiian walls,

FIGURE 88 *(left).* Stone relief of a phallus from the entrance of a house at Pompeii, with the inscription "Herein dwells happiness." FIGURE 89 *(right).* Worth its weight in gold? Fresco of Priapus from Pompeii's House of the Vettii.

"Thysas, don't love Fortunas," and "Sarra, you're not acting very nicely, leaving me all alone" (*CIL* 4.4498; 1951)

A closer look, however, at the ithyphallic figure of Priapus (Figure 89) and a wider look at sexuality in the general Pauline era reveal things other than a simple and benign attitude toward the body. According to some of the myths, Priapus's parents were Dionysos and either a nymph or Aphrodite herself. By the third century B.C.E., Priapus was popular in the Troad region of today's northwestern Turkey, but his popularity spread rapidly in the Hellenistic period and into Roman imperial times. That progress was helped in part by first Greek and then Latin obscene poems known as the *Priapae*. He was a minor and mischievous god, associated of course with sex and virility, but also with the fertility of herbs and gardens, which in the poems he was frequently said to guard. Although the earlier Greek poems bore some religious content, the later Latin ones almost exclusively depict him as a ribald character with an anal fixation. His chief purpose in both poetry and popular lore and the placement of his statues in gardens was to warn away thieves with the threat of rape and to chase down intruders and sodomize them. Amy Richlin's *The Garden of Priapus* is subtitled *Sexuality and Aggression in Roman Humor,* and it emphasizes that, even though Priapus is amusing in poem, myth, and statue, his humor becomes very different when one realizes that he embodies the essential sexuality of Roman texts: "male, aggressive, and bent on controlling boundaries" (xvi).

Priapus alerts us to the essential public scripting of normative sexual behavior in the Roman Empire at the time of Paul. Even at best, it was based on control and power. At worst, and that was mostly, it was based on subjugation and humiliation. We look next at more private details, at elements not from public or official civic life, but from the private life of brothel and bedroom from across the Roman world in general and from Pompeian graffiti and frescoes in particular. We examine lines and slogans scribbled in bathhouse corners and small erotic scenes painted on bedroom walls, images the otherwise racy *Elegies* of Propertius called "lewd panels" and "indecent pictures" that "corrupted the innocent eyes of girls"—but not boys, apparently? (2.6.29). We repeat what we said above about the deeper presuppositions of such items: They were much less about egalitarian sexual mutuality and much more about sexual patriarchy as a microcosm of martial imperialism. They indicate male control, abuse, and even humiliation of female bodies. They specify male power, possession, and penetration of female bodies.

Power and Possession

Most of the erotic images on lamps, medallions, or walls were intended to evoke feelings of pleasure and sensuality. But we look beneath that surface to see how those images unveil attitudes about possession and subordination. Remember, at the outset, that those Augustan marriage laws were mostly concerned with controlling female promiscuity and elite procreation. Those imperial women depicted on the *Ara Pacis Augustae,* for example, were cloaked in *stolae* less for female modesty about their bodies and more for male control over those same bodies. Horace's *Odes* describes Rome as "teeming with sin" because "our times have sullied first the marriage-bed, our offspring, and our homes." Next, "the maiden . . . plans unholy amours, with passion unrestrained." Finally, amid "her husband's revels she seeks younger paramours." But then to sex and war. He concludes by comparing a present wife's promiscuity, "lavish purchaser of shame" and "not without her husband's knowledge," with past parents "of whom were sprung the youth that dyed the sea with Punic blood" when Hannibal threatened the very future of Rome (3.6.17–36). If you make love virtuously, you will make war vigorously.

That attitude is captured in a graffito from the House of the Moralist in Pompeii that warns, "Don't cast lustful glances, or make eyes at other men's wives" (*CIL* 4.7698b). But although men protected their women from others, they sought to conquer the daughters or wives of those same others with near impunity, and the number of those conquests served to establish intramale ascendancy. We find these boasts on walls near a brothel: "I have screwed many girls here"; "When I came here, I screwed. Then I returned home"; and even one Restitutus bragged that he "seduced often many girls" (*CIL* 4.2175, 2246, 5251). And again, "Few women have known that I, Floronius, great cocksman, soldier in the VII Legion, was here: and I will do me only six" (*CIL* 4.8767).

These texts preserve the crude machismo urge to "do" or "take" a woman. But many frescoes from Pompeii reveal a more subtle sense in which possession or subordination is scripted in the sexual behavior of the well-to-do. Many scenes—surprising if not discomforting to current sensibilities—depict slaves preparing and pouring wine or attending to the lamps beside a couple who are having intercourse (Figure 90). That was a clear display of power relations, and Antonio Varone, in *Eroticism in Pompeii,* captures the essence of that kind of humiliation: "Just as they could freely dispose of

FIGURE 90. Fresco from Pompeii of a slave attending while a women is in bed with a man.

their slaves for sexual purposes, the master and mistress could also formally consider them as little more than domestic animals, under whose gaze it was licit not to feel the slightest embarrassment" (75). One of Martial's witty epigrams, in which he demanded more effort and adventure from his wife in bed, hints at his desire for such condescending exhibitionism common among slave owners by declaring that even "Trojan slaves used to masturbate themselves behind the doors whenever Andromache had taken her seat on Hector as her horse" (11.104.13–14).

Power and Penetration

The crucial role that power played in the social scripts of ancient sexuality is also apparent in the way Greek and Roman authors distinguished between "active" and "passive" roles, with superiority defined as active male penetration. We saw that already in Martial's sarcastic remarks about the *galli* priests of the Great Mother goddess. It is also evident in the erotic scenes on the disk-shaped oil lamps that were widespread household artifacts across the Mediterranean, even in Judea, which was notoriously prudish by Roman standards. Almost without exception, these lamps reveal a set of positions in which the man is what the Romans would think of as "active" and the woman as "passive." But even when the female seems to be "active" by being on top during intercourse or by performing oral sex, that "activity" is portrayed as service to the male and is depicted iconographically by the man holding and controlling her head or by the man extending his arm back behind his head, such as on a bas-relief from Pompeii (Figure 91). That latter gesture may show a certain amount of narcissistic aloofness or may just reflect an attempt to get out of the way. Be that as it may, women only extend a hand to touch or caress the man. Further, a woman's activity in oral sex was considered not only servile but degrading, for example, in the crude graffito from Pompeii, "Veneria sucked the cock of Maximus through the whole grape harvest, leaving both her holes empty and only her mouth full" (*CIL* 4.1391), or, again, on some lines scribbled in Pompeii's Stabian baths, the command to "go down with your mouth along the shaft, licking it, then still licking withdraw it upwards. Ah, there, I'm coming!" (*CIL* 4.760).

Notions of activity and penetration were not demarcated only by gender. Class and status factored into the equation to such an extent that maleness and femaleness were not the sole criteria for normative behavior. The wealthy man was free to penetrate actively almost anyone; his object could be a woman, boy, or lower-class man. This is how the widespread and seeming acceptance of homosexuality in Greece and Rome must be understood. In Greece it had long been common for landowning adult men to penetrate, not other adult men of similar status, but young teenage boys. In Rome it

FIGURE 91. Bas-relief of intercourse from Pompeii; note the man's arm gesture, which indicates his passivity and therefore the woman's servile status.

FIGURE 92. Cameo with a man and what appears to be a young boy.

was almost axiomatic that wealthy men include in their household teenage boy slaves, and, for example, curly haired imports from Asia Minor were particularly prized for sexual usage (Figure 92). They were pursued and penetrated like women, discarded and replaced when they reached manhood and grew facial hair, but they never, ever, were to penetrate their masters.

The poet Tibullus dedicated several of his first erotic poems to his mistress Delia (1, 2, 3, 5, 6), but then others to a servant boy, Marathus (4, 8, 9). That was scandalous, but mainly because he admitted that his affections for mistress and boy had made him a servant. To be penetrated was something for slaves, boys, or women. And they were shamed in the process, as this libel from Pompeii makes clear: "Equitias's slave Cosmus is a big queer and cocksucker with his legs wide open" (Diehl 648). Read through all the Latin erotic poems or Greek epigrams, and you will agree with the depressing conclusion of Amy Richlin's just-cited book:

> The content is determined by the central figure: the man, the poet, the narrator, the lover, the pursuer. The objects of his love are women and boys, whom he perceives as delicate (in comparison to himself) and soft (the better to receive him). They are younger than he and their assets are defined by his assessment. Their elusiveness is a function of their value and can be expressed in terms of cash value or the price of a slave; a high degree of the recognized physically attractive features produces demand and makes the object of desire harder to

obtain. . . . Women rarely, and *pueri* [boys] never, are the narrators of erotic poems; they have no voice here. (55)

What was unimaginable was an egalitarian position, an egalitarian escapade, an egalitarian relationship. Equality was not in any script, whether between man and woman, man and boy, man and man. Jewish morality, of course, was emphatically different in both theory and practice. Simply put, in the Jewish ideal, sex was restricted to marriage between husband and wife and for the purpose of procreation. Nudity was shameful, and an especially sensitive issue for Jewish circumcised men in the public baths. Given all that we have seen and read, it's not at all surprising that after the initial eruption of Vesuvius and right before Pompeii was engulfed in ashes, a Jew scribbled on the walls: "Sodom and Gomorrah!"

Power and Imperialism

Although Augustus and his wife Livia portrayed themselves as chaste models of his marital legislation, that program was surely his greatest failure. It was repealed later by the Senate but, more significant, it was totally ignored if not mocked by his own family and dynastic successors. In fact, Augustus himself might not have been so pure, as the banished Ovid's more or less repentant *Tristia* suggests that the *divi filius* himself had some of those erotic scenes on his own household walls:

> Surely in our houses, even as figures of old heroes shine,
> 　　painted by an artist's hand,
> so in some place a small tablet
> 　　depicts the varying unions and forms of love. (2.521–24)

But that is very mild and nothing compared to what the gossipy historian Suetonius in his *Lives of the Caesars* records about Augustus's successors. First, his *Tiberius* tells us that the emperor spent much of his reign on the island of Capri, where "he acquired a reputation for still grosser depravities that one can hardly bear to tell or be told, let alone believe," but of course Suetonius's gossip as history bears up well under the strain of both telling and believing (44.1). Next, in his *Caligula,* the emperor thought himself the incestuous son of Augustus and his daughter, Julia, and therefore committed incest with his own sisters. He "respected neither his own chastity nor that of anyone else" by seducing or raping any noblewomen he wanted, often at dinners with their husbands present (36.1–2). Then, in *The Deified Claudius,* the emperor's impotence was lampooned; he divorced one wife "because of scandalous lewdness" and another for the same, and his last wife even married another man while still wed to the emperor (26.2). Finally, in *Nero,* that emperor's various perversions and cruelties were legendary. He debauched even one of the Vestal Virgins, and he castrated and tried to make a woman of the boy Sporus in order to marry him. But, most shamefully, Nero later married another man, but made himself the woman, "going so far as to make the cries and lamentations of a maiden being deflowered" (29).

We deliberately concluded this section with Suetonius's gossip about the Caesars' insatiable desire for sexual control and domination for one very specific reason. Even if all of those stories of Caesarian sexual perversity are just overdone facts, unfounded rumors, or prurient imaginings, they indicate, expect, and take for granted a certain dialectic of patriarchal power and penetrative possession on both sexual and imperial levels. That dialectic of sex and war is made visually obvious in the magnificent Sebasteion seen already in Chapter 1. We look now at imperial war on that monument, in the city of Aphrodite-Venus, goddess of love, consort of the war god Mars, and legendary ancestor of the Julian clan.

By Phallus and by Sword

We presume here the general description of the Sebasteion from Chapter 1 and especially those articles by R. R. R. Smith cited in our References. But we focus now on certain very specific aspects from those north and south relief-studded galleries. On the north wall, as you may recall, the top level contained allegorical figures for time and place, night and day, and the middle level had a series of personified nations (*ethnē,* "peoples") conquered by Rome. "The overall purpose of the north-portico allegories and provinces seems to be to suggest and illustrate a grandiose identification of the physical world and the Roman empire," as R. R. R. Smith concludes from the extant evidence. "Taken together, the north-portico reliefs seem to speak the language of empire without end, imperial conquest by land and sea, night and day" (1987: 96).

There were fifty statues of personified conquered nations in that gallery, sculpted in native dress and characteristics and accompanied by their names on the statue bases. Among them, excavators have recovered the inscriptions from the bases of Jewish, Egyptian, Cretan, and Cypriot statues. "The selection of outlandish peoples was meant to stand as a visual account of the extent of the Augustan empire," notes R. R. R. Smith, "and by the sheer numbers and impressive unfamiliarity of the names, to suggest that it is coterminous with the ends of the earth" (1988: 77). But we stress in this chapter's context that those provinces were all personified as *women*, having been conquered by Augustus and now submissive to the *pater patriae* in the Roman family. It was not uncommon to depict the provinces in imperial art as women; they can be found as such on the inner altar of the *Ara Pacis Augustae* and the cuirass of Augustus's Prima Porta statue. The series at Aphrodisias might even have been modeled on those in the Augustan Forum at Rome, though its world-famous sculptural school would hardly have slavishly copied even that most important model.

Keep those *female* personifications of conquered peoples in mind as we turn from the north to the better-preserved south portico. Its overall theme is the integration of the older Greek and the newer Roman imperial theology. As you may recall, the top level has historical and symbolical scenes of the imperial family, and the middle level has scenes from classical Greek myths and legends. For our present topic, we focus particularly on two panels built sometime after the mid-first-century earthquake and just before the complex's completion in the reign of Nero.

One shows the emperor Claudius victorious over defeated Britannia (Figure 93), and the other depicts Nero victorious over defeated Armenia (Figure 94). Each relief shares some affinity with earlier Hellenistic statuary groups of battles with those great women warriors the Amazons. But, of course, these female figures are not armed combatants, but unarmed women. The two reliefs are striking in their not so subtle sexual imagery, an imagery less sensually erotic in context than violently pornographic. In the first, Claudius stands nude, apart from billowing cape and helmet, poised to pierce the female figure of Britannia with a spear. She is pinned by his knee to the ground and is dressed with a belted tunic completely off her shoulder to expose her right breast. One hand grasps that garment at her left shoulder to keep it from sliding off, and the other is held up in a futile attempt to protect herself. Claudius's left hand holds her by the hair, which is long and loosened to indicate iconographically the uncontrolled barbarian.

In the other and very similar relief, Nero's youthful, muscular nude body stands astride a slumped Armenia. He holds her up from complete collapse with a firm grasp of her left arm, but holds his sword ready in the other

<small>FIGURE 93 *(left)*. Claudius victorious over the female personification of Britain, from the Sebasteion at Aphrodisias. FIGURE 94 *(right)*. Nero victorious over the female personification of Armenia, from the Sebasteion at Aphrodisias.</small>

hand. She is completely naked except for the Roman iconographic symbols for all Orientals, high boots, a Phrygian cap, and barbarian-style hair flowing out to shoulder length.

Each of the Caesars is about to pierce and kill his conquest with a weapon, but as we know from the gallery's total north-south context, those two women/peoples will not be permanently dead after defeat. They will be raised up, as it were, from the south gallery to join the rest of those conquered personifications in the north gallery. They will become part of the empire, concubines of the *pater patriae,* part of his imperial harem, members of his global family. There they will stand as trophies, quiet and submissive under Caesar's control, and by adding them he will ascend to even greater glory. The emperors all rose to power by dominating and conquering others, they expanded and vigorously defended those acquired boundaries through war, and the gallery at Aphrodisias shows how they first humiliate the female provinces only to raise them up and place them in their empire. They were, to use Amy Richlin's earlier-cited words about Priapus, "male, aggressive, and bent on controlling boundaries." Whether in the bedroom or on the battlefield, men rose in status by exerting power and subordinating others.

The Gospel of Jesus Christ as Lord

The content of the imperial gospel that we have just seen made eminent sense to at least male elites across the Mediterranean. They recognized only too clearly that Augustus's ascendancy had saved their world from either the continual destruction of Roman civil war or the final disintegration of Roman imperial control. They also accepted the successful use of force and violence to establish peace and control by patriarchy between the sexes as by imperialism between the nations. All of that was clear enough from *pater-familias* to *pater patriae*. But what exactly was the content of Paul's impertinently alternative gospel? Epithets and titles, assertions and proclamations are all quite similar with, of course, the imperial usage preceding the polemically deliberate Pauline usurpation. What, beyond the personal and individual, is the structural and systemic difference between Lord or Savior, Divine One or Son of God, gospel or good news as applied first to Augustus and then to Jesus? What exactly is the content of the Pauline gospel?

Here, just as overture, is a medley of Pauline phrases about the gospel of freedom establishing not just a new world, but a new creation. It is, says Paul, my gospel, our gospel, the gospel of God, the gospel of his Son, the gospel of Christ. And, in a first climactic summary, it is the gospel of the glory of Christ, who is the image of God. It is, continues Paul, a call to freedom, the freedom for which Christ has set us free, the freedom we have in Christ Jesus, because the Lord is the Spirit and where the Spirit of the Lord is, there is freedom. And, in a second climactic summary, it is the freedom whereby creation itself will be set free from its bondage to decay and will obtain the freedom of the glory of the children of God. It is, concludes Paul, about a new covenant with God, a new life in the Spirit. And, in a third climactic summary, it is a new creation. It is the good news of global freedom for all creation. But, once again, what is the *content* and not just the *claim* of that gospel, that freedom, and that new creation?

Deep down beneath an Augustus or a Jesus, a Paul or a Nero, two giant tectonic plates ground relentlessly against one another in that first century. Each was formed from a powerfully creative transmutation within prior tradition, one within paganism, the other within Judaism. The tectonic plate of Hellenistic tradition mutated under the Roman challenge until, at least for many, Caesar's apotheosis meant not just the promise, but the start of the world's salvation, redemption, and justification. The tectonic plate of Judaism mutated under the Christian challenge until, at least for some, Christ's resurrection meant not just the promise, but the start of the world's salvation, redemption, and justification. But, as always, the end of evil and injustice, and even the start of that end, was about means.

For the Defense of the Gospel

Luke's Acts tells a fascinating story about Paul at Ephesus. Demetrius and his fellow silversmiths caused "no little disturbance concerning the Way" (19:23). They had a twofold complaint, one commercial and one religious. Because of "the Way's" antagonism toward paganism, "there is danger not only that this trade of ours may come into disrepute but also that the temple of the great goddess Artemis will be scorned, and she will be deprived of her majesty that brought all Asia and the world to worship her" (19:27). People rushed into the great theater "dragging with them Gaius and Aristarchus, Macedonians who were Paul's travel companions" (19:29), but not Paul himself, who, "wished to go into the crowd, but the disciples would not let him; even some officials of the province of Asia, who were friendly to him, sent him a message urging him not to venture into the theater" (19:30–31). The town clerk commands the crowd to proceed legally, to take their grievances to the proconsul, and to avoid "being charged with rioting today" (19:38–40). What is striking about that story, no matter how you judge its particular or even general historicity, is that Paul is not directly involved, attacked, or imprisoned. We know about an Ephesian imprisonment not from Luke, but from Paul himself.

In Proconsular Chains

We mentioned in Chapter 2, but only in passing, that Paul was in prison when he wrote the letter to Philemon. In the first half of that very brief letter Paul mentions his imprisonment four times in its thirteen verses, using two different but connected Greek words: prisoner (*desmios*) and chain (*desmos*). The opening words in Greek are "Paul prisoner (*desmios*) of Christ Jesus" and that is repeated again later, "prisoner (*desmios*) of Christ Jesus" (1:1, 9). But the other two expressions are rather more specific. The English text has the phrase "during my imprisonment" twice but, more literally, it should read, "in chains (*desmois*)" twice (1:10, 13). Paul emphasizes that he is a *prisoner* for Jesus Christ *in chains* for the gospel. Furthermore, the "for" in the last sentence translates the Greek genitive case, and it is necessary to read "of" rather than "for" and take that "of" very seriously. In Paul's mind, as we shall see, he is a prisoner *of* Christ in the chains *of* the gospel.

Paul's letter to the Philippians was also written from prison and, once again, the English translation has "my imprisonment" twice but, more literally, it should read "my chains" twice (*desmois* in 1:7, 13). Everything about that imprisonment is disputed, and most conclusions are beyond either final proof or disproof. We work with the following basic hypothesis: *The letters to Philemon and the Philippians come from the same imprisonment at Ephesus, rather than from later ones at either Caesarea or Rome.* The former location is from hints in Paul, while those latter two-year locations are from statements in Acts (24:17; 28:30). Granted that general background, what precisely is Paul's situation?

Paul was not held in the hard extremity of Roman *underground incarceration,* as was King Perseus of Macedonia in 167 B.C.E. according to Diodorus Siculus's *Library of History,* written around 30 B.C.E.:

> This prison is a deep underground dungeon, no larger than a nine-couch room, dark, and noisome from the large numbers committed to the place, who were men under condemnation on capital charges, for most of this category were incarcerated there at that period. With so many shut up in such close quarters, the poor wretches were reduced to the physical appearance of brutes, and since their food and everything pertaining to their other needs was all foully commingled, a stench so terrible assailed anyone who drew near that it could scarcely be endured. (31.9.2)

Instead, Paul was held in *military custody,* chained to a soldier. Everything thereafter depended on what friends could do, what custodians would allow, and on how humanity and bribery might prevail over inhumanity and cruelty. According to Josephus's *Jewish Antiquities,* for example, Herod Agrippa I was placed under such a guard in 37 C.E. when he rejoiced too openly and too early upon the emperor Tiberius's death. This, however, was the style of Agrippa's imprisonment:

> [Antonia arranged that] the soldiers who were to guard him and that the centurion who would be in charge of them and would also be handcuffed to him should be of humane character, that he should be permitted to bathe every day and receive visits from his freedmen and

friends, and that he should have other bodily comforts too. His friend Silas and two of his freedmen, Marysyas and Stoecheus, visited him bringing him his favorite viands and doing whatever service they could. They brought him garments that they pretended to sell, but, when night came, they made him a bed with the connivance of the soldiers. (18.203–4)

Although such amenities were surely very welcome and certainly much better than their absence, they did not mitigate the ever present possibility of immediate execution. And Paul's position was extremely precarious.

He tells the Philippians, "It has become known throughout the whole imperial guard and to everyone else that my imprisonment is for Christ" (1:13). That phrase "imperial guard" is literally "pretorium" and means not the imperial Pretorian Guard in Rome, but the official judgment seat and punishment barracks of any governor. In the present case, therefore, Paul is not imprisoned by some lower official in some minor city, but by the official provincial representative of the Senate and People of Rome at Ephesus in Asia.

"By Life or by Death"

Throughout Philippians Paul vacillates between life and death, deliverance and execution, but hope always triumphs over despair. Watch that dialectic in these verses, and notice how he talks himself into ultimate confidence:

For I know that through your prayers and the help of the Spirit of Jesus Christ this will turn out for my deliverance. It is my eager expectation and hope that I will not be put to shame in any way, but that by my speaking with all boldness, Christ will be exalted now as always in my body, whether by life or by death. For to me, living is Christ and dying is gain. If I am to live in the flesh, that means fruitful labor for me; and I do not know which I prefer. I am hard pressed between the two: my desire is to depart and be with Christ, for that is far better; but to remain in the flesh is more necessary for you. Since I am convinced of this, I know that I will remain and continue with all of you for your progress and joy in faith, so that I may share abundantly in your boasting in Christ Jesus when I come to you again. (1:19–26)

A short while later he reverts to the possibility of his execution, but once again he moves from that possibility to speak of imminent deliverance:

But even if I am being poured out as a libation over the sacrifice and the offering of your faith, I am glad and rejoice with all of you—and in the same way you also must be glad and rejoice with me. I hope in the Lord Jesus to send Timothy to you soon, so that I may be cheered by news of you. . . . I hope therefore to send him as soon as I see how things go with me; and I trust in the Lord that I will also come soon. (2:17–19, 23–24)

We will see below that Paul's confident tone may have been more to console the Philippians than to reassure himself and that the terror of that imprisonment was far greater than we glimpse from those letters to either Philemon or the Philippians.

One further point. Paul also admits that there was a split among the Ephesian Christians and, although he gave no precise details, it was probably over his program and his imprisonment.

Some proclaim Christ from envy and rivalry, but others from good-will. These proclaim Christ out of love, knowing that I have been put here for the defense of the gospel; the others proclaim Christ out of selfish ambition, not sincerely but intending to increase my suffering in my imprisonment. What does it matter? Just this, that Christ is proclaimed in every way, whether out of false motives or true; and in that I rejoice. (1:15–18)

Some Christians may have resisted anything liable to draw Roman attention or opposition to their community and argued that Paul's imprisonment vindicated their position. It is striking that, although he mentions community persecution at Philippi, he says nothing about any such general reprisals at Ephesus. Many there may not have agreed with whatever Paul did to result in his arrest.

Epaphras and Epaphroditus

In his letter to Philemon, Paul mentions a person named Epaphras whom he describes as "my fellow prisoner in Christ Jesus" (1:23). In the other letter from that same Ephesian imprisonment, Paul mentions an Epaphroditus sent to him with assistance by the Philippians. But Epaphras and Epaphroditus are simply the shorter and longer forms of the *same name*. So, for example, Luke uses the shorter form Silas repeatedly in Acts 15–18, but Paul uses the longer Silvanus in 1 Thessalonians 1:1 and 2 Corinthians 1:19. Conversely,

Luke uses the longer form Priscilla in Acts 18:2, 18, 26, but Paul uses the shorter Prisca in 1 Corinthians 16:19 and Romans 16:3. In those instances we are dealing with shorter and longer forms of the *same name* for the *same person*. Here, then, is the question. Granted that Epaphras and Epaphroditus are the *same name,* are Epaphras of the Philemon letter and Epaphroditus of the Philippians letter the *same person*?

On the one hand, as we see below, Paul's Epaphroditus is obviously from Philippi, but in the pseudo-Pauline letter to the Colossians, an Epaphras is called "one of you"; that is, he is from Colossae (1:7; 4:12). On the other, it is surely too coincidental to have two persons with the same name playing significant roles in Paul's Ephesian imprisonment. It might even be too coincidental to have two different persons with the same name playing significant roles in two different Pauline imprisonments. Tentatively, then, and despite Colossians, we take Epaphroditus and Epaphras as the same name for the same person during Paul's Ephesian imprisonment. What do we know about this Epaphras/Epaphroditus from Paul's two prison letters that mention his name?

In his letter to the Philippians Paul thanks them for their consistent assistance to him from the very beginning of their relationship. In this context he mentions the financial aid they just sent to him with Epaphroditus:

> For even when I was in Thessalonica, you sent me help for my needs more than once. Not that I seek the gift, but I seek the profit that accumulates to your account. I have been paid in full and have more than enough; I am fully satisfied, now that I have received from Epaphroditus the gifts you sent, a fragrant offering, a sacrifice acceptable and pleasing to God. And my God will fully satisfy every need of yours according to his riches in glory in Christ Jesus. (4:16–19)

Apparently Epaphroditus did not simply deliver financial aid from Philippi, he also stayed to help Paul personally and, when that generosity endangered his very life, Paul decided to send him home.

> Still, I think it necessary to send to you Epaphroditus—my brother and co-worker and fellow soldier, your messenger and minister to my need; for he has been longing for all of you, and has been distressed because you heard that he was ill. He was indeed so ill that he nearly died. But God had mercy on him, and not only on him but on me also, so that I would not have one sorrow after another. I am the more eager to send him, therefore, in order that you may rejoice at seeing him again, and

that I may be less anxious. Welcome him then in the Lord with all joy, and honor such people, because he came close to death for the work of Christ, risking his life to make up for those services that you could not give me. (2:25–30)

Was there some connection between Epahroditus's illness and his personal service to Paul? Paul calls the Epaphras of the letter to Philemon "my fellow prisoner in Christ Jesus" (1:23) and in that to the Philippians he is "my brother and co-worker and fellow soldier" (2:25). Does that mean that Epaphras/Epaphroditus was like Paul himself, a chained prisoner? In context, that is not possible. They can decide whether he stays or returns and, indeed, it seems that Epaphroditus wanted to stay, but Paul insisted on sending him home ("I think it is necessary to send" him back). There is, however, another possible interpretation that explains both his title of "fellow prisoner" and his endangered health. Epaphras may have requested and been allowed to live with Paul, but *in service rather than in custody*.

Lucian of Samosata, the mid-second-century satirist, described in his essay *On Friendship* how Demetrius had assisted Antiphilus in prison:

Then he bade him have no fear, and tearing his short cloak in two, put on one of the halves himself and gave the remainder to Antiphilus, after stripping from him the filthy, worn-out rags that he was wearing. From that time forth, too, he shared his life in every way, attending and cherishing him; for by hiring himself out to the shipmen in the harbour from early morning until noon, he earned a good deal of money as a stevedore. Then, on returning from his work, he would give part of his pay to the keeper, thus rendering him tractable and peaceful, and the rest sufficed well enough for the maintenance of his friend. Each afternoon he remained with Antiphilus, keeping him in heart; and when night overtook him, he slept just in front of the prison door, where he had made a place to lie and had put down some leaves. (30–31)

Lucian actually mentions such assistance offered to the Christian prophet Peregrinus by fellow Christians in *The Passing of Peregrinus,* but in this case it is told with utter contempt:

Every other form of attention was shown him [Peregrinus], not in any casual way but with assiduity, and from the very break of day aged widows and orphan children could be seen waiting near the prison, while their officials even slept inside with him after bribing the guards. Then elaborate meals were brought in, and sacred books of theirs were read aloud, and excellent Peregrinus—for he still went by that name—was called by them "the new Socrates." (12)

Such definitely difficult and possibly dangerous service may have been what Paul meant by calling Epaphras his "fellow prisoner."

One small footnote. In writing to the Philippians about Epaphroditus, Paul gives us a rather precious piece of biographical information almost in passing. "You Philippians," he says, "indeed know that in the early days of the gospel, when I left Macedonia, no church shared with me in the matter of giving and receiving, except you alone" (4:15). In other words, there were other Pauline churches before Macedonia and that probably indicates Galatia. But the Galatians did not send assistance—because of distance or indifference?

Paul's Sufferings in Christ

In 1 Corinthians Paul says that he had "fought with wild animals at Ephesus" (15:32), metaphorically describing those guards to whom he had been chained as a prisoner. Had he literally fought wild beasts in the arena, he would not have lived to record it. Ignatius of Antioch understood Paul's phrase metaphorically when, in the early second century C.E., he used it as a deliberate echo and a calculated imitation of Paul. He had been condemned to the beasts (literally) and sent under chained guard to martyrdom at Rome. In his own *Letter to the Romans* he says, "From Syria to Rome I am fighting with wild beasts, by land and sea, by night and day, bound to ten 'leopards'—that is, a company of soldiers—and they become worse for kind treatment." But Paul's passing mention of "wild beasts at Ephesus" in 1 Corinthians 15:32 is minimal compared to the emphasis on suffering in 2 Corinthians.

Suffering and Mysticism

At the very start of that second Corinthian letter Paul counterpoints two themes, *affliction/suffering* and *consolation,* repeating them over and over like drumbeats, the former seven times, the latter ten times in five verses (2 Cor. 1:3–7). But those mantric refrains serve primarily as prologue to the next section in 2 Corinthians:

We do not want you to be unaware, brothers and sisters, of the affliction we experienced in Asia [i.e., at Ephesus]; for we were so utterly,
unbearably crushed that we despaired of life itself. Indeed, we felt that
we had received the sentence of death so that we would rely not on
ourselves but on God who raises the dead. He who rescued us from so
deadly a peril will continue to rescue us; on him we have set our hope
that he will rescue us again, as you also join in helping us by your
prayers, so that many will give thanks on our behalf for the blessing
granted us through the prayers of many. (1:8–11)

Like all autobiographical data in Paul's letters, that information is included
only because of the immediate situation at Corinth. The more the Corinthians boast of their accomplishments, the more Paul counterboasts or anti-
boasts of his sufferings, because they exalt God's power and allow him to
participate here and now in Christ's death. Later, in that same 2 Corinthians, he says,

We are afflicted in every way, but not crushed; perplexed, but not
driven to despair; persecuted, but not forsaken; struck down, but not
destroyed; always carrying in the body the death of Jesus, so that the
life of Jesus may also be made visible in our bodies. For while we live,
we are always being given up to death for Jesus' sake, so that the life of
Jesus may be made visible in our mortal flesh. So [very sarcastically]
death is at work in us, but life in you. (4:8–12)

Both the death of Christ and the life of Christ are continuously and dialec-
tically manifested here and now in Paul's own mortal body.

Paul uses the phrase "*in* Christ" or "*in* Christ Jesus" or "*in* Christ Jesus
our Lord" so often that you can hardly keep count. Even if we lose count,
we must take it very seriously, because he intends that word *in* more organically than we can ever imagine. For Paul, being "*in* Christ" is not just
metaphorical trope, but mystical identity. It determines everything in his
theology, so that Paul does not think that those "*in* Christ" need to be given
ethical norms, legal rules, or communal instructions. They should know
them internally, intrinsically, organically (the way a trained athlete reacts correctly and properly, but spontaneously and immediately). When he answers
the ethical questions raised by the Corinthians, for example, he never refers
to his earlier on-site instructions. That *in* is the beating heart of Paul's theology, and everything else flows from it in life and in death. The character of

Christ has been totally assumed by Paul, and Paul's own character has been totally subsumed by Christ.

Almost a century ago and after two tours of Pauline geography, Gustav Adolf Deissmann emphasized that basic point in *Paul: A Study in Social and Religious History*.

> Whoever takes away the mystical element from Paul, the man of antiquity, sins against the Pauline word: "Quench not the Spirit" (1 Thessalonians 5:19). . . . This primitive Pauline watch-word "in Christ" is meant vividly and mystically, as is the corresponding "Christ in me." The formula "in Christ" (or "in the Lord") occurs 164 times in Paul's writing: it is really the characteristic expression of his Christianity. . . . The constitutive element in mysticism is immediacy of contact with the deity. (80, 140, 147)

Recall those two phrases about "my chains" at the start of Philippians (1:7, 13). In our English translation that second enchainment is described as being *"for* Christ." But the Greek is, more literally, "my chains are *in* Christ." Paul, in other words, experiences an immersion of his own sufferings under Rome at Ephesus *in* those of Jesus under Rome at Jerusalem.

Mystics are those who experience union with the Holy itself. Whether that is good or bad depends, of course, on the character of their Holy. Think of Jewish mystics living fully in that state to which God called everyone in Leviticus 19:2: "You shall be holy, for I the Lord your God am holy." They live completely in that state to which God invited everyone in Deuteronomy 6:5: "You shall love the Lord your God with all your heart, and with all your soul, and with all your might." Also, with all your intellect and all your will, with all your life and all your death.

Ecstatics are those who experience the altered state of consciousness known as trance, a possibility that, like dreaming, seems to be hard-wired into our brains. Ecstatic trance can be achieved in many different ways, from church to laboratory, from meditation to medication. It is not just a faith's theology, but also the brain's chemistry. Think of it as a temporary but repeated, a passing but profound cessation of the mind's normal separation processes, its usual distinctions between self and other. And, of course, there is nothing more powerful than theology corroborated by chemistry. People speaking in tongues, for example, do so in ecstatic trance and, as Paul says in 1 Corinthians, "I thank God that I speak in tongues more than all of you" (14:18). Many scholars, by the way, see in Pauline thought parallels to

Stoicism or other ancient philosophical systems but, at least in terms of ecstatic speech, Paul would have been seen as more akin to those devotees of Dionysos or Cybele who were, from the Roman perspective, out of control, hysterical, or even mad.

Mysticism and ecstasy are not synonymous, and one can be either, neither, or both. As far as we can tell, Paul was both an ecstatic and a mystic. And no matter how one explains or interprets ecstatic mysticism, it is absolutely fundamental for any understanding of Paul. Luke agrees on Paul's ecstatic experiences, and here are two examples that may well refer to the same event:

> It is necessary to boast; nothing is to be gained by it, but I will go on to visions and revelations of the Lord. I know a person in Christ who fourteen years ago was caught up to the third heaven—whether in the body or out of the body I do not know; God knows. And I know that such a person—whether in the body or out of the body I do not know; God knows—was caught up into Paradise and heard things that are not to be told, that no mortal is permitted to repeat. On behalf of such a one I will boast, but on my own behalf I will not boast, except of my weaknesses. (2 Cor. 12:1–5)

> After I had returned to Jerusalem and while I was praying in the temple, I fell into a trance and saw Jesus saying to me, "Hurry and get out of Jerusalem quickly, because they will not accept your testimony about me. . . . Go, for I will send you far away to the Gentiles." (Acts 22:17–21)

When Paul tells the Galatians, "It is no longer I who live, but it is Christ who lives in me" (2:20), we must take his statement as literally as possible, because Paul, as an ecstatic mystic, *experiences* his relationship to Christ within such a blurred distinction and inside such a combined identity. In a world where identity was often shaped by one's relationship to Rome, by being, as it were, "in Rome," insisting on a self-definition exclusively by being "in Christ" was subversive at best and treasonous at worst.

Mysticism and Resurrection

Does Paul think, therefore, that only mystics can be Christians or that all Christians must be mystics? In a word, yes. And the reason is because they have accepted the gift of life within the resurrection as era. They are already living in/by/with the Spirit of Christ and in/by/with the Body of Christ.

THE SPIRIT OF CHRIST. Throughout his letters Paul speaks repeatedly of "the Spirit" or "the Holy Spirit." He identifies that Holy Spirit in one single chapter of Romans as "the Spirit of life in Christ Jesus" (8:2) and also as "the Spirit of God" (8:14). But he also tells his readers, "You are in the Spirit, since the Spirit of God dwells in you. Anyone who does not have the Spirit of Christ does not belong to him" (8:9).

First, of course, those phrases emphasize the equation between "the Spirit of God" and "the Spirit of Christ." For Paul and by whatever exact term, there is only one Spirit, the Holy Spirit of God in Christ. But, although he speaks, for example, of "the Spirit of [God's] Son" (Gal. 4:6) and the "Spirit of Jesus Christ" (Phil. 1:19), he speaks more usually about the (Holy) Spirit (of God). Second, Romans 8:9 emphasizes a two-way mutuality. To say "You are in the Spirit" means "The Spirit is in you," and to claim "You have the Spirit" means "The Spirit has you." It is absolutely a two-way process but, of course, the basis is a *charis,* a grace, a free gift from God.

In itself, Spirit or spirit is clear enough as the invisible glue that holds any group together around some past memory, present purpose, or future project. It is what turns a collectivity of people into a community of commitment either permanently or temporarily. It manifests itself in what that community thinks, says, and does; plans, decides, and accepts; believes, hopes, and loves. Everything thereafter depends on the *content* of that Spirit. And if you speak of a Holy Spirit, everything depends on the *nature* of that holiness. Finally, if you invoke the Spirit of God, everything depends on the *character* of that God.

You can insist, with Paul, that God's Spirit is a *charis,* a grace, a free gift like, for example, air or gravity. From those analogies, God's Spirit is that which you can neither create by your own action nor deserve by your own virtue. But it is also permanently available for anyone and demands only that you accept it freely and cooperate with it fully. But, even so, you still have to face this question: What is the *character* of that God whose Spirit has overtaken you as a free gift?

THE BODY OF CHRIST. On the one hand, the body is a simple and rather obvious metaphor for any assembly of members united into a community. Any ancient ruler, for example, had both a body personal and a body political. At great length in 1 Corinthians 12:4–31 and in much shorter summary in Romans 12:4–8, Paul compares the multiple talents and gifts within the Christian community to the divergent members and functions of the human body. The body cannot be all head, all hand, or all foot, but needs a variety of members to work successfully. Similarly with the Christian assembly: "There are varieties of gifts, but the same Spirit; and there are varieties of services, but the same Lord; and there are varieties of activities, but it is the same God who activates all of them in everyone" (1 Cor. 12:4–6). So far, so good. And although that metaphor is therapeutically necessary for all community leadership, it is quite standard ancient thinking.

On the other hand, there are delicate hints that Paul intends a deeper meaning for the Christian assembly or assemblies as the communal "body of Christ." Sense the ambiguity in these three sentences: "Just as the body is one and has many members, and all the members of the body, though many, are one body, so it is with Christ" (1 Cor. 12:12); "You are the body of Christ and individually members of it" (1 Cor. 12:27); and "So we, who are many, are one body in Christ, and individually we are members one of another" (Rom. 12:5). There and elsewhere in Paul the metaphorical usage of the assembly body of Christians cedes place to what has been called the *mystical body* of Christ (a term never found in Paul, by the way). Ordinary language expects *mystical spirit* or *physical body,* but the term *mystical body* attempts to express a mystical unity between the Christian assembly and Christ himself—*but in their bodies.* As distinct from the Spirit of Christ, the Body of Christ places emphasis on the crucified and glorified body present in history, Eucharist, and community.

One Spirit of God and one Body of Christ. You are in them and they are in you. Think of these sentences: "For in the one Spirit we were all baptized into one body—Jews or Greeks, slaves or free—and we were all made to drink of one Spirit" (1 Cor. 12:13); and "As many of you as were baptized into Christ have clothed yourselves with Christ" (Gal. 3:27). Those and many, many other Pauline metaphors and statements emphasize the organic unity wherein Christians are intrinsically empowered and internally enabled by God's Spirit within Christ's Body.

Paul's understanding of that organic unity between Christ and Christians receives a rather extraordinary confirmation in one particular place. Writing to the Corinthians, Paul had to answer a question about sexual immorality (*porneia*). It may possibly have been provoked by the practice of sacred prostitution associated with the temple of Aphrodite atop the Acrocorinth. In any case, here is Paul's reaction:

Do you not know that your bodies are members of Christ? Should I therefore take the members of Christ and make them members of a prostitute (*pornēs*)? Never! Do you not know that whoever is united to a prostitute (*pornē*) becomes one body with her? For it is said, "The two shall be one flesh." But anyone united to the Lord becomes one Spirit with him. (1 Cor. 6:15–17; uppercase for "Spirit" added)

Just before that section, Paul gives a list of sinners who would "not inherit the Kingdom of God" and puts "fornicators" (*pornoi*) in first place (1 Cor. 6:9–10). Just after it, he tells his readers,

Shun fornication (*porneian*)! Every sin that a person commits is outside the body; but the fornicator (*porneuōn*) sins against the body itself. Or do you not know that your body is a temple of the Holy Spirit within you, which you have from God, and that you are not your own? For you were bought with a price; therefore glorify God in your body. (1 Cor. 6:18–20)

What is striking, of course, is the rather stunning physicality of that "members of Christ" argument. Christians are not only united in the Spirit of Christ; they are united in the Body of Christ. And that bodily unity not only has negative implications for prostitution; it has positive implications for all the rest of a Christian's bodily life. It also had profound implications for Paul in Roman chains at Ephesus not just *for* Christ, but *in* Christ.

Paul is a mystic. He thinks mystically, writes mystically, teaches mystically, and lives mystically. He also expects other Christians to do likewise. All live together within the Christian understanding of the general bodily resurrection as era rather than moment and as process rather than instant. Mystics, however, stand on the mountaintop and get there from the top downward rather than the bottom upward. That gives them tremendous strength, conviction, and assurance, which makes them rhetorically magnificent as long, of course, as they are united, as Paul was, with a holiness that is itself transcendentally magnificent. But sometimes mystics can be impatient with the slow progress of nonmystics over necessary foothills, indifferent to technical teaching about climbing techniques, and slow about establishing safeguards against the dangers of falling. Not all the problems in Paul's communities came from opponents and enemies. Some also came from having a mystic as mentor.

A footnote. We wonder if Paul's converts would have been different if they had received a prebaptismal copy of the *Didache,* a training manual written by a Christian Jewish community for its new pagan converts probably in Syria and probably contemporary with Paul's own letters. It would have told them clearly and explicitly what was and was not expected from them in this new faith as lifestyle. And then, of course, all those expectations would have had to become fully internalized in them and not just externally legislated. Of course! So it is with every training program, from athletics to war and from ministry to sanctity. But the fact that to be successful every training must eventually become instinctive, second nature, and effortless cannot negate the inevitable necessity of its presence at the start.

The Normalcy of Imperial Divinity

The Roman Empire's divine mandate for cosmic supremacy and prophetic destiny for global ascendancy appeared in written texts, carved images, and urban structures. The Boscoreale Cups, one more example from narrative images, depict the normalcy of Rome's imperial rule as an incarnation here below of the normalcy of heaven's divine dominion (Figures 95–99).

We saw earlier the sequential images of Piety, War, Victory, and Peace on the *Ara Pacis Augustae* in Rome. But, there, any too-overt imperial divinity was carefully muted, if not completely avoided. Not so with these next examples. Here is the "form of God" as piety, war, victory, and peace. Here, in other words, is what the normalcy of civilization would expect from anyone holding "the form of God." Not despotism, of course, but not *kenōsis* either.

A conjunction of divinity and victory, with both flowing from Augustus to Tiberius, is beautifully illustrated on two silver drinking cups from a vineyard villa at Boscoreale on the southeastern slopes of Mt. Vesuvius.

FIGURE 95. One of the Boscoreale Cups, with sacrificial scene.

Somewhat worn even in antiquity, they were buried in a cistern during the eruption of 79 C.E., excavated in 1895 among a hoard of gold and silver objects, stolen, smuggled abroad, and finally bought for the Louvre by Baron Edouard Rothschild. He initially kept the cups for himself, but had them recorded and pictured with the entire collection in 1899. That was rather fortunate because, when his heirs finally donated them to the Louvre in 1991, they were in a much worse state than before, and much is now dependent on the 1899 data.

The cups are a matched pair, form a visual unity, and create a rather extraordinary merging of theology, history, and streaming video. Those narratives appear in very high relief, as the cups are surrounded by a silver shell hammered outward in *repoussé* style, which also made it easy accidentally to damage or even deliberately to vandalize the images. Each cup features two story panels divided by the handles on either side. It is also of great significance that, as Ann Kuttner argues in her superb book *Dynasty and Empire in the Age of Augustus: The Case of the Boscoreale Cups,*

> the cups were made in the lifetime of Augustus before Tiberius' accession in A.D. 14, indeed before his exile in 6 B.C., copying a set of monumental reliefs commissioned by or for the emperor and his heirs in the city of Rome. These reliefs (which can be linked to the Ara Pacis) were made around the time of Tiberius' triumph awarded in 8 and celebrated in 7 B.C., associating with Tiberius' *gloria* projects completed by his brother Drusus shortly before Drusus' death in 9 B.C., both brothers acting under the *auspicia* and to augment the glory of the emperor Augustus. (5)

It is as if the *Ara Pacis Augustae* was totally lost and completely unknown except for images on a pair of silver drinking cups.

One panel of the Augustus cup has him centrally seated in civil toga, not military uniform, and spatially separated from figures approaching on both sides (Figure 96). From the left comes the goddess Roma, the Genius or Spirit of the Roman people, young Amor below, son of Mars and Venus, and, finally, the goddess Venus, who places a small winged image of the goddess Victory on the globe of cosmic authority that Augustus holds in his extended right hand—a scroll is in his left hand. From the right, the war god Mars leads personifications of conquered nations coming (willingly!) from east and west. Note that only Augustus is seated; all other divinities stand to approach him.

FIGURE 96. Panel 1 of the Boscoreale Cups, with seated Augustus receiving the goddess Venus and the war god Mars leading personified barbarian nations.

FIGURE 97. Panel 2 of the Boscoreale Cups, with seated Augustus, surrounded by his court, offering clemency.

The other panel of the Augustus cup has a very similar and centrally seated toga-clad image, but now he is surrounded and even crowded by military officers (Figure 97). On the left, Tiberius's brother, the elder Drusus, appears in armor leading a group of barbarians who offer their children (willingly!) to Augustus. Circled around Augustus are officials carrying symbols of authority; two imperial guards stand to the right. There is a striking parallel as Augustus extends his right hand on each panel: on the first, his extended hand receives victory; on the second, his extended hand offers clemency. If the first panel is narrative theology, the second is narrative history. They are a unity created by a double, twinned image rather than by a single, continuous scenario, as on the Tiberius cup.

FIGURE 98. Panel 3 of the Boscoreale Cups, with armor-clad Tiberius before the Capitoline Temple of Jupiter, sacrificing a bull.

FIGURE 99. Panel 4 of the Boscoreale Cups, with Tiberius riding triumphantly in his chariot.

One panel of the Tiberius cup shows him in armor beside a centrally positioned portable tripod altar (Figure 98). On the left, attendants and officials approach the altar. On the right, four attendants prepare the huge bull for sacrifice before the Capitoline Temple of Jupiter. Piety before victory.

The other panel of the Tiberius cup is split between two scenes. On the right, that bull is being led in ritual procession around to the other side. On the left is the sequence's grand finale as Tiberius stands in a four-horse triumphal chariot (Figure 99). Since the cups are a pair, the overall message is clear. Augustus's divinity (see Figure 96) flows into his own military success (see Figure 97) and, through Tiberius's piety (see Figure 98), into Tiberius's victory (see Figure 99). For Tiberius, all of that is achieved, of course, under, for, and by the auspices of his divine stepfather. Piety leads to victory and victory leads to peace, but all under the serene control of the divine Augustus.

Two short footnotes. First, since only a few percent within the Roman Empire could ever have read or would ever have heard a Virgil, a Horace, or an Ovid, it was images, from smallest coin to largest forum, that were most significant for most people most of the time. Second, did some, most, or all hearers or viewers take that all fictionally or factually, literally or metaphorically, historically or symbolically? Ancients understood those distinctions in the abstract just as well as we do. But, as with advertising for us, those images came in under the radar scope of those distinctions. Do we see a supreme athlete in a TV car commercial literally or metaphorically? If, indeed, we applied that distinction, the advertisement would dissolve into vacuity. It is neither literal nor metaphorical; it is commercial. See the image, get the message, buy the product. Roman imperial theology worked well as a magnificent advertisement for what many people wanted to believe. Was there, in any case, an alternative? Yes, there was, in this next extraordinary claim by Paul.

The Challenge of Kenotic Divinity

The Greek word *kenos* means "empty," the verb *kenoō* means "make empty," and we have created an English adjectival form, *kenotic,* which is intended to sound as strange a word as it is a concept, at least in the context of imperial rule or divine control. It is hard to imagine anything less humanly or divinely normal across place and time, past, present, or presumably future. As is clear from those preceding texts and images, the "form of God" present in an Augustus or any divine emperor manifested itself exactly as expected. It was divinity revealed through that sequence of Piety, War, Victory, and Peace. It was simply normal imperial divinity. And the comparison, now, is not between despotic and kenotic rule, but between divine normalcy and divine kenosis. What, on earth or in heaven, is the "form of God" that empties itself to the opposite, the "form of slave"?

The famous hymn to Christ in Philippians 2:6–11 is often accepted as a pre-Pauline composition adopted and adapted by Paul to inculcate humility in the Philippians. It does seem, however, to be theological overkill for such an ordinary admonition, and it could just as well be Paul's own creation integrating the deep horror of his Ephesian near execution organically and mystically with the execution on the cross of Christ himself.

It is God, he tells the Philippians, who "has graciously granted you the privilege not only of believing in Christ, but of suffering for him as well—since you are having the same struggle that you saw I had and now hear that I still have" (1:29–30). There is, Paul concludes, a profound internal unity between the status of Christ, of Paul, and of the Philippian Christians. All must have "the same mind," like this:

> Christ Jesus . . . though he was in the form of God, did not regard equality with God as something to be exploited, but emptied himself, taking the form of a slave, being born in human likeness. And being found in human form, he humbled himself and became obedient to the point of death—even death on a cross.
>
> Therefore God also highly exalted him and gave him the name that is above every name, so that at the name of Jesus every knee should bend, in heaven and on earth and under the earth, and every tongue should confess that Jesus Christ is Lord, to the glory of God the Father.

It is important not to lose sight of that hymn's extraordinary double challenge, and the second, or internal, one is even more mysterious than the first, or external, one.

The first and more obvious challenge is to Roman imperial theology as the normalcy of civilization in its own time and place. The hymn subverts and even lampoons how millions within the Roman Empire took it for granted that somebody with the "form of God" should act. It probably does the same, actually, for most Christians today. That former challenge could hardly be missed by anyone aware of how the "form of God" was celebrated from Augustus to Nero and especially by anyone aware that it came from a prisoner under investigation and held chained within a proconsular praetorium. Think, once again, and as always in both texts and images, of what Augustus had established as the proper or even normal way to accept and proclaim the "form of God."

The second, less obvious, and more internal challenge is not just to Christians with regard to their own lives as kenotic, or emptied, of those standard hierarchical distinctions of race, class, and gender. Their lives are to be a kenosis of all such distinctions except for, as we see in Chapter 6, the distinction that maintains the primacy of those who best serve and most love the community. There is, however, an even more radical challenge to Christ the Lord and also to God the Father. We articulate that challenge in the form of three questions.

First, was Christ's downward motion, from heaven to earth and earth to cross, just a random test, an accidental trial, a deliberately severe humiliation ritual? Could it have been anything else as long as it was an act of divine obedience? For example, would all have been the same if Jesus had become a leper, suffered for years both humiliation or rejection, and finally died alone and in agony? We think Paul would have insisted that the cross was not just slow, terrible, or humiliating suffering, but also official, legal, and formal Roman public execution. That displayed unmistakably in Christ the clash of gods and gospels between Jewish covenantal justice and Roman imperial normalcy.

Second, granted that Pauline response, did kenosis have implications for the subsequent exaltation process? Was it just a case of accepting crucifixion and then obtaining exaltation, or did that kenotic crucifixion establish a very different mode of exaltation? Did that downward kenosis forever change the upward exaltation in its type, its mode, and its practice? In other words, is the Lordship of Christ, now in Christian heaven, irrevocably different from the Lordship of Caesar, now in Roman heaven? We are not sure how Paul would answer this second question, but it seems that, unless Christ's kenosis was merely a test of obedience, it would mark forever the mode of any subsequent exaltation. Jesus Christ in Christian heaven is not just Julius Caesar in Roman heaven with simply a different name.

Third, does that paradox of kenotic exaltation reflect not only God's Kingdom on earth, but also God's character in heaven? Is kenosis not just about Christ, but about God? We are even less sure how Paul might have answered this question, but we suggest two pointers in a possible direction of response. One is that a single upward motion from humanity to divinity, as with the divine emperor, tells us more about humanity than divinity. But a double motion, from divinity to humanity to divinity, first downward and then upward, tells us more about divinity than humanity. The "form of God" given up by Jesus could hardly be different from the very form of God itself. Is kenosis, therefore, not a passing exercise in ultimate obedience, but a permanent revelation about the nature of God? After all, Paul insisted that Christ was "the image of God" (2 Cor. 4:4). Does, then, a kenotic Son reveal a kenotic Father, a kenotic Christ image a kenotic God?

We started this chapter with two visions of gospel, two tectonic plates grinding steadily against one another beneath the surface of history. Paul's Christian gospel emphasized the equality of all those "in Christ" with one another, a kenosis of background in race and religion, class and gender. We now catch a glimpse of that gospel's deepest foundation. That kenosis within Christian community is basically established by organic and mystical union with a kenotic Christ. But, for Christians, is not Christ *the* revelation of God and, then, is that kenotic Christ not the supreme revelation of a kenotic God? But what, on earth—or in heaven—is a kenotic God? Maybe this? A God whose gracious presence as free gift (Paul's *charis*) is the beating heart of the universe and does not need to threaten, to intervene, to punish, or to control. A God whose presence is justice and life, but whose absence is injustice and death?

6

Who and What Controls
Your Banquet?

The Roman house was no island of privacy, protected by watertight barriers against the world of public life outside. It was porous, constantly penetrated by the outside world; and from its ability to control and exploit this penetration it drew power, status, and profit.

> —Andrew Wallace-Hadrill, *Houses and Society*
> *in Pompeii and Herculaneum* (1994)

The Christian confession and the design of Graeco-Roman houses were at odds with each other.

> —Carolyn Osiek and David L. Balch, *Families in the New Testament*
> *World: Households and House Churches* (1997)

[The Roman Empire] was a society based on patronage, not class stratification. . . . Thus society resembled a mass of little pyramids of influence, each headed by a major family—or one giant pyramid headed by an autocrat—not the three-decker sandwich of upper, middle, and lower classes familiar to us from industrial society. . . . The client of a power wielder thus becomes a powerful man and himself in turn attracts clients. Even those marginal hangers-on to power attract others, more disadvantageously placed, as their clients. . . . It is quite different from the three-layer sandwich of a class society. . . . Patronage virtually precludes independent political relations for those patronized. It also precludes the emergence of class consciousness. Hence the infrequency of concerted political action, aimed at improving their lot, on the part of the disadvantaged masses. . . . Under the divisive local loyalties of patronage, and sundered by ethnic, religious or status differences, the latter were unaware of its class interests. Potential warlords there were, aplenty. But no revolutionaries with alternative programs for setting society to rights.

Indeed, society's wrongs were misguidedly diagnosed (when any form of diagnosis existed).

—Thomas Francis Carney, *The Shape of the Past: Models and Antiquity* (1975)

✑   ✑   ✑

A Eucharist at Corinth

Overture

You come to Corinth from Philippi and Thessaloniki, as Paul did at least twice, but not by the same route or from the same direction. He came across that north-south isthmus whose four-mile width barely holds mainland Greece to the Peloponnese. That connection is now cut by an east-west canal, but then it was only scarred by the *diolkos,* or paved roadway on which ships were hauled between the Ionian and the Aegean seas. Better that than risking Cape Maleas, the Cape Horn of the Mediterranean, at the southeastern tip of the Peloponnese! You are traveling for weeks in the footsteps of Paul through Greece and Turkey. You came from Macedonia through the mountains of central Greece, crossed the western-end narrows of the Corinthian Gulf by ferry that early afternoon, and then came east on the coastal road from Patras to Athens. You are now standing in the middle of the agora or forum of first-century Roman Corinth, looking southward to where the crag of the Acrocorinth looms above the city's battered ruins.

It is Wednesday, May 10, 2000, and the site is relatively empty except for an American pilgrimage group of around forty people listening intently as their Greek guide tells the story of Paul's judgment before Gallio at Corinth from Acts 18:12–17. She mentions that the governor's "tribunal" is termed *bēma* in the Greek of Acts, that it stands right there in front of you with five levels of cut stone still firmly in place, and that, as you can easily see, there is a sign on its front that says in Greek BHMA above the English BEMA. You yourself are thinking about questions like those raised in Chapter 1, about Luke's polemical apologetics on Pauline innocence, Jewish responsibility, and Roman indifference. It hardly seems the best time or place to ask whether Luke is telling history or creating parable in Acts 18:12–17. Besides, that *bēma* was not what was most important, most memorable, and most Pauline about that sunlit day in Corinth as far as you were concerned.

You leave the forum, pass between what the archaeologists have designated as Temples F–G and H–J, and turn north between them and the West Shops forming the frontage for the Roman imperial Temple E some distance behind them. At the end of those shops, off the northwest corner of the forum, is a small Temple C, whose shattered columns and broken stones now serve as seats for that group of forty, who sit together in the shade of a tree nobody can identify. There are pines and cypresses everywhere among the ruins, but this tree has green leaves and large clusters of what look like yellow cherries. The group sits facing the road to Sikyon, one of the most ancient cities in Greece, and across the road is the Temple of Apollo, one of the most ancient temples in Greece (Figure 100). You sit directly off that temple's southwest corner with the right angle of those Doric-capped and still pedimented monolithic columns pointing straight at you. You stand for a moment on top of a solid wall to see beyond road and temple the sparkle of sunlight on water toward the small peninsula dividing into two bays the east-end narrows of the gulf.

FIGURE 100. The Temple of Apollo at Corinth, looking north across the Corinthian Gulf onto the Greek mainland.

The pilgrimage group is seated in Paul's city of Corinth, among ruins he would never have imagined, and under the shade not of urban portico, but of rural tree. They are there at that moment to celebrate the Eucharist. The celebrant consecrates the bread and wine using the traditional words for the Lord's Supper from Paul's first letter to the Corinthians:

> I received from the Lord what I also handed on to you, that the Lord Jesus on the night when he was betrayed took a loaf of bread, and when he had given thanks, he broke it and said, "This is my body that is for you. Do this in remembrance of me." In the same way he took the cup also, after supper, saying, "This cup is the new covenant in my blood. Do this, as often as you drink it, in remembrance of me." (11:23–25)

Those verses, however, were not what made this Eucharist particularly and most appropriately Pauline. Their citation was not only in textual continuity with his letter, but the celebrant was in living continuity with his tradition. Recall, from Galatians 3:28 in Chapter 4, that Paul denied the validity of any outside hierarchies for converted Christians. "In Christ," or as we might say more institutionally and ecclesiastically than mystically and organically, "inside Christianity," a Christian Jew was not superior to a pagan Christian, a free Christian to an enslaved Christian, or a male Christian to a female Christian. Paul took it for granted, therefore, that, within Christianity, women just as well as men could receive the same gifts, offer the same services, and perform the same activities.

What was most Pauline about that day at Corinth for you was not the *bēma* itself. The story about Paul's trial before Gallio and the latter's declaration of Pauline innocence is almost certainly Lukan fiction rather than Pauline fact. It did not happen there to Paul, but is imagined there by Luke. What was definitely Pauline and definitely not Lukan, what was most vitally and importantly in continuity with Paul and not Luke that day at Corinth, was that the eucharistic celebrant was an Episcopal priest, a Cathedral canon, and a woman.

Overview

This chapter works with a series of interfaces—between public space and private house, between sacrificial ritual and social meal, and between artisan's shop and aristocrat's villa. As foundation for it all, we emphasize the hierarchical normalcy of patrons, brokers, and clients as the social *morality* that held Roman society together and, like the air, permeated everyone and everything in that Mediterranean world. Our hypothesis is that especially or maybe even uniquely at Corinth, Paul's radical horizontal Christian equality clashed forcibly with Roman society's normal vertical hierarchy.

We begin with the normalcy of Roman patronal society as evidenced in public areas, public offices, and public meals. We move next from public to private life, as the Greek-style house cedes place to its Roman-style replacement. We accept John Chow's suggestion in *Patronage and Power: A Study of Social Networks in Corinth* that there was a "relationship between many of the problems in 1 Corinthians and the activity of some powerful patrons in the Corinthian church" (189). But we ask especially how Paul, an artisan working with and under an artisan couple like Prisca and Aquila, would ever have encountered "powerful patrons" with normal social expectations that he would behave like an appropriately deferential client, like, say, a financially maintained household philosopher.

Next, an important interlude studies the architectural interchange between shop, apartment, and villa on main-street urban frontage and the consequent social interchange between the freeborn, the freed, and the enslaved in those situations. Patronage, of course, once again. We exemplify not from Corinth, but from Herculaneum and Pompeii because, through the horror of Vesuvius's eruption, those Campanian cities now best exemplify those intertwined factors. As always, we go not just where Paul went, but where we still best see his religious, political, social, and economic world.

Finally, we turn to Paul's volatile relationship with his Corinthian converts across multiple visits and letters. His inaugural insistence in 1 Corinthians 1–4 that God's *power* or *wisdom* is what the normal world calls *weakness* or *stupidity,* and vice versa, is both the best possible commentary on that kenotic divinity from Philippians 2:6–11, just seen in Chapter 5, and a frontal assault on Corinth's patronal normalcy entering the Christian assembly.

We exemplify that devastatingly polemical opener with three case studies. In one, Paul discusses the Corinthians' view of power in refusing, as good patrons, to accept the equality of the Lord's communal supper. In another, he discusses their view of wisdom in refusing, as good Platonists, to accept the materiality of Christ's bodily resurrection. In a final one, he counters their focus on spiritual superiority by admitting that there is superiority, but the superior one is whoever best loves and most serves the assembly.

The Moral Glue of Ancient Public Life

Think of two types of human society at either end of an ideal spectrum. At one end is a *patronal* society whose moral ideology expects offices, benefits, goods, and services by right of assistance from an influential power broker. At the other end is a *universal* society whose ethical theory expects those same benefits by right of request to an appropriate civil servant, commercial agent, or legal advocate. Patronal relations were the ethical mainspring and moral bedrock of the Roman world. They were utterly presumed and ubiquitously normal, just as democratic processes or commercial advertisements are for us. Patronage permeated every level of society, from gods to emperors, emperors to countries, aristocrats to cities, and, indeed, from any have to any have-not. Think of our own still more or less acceptable *political patronage,* enlarge it to structure all of society at every level, consider it morally right, and you have the Roman system. It was needed by rulers, praised by philosophers, proclaimed by inscriptions, and used by everyone.

The ubiquity, universality, and normalcy of patronage and clientage in the Roman world meant that Paul could never have avoided it, and neither could his converts or anyone else. There would always be an inevitable pull to understand Christianity as a new and improved patronal system. People could see patronage as descending from God to Christ to Paul to the assembly, and it could all be understood as a better patronage program than the Roman one all around them. The problem of such an interpretation could have arisen anywhere and could have been created totally from inside any given Christian community. But it would certainly arise where a Christian assembly contained one or more members who were also important in the outside pagan world and who, working with patronage outside Christianity, took it for granted that it would also prevail inside Christianity.

Meeting and Eating in Public

As we saw on the island of Delos in Chapter 1, the sacrifice of animals at temple altars was an indispensable part of ancient civic life. Priests slaughtered, butchered, and burned sacrificial meat on altars, and scholars have explained those rituals in two dimensions. The vertical dimension fostered divine-human relations and preserved what the Romans called the *pax deorum,* the peace with the gods. The horizontal dimension solidified relations between humans and drew the community closer together. Your offered animal became sacred by sacrifice (from Latin *sacrum facere,* "to make sacred") and was returned to you and others as a communal meal. There was no clear separation between those vertical and horizontal dimensions, since the patronal system permeated animal sacrifices, priestly offices, and civic meals as much as any other aspect of ancient life. Public sacrifices did not so much distinguish between immortal gods and mortal humans as announce and reinforce the hierarchy from the gods down along a scale of human participants and spectators. Do not imagine those rituals preoccupied with the vast chasm between divinity and humanity as modern monotheistic religions might be. Imagine, instead, a downward spectrum of patrons from divinity, through royalty, priesthood, aristocracy, and citizens, to the free, the freed, the servile, and the enslaved. Think of sacrificial ritual as strengthening the bonds of loyalty among the many little pyramids built atop each other and made up of layers and layers of patrons and clients. Traces of this system are scattered in the architecture, inscriptions, papyri, and dining rooms of the empire, including in the center of Paul's Corinth.

Augustus in the Agora

TEMPLES. The emperor was at the very tip of the Roman Empire's patronal pyramid. That was as clear at Corinth as it was across those many Mediterranean sites we have already seen. A number of structures, statues, and inscriptions honoring the Roman emperors existed both around and in the midst of this Roman colony's forum—an area some three football fields in size.

First, on the eastern end was the Julian Basilica, a commercial building where excavators found many Julio-Claudian statues placed there by wealthy Corinthians. Second, one of the earliest inscriptions to the divine Julius Caesar, DIVO IUL[IO] CAESARI, was found among Corinth's rubble. Third, a marble architrave testifies to a shrine and statue of Apollo Augustus connected to a series of shops (*Corinth* 8.2, no. 120). Fourth, the forum's western side was made up of temples variously referring to the emperors. One example is the Temple of Venus (Temple F), built under Augustus to honor her as his divine ancestress and as the mother of the Romans. Another is the temple of Augustus's favorite god, Apollo (Temple G), built under Tiberius. Fifth, through a large gap between those smaller temples, stairs led up to a higher terrace upon which stood an exceptionally large temple (Temple E). Although now in a very poor state of preservation, it belonged either particularly to Augustus's sister Octavia or more generally to the imperial cult. It was built at a later date than those smaller temples in front of it but was nevertheless arranged so as not to overshadow them and the entire Corinthian Forum.

FLAMINES. It is clear from the forum's plan that the city architects abandoned strict axiality to create a clear view from Temple E toward the forum's main altar (Figure 101). That altar, along with a nearly complete inscription from 54/55 C.E., point not only to the centrality of sacrifice in civic religion, but also to the importance of patronage. The inscription, on a base whose statue is long gone, honors one Gaius Iulius Spartiaticus, a wealthy and influential Spartan magnate and Corinthian citizen with a long and distinguished record of service to the imperial family. His patron, the divine Claudius, awarded him equestrian rank, and later Nero bestowed upon him various honors for services rendered. The most important of those was to make him *flamen* of the divine Julius and high priest for life in the Augustan house (*Corinth* 8.2, no. 6).

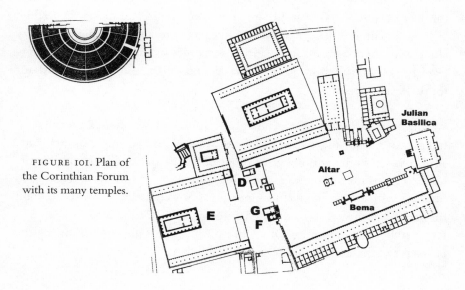

FIGURE 101. Plan of the Corinthian Forum with its many temples.

The *flamines* were one of the priesthoods revived by Augustus, and in Roman colonies they were associated with the imperial cult. As the name implies, the *flamines* symbolically stoked the flames of sacrificial altars, but what that meant in practice was sponsoring entire festivals on behalf of the divine Caesars. That statue base bears the indelible imprint of the patronal system's topmost pyramidal point: Nero is Spartiaticus's patron, and he is Nero's client. But Spartiaticus in turn was patron to the Calpurina tribe, one of the subdivisions in Corinth's citizen body, and their members were his clients. In fact, that tribe had paid for the statue's placement in the forum, which linked them publicly to one of the city's most influential patrons and through him to the emperor himself.

AUGUSTALES. Other groups also sought the emperor's patronage. The *Augustales,* a lower-class group of freed slaves, are known to have existed in cities throughout the empire and especially in Roman colonies like Corinth. In that city's forum, they erected a huge blue marble step with an enormous statue of Augustus, to judge from the large footprints, impression of a spear or staff, and the inscription to the *lares Augusti,* Augustus's own ancestral spirits. None of these Corinthian freed slaves could ever have ascended alone to any height on the pyramidal blocks of Corinth's patronal system. Indeed, each was certainly a client of this or that wealthier and more influential patron. But by banding together as a group, they could collectively purchase such a public monument and thereby demonstrate to city and visitor their devotion to Caesar, hoping, if not for his direct imperial favor, then at least for attention from someone like Spartiaticus. That high visibility along with their semi-exclusive group dynamics would attract many lower-level hangers-on to become potential clients of the *Augustales's* third- or fourth-level patrons.

MEALS. Both of those preceding inscriptions were situated on the central axis of the forum, where sacrifices were offered on imperial birthdays, anniversaries, and any number of other occasions. Though the sacrifice itself was the central ceremony, the often daylong festivities were recognized holidays with a marketlike atmosphere; games were held, and at some point the sacrificial meat was distributed to Corinth's citizens. The *Discourses* of Paul's older contemporary Dio Chyrsostom give some indication of the character of these imperial festivals. He says they, bring together a huge throng of people, litigants, jurors, orators, governors, attendants, slaves, pimps, muleteers, tinkers, prostitutes and craftsmen. Consequently those who have goods to sell get the highest price and there is no lack of work in the city, whether for the transport, or houses or women. (35.15)

We can well imagine the hustle and bustle of Corinth's forum packed with citizens and slaves, local residents and foreign visitors during the various imperial feast days. Processions of priests and officials marched through the city and wound toward the forum's altars, where, with accompanying pomp, prayer, and libation, beast after beast was slaughtered. The meat was then distributed by key priests like Spartiaticus first to honored guests and the city's leading citizens, who in turn took it to their neighborhoods or homes to pass it on to their clients. These in turn, would preside over a banquet with their families, clients, and slaves. Many others would have barbecued right there in the forum and ate the meat as part of a public meal. The entire ceremony, of course, took place under the watchful eyes of the imperial family, whose statues stood in the forum and its surrounding temples.

Reclining at the Asclepeion

In addition to banqueting at citywide festivals and the routine purchase of sacrificial meat at the *macellum,* the meat market supplied by the nearly daily sacrifices at Corinth's other temples, there were other contexts that intimately connected religion and food at Corinth and were likewise permeated by the patronal system. Many pagan temples had accommodations for dining within their sacred precincts, as one might guess from this rhetorical question in, once again, Dio Chrysostom's *Discourses*: "What sacrifice is acceptable to the gods without the participants in the feast?" (3.97).

For such dining, the Corinthian *Asclepeion,* or shrine to Asclepius, is the best-preserved example. Located about a quarter mile down the slope from the Corinthian Forum and just west of the Lecheion Road, the complex was almost entirely excavated by the American School of Classical Studies at Athens in the first half of the 1900s. Although a latecomer to the pagan pantheon, the healer god Asclepius enjoyed tremendous popularity by the first century, largely because his Asclepeia were part shrine, part hospital, part spa, and part country club. Located away from the bustle of the city center and near a spring with ample greenery and shade, the complex had two distinct levels (Figures 102 and 103). On the eastern and upper terrace stood the actual temple and, to the west of it, the *abaton,* where patients "incubated" or slept for a few days, perhaps in a drugged state, under the special care of Asclepius himself. That procedure worked, by the way, to judge from hundreds of terra-cotta body parts left behind as testimonial offerings by those who were cured.

On the western and lower terrace a colonnade surrounded a pool, and on its eastern side three dining rooms (*triclinia*) made up the lower story of the *abaton.* Each of these banquet rooms opened onto the pool, each had permanent stone couches along their internal walls, and those were divided into eleven spaces for guests (the door opening disallowed a twelfth seat). No doubt the sacrifices to Asclepius in that upper-terrace temple provided at least part of the meals. And such meat included pork, to judge from a stat-

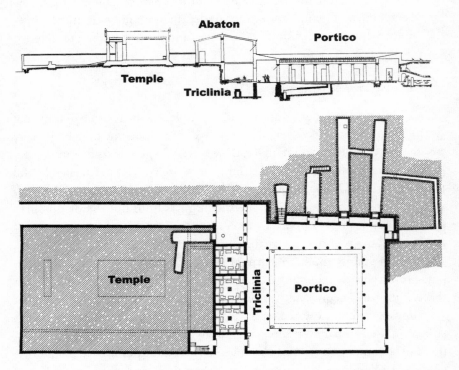

FIGURE 102 *(top).* Section drawing of the Asclepeion, with banquet rooms (*triclinia*) on the lower level opening onto the portico and pool. FIGURE 103 *(bottom).* Plan of the Asclepeion; in the center are three *triclinia* with dining couches around the walls.

uary relief of a reclining Asclepius reaching for a libation of wine, some cakes, and a sacrificed pig. A fire-blackened square stone in the center of each room was used as a place to keep food warm on a brazier.

Those undergoing cures at the shrine were not the only ones to dine there, since Asclepeia were a favorite place for local men of wealth to dine and hold banquets, and the most pressing question for those arriving was their place among those eleven seats. As with every meal in antiquity, there was a clear ranking in the seating arrangement. The most important person or host took the seat in the middle bench looking out onto the pool and was flanked on either side by those next in line. The rest arranged themselves in descending manner to the right and left, with their importance articulated by the distance from the host. Even at a small dinner with eleven or fewer guests, one's social rank and relation to one's patron were matters of public record, and it was always clear who the most important person was, who, that is to say, paid for the banquet. Think, for a moment, about those sacred dining rooms at Corinth's Asclepeion against the background of the following texts from elsewhere in the Mediterranean.

Hierarchy from Outside to Inside

First, an Egyptian papyrus from the middle of the first century B.C.E. preserves the statutes of a group that met probably in the city of Philadelphia and that called itself "the association of *Zeus Hypsistos*" ("the Most High Zeus"). By the way, as you recall from Chapters 1 and 4, many Jews called their God *Theos Hypsistos* ("the Most High God"). This papyrus, now in the British Museum, sheds light not only generally on patronage at meals but also particularly on some of Paul's problems at Corinth. The Egyptian group assembled in the sanctuary of Zeus, probably in a side room like those in the Corinthian Asclepeion, for the express purposes of sharing a meal on at least a monthly basis. The meal was the main event, and the papyrus text tells how they sacrificed, poured out libations, and prayed to (*euchesthai*) Zeus Hypsistos. All of that was apparently followed by heavy drinking.

There was an unmistakable hierarchy inside the group that paralleled the outside world. First and foremost, this group in pre-Roman Egypt honored their Ptolemaic ruler and vowed to "perform the other customary rites on behalf of the god and lord, the king." In addition to acknowledging the king's ultimate patronage, the group's immediate patron was a president named Teephbennis, "a man of parts, worthy of the place and of the company." He and his vice president or assistant, whom also "all are to obey," provided for a monthly banquet. The president was the banquet's host and hence the focus of group loyalty, as stipulated in the papyrus: "It shall not be permissible . . . to leave the brotherhood of the president for another." All the members were seated down the line according to their recognized social rank, which was a contentious and sore point, so that members were prohibited "to enter into one another's pedigrees at the banquet" by challenging their seating location. Order and group cohesion was the ideal, but when members became emboldened or inebriated with wine, the meetings often became more rambunctious; the papyrus warns members "not to speak abusively at the banquet" and even forbids them to "accuse or indict another" in public courts. As Paul commanded in 1 Corinthians 6:1–8, internal disputes should be handled internally. Notice, of course, that it required some degree of economic and political standing, whether as patron or client, to attend such a meal, have such a row, and consider such a public litigation.

Second, a more detailed account of such an association that met for meals, rites, and lots of drinking survives on an inscription from Athens. The inscription, found on a column by German archaeologists in the late nineteenth century, records something like the minutes along with the often amusing rules of an all-male group of devotees to Dionysos, or Bacchus, a group that called itself the *Iobacchoi* (*IG* 2.2.1368; Figure 104). Though the inscription itself dates to the second century C.E., the association had been in place for some time and had built its own meeting hall west of the Acropolis, near the Aereopagus, and in an area long sacred to Dionysos. The 36-by-60-foot hall was divided basilica-like by two rows of columns, with an apselike room at the end where an altar and the inscription were placed (Figure 105). Chiseled into the top of the column above the inscription were two panthers and a *bucranium*, a bull skull wreathed for sacrifice. That indicated that the group sacrificed to Dionysos, and the text itself specifies how the sacrifices were performed and the meat distributed by the *archibakchos* (*archē* literally means "head" or "ruler"; the term *archibakchos* is akin to *archisynagōgos*, the term for the Jewish leader of the synagogue). A series of offices and positions are then spelled out for the sequence of events after the sacrifice: "The *archibakchos* shall offer the sacrifice to the god and set forth the libation . . . and when portions are distributed, let them be taken by the priest, vice-priest, *archibakchos*, treasurer, *boukolikos*, . . ." Hierarchy was everywhere apparent and although, no doubt, it helped to maintain order,

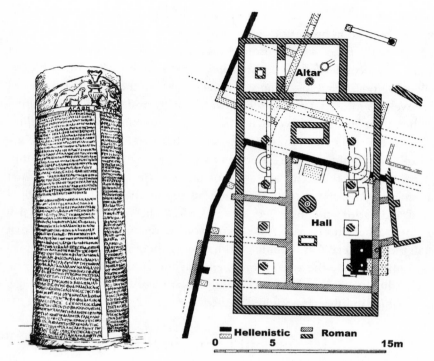

FIGURE 104 *(left).* The inscribed column of the Iobacchoi, who met and drank in honor of Dionysos. FIGURE 105 *(right).* Plan of the meeting hall of the Iobacchoi; note the location of the altar at the very end of the structure.

it also firmly modeled within this inside world what all knew from the outside world.

Small associations like the Iobacchoi, which met inside a room that could accommodate no more than fifty members if standing and much fewer if reclining, replicated the set of patronal pyramids in the outer society. For example, the rules of the Iobacchoi state that "whoever of the Iobacchoi obtains a legacy or an honor or an appointment, shall set before the Iobacchoi a libation worthy of the appointment." Any gain in a member's social status in the civic realm required a corresponding recognition inside the community, and Iobacchoi who received "the office of ward-bearer, membership in the council, presidency of the games, councilorship in the Panhellenic league, membership in the senate, position as legislator, or any position of authority at all" had to pay for drinks; these drinks were at his expense but also in his honor.

Since the outside world's patron-client relations were mirrored within the group, this second-century-C.E. inscription praises especially "the most excellent Herodes Claudios," who was none other than the fabulously rich and very well-connected Tiberius Claudius Atticus Herodes. He had been first teacher, then client, and eventually friend of the emperor Marcus Aurelius, whose patronage made him the best-known benefactor of cities and sponsor of civic buildings in second-century Greece, including his famous odeon south of the Acropolis and not far from the meeting hall of the Iobacchoi. No wonder, then, that upon his appointment as their new chief priest and patron, the inscribed stele records, "They cried out: 'Long live the most excellent priest Herodes! Now you are fortunate; now we are first of all the Bakcheia!'" Although a brotherhood, there was not only competitive ranking inside the association; there was also competition outside even among the various Bacchic associations. Under Herodes Atticus's patronage, these Athenian Iobacchoi vaulted to the top rung.

Meeting and Eating in Private

Archaeologists tend to devote much more attention to public settings with monumental architecture, *euergistic* (from the Greek for "good works") or patronal inscriptions, and artistic sculpture. But the private sphere of homes and households has drawn increased attention of late, and in addition to a few houses here and there across the Mediterranean, the ash- and lava-covered sites of Pompeii and Herculaneum provide, as we see below, something like a tragic open-air museum for ancient domestic life. In what ways should we imagine meeting and dining in private homes? Remember that, as we saw in public space, whether we start with *eating places, meeting spaces,* or *religious rites* in homes, these three areas overlap and intertwine to such an extent that any division is purely artificial. And, to emphasize this once again, none exists in isolation from patronage.

The Greek House

We must start by "thinking away," as Andrew Wallace-Hadrill proposed in that book from this chapter's first epigraph, "the assumptions of the industrial city of the modern Western world" (141) with regard to both antiquity's domestic architecture and social interaction. To do so we return once again to Delos, in the center of the Aegean's Cycladic Islands, for a full set of examples that allow us to begin rethinking our models with the pre-Roman Greek house.

The École Français d'Archéologie in Athens has excavated over one hundred homes on the island, and those, along with others from Olympos, Priene, and Pergamum, provide the basic framework of houses that developed within the Greek cultural tradition and were common from Asia Minor to southern Italy during the Hellenistic era and the centuries leading up to the common era. Although there were differences with regard to size, layout, and decoration among these many houses, they tend to share a set of typical features, some of which are important for understanding the antecedents of later houses in the Roman Empire at the time of Paul.

First, with regard to general shape, most houses were elongated rectangles with one central courtyard onto which rooms opened from both front and rear. In the front by the street were smaller closets and service rooms, latrines and washing rooms, and in the back was typically at least one large room (*oecus maior*), where the family could dine, meet, or receive guests. Over half of the houses on Delos were of this basic type, with a size between 650 and 1,800 square feet. If, just to think about it, Paul were to have gathered in such a home's *oecus maior,* there would have been space for no more than a dozen people, more if they overflowed into the courtyard, which was almost always a possibility in the warmth of the Mediterranean climate.

Second, with regard to status and wealth, more affluent houses distinguished themselves from most ordinary ones by an increased size of between 2,700 to 7,500 square feet, but also by the addition of columns and more rooms around the courtyard. The columns within these so-called peristyle houses (from the Greek *peristylos,* "surrounded by columns") supported a roofed walkway reminiscent of the civic center's porticoed stoa. The added rooms flanked the peristyle courtyard on all sides, were richly decorated with high-quality mosaic floors and well-executed fresco walls, and served as reception rooms for the owner's guests or clients.

Third, with regard to access, most houses in the Greek tradition had a single entrance with a corridor leading to the courtyard, which meant that the courtyard could be tightly controlled with regard to both access and visibility. But many of the more affluent homes, like the House of the Comedians, had two doors (Figure 106). A smaller one led through a vestibule to other service rooms or servants' quarters and only indirectly through a series of internal doors to the courtyard, and a larger one or a double door opened directly onto the elegant peristyle courtyard (Figure 107). When these doors were open, all could see inside with its lavish decorations and appreciate the status of the owner, but certainly not all could enter; many, no doubt, would have to enter through the smaller door and could penetrate no farther than the service areas. It is quite possible, if you follow the Roman architect Vitruvius's description of the Greek house in his treatise *On Architecture,* that there was a threefold division in those houses on Delos. The front part and sides consisted of service areas and shops, as in the House of the Comedians; the center area immediately around the peristyle was what he calls the *andronikon,* the realm of male and public representation, where banquets were held and business transacted; and the rear area was domestic, what he calls the *gynaikonitis* and the realm of women (6.71–75).

Fourth, with regard to distribution, houses on Delos did not cluster into "good" and "bad" neighborhoods as they sometimes do today, and this will be crucial for our understanding of Paul's patronal problems at Corinth.

FIGURE 106. Sketch of the entrance and vestibule of the House of the Comedians on Delos.

Larger and lavishly decorated houses were built next to and mingled with smaller and less luxurious houses, both of which might be fronted with shops or workshops. This pattern is also clear at Asia Minor's Pergamum in an excavated first-century *insula* (Latin for "island"), a term the Romans used for a city's blocks distinguished from one another by different owners, but excavators today use for a city's blocks separated from one another by streets on all four sides. The units within that pie-shaped insula consisted, first, of one enormous peristyle house of some 6,900 square feet; another, smaller peristyle house of 3,500 square feet; and three courtyard houses of around 1,400 square feet apiece. Next, there was a small apartment complex with three rooms on the bottom floor and an unknown number on the now lost upper stories. Finally, there was a series of fourteen shops, workshops, or service rooms on all but one of the sides of the insula that faced the street (Figure 108). We must think about neighborhoods shaped along patronal lines with these Pergameme houses in the Greek tradition but will see it even more with Vesuvian houses in the Roman tradition. A wealthy patron occupied a large and elegant house with his family and slaves. Clustered around that house in descending size were the homes of slaves manumitted by that

FIGURE 107. Sketch of the peristyle courtyard of the House of the Comedians on Delos.

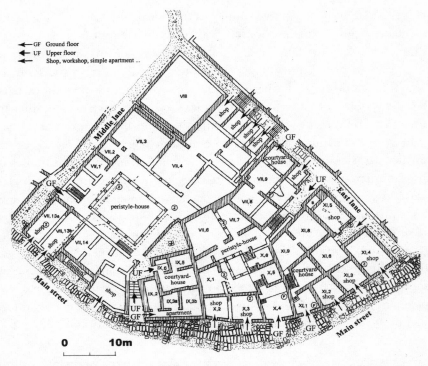

FIGURE 108. Plan of one neighborhood at Pergamum; note the variety of dwellings clustered around the large peristyle house.

family (and their own clients?), other slaves working on commission, and itinerant artisans renting shops and in apartments.

The Roman House

What we mean by the *Roman house* is the continual domestic tradition all across the empire as wealthy owners strove toward greater wealth and their less wealthy neighbors copied the ideal villa of the Roman Empire's urban monoculture. There are, of course, cultural differences between the Italian atrium-and-peristyle villa with double or multiple courtyards as against the Greek single-peristyle house. But we write this section more for the sake of contrasting the modern postindustrial house and family with its ancient Roman and patronal counterpart. We cite once again Andrew Wallace-Hadrill's superb book *Houses and Society in Pompeii and Herculaneum:*

We distinguish the commercial from the residential; shops, workshops, offices, and factories from houses. The Roman town draws the lines elsewhere, and though spatial, architectural, and decorative contrasts were constructed between petty trade and dignified sociability, they might nevertheless coexist in the same house. . . . We must reconstruct a world in which the rich frequently lived in close contiguity with their dependents, slaves and freedmen, clients and tenants, the sources of their economic and social power. (141)

And we stress throughout that Paul, his correspondence, and his problems must be placed in that context, whose essential elements we will try to sketch from bits and pieces of evidence.

In its basic plan, the Roman house usually had two open areas, an atrium with its top open to light and rain and a peristyle courtyard that was usually a garden area. Shops and service areas usually flanked the main entrance. Most notable about the Roman house is that the sleeping rooms were remarkably small and were usually right off or upstairs and overlooking the atrium or peristyle courtyard. Most of life's activities would have taken place around the atrium, in the reception area where the father would greet clients, or in the office where business could be conducted.

RELIGIOUS RITUAL. Unlike homes in the modern West, even the humblest house in the Roman world had an area dedicated to the household gods, the so-called *lares* or *penates*. This could be a small niche in a wall for tiny statuettes or, in smaller houses, a wall painting of a liturgical nature, as often found on Delos. Mid-level to larger homes had an area that was almost shrinelike called a *lararium*. There, the household gathered under the head of the household's supervision, perhaps even on a daily basis, for various rituals. These *lararia* were usually in the atrium or the kitchen, which were areas suitable for sacrifices. One of the most elaborate and certainly expensive household shrines was found in Pompeii's House of the Vettii. At over 10 feet tall, the shrine was a set of columns and pediment in half-relief. It had a bright blue tympanum with a *patera,* or flat dish that was used in sacrifices, and a central fresco with two dancing *lares* whose drinking horns suggest libations. Below, a snake as a sign of fertility slithers toward the altar (Figure 109).

But the very rich could set aside more than a wall space, however well decorated, for their religious observances. Two examples. Neapolitan Cumae

FIGURE 109. The household shrine, or *lararium,* from the House of the Vettii in Pompeii.

was famous of old as the location of the Sybil's prophetic oracles, but possibly more famous in the first century as a wealthy resort area. In 1992 excavations, archaeologists found what they first thought was an Isis temple, with a set of three granite statues, a little over a foot tall, and a podium. The three headless statues were of Isis, a sphinx, and a priest that was inscribed with hieroglyphics. After three more seasons of fieldwork, however, the excavators concluded that the structure was in fact a small private shrine, or *sacellum,* within a private seaside mansion. Was that *lararium* only for the family's rituals, or was it open to all those under its patronage, even and especially those not dwelling in his house?

An even more spectacular discovery was made at Pompeii in 1909. Italian archaeologists uncovered perhaps the world's most famous frescoes in a house outside the city that they later called the Villa of the Mysteries (Figures 110 and 111). Wall murals on all sides of its Room 5 depict various scenes relating to the rituals of the god Dionysos, and an extremely large number of women are represented in them. Among the mural depictions are a woman startled by Dionysos, a scroll being read (some sacred text?), a revelation behind a sheet (of the phallus?), a daemon flagellating a young girl (an initiate?), dancing maenads, and a woman with cupids grooming herself as a matron looks on (the initiate as bride?). This room was separated from the atrium by at least one other room and was thus relatively inaccessible and invisible, and the function of that frescoed room is intensely debated. Was it hidden as a cultic room for initiation into the mysteries? And, if so, we emphasize its location inside a private villa. Was it a bridal prepara-

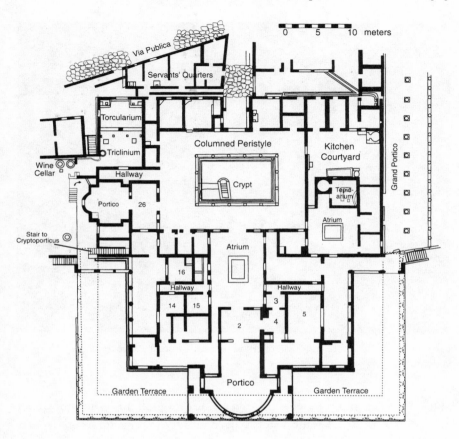

FIGURE 110. Plan of the Villa of the Mysteries; Room 5 is where the Dionysian frescoes were discovered.

tory room? (If you go there on Saturday afternoons—at least in summer—several Neapolitan couples will be having their wedding photos taken in that room!) Was it the master bedroom? A *triclinium,* or dining room, for family and guests?

It is very hard to decide, but keep this in mind. There is no other evidence of Dionysos's worship anywhere within that villa, although two other shrines were discovered there. One was in the north courtyard with a tufa altar and statues of Hercules and an unidentifiable goddess. The other was near the hearth with painted images of the Roman handicraft goddess Minerva and, ironically, the fire god Vulcan. A tile was also found dedicated to the grain goddess Ceres. But there was no other evidence for Dionysos. In

FIGURE III. Reading of a scroll and offerings on a plate from the frescoes of the Villa of the Mysteries in Pompeii.

the end, we are not sure what to make of that room, but for our purposes it shows how religion was intimately woven into the architectural and decorative fabric of life in the Roman house.

The preponderance of religious imagery in Roman urban houses, particularly in that most decorated room, the *triclinium,* for banquets and dinners, can also be seen at Ephesus, the city from which Paul wrote his letters to the Corinthians. A set of seven residential units from around the time of Paul were excavated at Ephesus. They slope upward on a terrace, and those on the lowest level have shops and taverns fronting Curetes Street, which funnels modern-day tourists through the ruins from entrance to exit. Today access is restricted for the sake of ongoing conservation, but in antiquity pedestrians on that same street or along one of its steep alleys caught passing glimpses of wealth and decoration inside those villas. They saw marble and mosaic floors, walls painted with faux marble in geometric and floral patterns, and rich religious or cultural decorations. They saw a niche with Dionysos's wedding to Ariadne in glass mosaic; Pan and a Satyr, associates of the wine god, in a vaulted ceiling's stucco; and a painted bust of the philosopher

Socrates. They saw, but this was a century after Paul, a set of panels depicting Apuleius's religio-erotic novel *The Golden Ass,* a tale of one believer's conversion and initiation into the worship of the Egyptian mother goddess Isis.

Very few houses have been excavated at Corinth from the time of Paul, but one badly damaged *triclinium* mosaic survives from the first century in the Anaploga Villa. The banquet room was probably about 375 square feet and could easily hold the usual nine reclining guests. More of course, and perhaps as many as two to three dozen, could be accommodated in the atrium around the pool that collected rainwater. But a better-preserved example survives from central Greece.

RELIGIOUS DINING. In Dion, at the foot of Greece's Mt. Olympus, a large and magnificent villa was discovered in 1982, and it sheds light on the combination of religion and dining in Roman houses. The complex consisted of an entire city block, of which the southern third was made up of a bathhouse, apparently public judging by its sheer size, that was connected to the villa by a corridor from one of several atriums. To that atrium's south a wide opening flanked by two columns led to several rooms, the largest of which was a small temple or large shrine dedicated to the god Dionysos. It was an elongated rectangular room at whose eastern end was a beautiful larger-than-life statue of a now headless Dionysos. His legs strike the classical weight-shifting counterpose, his hair flows down each shoulder, and grape clusters are positioned to his left. On the floor was a mosaic depicting the enthroned wine god, scepter in hand and ivy wreath on head. Clearly, Dionysos was worshiped there by that household.

Just through the atrium there was a nearly 1,000-square-foot *triclinium* decorated with an exquisite mosaic with Dionysiac themes. It was laid out in a typical fashion, bordered on three sides by large white-colored areas without any mosaic but with marks for the couches. Those wooden couches have not survived, but some of their bronze decorative attachments are still extant. One is shaped like a horse's head, another like a satyr's bust, another like Heracles's head, and all are masterpieces of Macedonian metalworking. The central panel of the mosaic itself shows Dionysos riding his chariot and emerging from the sea, wreath and staff in one hand, drinking cup in the other, surrounded by two centaurs holding a vase and wine krater. Is this banquet hall evidence that the cult of Dionysos met in this house? Diners were certainly invited to enjoy wine, but also to do so in luxury, especially in the luxury of what the Romans called *otium,* or "leisure." The patron of the house was no doubt honored to the point of worship by some of those clients lucky enough to taste both wine and *otium*.

Social Patronage and Street Frontage

If, as John Chow has argued persuasively, Paul first encountered "powerful patrons" at Corinth, how did he get into contact with them? Furthermore, what about that married couple, Prisc[ill]a and her husband Aquila, who, on the one hand, seem to be patrons of Paul at Corinth, but, on the other, continue as his employers, friends, and co-working artisans?

Notice, first of all, that Priscilla is often mentioned in first place, as being more important than her husband. They are located sequentially in Rome, Corinth, Ephesus, and finally back in Rome. They are clearly very, very important, something on which both Luke's Acts and Paul's letters agree.

They are at Corinth in Acts 18:2–3: "There he [Paul] found a Jew named Aquila, a native of Pontus, who had recently come from Italy with his wife Priscilla, because Claudius had ordered all Jews to leave Rome. Paul went to see them, and, because he was of the same trade, he stayed with them, and they worked together—by trade they were tentmakers." That, by the way, was a difficult trade, whether in linen or leather, because much of it was monopolized by the military or for the military. Then, in Acts 18:18–19, they move to Ephesus: "After staying there [at Corinth] for a considerable time, Paul said farewell to the believers and sailed for Syria, accompanied by Priscilla and Aquila. . . . When they reached Ephesus, he left them there, but first he himself went into the synagogue and had a discussion with the Jews." They are still there in Acts 18:26: "He [the missionary Apollos] began to speak boldly in the synagogue; but when Priscilla and Aquila heard him, they took him aside and explained the Way of God to him more accurately."

Later when Paul writes to Corinth from Ephesus he adds, "The churches of Asia send greetings. Aquila and Prisca, together with the church in their *house,* greet you warmly in the Lord" (1 Cor. 16:19). Finally, they move back to Rome, presumably after the death of Claudius and the accession of Nero in 54 C.E. They are there when Paul says, "Greet Prisca and Aquila, who work with me in Christ Jesus, and who risked their necks for my life, to whom not only I give thanks, but also all the churches of the Gentiles. Greet also the church in their *house*" (Rom. 16:3–5, italics added).

What does Paul mean and do we understand by that *house* of Priscilla and Aquila at Ephesus and Rome? What type of *house* and *house*-assembly did that couple maintain in those two cities. Was *house* a shop, an apartment, or a villa? If a shop, was it a workshop with a back room or an attic? And here is the key question: If a workshop, was it rented from an adjacent villa? Was some shop-villa interaction the way in which artisans like Priscilla, Aquila, and Paul came into contact with "powerful patrons" at Corinth? We are trying to understand Paul's world not so much by going where he actually was as by going where, in the vagaries of time and place, his world is still preserved most fully and can still be seen most clearly. For shop and villa interaction, therefore, you go to Herculaneum or Pompeii in order to understand Corinth or Ephesus.

Interlude: The World's Last and Eternal Night

"Many lifted up their hands to their gods," the younger Pliny wrote to his friend Tacitus at the end of the first century, "but a great number believed there were no gods, and that this night was to be the world's last, eternal one" (*Letters* 5.16; 5.20). It was the night of August 24, 79 C.E., and since noon of that day Vesuvius had hurled gas, ash, and pumice 12 miles into the air above the cities of Pompeii and Herculaneum. Pliny said that the initial eruption looked like a huge umbrella pine (we would have said a giant mushroom cloud). "Like an immense tree trunk it was projected into the air, and opened out with branches. I believe that it was carried up by a violent gust, then left as the gust faltered; or, overcome by its own weight, it scattered widely—sometimes white, sometimes dark and mottled, depending on whether it bore ash or cinders." The younger Pliny watched from the relative safety of his uncle's official residence at Misenum about 20 miles across the Gulf of Naples from Vesuvius. The elder Pliny lived there as prefect of Rome's Mediterranean battle fleet. A messenger had come from Stabia, presumably by boat, to ask him for help after the eruption started. He took a squadron of fast warships on a search and rescue mission straight across the bay and lost his life in an action as brave in intention as it was foolish in execution (he slept there that night).

That first day meant lethal danger at worst and timely flight at best. But around midnight the second and far more terrible act began. Down its southern side toward Pompeii (Figure 112), 6 miles away with twenty thousand inhabitants, and down its western side toward Herculaneum, 4 miles away with five thousand inhabitants, Vesuvius poured a ground surge and pyroclastic flow, a hot, molten avalanche of gas, ash, and pumice (but not red–hot lava). It moved at over 50 miles an hour with a temperature of about 750 degrees Fahrenheit and buried Pompeii to a depth of almost 20 feet, Herculaneum to a depth of almost 70 feet.

In the artificial darkness of the next day's non-dawn our only extant eye-witness described that flow as a "horrible black cloud ripped by sudden bursts of fire, writhing snakelike and revealing sudden flashes larger than lightning." The Vesuvian cities were sealed in tufa, that volcanic stone that is strong enough to allow five-story-deep catacombs around Rome. The dead lay where ash had suffocated them, the sea had trapped them, or the flow had engulfed them. Their food, down to an eggshell, is often undamaged, and their unfinished meals remain on the tables from which they fled. Their furniture and artifacts stayed where they left them, the wood often completely intact, but also completely carbonized. Sexual images, graffiti, and symbols survived abundantly, election slogans remained on walls, and in a few cases legal documents remained in homes. Finally, there was a line from Virgil that some graffitist began to write but never got to finish: "All were silent . . ."

It is early September of 2003 in Naples, Italy. Europe's deadly summer heat wave has just broken, first with sudden thunderstorms that flooded downtown areas near the port, and then with strong breezes that cleared completely the usual shroud of summer haze. Tiberius's island retreat at Capri, the entire Sorrento peninsula, and the volcano within a volcano of Vesuvius are all etched sharply against a clear blue sky. You are there that

FIGURE 112. Forum of Pompeii with Vesuvius in the background.

week to study two archaeological sites not mentioned in the New Testament and never visited by Paul. You are there to look at the architectural relationship between villa and shop in Herculaneum and Pompeii, to think about that relationship in terms of the ubiquitous normalcy of social patronage in the Mediterranean world, and to bring together social patronage and street frontage with the help, once more, of Andrew Wallace-Hadrill's plans, diagrams, and texts. You are in Campania because volcanic horror preserved there far more, far better, and far fuller examples of those villa-and-shop combinations than you can see at Corinth or Ephesus.

House of the Bicentenary

You go first to the House of the Bicentenary on the main street, Decumanus Maximus, of Herculaneum (Figure 113). It is named for its discovery in 1938, on the two hundredth anniversary of that buried city's first "excavations." Behind you is a high, buttressed tufa wall supporting a built-up section of the modern town of Ercolano-Resina with the ancient city's forum buried somewhere beneath it. The first century's molten mud eventually

FIGURE 113. The Decumanus Maximus at Herculaneum, with Insula V and the House of the Bicentenary on the left.

became enshrouding stone, and you stand where the depth of the volcanic effect obscures any sight of the volcanic cause. But you cannot even get close to the excavated frontage of the House of the Bicentenary or its adjacent buildings, as steel barriers keep visitors at a distance that seems to expect the entire two-storied edifice to come tumbling down at any moment. You are reminded, forcibly, that excavation without conservation is simply postponed destruction. But at least you can see two stories and even the holes for the upper balcony's beam supports are still extant all along the front.

Why search for Paul at the House of the Bicentenary? In a very small second-story room overlooking the open courtyard of the House of the Bicentenary there was a cross-shaped mark against a painted white background with a now carbonized wooden cabinet below it. Some have seen that as the earliest Christian cross and described the room as a Christian oratory with a prie-dieu before a crucifix. Both are unlikely and close even to anachronistically impossible; the cross did not become a widely used symbol until the fourth century and very probably the cross shape was an imprint of a device for suspending another chest from the wall. It may even have been a *lararium,* that is, as you may recall, a shrine for the household gods. But, in any case, you are not there for that "sign of the cross" or because that House of the Bicentenary may have once housed "Christians" in an upstairs apartment. You examine that house and others around it to understand the architectural and social relationships of those houses, all as crucial contemporary background for Paul's house-assemblies and especially for his difficulties with patronage at Corinth.

The insula here is actually a complex of one large elegant dwelling with rental apartments upstairs and frontage shops downstairs. It is precisely that three-way usage that is your focus. You are interested in the House of the Bicentenary as an example of the porous architectural and social relationships between house, apartment, and shop. For example, the long hallway of the house was necessitated by the shops on either side. Behind them, the house opened up to its full splendor.

There are six doors facing you from right to left as you look at what the archaeologists term Insula V, Nos. 13–18 (Figure 114). One double-width door, deliberately taller than all the others, is the entrance to the main villa, the House of the Bicentenary, which, with its 6,500 square feet of space, is among the finest villas so far excavated at Herculaneum. Two single-width doors open onto stairs and allow private access to two elegantly decorated upstairs apartments with several rooms in each. The final three triple-width

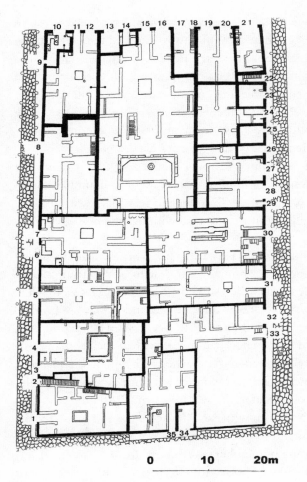

FIGURE 114. Plan of Insula V and the House of the Bicentenary at Herculaneum; note the proximity of doors Nos. 13–18.

doors all indicate shops. One with a back room has about 430 square feet of space. Another with 279 square feet connects internally to one of the two apartments. And the final one has a back room and connects internally to the House of the Bicentenary's atrium. Six doors: one for a villa, two for apartments, and three for shops. Think about the architectural and social interconnections of those three categories. Who owns what and how much? Do enslaved or freed persons run the shops? Are they sold, rented, or sublet? Within that triple complex what were the relationships between patrons and clients, friends and neighbors, the free, the freed, and the enslaved?

Luckily an archive of legal documents found in an apartment overlooking the peristyle garden at the back of the House of the Bicentenary provides a gold mine of information. The seventeen wooden tablets of several waxed sheets apiece were court-sealed to prevent tampering, and they tell a fascinating if unfinished story about the intricate and intimate relationships within a single extended family between the husband, wife, and child, on the one hand, and between the freeborn, freed, and enslaved, on the other.

The freeborn Caius Petronius Stephanus married the freedwoman Calatoria Themis. He bought her a slave woman, Vitalis, who bore a daughter, Justa, to an unidentified father (well, yes, that's what we think too, probably!). Vitalis was freed and renamed Petronia Vitalis, and Justa was brought up "like a daughter" within the family. For years all went well until Petronius and Calatoria had their own children. Trouble then arose between Calatoria and Vitalis, so Vitalis decided to leave and take with her the now grown-up Justa.

First, Vitalis sued Petronius and was awarded Justa, but with all the child's earlier upkeep costs going to Petronius. Next, Vitalis and Petronius both died. Then, Calatoria sued Justa. She claimed Vitalis was still a slave when Justa was born, so Justa was slave-born, and she demanded that Justa and all her by then extensive property be returned to her. Justa defended herself, but Vitalis had been freed by oral declaration rather than formal manumission, so there was no written evidence of when it happened, and none, therefore, on whether Justa was born before or after her mother's freedom. If before, she was slave-born; if after, she was freeborn. With no documents available, everything depended on witnesses. The case was too much for the Herculaneum authorities, and it was relegated to the urban praetor in the Forum of Augustus at Rome (remember those courts from Chapter 2?).

Two witnesses, both freedmen, spoke for Calatoria. Five witnesses, two freeborn, two freed, and one whose name is lost, spoke for Justa. Of those the most important voice was that of the freedman Caius Petronius Telesphorus, whose Greek name was now preceded as usual by the first two names of the master who had manumitted him. For the first act of the drama, in December of 75, Telesphorus, who, as Calatoria's tutor, had come with her to Petronius's house, stood bail for her reappearance in court. But, in the second act, Calatoria has a new bondsman, and Telesphorus swore that Vitalis was his *colliberta,* freed along with him, that he himself (probably as Petronius's steward) had overseen the repayment of those upkeep costs for Justa, and that he knew her to have been freeborn.

You do not know the outcome of the case or whether that dossier belonged to Calatoria or Justa. Apparently no decision was handed down from

Rome between 75 and 78, and by 79 Vesuvius rendered the case quite terribly moot. But you think long about its implications. Justa must have done very well to have sustained a long-distance court case at Rome with all the attendant expenses for herself and her witnesses. Female and male, freeborn and freed interacted within boundaries that might have been all quite clear in theory, but were marvelously messy in practice. In Herculaneum's Insula V.13–18 ambiguities of architecture and structure intersect with those of social status and family relationship.

Shrine of the Augustales

You walk northwest from the House of Bicentenary along the façade of Insula VI and think about another case where text and architecture intersect. Before you are eleven doors designated as Nos. 12–22. Two are to villas, and seven are to shops, but both of those villas have a street-frontage shop on either side of their long hallways. Also, in the case of the villa designated as No. 17, the twin shops at Nos. 16 and 18 open directly into that villa at the back. Finally, at the corner of the insula there are two front entrances (and two side entrances) into the Hall of the Augustales (Figure 115).

Luckily, once again, two sets of extant texts shed light on the interaction of architecture and society, house and patronage in Insula VI. A dossier of tablets was found in the House of the Dark Salon, No. 13 at the insula's east end, and fragments of inscribed marble plaques were found in the west-end Hall of the Augustales, Nos. 21–22. These tablets concern one Lucius Venidius Ennychus, whose characteristically Greek cognomen is embedded in a standard Roman triple name. That indicates that he was a freed slave, but he was also the owner of that House of the Dark Salon, which, at 6,400 square feet, was the same size as the House of the Bicentenary.

The texts show his arduous climb up the steps of the city's patronage pyramid. Two tablets from 60 C.E. show that Venidius and his wife, Livia Acte, had a one-year-old daughter. That record was crucial since, on her first birthday, the father had fulfilled the final legal requirement for a freed slave to become a Roman citizen, namely, bearing a child who lived to one year of age. When she survived her first year, he issued a declaration before a magistrate and became a full citizen, which accorded him not only a measure of status, but prevented his property from reverting to his former owner-patron upon his death. He was thus poised to become a patron to more disadvantageously placed freedmen or slaves.

Another set of documents records how Venidius first testified before the local official that he merited the "right to honor," and he provided the court with a list of ten men, apparently either *decurions* (councillors) or Augustales, to adjudicate his case. Since a freed slave, even one who became a citizen, could not hold public office, the honor to which he aspired was very likely as priest of Augustus and member of the Augustales, one of the few ways that well-to-do freedmen could gain honor and a measure of civic status. The next document records how Venidius, in turn, would be adjudicator for another. The Augustales in a way circumvented the rigid patronal system by allowing freedmen to form a group in the city that was linked more directly to the emperor's patronage, a move that in turn made them patrons to freedmen aspiring to join the Augustales. Groups like the Augustales functioned as a sort of social pressure valve and antidote to social unrest by permitting a measure of patronage among the most successful freedmen through honoring and pledging loyalty to the emperor.

Venidius became a member of the Augustales and his name is recorded on a marble list in the Hall of the Augustales on the Insula VI's opposite corner. He is listed on that inscription for helping to elect two brothers as new members and celebrating their election with a feast. They, of course, were

FIGURE 115. Hall of the Augustales at Herculaneum, where Venidius was able to climb the social pyramid.

now his clients. The patronal system had a circular and spiraling effect. The freed Venidius had accumulated wealth and citizenship, but, more important, enough connections to list ten members of the Augustales, any one of whom picked by the *duumvir,* or head councillors, would support his candidacy. He was then elected to that group and put on a banquet for them at enormous expense. Thereafter, in turn, he made it on other applicants' ten-man lists, had his name inscribed on marble, and feasted at subsequent banquets.

The House of the Dark Salon, just down the street from the Hall of the Augustales and both facing the forum, was quite a reward for the hardworking and now well-connected Venidius, but his status in the eyes of others and especially the number of his clients were certainly his greatest honors. The *taverna,* or bar, next door to his house had a painted advertisement for drink prices, but the real advertisement was for Venidius's success and new status. With the words "AD SANC(tum)" he named his little *taverna* "At the Sign of the Holy Man" and depicted a laureled priest with scepter and *patera* in hand above its entrance. Venidius could now revel in his emergence as a patron and social personality.

House of the Faun

You stand next before the second-century-B.C.E. House of the Faun in Pompeii (Figure 116). It is located in the northwestern area of the excavations and archaeologically designated as Insula 12 of Region VI. It is sometimes abbreviated as VI.12.2 because No. 2 is its very main, very high, and very formal doorway. Actually, however, at 6 acres, or 31,000 square feet, it takes up the entire insula block and is more a palatial mansion than a house. Like other insulae blocks in that area, its axis is northwest to southeast, with the primary street to the south, a secondary one to the north, and smaller alleys to the west and east. Even today you can enter from either that primary or secondary street. You are now standing on the main street, appropriately called Via della Fortuna today, and immediately in front of that most imposing main entrance. From where you are standing you can see to your right another entrance, but what interests you is that each of those entrances is flanked by two shops. There are six doors in all, but the main entrance dominates all the others. The mansion's primary-street frontage displays two entrances at Nos. 2 and 5 along with four shops at Nos. 1 and 3, 4 and 6. And those two shops flanking that striking main entrance open not only, of course, to the street, but also inward to the villa's atria. After looking at this "palatial mansion" and others near it, Paul Zanker, in *Pompeii: Public and Private Life,* concludes,

The grandest houses lay in the most important commercial thorough-fares. Rich families employed the advantages of these sites by includ-ing space for shops on the street side of their new houses from at least the early second century B.C. Such premises often had access to a bed-room on a mezzanine floor above the shop, called a *pergula* in Latin. The phrase *natus* [born] *in pergula* was used to refer to someone of humble origins. These shops were run by dependents of the wealthy owners, in most cases probably slaves or freedmen. (41–42)

Those two main-street entrances apparently set a standard, since this con-spicuously luxurious villa has two of everything important. Those two frontal entrances open into two separate atria, the western one continuing into the villa's *tablinum,* or reception room, the eastern one opening into a bath complex. There are also two open-air gardens with columned and cov-ered porticos on all four sides. With a normal-sized one to south and a far

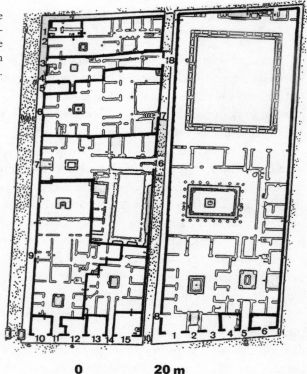

FIGURE 116. House of the Faun at Pompeii (right-hand section), showing the close connection between shops and house.

0   20 m

larger one to north, those two peristyles take up about two-thirds of the villa's entire space. The luxury of those open spaces is matched by the splendor of the villa's mosaics. Some with geometric designs were left on the entrance and reception room floors, but the three most famous examples have been removed to the walls of the National Archaeological Museum in Naples. An erotically suggestive mosaic of satyr and nymph came from an upstairs bedroom immediately to the right of the main entrance. An anatomically detailed mosaic of fish and seafood came from a *triclinium* between the main atrium and the first peristyle. But, above all else, this villa once contained one of the most famous mosaics in the world.

Between those two peristyle gardens was a special space that could be seen from either direction. On the floor, surely for looking at rather than walking on, was a mosaic of around a million and a half tiny tiles, or tesserae. It was copied from a Hellenistic painting of around 300 B.C.E. depicting a battle between Alexander the Great and Darius of Persia (Figure 117). Its

FIGURE 117. Detail of the Alexander mosaic at the House of the Faun.

master artisan froze in eloquent stone the ferocity of Alexander and the fright of Darius at the battle of Issus. You may remember meeting this image at the beginning of Chapter 3. The mansion's spatial and aesthetic luxury serve only to underline the normalcy of frontage shops owned directly or indirectly by the mansion's aristocrats. Nos. 1 and 3 connect into the mansion's western atrium, but Nos. 4 and 6 do not. Those latter shops are each about 270 square feet, and No. 4 has stairs to a second floor. "An excellent example," as Wallace-Hadrill says, "of the irrelevance of shops in the façade to the standing of a house" (210).

A very helpful Italian-English plan of the excavation on sale at Pompeii's bookstore color-codes nine different types of excavated structures: public buildings, temples, urban supply systems, guilds and associations, shops, inns and taverns, private homes with workshops, private homes, and market gardens. Even a glance across that color-coded map shows the extent of "shops" (yellow) along the street frontage of "private dwellings" (buff), not to speak about those "private homes incorporating workshops" (purple).

Mansion and Shop

Those complexes are only three examples of the intimate architectural and social relationship between villa and shop on main-street frontages in both Herculaneum and Pompeii, that is, in two places where we still have abundant evidence of that connection. From his detailed analyses of those buried Campanian cities, Wallace-Hadrill draws these general conclusions:

> The urban elite, best defined by their tenure of public office, drew revenue from trade and agriculture without discrimination and distanced themselves from commercial activity by the pattern of their lives (i.e., by not engaging in "sordid occupations" in person) without feeling any need to distance themselves physically. . . . Massive social contrasts are apparent, in the gulf between the most magnificent mansions and the humblest tabernae [shops, workshops, taverns] or cenacula [apartments]. Yet the gulf is constantly bridged, by contiguity and mutual dependence. We have seen, not so much a gulf between "rich families" and "poor families," but the promiscuity of the big household, in which rich and poor, and indeed male and female, young and old, inhabit the same spaces, separated by social rituals rather than physical environment. We have seen the (to Roman eyes) "sordid"

world of trade and commerce intertwined with the world of luxury and grandeur. (127, 185–86)

With that always in mind, you turn back from Herculaneum and Pompeii to Corinth, from those towns where Paul never visited to one he visited more often than he wanted. You take with you certain questions. When you speak of a *house*-church in Paul's urban world, what type of building are you imagining? Is it a freestanding *villa,* the rarest dwelling in a Roman city? Is it an *apartment,* say on the ground floor of a five-story building, maybe opening into a garden courtyard? Is it a *shop* or *workshop,* separated from the street by its counter and with the dwelling behind it or upstairs? Comings and goings to a shop would not be too noticeable especially before it opened or after it closed. Is it, above all else, a shop that is directly or indirectly part of a villa, a shop run by the villa's slaves, freedmen, freedwomen, or dependents? And what, in that case, about the architectural and social osmosis between shop and mansion, artisan and aristocrat? That gives us another hypothesis for this chapter, but secondary to and dependent on that first one about the problem of "powerful patrons" at Corinth. It combines social patronage with street frontage.

Recall that, as we saw above, Priscilla and Aquila employed Paul in their workshop at Corinth according to Acts 18:2 and that they had a house-assembly according to 1 Corinthians 16:19. Since they moved around so much, that must have been rented space. Our second hypothesis is that their rented workshop was a functional part of a villa on a main street in Corinth and that its ownership brought them all, willy-nilly, into contact with more elevated circles than Paul had experienced up to that point.

There is even tantalizing archaeological evidence for that level of higher patronage at Paul's Corinth. In 1929 American excavators working just below the theater discovered a paving stone from the first century that once bore an inlaid bronze inscription (Figure 118). The bronze had been long since removed, but the hollowed-out spaces could still be read: ERASTVS. PRO. AED. S. P. STRAVIT, "Erastus, in return for his aedileship, laid this pavement at his own expense." This Erastus was elected to civic office as an *aedilis* in charge of public buildings and facilities and in exchange paid for the pavement (patronage then, bribery now?). In his letter to the Romans Paul mentions one Erastus, "the city treasurer" (*oikonomos*), who sends his greetings from Corinth to Rome (16:23), but an *oikonomos* in Greek or an *ararius* in Latin is a notch below the office of *aedilis.* Maybe it is not the same person, or maybe Paul did not know about those civic distinctions. We are

FIGURE 118. Inscription from Corinth naming Erastus (mentioned also in Romans 16:23), still readable even though the bronze letters have long since been removed.

inclined to think, however, that Erastus was *ararius* while Paul was at Corinth, but had sponsored (recall *euergetism* as public good works) his way up the ladder to become an *aedilis* by the time he laid that pavement.

Visits, Reports, Letters, and Problems

When Paul was at Ephesus it was a major port on the eastern coast of the Aegean, a governor's seat, for Roman Asia, and a city with over a quarter of a million people. Today, with its harbor silted up and its glory long gone, it is a spectacular inland ruin near Selçuk off the road from Kusadasi, but at times it seems to hold as many students, pilgrims, and tourists as once it held inhabitants. Corinth was then a twin-harbored city in the western Aegean, also a governor's seat, for Roman Achaia, and another city with around a quarter of a million people. Located strategically at the western end of the isthmus separating central Greece from the Peloponnese on a north-south axis and the Ionian from the Aegean seas on an east-west axis, it had one harbor at Lechaion on the Corinthian Gulf and another at Cenchreae on the Saronic Gulf. Today, as with Ephesus, its glory is long gone, and those students, tourists, and pilgrims replace its ancient inhabitants beneath that same craggy Acrocorinth. Modern Corinth to the northeast holds a tenth of ancient Corinth, but a lockless canal across the isthmus cuts 250 miles from Brindisi to Piraeus and guarantees a permanent Corinth in Greece's European Union destiny.

In Paul's days a ship sailing due east from Corinth's Cenchreae could take a messenger to Ephesus at best in two weeks and at worst in many more, depending on island hops and cargo stops, not to mention omens, winds, and storms. The Christian community Paul had founded at Corinth sent him a list of questions when he was in Ephesus in the mid-50s. They were clearly matters not just of curiosity, but of controversy within a seriously divided group. But they were not simply offering problems to Paul for his solution. At the heart of the trouble were their divergent views of Paul's competence and importance, authority and even integrity.

Paul's letters to the Corinthians were written after his release from that Ephesian prison where he had written to Philemon and the Philippians. But if he could refer to that past experience as having "fought with wild animals at Ephesus" in 1 Corinthians 15:32, he might have described his present experience as fighting with wild animals at Corinth. Was there some basic root problem at Corinth that generated so much discord about and antagonism toward Paul? Think of the contrast, for example, between Philippi and Corinth as seen in the letters Paul wrote to each assembly. Both were Roman colonies officially founded for disbanded veterans, to repay them for their services, to keep them out of Italy, to stimulate the local economy, and to foster *Romanitas* in a Greek world. But Paul wrote to Philippi as warmly and to Corinth as nastily as he ever wrote to anyone anywhere (even including the Galatians). What went so spectacularly wrong at Corinth?

VISIT 1. Paul's difficulties at Corinth started early and became steadily worse before they became finally better. "This," says Paul in 1 Corinthians, looking back on that inaugural visit, "is my defense to those who would examine me" concerning it (9:3). After a long defense of his right to support, Paul concludes in that same letter, "We have not made use of this right, but we endure anything rather than put an obstacle in the way of the gospel of Christ," and again, "I have made no use of any of these rights, nor am I writing this so that they may be applied in my case. Indeed, I would rather die than that—no one will deprive me of my ground for boasting" (9:12, 15). Why did Paul refuse their generosity and hospitality?

It sounds from those final sentences that he did it out of general principles but, for example, he never refused such support from the Philippians. Recall, from Chapter 6, that they had helped him first at Thessalonica and later at Ephesus according to Philippians 4:15–19. Paul even admits in 2 Corinthians that the Philippians had helped him in between while he was on his first visit at Corinth itself:

> I robbed other churches by accepting support from them in order to
> serve you. And when I was with you and was in need, I did not burden

anyone, for my needs were supplied by the friends who came from
Macedonia. So I refrained and will continue to refrain from burdening
you in any way. (11:8–9)

The question, in other words, is very specific: Why did Paul refuse support
precisely at Corinth and not elsewhere? What was wrong with Corinthian
support?

LETTER 1. Paul's first letter to the Corinthians is lost, and we know
about it only from his comment in 1 Corinthians 5:9: "I wrote to you in my
letter." But it is a second indication of previous trouble. He had warned
them in it "not to associate with anyone who bears the name of brother or
sister who is sexually immoral or greedy, or is an idolater, reviler, drunkard,
or robber. Do not even eat with such a one," as he put it in 1 Corinthians
5:11. How did such individuals come to be within Corinthian Christianity?
And did the community not recognize that problem and have to be told by
Paul to do something about it?

LETTER 2. Letter 2 is our 1 Corinthians. After a long, powerful, and im-
passioned overture (chaps. 1–4), Paul reacts to several problems reported to
him most likely by "Chloe's people" (5–6) and then responds to several
questions posed by the Corinthians (7–16). He must also have been updated
on Corinth by "the coming of Stephanas and Fortunatus and Achaicus"
(16:17). They were presumably on his side in the disputes with some at
Corinth because he himself "did baptize also the household of Stephanas"
and "members of the household of Stephanas were the first converts in
Achaia" (1:16; 16:15).

VISIT 2. Paul sent Timothy to Corinth, but with some trepidation, as he
noted in 1 Corinthians 4:17 and 16:10. Timothy's report was so serious that
Paul made a short visit directly from Ephesus to Corinth and back. He refers
later to it as a "painful visit" in 2 Corinthians 2:1 and 13:2. But matters continued to get worse.

LETTER 3. This is another now lost letter and is known only because
Paul mentions later that he wrote this letter to avoid making another
"painful" visit. He also refers to it repeatedly in 2 Corinthians:

I wrote you out of much distress and anguish of heart and with many
tears, not to cause you pain, but to let you know the abundant love

that I have for you. . . . For even if I made you sorry with my letter, I do not regret it (though I did regret it, for I see that I grieved you with that letter, though only briefly). . . . I do not want to seem as though I am trying to frighten you with my letters. (2:4; 7:8; 10:9)

The second, or painful, visit did not help, and neither did the third, or tearful, letter. Quite clearly, therefore, things are still getting worse rather than better, and this intensifies our basic question: What went bad and got steadily worse between Paul and Corinth?

LETTER 4. There are two separate letters now contained and reversed in the text we know as 2 Corinthians. The chronologically first one is 2 Corinthians 10–13, and it is so bitter that the trouble has clearly escalated into an out-and-out attack on Paul himself. It involves other Christian Jewish missionary opponents whom Paul sarcastically calls "super-apostles," but regardless of them and their purpose, the question is Why are some, most, or all the Corinthians ready to follow them and not Paul?

LETTER 5. After sending that Letter 4, Paul sent Titus ahead of him to see how things stood at Corinth. Paul traveled north from Ephesus expecting to meet Titus either at Troas on the Asian side or Philippi on the European side of the upper Aegean, according to 2 Corinthians 2:12–13. They met in Macedonia, and the news was very, very good, as Paul exults in 2 Corinthians 7:5–15. Paul then wrote the letter we know as 2 Corinthians 1–9, a letter of joyful reconciliation.

VISIT 3. After receiving Titus's report and sending that Letter 5, we may presume that all went well at Corinth, and we will have to return there and consider 2 Corinthians 8–9 and the Great Collection in the next chapter.

PROBLEMS. What underlay that complicated weave of visits, reports, and letters was a fundamental clash between two visions of moral community and, even more important, of two fundamental theologies on which those discordant visions were based. At Corinth, Paul and his vision encountered more forcefully than ever before the full normalcy of high-powered Roman patronage backed, of course, by Roman imperial theology. What, after all, was a divine emperor but a supreme patron?

First, recall that egalitarian negation of privilege between Jew and Greek, slave and free, male and female "in Christ Jesus," that is to say, within the

Christian assembly, seen earlier in Galatians 3:28. Paul repeats it here in 1 Corinthians 12:13 by saying, "In the one Spirit we were all baptized into one body—Jews or Greeks, slaves or free—and we were all made to drink of one Spirit." None of that arises, for Paul, from ideas about general political democracy or universal inalienable rights, but from the common status of Christians as equals before and under God. As he himself put it in Romans 8:29, those whom God "foreknew he also predestined to be conformed to the image of his Son, in order that he might be the firstborn within a large family." We already saw the practical results of that intra-Christian equality with regard to slavery and patriarchy in Chapter 2.

Second, the foundation of that equality is imitation of (better, participation *in*) the kenosis, or self-emptying, of Christ as told to the Philippians. Before he proclaimed that hymn to the kenotic Christ in 2:6–11, he pleaded with the Philippians to "let the same mind be in you that was in Christ Jesus" (2:5), and after it he warned them, in a magnificently accurate paradox, to "work out your own salvation with fear and trembling; for it is God who is at work in you, enabling you both to will and to work for his good pleasure" (2:12–13). How, indeed, could one live personal or communal kenosis without the empowerment of a kenotic Christ and a kenotic God?

Third, over against that startling vision of a kenotic community stands the utter normalcy of human civilization in general and Roman patronage in particular. For that normalcy, Paul's vision is quite simply inhuman, impossible, idiotic, and absurd. But what is at stake is very clear. *A kenotic community begets equality, a patronal community begets inequality; kenosis begets cooperation, patronage begets competition.* On his very first visit, Paul walked right into that problem and maybe even caused some of it inadvertently. On the one hand, Paul mentions in 1 Corinthians 1:14–16 that he himself baptized only Crispus, Gaius, and the household of Stephanas at Corinth. But Crispus is "the official of the synagogue" in Acts 18:8, Gaius is "host to me and to the whole church" in Romans 16:23, the household of Stephanas "devoted themselves to the service of the saints," and, as seen in the preceding section, Stephanas himself visited Paul at Ephesus in 1 Corinthians 16:15–17. Maybe they considered him their patron or, if not, maybe others considered them as his? In any case, and immediately, Paul absolutely refused *patronal* support from the Corinthians while always accepting *communal* support from the Philippians. And the clearest reason for that refusal is given by his brilliant overture in 1 Corinthians 1–4.

Wise Power or Foolish Weakness?

It is not enough to admire the soaring rhetoric and the mantric or even hypnotic repetition of Paul's paradoxes about humanity and divinity, wisdom and foolishness, power and weakness in 1 Corinthians 1–4. You must also ask yourself exactly what it means. It is, of course, the best commentary ever written on the *communal* implications of that kenotic divinity in Philippians 2:6–11. But, still, what exactly does it mean both negatively and positively? The most important clue is in this comment from 1 Corinthians 1:26–29:

> Consider your own call, brothers and sisters: not many of you were wise by human standards, not many were powerful, not many were of noble birth. But God chose what is foolish in the world to shame the wise; God chose what is weak in the world to shame the strong; God chose what is low and despised in the world, things that are not, to reduce to nothing things that are, so that no one might boast in the presence of God.

But *not many* means *some* or *a few* or at least *one* in Corinth's Christian community whom the surrounding non-Christian community considered to be wise, powerful, and highborn. And those sentences not only set up paradoxical oppositions between what is human and what is divine; they also introduce certain key terms that weave and interweave throughout the entire section in 1 Corinthians 1–4.

First, the phrase *by human standards*, literally, *according to the flesh* or *fleshly* (mentioned four times), means the same as *this age* (four times), or *the world* (ten times), or *that which is human* (twelve times) in these four chapters. That is not a narrow and specific reference to certain contemporary evils in Paul's own times, but a sweeping and repeated reference to what we call the *normalcy of civilization*. Next, the terms *wise* and *wisdom* and their opposites, *foolish* and *foolishness*, resonate through the entire section. Then, the terms *powerful* and *power* and their opposites, *weak* and *weakness*, resonate likewise though this entire overture (with *strong* or *strength* sometimes used as equivalent to *powerful* or *power*). In other words, in the light of 1 Corinthians 1:26–27, that entire section in 1 Corinthians 1–4 is not just aimed at abstract categories of human life, but at real persons in Corinth and at them precisely in their general human normalcy rather than in their specific evil abnormalcy.

It is possible to be powerful without being wise or wise without being powerful, so we take seriously Paul's double criticism of certain Christians at Corinth whose importance derives from being accepted as both. Emphatically, implacably, and with drumbeat repetition Paul claims that human wisdom or power are divine foolishness or weakness and vice versa. (By the way, the Greek term behind "foolish/ness" is actually the root from which we get "moron" and "moronic," so those latter terms would be even more appropriate translations.) As seen above, some of Paul's earliest Corinthian converts were important enough to be involved in the standard and competitive patronal relationships basic to their culture's normalcy. That is why he refused to become financially dependent on them and why, in 1 Corinthians 2:2–8, he says,

> I decided to know nothing among you except Jesus Christ, and him crucified. And I came to you in weakness and in fear and in much trembling. My speech and my proclamation were not with plausible words of wisdom, but with a demonstration of the Spirit and of power, so that your faith might rest not on human wisdom but on the power of God. Yet among the mature we do speak wisdom, though it is not a wisdom of this age or of the rulers of this age, who are doomed to perish. But we speak God's wisdom, secret and hidden, which God decreed before the ages for our glory. None of the rulers of this age understood this; for if they had, they would not have crucified the Lord of glory.

The rulers of this age are, proximately, the Roman authorities who executed Jesus, but they are, ultimately, the cosmic powers that make imperial violence and human injustice the normalcy of human history and the permanent patina of civilization.

Paul's counterpointed reversals of divine power or wisdom and human weakness or foolishness appear intensively not only at the start of 1 Corinthians, but also at the end of 2 Corinthians. The emphasis in 1 Corinthians 1–4 is primarily on Christ's crucifixion being the supreme example of divine power and wisdom as human weakness and foolishness. In 2 Corinthians 10–13 it is on Paul's own life being a further example of divine power and wisdom seen as human weakness and foolishness. But, of course, that Paul is *in* Christ and that Christ is *in* Paul. The root problem behind both 1 Corinthians 1–4 and 2 Corinthians 10–13 is the same. It is that those who were wise and powerful in the Corinthian church resented Paul's refusal to enter into their competing patronal networks and, even before that or maybe only after it, they claimed that, as Paul quotes them in 2 Corinthians 10:10, "'his letters are weighty and strong, but his bodily presence is weak, and his speech contemptible.'" Already in 1 Corinthians 1:12 and 3:4 the wise and powerful ones preferred Apollos to Paul, although all evidence is that Apollos resisted that competitiveness just as much as Paul did. But in 2 Corinthians 10–13, the Pauline opponents are readily accepting other Christian apostles whose Jewish credentials are as good as Paul's but before whose rhetorical eloquence he must admit defensively in 2 Corinthians 11:5–6, "I am not in the least inferior to these super-apostles" since "I may be untrained in speech, but not in knowledge." His basic response to their boasting of power is to lampoon it with a boasting of weakness in 2 Corinthians 11:23–33:

> Are they ministers of Christ? I am talking like a madman—I am a better one: with far greater labors, far more imprisonments, with countless floggings, and often near death. Five times I have received from the Jews the forty lashes minus one. Three times I was beaten with rods. Once I received a stoning. Three times I was shipwrecked; for a night and a day I was adrift at sea; on frequent journeys, in danger from rivers, danger from bandits, danger from my own people, danger from Gentiles, danger in the city, danger in the wilderness, danger at sea, danger from false brothers and sisters; in toil and hardship, through many a sleepless night, hungry and thirsty, often without food, cold and naked. . . . If I must boast, I will boast of the things that show my weakness. The God and Father of the Lord Jesus (blessed be he forever!) knows that I do not lie. In Damascus, the governor under King Aretas guarded the city of Damascus in order to seize me, but I was let down in a basket through a window in the wall, and escaped from his hands.

That is a marvelous and humorous finale. The Roman legionary soldier who swore he was first over the enemy's city walls received the *corona muralis,* a battlemented gold crown for conspicuous bravery. I got, says Paul, in climaxing this lampoon of superior achievements, the *corona ex-muralis,* for getting away safely, for being first over the wall in the opposite direction. "I am content," he concludes in 2 Corinthians 12:10, "with weaknesses, insults, hardships, persecutions, and calamities for the sake of Christ; for whenever I am weak, then I am strong."

Power and the Eucharist

Most of the problems at Corinth stem, as John Chow has shown, from powerful patrons within the assembly, important people both very good for help, support, and protection, but also very bad for unity, equality, and commonality. It was those whom Paul calls the Corinthian *powerfuls* who could take financial disputes outside the Christian assembly and into the civil courts (1 Cor. 6:1–8), who could countenance marriage between stepson and widowed stepmother to protect patrimony (5:1–13), and who could argue for attending celebratory meals in pagan temples, buying such meat in the market, and eating it at private dinners (10:14–33). All such problems involved not just their position inside the Christian assembly, but their contacts with friends, freedmen, and clients outside it. Those were problems for the haves rather than the have-nots. What happened at the eucharistic meal or Lord's Supper in 1 Corinthians 11:17–34 is a fascinating example.

Greco-Roman moralists argued whether it was ethically correct to serve superior food and wine to friends and equals, but inferior food and wine to freedmen and clients at a patronal banquet. Was it right, in other words, to turn that banquet into one more display of social stratification that exalted the haves and humiliated the have-nots?

In the last decades of the first century, the Spanish poet Martial, surviving at Rome as a literary client dependent on rich patrons, complained bitterly about such banquet humiliations in his *Epigrams*. "While the throng of invited guests looks on, you, Caecilianus, alone devour the mushrooms" (1.20), and again, "Why do I dine without you although, Ponticus, I am dining with you . . . let us eat the same fare" (3.60). His friend (and patron!) Pliny the Younger, who finally helped him back to Spain, found such patronal discrimination most inappropriate and tells this story in his *Letters:*

> Some very elegant dishes were served up to [the host] and few more of the company; while those which were placed before the rest were cheap and paltry. He had apportioned in small flagons three different sorts of wine. . . . One was for himself and me; the next for his friends of a lower order; . . . and the third for his own freedmen and mine. One who sat next to me took notice of this, and asked me if I approved of it. "Not at all," I told him. "Pray, then," said he, "what is your method on such occasions?" "Mine," I returned, "is to give all my company the same fare; for when I make an invitation, it is to sup,

not to be censoring. Every man whom I have placed on an equality with myself by admitting him to my table, I treat as an equal in all particulars." "Even freedmen?" he asked. "Even them," I said; "for on these occasions I regard them not as freedmen, but boon companions." "This must put you to great expense," says he. I assured him not at all; and on his asking how that could be, I said, "Why you must know my freedmen don't drink the same wine I do—but *I* drink what *they* do." (2.6)

You will notice that last sentence, uttered, no doubt, with no narrative irony and full aristocratic complacency. The two options were patronal discrimination or patronal slumming. Not even Pliny considered the third option—give all alike the best wine.

When, later, Paul wrote his letter to the Romans from Corinth, he added, "Gaius, who is host to me and to the whole church, greets you" (16:23). The problem that arose in 1 Corinthians 11:17–34 is exactly what would occur when Gaius or some other Corinthian Christian patron hosted all the assemblies for a eucharistic supper within the expected normalcies of Greco-Roman patronal banquets.

In Christian churches today the Eucharist is a morsel of bread and a sip of wine as ritual memorial and sacramental participation in the Lord's (Last) Supper. First-century Christian Eucharists, however, involved that latter function within the context of a full meal, supper, or banquet (*deipnon*). But Paul calls that real but special meal the *kyriakon deipnon* and distinguishes it from *idion deipnon* in 1 Corinthians 11:20–21. The "Lord's-style supper" is not the same as "one's own-style supper." What made them different?

Could one have a *kyriakon deipnon* at home simply by saying certain prayers before and after the meal or by reciting special words of remembrance over the bread ("This is my Body") and the wine ("This is my Blood")? Absolutely not. But why? Because what made the supper *kyriakon,* or Lord's-style, was never just those words, but the fact of a communal share-meal, a supper to which those early Christians brought whatever they had and shared it among one another. That is what made it intrinsically sacred and placed it in continuity with the share-meals of the historical Jesus. It was not handout, charity, or welfare, but an attempt to participate in a new creation that acknowledged God as owner of all things and humans as but stewards of a world not their own. Telling evidence of these share-meal Eucharists was seen already at the end of Chapter 3, where both the Pauline

1 Thessalonians and the post-Pauline 2 Thessalonians insist against freeload-ers that individual work must precede common food. The sequence is: work, share, eat.

Mutuality and commonality worked well, even granted some freeloader problems, as long as Christian assemblies contained primarily those who, in Roman terms, lived in *negotium* rather than in *otium,* by manufacturing in workshops or selling in shops rather than in landed leisure and patronal ease. But with Gaius or maybe even a competing patron, here is what happened according to 1 Corinthians. A well-to-do patron invited all the assemblies to a common celebration of the Lord's Supper and, as usual, each brought food and drink to share with all. But, then, "when the time comes to eat, each of you goes ahead with your own supper, and one goes hungry and another becomes drunk" (11:21). Instead of a common sharing, there was a private eating, and of course those better off had better food and drink than those of lesser means. Some ate in the *triclinium* but others in the atrium, or some in the master *triclinium,* others in a lesser one, or else most ate in the atrium and perhaps some in the service areas. "Do you," asks Paul, "show contempt for the church of God and humiliate those who have nothing?" (11:22). And, with individual eating, some started before all arrived. "When you come together to eat," Paul admonished them, "wait for one another" (11:33).

Paul's solution is actually a compromise and maybe a little too close for comfort to Pliny's aristocratic complacency. He might have insisted that all members should bring the best they could but, instead, he made two sug-gestions. On the one hand, the haves should eat their better food at home before attending the Eucharist: "What! Do you not have homes to eat and drink in?" (11:22), and, again, "If you are hungry, eat at home, so that when you come together, it will not be for your condemnation" (11:34). On the other, the order of the Lord's Supper is this sequence:

(1) Invocation and *breaking* of the bread (11:23–24)

(2) The supper itself (11:25a)

(3) Invocation and *passing* of the cup (11:25b–26)

Paul insists on the traditional nature of that sequence. The twin frames em-phasize commonality by that *breaking* of bread and *passing* of the wine cup. Furthermore, the supper itself takes place totally in between them and not in any way before them. It must be, therefore, a common share-meal just as are its frames. That was maybe the best that Paul could get. The haves could still bring cheaper food for all to eat, but at least everyone had to eat together at the same place and the same time from the same food and the same drink. Still, the Eucharist or Lord's Supper, the central symbolism of Christianity's divine responsibility for a shared earth, was fractured badly at Corinth, and Paul knew it. Those terminal warnings about illness and death, judgment and condemnation (11:27–34) indicate very clearly that much more was at stake than common courtesy and public politeness.

Wisdom and the Resurrection

Paul twice emphasizes forcibly that he had *handed on* to the Corinthians traditions that he himself had *received* from, presumably, Jerusalem (1 Cor. 11:23; 15:3). One such case, just seen, concerned the powerful and their reaction to the Lord's communal supper. The other concerned the wise and their reaction to the Lord's bodily resurrection.

Imagine Corinthians whose wisdom about human destiny came from the by then almost commonplaces of Platonic philosophy. What would they have thought about the body and the soul, about the proper relationship between them, and about what happened to each at death? Socrates, having refused to escape legal death by illegal escape, spent his last day in conversation with friends about the immortality of the soul. Here is a medley of his comments from Plato's *Phaedo:*

> [The soul must] have its dwelling, so far as it can, both now and in the future, alone by itself, freed from the shackles of the body. . . . The soul is most like that which is divine, immortal . . . whereas body is most like that which is human, mortal. . . . [At death] the soul, the invisible part, which goes away to a place that is like itself . . . into the presence of the good and wise God, where, if God so will, my [Socrates's] soul must shortly go. . . . Every seeker after wisdom knows that up to the time when philosophy takes it over his soul is a helpless prisoner, chained hand and foot in the body, compelled to view reality not directly but only through its prison bars, and wallowing in utter ignorance. (67d, 80bd, 82e)

What would Platonic wisdom at Corinth make of a Paul proclaiming the *bodily* resurrection of Jesus, proclaiming not the liberation of his soul from his body at death, like that of the martyred Socrates centuries earlier, but the reintegration of his body and his soul in eternal life? They would have called it foolishness or, more politely, they would have heard *resurrection of the body* and smoothly translated it into *immortality of the soul*. They would probably have had no problem with apotheosis for Jesus's soul into a unique relationship with the divine, but *bodily resurrection* would be, in good Platonic fashion, like taking the shackles of prison with them into eternity.

Paul's first argument is to repeat the basic tradition about the death and resurrection of Jesus, emphasizing especially that, after his death and burial, he "was seen" by many people including himself (15:3–11). That, of course, would not have actually helped him with those wise Corinthians. They would probably have replied that, in their past Greco-Roman tradition, individuals had often come back from the dead to visit the living. Think, Paul, they might have said, of dead Hector appearing to Aeneas at the start of Virgil's *Aeneid* and warning him to flee the toppling towers of Ilium (2.268–97).

The second argument closes down that avenue of misunderstanding. There is, insists Paul, only one meaning for the term *resurrection,* namely, the *general bodily resurrection* at the end of this evil aeon when God raises all the dead for judgment in prelude to transforming this earth into eschatological perfection and utopian peace. Since this great future moment will not destroy but transform the world, will not annul creation but perfect it, will not take earth to heaven but heaven to earth, there must be, first and above all, a great scene of public justice. All of that, so far, is completely without the expectation of Jewish eschatology in general and Pharisaic theology in particular. But then Paul adds in the stunningly original adaptation, the totally original variation, the utterly creative revision that Christian Judaism had already made to that Pharisaic theology. That general bodily resurrection *has already begun* with the bodily resurrection of Jesus, and therefore that start and finish, that beginning and ending, stand or fall together:

> Now if Christ is proclaimed as raised from the dead, how can some of you say there is no resurrection of the dead? If there is no resurrection of the dead, then Christ has not been raised. . . . We testified of God that he raised Christ—whom he did not raise if it is true that the dead are not raised. For if the dead are not raised, then Christ has not been raised. (15:12–13,15b–16)

The argument is very clear: no Jesus resurrection, no general resurrection; no general resurrection, no Jesus resurrection. In other words, using the metaphor of harvest, "Christ has been raised from the dead, the first fruits of those who have died" (15:20). Jesus's resurrection is to the general resurrection as first fruits are to the rest of the harvest. There is no possibility of Christ's resurrection as a special, unique, peculiar privilege accorded to him alone. Had such occurred, it would have been termed assumption, exaltation, or even apotheosis. But the term *resurrection* meant one thing and only thing at that time—it meant the general bodily resurrection as God finally began the great cleanup of the world's mess. As we said in Chapter 3, using that term of Jesus meant that the general bodily resurrection had begun with him. The special, particular, and unique claim of Christian Judaism is that what Pharisaic Judaism expected as a single instant has come as an extended span of time (but presumably brief), what was awaited as a moment has come as a process (but presumably short).

The third argument goes to the heart of the debate with those wise Corinthians. "But someone will ask," says Paul, " 'How are the dead raised? With what kind of body do they come?' " (15:35). Hear again the voice of Platonic tradition in the background. The soul is in the body (*sōma*) as in a tomb (*sēma*) for the *Cratylus* (400c) or as an oyster in its shell for the *Phaedrus* (250c). What is a resurrected body like and, in any case, who would want one?

> Soul is utterly superior to the body, and that which gives each one of us his being is nothing else but his soul, whereas the body is no more than a shadow which keeps us company. So 'tis well said of the deceased that the corpse is but a ghost; the real man—the undying thing called the soul—departs to give account to the gods of another world, even as we are taught by ancestral tradition—an account to which the good may look forward without misgiving, but the evil with grievous dismay. (*Laws* 12.959b)

Paul's answer holds alike to continuity *and* discontinuity. Continuity because "what you sow does not come to life unless it dies" (15:36), so that the buried body is to the resurrected body as planted seed to grown grain. Discontinuity because "it is sown a physical body, it is raised a spiritual body. If there is a physical body, there is also a spiritual body" (15:44). That is probably a bad translation; better this: "It is sown a soul-body, it is raised a Spirit-body." For Paul, a "spiritual body" is not just a square circle, but the normal human body transformed by the Spirit of God. Read it, in other words, as a "Spiritual body," a body transfigured by divine empowerment. Recall, Paul might have said, all those ancient promises of an eschatologically transformed world here below upon this earth. What other than transformed Spirit-bodies could exist in such a world? Here is his grand finale in 15:21–26:

> For since death came through a human being, the resurrection of the dead has also come through a human being; for as all die in Adam, so all will be made alive in Christ. But each in his own order: Christ the first fruits, then at his coming those who belong to Christ. Then comes the end, when he hands over the kingdom to God the Father, after he has destroyed every ruler and every authority and power. For he must reign until he has put all his enemies under his feet. The last enemy to be destroyed is death.

We will see that last assertion again in Chapter 7. But we ask one question about it immediately. From Genesis 2–3 Paul sees death as a divine punishment for Adamic disobedience, and so it is not a normal part of God's all-good creation. Is that correct or is death in itself simply part of the normalcy of divine creation? Further, is God's last enemy death *or* violence *or*, maybe better, violent death (violence understood, of course, as a human monopoly)? Maybe to understand what Paul meant by death we have only to watch local, national, or international news on any given evening? Violence, after all, has been civilization's drug of choice across the millennia of its addiction.

There is one final and even more basic question whose answer may serve as summary not only of 1 Corinthians 15, but of Paul's transmutation of both general Jewish apocalyptic eschatology and specific Pharisaic resurrection theology. Why did Paul not agree with his "wise" Corinthian converts by accepting Platonic theology and insisting that Christ's soul, as purer even than Socrates's, resided now with God in a state of such eternal holiness that it judged positively or negatively all other souls before or after it. Plato, after all, had insisted (against Homer's Hades) that the soul's immortality was necessary for divine justice, so that virtuous souls could be rewarded and evil souls punished after this life. Why not, at least, leave two options for Christian faith: the resurrection of the body or the immortality of the soul? Because, quite simply, *the general bodily resurrection was, first of all, about the justice of God amid the goodness of creation here below upon a transformed earth, and, second, within that, it was about the martyrs who had died for justice and from injustice with their bodies tortured, brutalized, and murdered.* Resurrection was not just about us and survival, but about God and this earth. It was not about the heavenly evacuation, but the earthly transfiguration of this bodily world. The soul's immortality, even with all due postmortem sanctions, did not restore a world disfigured by human evil, injustice, and violence. For the Jewish and Pharisaic Paul, divine justice was necessarily about transfigured bodies upon a transfigured earth.

Hierarchy Within the Community

Even a casual reading of the two Corinthian letters would make you very much aware of the multiplicity of problems within the assemblies and between them and Paul himself. If you calculated the priority Paul gave to those difficulties by the amount of space he accorded each, the content of 1 Corinthians 12–14 becomes immediately striking. Apart from the long and programmatic overture in 1 Corinthians 1–4, this is the longest sustained section in both letters. What was at stake in such a long discussion? It was about unity, diversity, and hierarchy. It was about the basic problems between a kenotic community of equals and a patronal society of unequals. But how could there be unity amid diversity without hierarchy?

Unity and Diversity

Once again the problem is superiority and inferiority, who is better than whom, who has the most important function, the best position, the greatest gift. Paul's basic principle is given immediately in 1 Corinthians 12:4–7:

There are varieties of gifts,	but the same Spirit;
and there are varieties of services,	but the same Lord;
and there are varieties of activities,	but it is the same God who activates all of them in everyone
To each is given the manifestation	of the Spirit for the common good.

Paul does not distinguish too precisely between gifts, services, and activities, since they are all manifestations of Spirit, Lord, and God. And they are not given for personal ascendancy but "for the common good." Here are the Spirit manifestations he lists; notice the overlap between what we might otherwise distinguish as nine gift activities in the first passage and nine service activities in the second:

> To one is given through the Spirit the utterance of wisdom, and to another the utterance of knowledge according to the same Spirit, to another faith by the same Spirit, to another gifts of healing by the one Spirit, to another the working of miracles, to another prophecy, to another the discernment of spirits, to another various kinds of tongues, to another the interpretation of tongues. (12:8–10)

> God has appointed in the church first apostles, second prophets, third teachers; then deeds of power [miracles], then gifts of healing, forms of assistance, forms of leadership, various kinds of tongues. Are all apostles? Are all prophets? Are all teachers? Do all work miracles? Do all possess gifts of healing? Do all speak in tongues? Do all interpret? (12:28–30)

In between those two lists, Paul gives the classical analogy of the diverse but unified members of a human or a social body.

In Livy's *History of Rome* Menenius Agrippa successfully used that comparison to show "how the internal disaffection amongst the parts of the body resembled the animosity of the plebeians against the patricians" and thereby prevented a class war of lower against upper classes:

> In the days when all the parts of the human body were not as now agreeing together, but each member took its own course and spoke its own speech, the other members, indignant at seeing that everything acquired by their care and labour and ministry went to the belly, whilst it, undisturbed in the middle of them, did nothing but enjoy the pleasures provided for it, entered into a conspiracy; the hands were not to bring food to the mouth, the mouth was not to accept it when offered, the teeth were not to masticate it. Whilst, in their resentment, they were anxious to coerce the belly by starving it, the members themselves wasted away, and the whole body was reduced to the last stage of exhaustion. Then it became evident that the belly rendered no idle service, and the nourishment it received was no greater than that which it bestowed by returning to all parts of the body this blood by which we live and are strong, equally distributed into the veins, after being matured by the digestion of the food. (2.32)

That, of course, is not exactly how Paul used the metaphor. His point is, "There are many members, yet one body" (12:20) and all depend on all. But the twin frames of the body image in 12:12–13 and 12:27 are of primary importance for Paul:

> For just as the body is one and has many members, and all the members of the body, though many, are one body, so it is with Christ. For in the one Spirit we were all baptized into one body—Jews or Greeks, slaves or free—and we were all made to drink of one Spirit.
>
> Now you are the body of Christ and individually members of it.

That means, minimally, that the Christian assembly is like a human body, but one that belongs to Christ. But it also means, maximally, that there is an organic fusion between Christ and the Christian community insofar as both are transfused with the same Holy Spirit.

Diversity and Hierarchy

Some Corinthians must have set up a hierarchy of gifts and services with "tongues" or "speaking in tongues," that is, the ecstatic utterance of non-speech, as the greatest of them all and those who possessed it as the most Spirit-filled Christians in the assemblies. In English the term for that spiritual gift is *glossolalia,* from the Greek words for tongue (*glossa*) and speaking (*lalein*), and Paul refers to such utterances over a dozen times from 12:10 to 14:39. But he not only opposes any primacy of glossolalia; he replaces that hierarchy with a completely different one.

First, there is the well-known rhapsody on "the more excellent way" (12:31), which begins, "If I speak in the tongues of mortals and of angels, but do not have love (*agapē*), I am a noisy gong or a clanging cymbal" (13:1), continues with the qualities of love (13:4–12), and concludes, "Now faith, hope, and love abide, these three; and the greatest of these is love" (13:13). That section in 1 Corinthians 13 and its wider ambience in 1 Corinthians 12–14 makes it clear that "to love" means "to share" and that all other Spirit gifts or Spirit functions are worthless unless received, used, and shared with all for the common good.

Second, and on that basic principle, prophets take precedence over glossolalists because "those who prophesy speak to other people for their upbuilding and encouragement and consolation," while "those who speak in a tongue build up themselves, but those who prophesy build up the church" (14:3–4). Once again, the principle of common good is clear: "Since you are eager for spiritual gifts, strive to excel in them for building up the church" (14:12).

Third, glossolalia speaks "to God," but does not speak to the human mind, not of believers and not of nonbelievers:

> I will pray with the spirit, but I will pray with the mind also; I will sing praise with the spirit, but I will sing praise with the mind also. . . . I thank God that I speak in tongues more than all of you; nevertheless, in church I would rather speak five words with my mind, in order to instruct others also, than ten thousand words in a tongue. (14:15–19)

Again and again, Paul reverts to his basic principle: "Let all things be done for building up" (14:26).

Finally, therefore, if there is glossolalia, there should also be interpretation, there should be somebody who can say what it means. Despite all those problems with that gift, however, Paul never says to stop it. Interpretation yes, order yes, peace yes, but "do not forbid speaking in tongues" (14:39). Still, the only hierarchy that Paul accepts is the primacy of those who best build up the community, and that can only be done by those who *love,* that is, those who *share* fully and completely what they have received as not their own to have, to use, or to boast about.

All of that is, quite simply, Paul's egalitarian vision in action of a Christian kenotic community that empties itself in love and service for others. But, as some at Corinth assured him, that is not how the wise and strong of this world operate, not outside Christianity and not inside it either. That is not, they could have said, the normalcy of either civilization or religion, which always work by wisdom and strength overpowering foolishness and weakness. To which Paul's only reply would have been: Yes, but "God's foolishness is wiser than human wisdom, and God's weakness is stronger than human strength" (1:25).

One World Under Divine Justice

On the one hand the Imperial system was based on the most glaring and flagrant form of idolatry, the worship of a living man as the incarnate god on earth; it was the direct enemy of Christ: its system was like a parody of the Christian Gospel. How could Paul do anything but hate it and condemn it? On the other hand it saved the world from worse evils: every one who lived in those times knew that the Emperor and the Imperial Government alone stood between the civilised world and destruction, and restrained the power of disorder, war and savagery, which had recently nearly overwhelmed society and put an end to civilisation. . . . The Empire was the servant, the bearer, the instrument of the Church, and yet it was also its irreconcilable and inevitable foe. . . . Paul was much more likely to see the character of the Empire than the Emperors to comprehend the nature of the Church. It is in truth as inconceivable that Paul could be insensible of the nature of the Imperial system, as it is that he could consent to any compromise with the Imperial worship. A purified Empire was the Pauline idea; but a purified Empire meant the elimination of the God-Emperor.

—William Mitchell Ramsay, *The Cities of St. Paul* (1907)

A Christianizing theory of religion which assumes that religion is essentially designed to provide guidance through the personal crises of life and to grant salvation into life everlasting imposes on the imperial cult a distinction between religion and politics. But a broader perspective suggests that religions need not provide answers to these particular questions, and the imposition of the conventional distinction between religion and politics obscures the basic similarity between politics and religion: both are ways of systematically constructing power. . . . The imperial cult stabilized the religious order of the world. The system of ritual was carefully structured; the symbolism evoked a picture of the relationship between the emperor and the gods. The ritual was also structuring; it imposed a definition of the world. The imperial cult, along with politics and diplomacy, constructed the reality of the Roman empire.

—S. R. F. Price, *Rituals and Power:*
The Roman Imperial Cult in Asia Minor (1984)

✑   ✑   ✑

Under the Arch of Titus

Overture

It is early on a beautiful mid-July morning in 2002, and the present human heat of the crowded Metropolitana B-train is even worse than the future solar heat of the Roman day. Upstairs from the subway, you emerge into the piazza, cross before the still uncrowded Flavian Amphitheater, ignore the Arch of Constantine, and walk directly to the Arch of Titus (Figure 119), erected under Titus's brother, the emperor Domitian, in 81–82 C.E. As always in Roman imperial theology, the sequence is clear: first victory, next peace, then divinity. Even if, as in this case, the great dynastic victory took many years to complete even against a small country like the Jewish homeland.

You now stand directly under the Arch of Titus as it opens westward to the Roman Forum and eastward to the Flavian Colosseum. You look to your left where, inside the northern curve of the arch, a deep-cut frieze shows the emperor Titus in a four-horse chariot with the goddess Roma preceding and the goddess Victory following his triumphal procession. You look to your right where, inside the southern curve of the arch, a parallel image shows Jerusalem's golden treasures being carried by the soldiers who burned the Temple to the ground (Figure 120). You look behind you and notice that both those scenes flow, as did that original triumphal procession in 71 C.E., westward to the temple of Capitoline Jupiter, for whose maintenance the Jewish Temple tax would henceforth be exacted. You look above you where, in the middle of the arch's topmost coffered curve, the bust of the now divine Titus is carried heavenward on the back of a Roman eagle (Figure 121). Like Julius Caesar and Augustus at the start of Rome's first imperial dynasty, Titus too ascends among the gods at the start of its second dynasty.

FIGURE 119. Arch of Titus with the Colosseum in the background.

You look before you, finally and climactically, at the largest amphitheater in the Roman Empire, the giant oval known as the Flavian Colosseum. Bracket for now the obscene slaughter that celebrated its dedication by Titus in 80 C.E. and focus on a marble lintel from inside the western entrance gateway. It announces a restoration under early-fifth-century emperors, but they had reused a block that once held a summary statement of the giant structure's original purpose. This can still be reconstructed from the holes left by the earlier bronze pins. It states that the emperor Vespasian commanded the construction of this "new amphitheater" from the share of the Jewish spoils that fell to him as general in the war of 66–74 C.E., which he had started and his son Titus had finished.

Against that background, precisely against that background, we revert from this chapter to Chapter 1, and ask again those two counterfactual questions. *Was there a serious chance for a Jewish Roman Empire and was it that very possibility that bred both approval and disapproval among pagan onlookers?* Recall that first response from Chapter 1 and consider these two other reactions as well.

FIGURE 120. Depiction on the Arch of Titus of the spoils from the Jewish Temple being brought to Rome by the legions.

BEFORE 70 C.E. How absurd, one might reply, recalling, for example, the great orator Cicero. In 59 B.C.E., a few years after Pompey had conquered Jerusalem, he was defending Flaccus, who, as governor of Asia, had confiscated that province's annual Jewish collection for the Temple at Jerusalem. "Even while Jerusalem was standing and the Jews were at peace with us," says his *Pro Flacco,* "the practice of their sacred rites was at variance with the glory of our empire, the dignity of our name, the customs of our ancestors. But now it is even more so, when that nation by its armed resistance has shown what it thinks of our rule" (28.67–69). But that equation of Jewish religion and Jewish rebellion remained a passing rhetorical attack and never became a permanent imperial accusation.

Still, one insists, the Roman establishment called the Jews atheistic, misanthropic, and superstitious. They were atheistic because they maintained exclusive worship; they were misanthropic because they maintained separate identity; and they were superstitious because they maintained both those actions as a divine mandate. So how could the Roman Empire have ever become Jewish? But, of course, those three accusations were exactly the same triad launched by the Roman establishment against the early Christians and

FIGURE 121.
Ascension of Titus
on the Arch of Titus.

eventually Rome became Christian. If, in other words, you told the philosopher Seneca around the year 50 C.E. that the Roman Empire would be *either* Jewish *or* Christian within three hundred years and asked him to wager his immense fortune on which one it would be, this is how he would have replied (after rolling on the floor with laughter and readjusting his toga). Both groups are weirdoes, he would have replied, but at least the Jews have been around for a long time, have their own country, and are our allies, so it must be the Jews (but, thank Jove, I will not be around to see that day).

AFTER 70 C.E. Well, all right, you respond, *maybe* such an event might have been imaginable in the year 50 C.E., but that was before the great revolt of 66–74 C.E. After that terrible war Rome could only see Judaism as a rebel religion, and your counterfactual questions are once again absurd. But consider this. Rome never combined religious separation and military rebellion into a single accusation, never claimed that the former caused the latter, and never concluded, as it might have done, that Judaism was an illicit religion.

Even after the first great revolt, for example, neither the historian Tacitus nor the satirist Juvenal makes any conflation of Jewish religious dissidence and Jewish military revolt. In his *Histories,* written in the first decade of the 100s C.E., Tacitus's view of Jewish origins is as nastily negative as Cicero's.

"Moses introduced new religious practices," he claimed, "quite opposed to those of all other religions. The Jews regard as profane all that we hold sacred; on the other hand, they permit all that we abhor" (5.4:1). But when Tacitus turns from ethnography to history, he never blames Jewish rebellion on Jewish religion. Indeed, he blames the Roman imperial governors rather than their Jewish colonial subjects. In 44 C.E., according to his indictment, "Claudius made Judaea a province, and entrusted it to Roman knights or freedmen; one of the latter, Antonius Felix [52–60] practiced every kind of cruelty and lust. . . . Still the Jews' patience lasted until Gessius Florus became procurator [62–66]" (5.9.3–10.1) That comes as close as Tacitus could to saying that the Jewish war of 66–74 was Rome's fault.

Juvenal's *Satire* 14 is particularly interesting because he notes the transition in some families from a father who "fears (*metuentem*) the Sabbath" to a son who "takes to circumcision," that is, from a God-fearer to a proselyte, so that "having been wont to flout the laws of Rome, they learn to practice and fear (*metuunt*) the Jewish law, and all that Moses handed down in his secret tome" (96–102). Satire only works when hearers recognize the individual or at least the type. So, then, how many such individuals were present in first-century Rome?

Once again, of course, our point is not to argue that the Roman Empire could have become Jewish not only before but even after that first great revolt. That is beyond proof or disproof. We ask our counterfactual questions only to listen for the reasons that dismiss or deride them and thereby reveal presuppositions, presumptions, and prejudices. We want, above all, to hold those counterfactual questions as background for Paul's letter to the Romans in order to cauterize the covert anti-Judaism or overt anti-Semitism that has so often been derived from its text.

Overview

When Jesus was born, Rome was the city of Augustus, but when Paul died it was the city of Nero. But by then the writing was already on the wall as the Julio-Claudian dynasty staggered toward its ignominious end. We start this chapter with one major contrast between Augustus and Nero (apart, of course, from character). Augustus spread his divine presence indirectly to every street corner of the city by creating offices and giving some status not just to the freeborn, but to the freed and even the enslaved. Nero, on the other hand, became infamous by being held directly responsible for the great fire of 64 C.E. That was probably a fiction, but the libel seemed confirmed by a subsequent urban renewal in which he constructed an unbelievably luxurious palace, the Golden House, just for his own use. And that was definitely a fact.

We conclude the section with another contrast, this time between that spatial Golden House, spread over three of Rome's seven hills, and the cramped and crowded tenements where Rome's Jews and Christians lived and the equally cramped catacombs where they were buried.

When Paul wrote his letter to the Romans from Corinth in the late mid-50s all of that was in the future. But with Claudius's death in 54 C.E., his expulsion of (some?) Jews and Jewish Christians quarreling over Jesus became moot, and they started to return under the new emperor, Nero. We begin our reading of this powerful letter with another warning about the nature of religious polemics (recall our first warning about the letter to the Galatians in Chapter 4). Paul is always bitingly, inaccurately, and unfairly offensive (in both senses of that word) against any Jews, Jewish Christians, or God-worshipers who threaten in any way his mission to convert pagans, especially those God-worshipers, to Christ.

We analyze the letter as a sweeping theology of human history seen by Paul as God's desire to create one world under global *justification* (or *making just*), under, in other words, the divine equity of distributive justice rather than under the divine threat of retributive justice. The letter is structured in three narrowing circles: unity under justice for, first, pagans and Jews (chaps. 1–8), then for Jews and Christians (9–11), and finally for Jewish Christians and pagan Christians (12–16).

At the moment of Paul's writing that vision of global unity under divine distributive justice was incarnated personally and concentrated symbolically for Paul in two magnificent initiatives (15:23–33). First, since the Jerusalem Conference, as he recalled in Galatians 2:10, Paul had been organizing a financial collection from his pagan converts for the common-life community known as "the poor" and assembled around James, the brother of Jesus, in Jerusalem. Representatives from the various provinces would bring it, and Paul was to accompany them to Jerusalem. That would emphasize and he hoped promote the religio-social unity of pagans and Jews, Jewish Christians and pagan Christians. Second, and thereafter, Paul intended to turn from the eastern to the western Roman Empire, and he planned to visit the Roman assemblies and obtain their assistance on his way to Spain. That would emphasize and he hoped promote the religio-geographical unity of

East and West under the justice of God as revealed in Christ. That was the global unity Paul described as a theology, lived as a geography, and served as a ministry. And, as it turned out, he died for it as well.

One final point and request. Throughout this book we have cited rather than simply referred to any passage in Paul's letters under discussion. We do not presume you have a New Testament always at hand. But because of the length and density of Paul's argument in Romans we have had to impose limitations in this case, so there will be more unquoted references than usual. You will be able to follow the discussion without a copy of Romans beside you, but it would be better if you had one available.

Augustus and Nero at Rome

The Arch of Titus was dedicated, high on its eastern side, to "The divine Titus Vespasian Augustus, son of the divine Vespasian." The Flavians, Rome's second imperial dynasty, lasted almost thirty years and had three emperors, but although Vespasian and his elder son, Titus, were officially divinized by the Senate, his younger son, Domitian, was assassinated and officially execrated by that same body. The Julio-Claudians, Rome's first imperial dynasty had lasted almost one hundred years and had five emperors. But only two, Augustus and Claudius, were senatorially divinized, and the last one, Nero, was finally "pronounced a public enemy by the Senate" and condemned, according to Suetonius's *The Lives of the Caesars: Nero,* to being "stripped, fastened by the neck in a fork, and then beaten to death with rods." He only avoided that fate by suicide, driving "a dagger into his throat, aided by Epaphroditus, his private secretary" (49.2–3). On June 9, 68 C.E., the Julio-Claudian dynasty came to an ignominious end and Rome was plunged once more into civil war.

Compare, however, across almost one hundred years, the imperial theological strategy of an Augustus and a Nero, and then ponder the supreme irony that not Augustus but Nero was claimed fled not dead, was imagined still alive somewhere in the East as, on the one hand, their once and future savior by the Parthians and, on the other, as their great anti-Messiah by the Jews.

Imperial Divinity at Every Corner

The blocks, or insulae, in Roman neighborhoods, for example, in across-the-Tiber Trastevere, were a far cry from the splendor of Rome's marbled and columned public architecture. But the message of that architecture's images was not isolated to the urban civic center or the great public plazas. Augustus made sure that imperial Roman theology penetrated deep into local districts among the urban plebs. Under the Republic, the many freedmen and slaves who made up that urban plebs were volatile, were often a threat to the established order, and were always a powerful tool for those who manipulated their discontent for political gain. Unrest always festered just beneath the surface of the urban landscape, and the Senate was always conscious of groups that met beyond the umbrella of their aristocratic control. Inside Rome, the *collegia,* or associations of freedmen and slaves who tended to the *lares compitales,* or neighborhood shrines, to the "guardian spirits of the crossroads," for example, were especially suspect inside Rome.

If the *lararium* was the focal point of religious piety for the household and especially for its *paterfamilias,* think of the *lares compitales* as the focal point of religious devotion for the blocklike insula and its plebeian inhabitants. Under their divine sanction they held local games, festivals, and sacrifices. Think of them as lower-class block parties with plenty of food and drink, based religiously of course, but also a possible crucible for subversive political activity. Those *collegia* were outlawed by the Senate in 64 B.C.E. but later reinstated, were then reduced in number by Julius Caesar, and initially outlawed by Augustus in 22 B.C.E. Later, however, Augustus cleverly refocused their structure and energy. He restructured the city into 14 districts and 265 wards, then appointed four officials from the freedmen and a number from the slaves for each of those neighborhood wards, and finally placed himself squarely in the middle of the process by transforming the *lares compitales* into the *lares Augusti* at the *compita,* or street corners.

The *lares* were visually represented by one or two dancing figures (Figure 125), but Augustus placed his own divine personification on those transformed crossroad altars (Figure 122). This strategic rearrangement gave some measure of honor and prestige to local freedmen and lower-level patrons, who could now identify with the emperor, supervise the sacrifices, and even see themselves represented on local altars. That can be seen on an altar from the Vicus Aesculeti on the Campus Martius dating to 2 B.C.E. showing a bull and a boar being sacrificed to Augustus (Figure 123). The new organization also provided opportunities for participation by slaves, who previously had no active role in any civic cult. A simple altar with oak wreath from a neighborhood on the Caelian Hill was sponsored by the slave officials Felix, Florus, Eudoxsus, and Polyclitus, who inscribed their names

FIGURE 122 *(left)*. Altar of the *lares* from the Vicus Sandaliarius in Rome, with Augustus in the center. FIGURE 123 *(right)*. Bull and boar shown sacrificed on an altar of the *lares compitales* in a Roman neighborhood.

but not their portraits on its side (Figure 124). Women could also join in those rites. One altar, though an unofficial rather than the official one, shows the two *lares* on one side and what must have been wealthy freedwomen sacrificing on the other (Figure 125).

The cult of the *lares Augusti* held a major celebration on August 1, the beginning of the month named after Augustus, and that celebration and cult continued long after his death. Since the *lares* had traditionally been ghost-like ancestral guardian spirits, the *lares Augusti* were appropriate throughout the entire Julio-Claudian dynasty and into Paul's lifetime. There is in fact evidence for their use and repair of their shrines through the third century. As Mary Beard, John North, and Simon Price note in their *Religions of Rome:*

> The cults were not a transient Augustan phenomenon, but played their part in permanently re-orienting Roman religion under the Empire. The creation of the new wards took the emphasis on place to every corner of the city; here we see the emperor inserted within a religious framework that incorporated the whole city, by creating an opportunity for local participation in the creation of imperial Rome's new mythology. (186)

FIGURE 124. Altar of the *lares Augusti* dedicated by slaves, whose names are encircled by a wreath.

Remember all of this when you think of those Roman Christians addressed by Paul. They lived precisely in the local places and among the lower classes specifically addressed by Roman imperial theology on the level of the *lares Augusti*. And now, as the Julio-Claudian dynasty shuddered to its extinction, compare those small but multiplied Augustan structures with Nero's single but massive construction.

The Great Fire and the Golden House

As you stood beneath the Arch of Titus where the Via Sacra crested the Velian Ridge you stood above the buried entrance to Nero's *Domus Aurea,* his Golden House, that megalomaniacal palace-garden-lake complex that sprawled across the heart of Rome in the middle of the first century C.E. It was, undoubtedly, the most grandiose and opulent private dwelling ever built inside or outside Rome. We look at it here not just to consider its architectural audacity, but to contrast its self-centered indulgence with Augustus's architectural program for restoring *pietas* to city and empire. Recall the use of images and structures as that first *divi filius* manifested a Roman imperial theology in which official *piety* led to military *victory* and imperial *peace*. Remember, from Chapter 2, Augustus's restoration of the dilapidated temples, his forum with the temple to the war god Mars *Ultor,* and his Altar of Augustan Peace. Then imagine how Romans might have looked at Nero's Golden House.

FIGURE 125. Altar of the *lares Augusti* dedicated by women, with *lares* on the front panel and women sacrificing on either side of the now fragmentary side panels.

Augustus's program spread among the city's inhabitants the wealth that victory and expansion brought to the capital, with a grain dole for the poor, entertainment and games for the masses, and water and baths for each neighborhood. Nero's narcissism in building the Golden House had its counterpart in his passion for the arts, of which he fancied himself a patron. He also saw to Rome's more basic needs with the construction of a large *macellum,* or meat market, and of public baths so splendid that Martial's *Epigrams* could declare, "What worse than Nero, what better than Nero's baths?" (7.34). We emphasize, however, not the abnormality of Nero's particularly cruel and selfish reign, but the normalcy of dynasties degenerating under the weight of absolute power. Even so, Nero's energies and expenses for his own palace overshadowed all other projects in scale and detail, and we contrast Paul not just with that one perversely evil Nero of long, long ago, but with the normalcy of all imperial power degenerating steadily as time passes.

Rome was built on seven hills, and Nero's Golden House spread across three of them. It covered the southern slope of the Esquiline Hill, the northern slope of the Caelian Hill, and almost the entire Palatine Hill, and although it is called a *house,* it was actually a set of gardens and vineyards, pavilions and palaces that covered over three hundred acres (Figure 126). While other Roman aristocrats built villas outside Rome in rustic settings, Nero brought

the countryside inside Rome and clustered various structures around an artificial lake. To shape an appropriate entrance for the Golden House, Nero
straightened out the revered but winding Via Sacra to create an axial view
from the Roman Forum into an enormous vestibule. In that entrance the
emperor placed, according to *Nero* in Suetonius's *The Lives of the Caesars,* a
120-foot nude statue of himself as the sun god Sol, or Helios (21). It was
modeled on the Colossus of Rhodes, one of the seven wonders of the ancient world.

Given its central urban location and Rome's constant rebuilding, archaeologists have uncovered only a fraction of the original Golden House. The
most extensive remnant is the Esquiline Wing, a suite of some 140 rooms
cut along a terrace in the hill, but later filled in for the foundations of the
Baths of Trajan. That wing was an insignificant portion of the whole, but
today it allows an appreciation of Nero's architectural creativity and decorative opulence. It faced south onto the artificial lake and, beyond that, onto
an enormous *nymphaeum,* or fountain-and-pool structure. That, by the way,
intruded into the unfinished Temple of the Divine Claudius, a project dedicated to Nero's stepfather and predecessor that Nero impiously suspended
to concentrate efforts on his own house. Furthermore, to fill that artificial

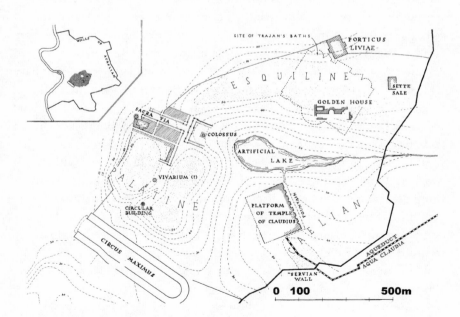

FIGURE 126. Area of Nero's Golden House in Rome.

lake Nero siphoned off the city's water supply by redirecting the Aqua Claudia aqueduct northward to his garden paradise. The Esquiline Wing's doors, windows, and roof openings shielded or harnessed sunlight according to the seasons, so that some were warm and well lit in winter, others shaded and fountain-cooled in summer. This western wing was divided into two sections on either side of a polygonal courtyard that opened toward the lake. At the east of that wing was an octagonal room and, apparently, those two western sections were paralleled but reversed in an eastern wing. A close look at one or two rooms suffices to establish Nero's self-indulgent tastes.

From the western wing, one room stands out. It mimicked a grotto, was darkened completely by the absence of natural light, had a vaulted ceiling and artificial stalactites made of pumice, and was decorated with a mosaic of Odysseus and the cave-dwelling Cyclops Polyphemus. It was part Disney World, part low fantasy, part high culture.

From the center of the still extant western and now lost eastern wings, the most innovative room was the Octagonal Suite, a large hall that opened web-like into rooms radiating from its center and whose upper stories the Italian archaeologist Laura Fabbrini has recently excavated (Figure 127). Although today only a brick, mortar, and concrete shell survives, the room's façades once dazzled and delighted visitors. From a few remnants as well as impressions in the plaster, we know that the floor was once *opus sectile,* a geometrically patterned and multicolored marble inlay, that the narrow walls were faced with revetments and white marble pilasters, and that the low domed ceiling was covered with blue, green, and translucent glass tessarae that have long since fallen to the floor. At the apex of the dome was a circular skylight, similar to and probably the inspiration for the rebuilt Pantheon. The Octagonal Suite was also backlit from the surrounding rooms, which had their own windows cut into the arches supporting the dome, but which were invisible from inside and below the suite. Light and airy within, the weighty dome was supported in a concealed manner by concrete struts along the radial walls of the adjacent rooms. It was cleverly disguised, an ingenious architectural trick. This may be the Golden House's circular banqueting room described in Suetonius's *The Lives of the Caesars.* It "constantly revolved day and night, like the heavens" according to his *Nero* (31). The Golden House was a pleasure palace that suited Nero's Greek and artistic inclination, but was also Roman at the same time.

Haunting the entire structure, however, was that fact that its grand scale was possible only after Rome's great fire in 64 C.E. Nearly four-fifths of the

FIGURE 127. Octagonal Suite of the Esquiline Wing of Nero's Golden House.

city was touched by that fire, and much of the city's center was razed. Nero owned the imperial estates on the Palatine Hill, inherited or acquired houses across the slopes of the Caelian and Esquiline hills, but in between were smaller commercial districts and densely populated tenement housing that prevented him from uniting his lands and constructing one vast palace. Once those warehouses and tenements were destroyed by fire, he unified the diverse urban sections into a single vast area for his parklike palace. But certain of Rome's fourteen districts were not affected. One was Nero's estate on the Palatine, which, combined with the fact that he so obviously exploited the fire for his own personal interests, fed the rumor that he himself had started the conflagration. Another area untouched by the fire was Augustus's newly created district of Transtiberium, "on the other side of the Tiber River," now called Trastevere, where a high concentration of Christians were living. We return at the end of this chapter to their use as Nero's scapegoats.

One footnote to the great fire, Nero, and his Golden House. His construction project was systematically rejected in the architectural programs of subsequent emperors. The materials lavished on his own personal pleasure and aesthetic satisfaction were cashed in for political gain. His successor, Vespasian, for example, plundered much of the complex, stripping it of marble that he used on his Temple of Peace, and also piously completed the

Temple of the Divine Claudius. Even though, or especially because, he was not a relative, he needed to link his new Flavian dynasty with the Julio-Claudian dynasty of Augustus. The next Flavian, that same Titus whose arch celebrated the destruction of Jerusalem's Temple, likewise razed Nero's palace to build public baths. The artificial lake was drained, and the Flavian Amphitheater was built in its place. Its name, the Coliseum or Colosseum, comes, ironically, from the Colossus of Nero, that giant statue that once stood in the vestibule of the Golden House. Domitian, the next and final Flavian, built an enormous palace on the Palatine Hill with a distinctly public character. Public entertainment replaced personal pleasure.

Judaism and Christianity at Rome

We look first at the Jewish communities and then at the Christian communities in Rome. But we emphasize that, when Paul wrote to the Romans in the mid-50s C.E., terms like "Jews" and "Christians" were much less clear and discrete than they would later become. What term would you use for a God-fearing pagan who became Christian but wanted to continue certain Jewish observances?

Jewish Expulsions and Returns

We know some major details about the Jewish communities in Rome during the two hundred years before Nero's imperial accession, and all of them are as ambiguous as our opening counterfactual questions. After all, three expulsions in two hundred years are a sign not of accepted weakness and acknowledged unimportance, but of disliked strength and rejected prominence.

The first expulsion is mentioned in the first-century-C.E. *On Superstitions* by Valerius Maximus. It records how in 139 B.C.E. the official in charge of foreigners had "expelled from Rome the astrologers and ordered them to leave Italy within ten days" and had also "banished the Jews from Rome because they attempted to transmit their sacred rites to the Romans, and he cast down their private altars from public places." In that and what follows, watch how Rome reacts against the too successful attraction of the East in general and of Judaism in particular.

The next expulsion occurred more than 150 years later, by Tiberius in 19 C.E., and again it had to do with oriental "superstitions" infiltrating Roman traditions. In his *Annals,* written a decade or so after the *Histories,*

Tacitus speaks of Tiberius's proscription "of the Egyptian and Jewish rites," his military absorption of "four thousand descendants of enfranchised slaves" to fight Sardinian bandits, and his orders for "the rest to leave *Italy,* unless they had renounced their impious ceremonial by a given date" (2.85:4). Suetonius's version of that story, published in his *Lives of the Caesars: Tiberius* around 120 C.E., says that Tiberius "abolished foreign cults, especially the Egyptian and the Jewish rites, compelling all who were addicted to such superstitions to burn their religious vestments and all their paraphernalia," absorbed "those of the Jews who were of military age" into the army, and banished others "from the *city,* on pain of slavery for life if they did not obey." Almost a century later, Cassius Dio's *Roman History* summarized it even more tersely: "As the Jews flocked to Rome in great numbers and were converting many of the natives to their ways, [Tiberius] banished most of them" (58.18:5a).

The archaeological background for those Roman Jews is found in many inscriptions from multiple synagogues named for a major patron (Agrippa), a local area (Sibura), a specific language (Hebrew), or a foreign origin (Tripolis). The Roman Jews, unlike their Alexandrian counterparts, were not under a single ethnarch, but those inscriptions show similar administrative structures and executive officers—a council of elders (*gerousia*) and their leader (*gerousiarch*), executives (*archontes*), a secretary (*grammateus*), a liturgical officer (*archisynagōgos*), and patrons, both female (mothers) and male (fathers).

The final expulsion happened only thirty years after that preceding one, which means, of course, that not "all" could have left under Tiberius. But the cause is now much more specific than either a general distaste for oriental sects or Jewish successes. In the first century, Luke's Acts says that when Paul arrived at Corinth "he found a Jew named Aquila, a native of Pontus, who had recently come from Italy with his wife Priscilla, because Claudius had ordered all Jews to leave Rome" (18:2). In the second century, Suetonius's *Lives of the Caesars: Divus Claudius* explains that "since the Jews constantly made disturbances at the instigation of Chrestus [i.e., Christ], he expelled them from Rome" (25.4). In the third century, Cassius Dio's *Roman History* gives a different account, dated to the start of Claudius's reign in 41:

> As for the Jews, who had again [after Tiberius's edict?] increased so greatly that by reason of their multitude it would have been hard without raising a tumult to bar them from the city, he [Claudius] did not drive them out, but ordered them, while continuing their traditional mode of life, not to hold meetings. (60.6:6)

In the fifth century, Orosius's *Against Pagans* cites the text from Suetonius quite accurately and also cites the date, "in the ninth year of Claudius" or 49 C.E. (7.6.15–16), as from Josephus, but there is no such text in our copy of that Jewish historian's writings. All in all, therefore, we can only be certain that sometime in the 40s Claudius moved against at least those synagogues or individuals responsible for public disturbances between, on the one side, Jewish Jews and Jewish God-worshipers and, on the opposing side, Christian Jews and Christian God-worshipers. Against *all* synagogues? Probably not. Against *all* individuals? Definitely not. Note, of course, that God-worshipers could have been on either or both sides of any such conflict between "Jews" and "Christians." In other words, you probably had pro-Jewish God-worshipers in conflict with pro-Christian God-worshipers in and around those Roman Jewish synagogues.

In the 40s, under Claudius, that dispute in Rome's synagogues was considered a totally "Jewish" matter to be solved by a totally anti-"Jewish" response. The Roman authorities lumped together as "Jews" what we might distinguish as Jewish Jews, pro-Jewish God-worshipers, pro-Christian God-worshipers, and pure Christian pagans. By the 60s, under Nero, *Christians* were so clearly distinguished from *Jews* that the former could be separately and independently persecuted for Rome's great fire in 64. In between, during the mid-50s, two events must be held in conjunction. In 54, as mentioned above, Nero became emperor, and within a year or two Paul wrote to the Romans. Priscilla and Aquila, for example, who had been in Corinth in Acts 18:2 and then in Ephesus in Acts 18:18–19 and 1 Corinthians 16:19 were back once more in Rome by the time of Romans 16:3. We may generalize their action and imagine that Claudius's death and Nero's accession permitted return for many other Jewish Jews and Christian Jews as well. And, as their numbers increased to as high as perhaps forty to fifty thousand, we find again that same ambiguity of Roman opposition because of Jewish strength.

On strength: Josephus calls Poppaea Sabina, successively Nero's mistress, wife, and victim, "a worshiper of God" (*theosebēs*) and records her defense of Jewish interests against accusations in the late 50s and early 60s by the Judean governors Felix, in *Jewish Antiquities* (20.195), and Festus, in *Life* (16). On opposition: Seneca, successively Nero's tutor, adviser, and victim, wrote of the Jews in his *On Superstition:* "The customs of this accused race have gained such influence that they are now received throughout all the world. The vanquished have given laws to the victors." Still, in that new Neronic environment, the situation of *Christian Jews* must have been doubly precari-ous. On the one hand, *Jewish Jews* would hardly welcome them since their presence had caused the disturbances and penalties under Claudius. On the other hand, *Christian pagans,* having grown strong and separate in their ab-sence, were unlikely to welcome them back as full fellow Christians. It is particularly those *weak,* or returning, Christians that Paul defends against the *strong,* or resident, Christians in Romans 12–13 generally and Romans 13–16 specifically.

Christian Locations and Catacombs

No Christian house from the time of Nero could ever be identified as such, since distinctive Christian material culture and iconic imagery did not develop until the late second century C.E. The rich body of early Christian archaeological remains in Rome is mostly from the third century, and it flourished dramatically after the fourth, when the empire became Christian. The shameful and subversive nature of the cross, for example, was not em-braced for Christian iconic self-expression until after the imperial conver-sion of Constantine the Great in the early fourth century C.E. In fact, figured crucifixes or even unfigured crosses cannot be found prior to Con-stantine. There is, however, one very noteworthy exception.

INSCRIPTIONS. A picture and graffito dating to around 200 C.E. is the earliest extant example of a crucifix or crucifixion scene, although, of course, it is an anti-Christian satire. It was discovered in 1856 scratched into the plastered wall of Room III within the imperial servants' quarters on the Palatine Hill. It is the earliest attestation of a crucifix, and it was found in the very area where Augustus had his own house, an area later incorporated into Nero's Golden House. The crude sketch (Figure 128) depicts a man in front of a cross on which a donkey-headed man is crucified, and the accompany-ing Greek scribble underneath pokes fun at a Christian: *Alexamenos sebete theon,* "Alexander worships God" (recall, by the way, that same word, *sebo-mai,* was often used for God-fearers). A pagan servant ridiculed the Chris-tian faith of a co-worker and used the shame of the cross, along with an ass's head, to lampoon early Christianity.

Another inscription provides evidence for an early Christian at a surpris-ingly high level within the imperial court. A sarcophagus belonging to the imperial freedman Marcus Aurelius Prosenes dating to the year 217 C.E. had

FIGURE 128. "Alexander worships God," a derisive caricature of a Christian worshiping a donkey-headed man on a cross, scratched into plaster in Rome.

two inscriptions. One, in a central and visible position between two cupids, pronounced that the interred was an

> ex-slave of the emperors, chamberlain of the emperor [Caracalla], steward of the treasury, steward of the imperial property, steward of the gladiatorial shows, steward of the wines, appointed by the divine Commodus to the court, his ex-slaves paid for the carving of the sarcophagus from their own money for their most pious master who well deserved it. (*CIL* 6:8498A)

That was the more official and public dedication, jointly commissioned by all of that successful freedman's clients, those former slaves whom he had in turn set free.

The second inscription, however, was written by one particular former slave of Prosenes named Ampelius. On the upper border of the sarcophagus's shorter and right side, just above a griffin and barely visible, was an inscription containing the distinctly Christian and Latin *receptus ad deum,* "taken back to God." It read,

> Prosenes was received unto God five days before the Nones of [March] at S[. . .]nia when Praesens and Extricatus were consuls, the latter for the second time [217 C.E.]. Ampelius his ex-slave on his return to the city from the campaign inscribed this. (*CIL* 6:8498B)

The loyal Ampelius had accompanied Prosenes on the emperor Caracalla's campaign against the Parthians in Mesopotamia, but his patron died there, so he took the costly and unusual step of forgoing cremation and bringing the body all the way back to Rome. Christians, like Jews, shunned cremation, a practice probably tied to their belief in the resurrection. It seems likely that Prosenes and Ampelius were fellow Christians, and that the latter ensured a theologically appropriate burial for the former. That meant not only avoiding cremation, but also eschewing overtly pagan decorations on the sarcophagus, which had only neutral dolphins, cupids, cornucopia, and griffin. It also lacked the common pagan phrase or one of the various abbreviations for *dis manibus (sanctum)*, "sacred to the deceased spirits," though the official inscription does refer to the "*divus* Commodus." Ampelius, perhaps later, added the second inscription in a clearly but unobtrusively Christian manner.

Should we assume, working back from a wall graffito and a sarcophagus inscription of the early third century, that Christianity's first foothold in Rome was on the Palatine among imperial servants and upwardly mobile imperial freedmen? And should we assume that most Christians met in homes or households in that geographical and political center? Those few archaeological remains and the occasional literary text suggest that some in fact did, but for the vast majority of Christians all indications point instead to the periphery, both topographically and socially.

BURIALS. No single Christian house from the time of Paul has—or will ever—be identified, but recall the brilliant studies of Peter Lampe on Rome's earliest Christians, introduced in Chapter 1. His work has shown with persuasive certainty that their highest concentrations were in marginal areas like Trastevere on the western banks of the Tiber and along the southern Via Appia, which led into Rome (Figure 129).

One would expect those two areas from later legends alone and earlier parish names, the titular churches that date back to the first two centuries. But Lampe also carefully surveyed the archaeological evidence, which, though rarely itself dating to the first century, has implications for the location of those first-century Roman Christians. He charted and traced the development around Rome of the earliest Christian burials, inside those well-known and frequently visited catacombs.

In antiquity almost everyone buried their dead outside the city's boundaries. Burials from the sacred island of Delos, for example, were on an

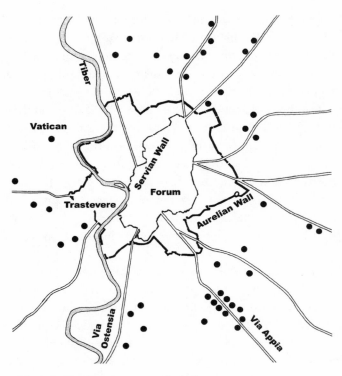

FIGURE 129. Map of early Christian catacombs in Rome.

adjacent islet and at Hierapolis, as you will recall from Chapter 3, the tombs of the dead stood along the major roads outside the city gates. So also on the roads leading into ancient Rome. There were the monumental above-ground tombs of the wealthy, and there were also some facilities shared by lower-class members of burial societies or guilds. These latter were located a row or two behind the mausoleums of the rich and famous or at a greater distance from the city gate. But as the city expanded and space grew sparse on the imperial city's periphery, less well off Romans—pagans, Jews, and Christians—dug beneath those roadside cemeteries and cut a maze of underground tunnels and chambers into the soft but firm volcanic tufa. Some of the dead were simply placed along the tunnels in tiers shelved with coffin-sized recesses, which were then covered on the side with tile slab; others were interred in arched recesses cut into chambers large enough for funerary and commemorative meals with the dead (Figure 130). Decorations and inscriptions provide a wealth of information about their users.

Among the around fifty known complexes that stretch over three hundred miles under modern-day Rome, many bear distinctly Christian decorations and inscriptions. The location of those earliest Christian catacombs along particular roads *outside* the city provides some indication of where the Christians had lived *inside* the city, since people buried their dead on the radial roads nearest their quarter. So we find, as Lampe has argued, that the earliest and most prominent Christian burials were, on the one hand, along the Via Appia, at San Callisto, with its famous crypt for some of the earliest popes, or farther south at San Sebastiano, where one early Christian scratched in the plaster of a pillar the Greek word for fish, ICHTHUS, an acrostic representing "Jesus—Christ—of God—Son—Savior," and at the Pretestato and Domitilla Catacombs. The next set of catacombs, on the other hand, were those on roads leading from Trastevere along the Via Aurelia and under the Vatican Hill (Figure 129).

MEMORIALS. Among those many early Christian tombs are two legendary burial sites, that of Paul himself, now under the church called St. Paul Outside the Walls on the Via Ostiensis, the road that left the city and

FIGURE 130. Early Christian catacombs of Priscilla in Rome; shafts would have been covered with tiles, like those still preserved at bottom left.

headed south to Ostia between Trastevere and the Via Appia, and that of Peter, today in the crypt of St. Peter's Basilica in the Vatican (Figure 131). Both are mentioned by the fourth-century Christian historian Eusebius quoting one Gaius from around 200 C.E., who wrote that Christians honored memorials to Paul and Peter at those locations (2.25.7). Though archaeologists have indeed found burials at those sites, we are less concerned here with arguing for or against their historicity than with their aid in locating the earliest Christian communities in Rome and the socioeconomic and theological information they provide about those earliest Christians.

First and in some detail, Peter's crypt. Over the years much archaeological energy has been spent under the Vatican, and the excavations tell a fascinating story—even if Peter was not actually buried there. Excavations reveal that by the middle of the second century Christians were venerating a simple grave in the Vatican Hill's aboveground cemetery, which excavators labeled "P." It was covered with a stone slab running west-southwest to east-northeast in an area used also by pagans. When two non-Christian mausoleums restructured the space between them by building stairs down the slope and a wall for some privacy or enclosure, that wall, painted red, cut obliquely over what was presumably Peter's grave. Christians were apparently unable to stop those pagan renovations by purchasing the space around their own revered tomb. Sometime after the red wall's construction, they did fashion an aedicula onto it with two niches and simple white columns

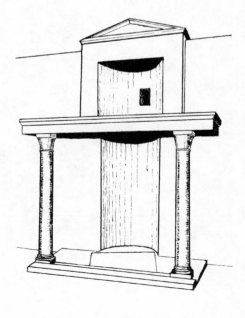

FIGURE 131. Reconstruction of St. Peter's tomb, with an aedicula built into the backside of another mausoleum's wall.

supporting a beam, but that was aligned awkwardly over the stone slab (Figure 131).

By all standards it was a relatively meager monument, though certainly more prestigious than many of the graves that crowded around Peter's tomb, many of which were simply shallow holes in the ground covered by brick tiles. As Lampe says in his book *From Paul to Valentinus,* "If we compare the sociology of the grave area 'P' with the sociology of the city region attached to the Vatican, Trastevere, both parts fit together seamlessly" (115). They both belonged to the *humiliores,* the common people of Rome.

Second and very briefly, Paul's grave. In 1823 the Church of St. Paul Outside the Walls burned down and a new one was subsequently rebuilt; unfortunately little excavation took place then, and now future excavation is all but impossible. What was discovered, however, was ironic but in a way appropriate. The area under and around that first church was a pagan burial place from first through third centuries C.E. We wonder if that's not how Paul would have wanted it. Paul, apostle of God to the Gentiles, was buried among the pagans to whom he had dedicated his life.

LOCATIONS. The neighborhoods of Trastevere and the Via Appia were in many ways similar districts. Both were, in Lampe's words, "perimeter areas" (43) that lay outside the old city wall and the *pomerium,* or sacred boundary, inside which worship of foreign deities was prohibited. Numerous Eastern religious shrines, for example, to the Syrian Dea and the Palmyran Sol, to the Egyptian Hadad and the mother goddess Isis, and to the Anatolian Cybele, were discovered in Trastevere, farther west on the Janiculum Hill, and northwest on the Vatican Hill. Martial tells us that the priests of Cybele washed statues and sacrificial knives in the Almone River along the southern Appian Way. Those of course were also the very areas in which Jews lived, which is indirect confirmation for placing the earliest Christian communities there. The Alexandrian Jewish philosopher Philo wrote after visiting Rome in *On the Embassy to Gaius,* "The great section of Rome on the other side of the Tiber River [Trastevere] was occupied and inhabited by Jews" (155). And the Roman Juvenal wrote in his *Satires* that Jews lived also "near the aging and damp Capena" (3.12), that is, just outside the Porta Capena in the swampy Appian lowland.

CLASSES. Religion, however, was not the reason so many Jews and other eastern immigrants lived outside the *pomerium,* in Trastevere, along the Via Appia, and in other peripheral areas. The primary reasons were socioeconomic, as both Juvenal and Philo suggest. Juvenal sneers that the old muses had fled the area outside the Porta Capena because so many Jews begged there now, and Philo describes the Jews in Trastevere as recently freed slaves. Since both the Tiber at Trastevere and the Via Appia were major traffic arteries that brought goods and people from the provinces, a heavily immigrant population is to be expected there. Trastevere was, again in Lampe's words,

> a harbor quarter, a workers quarter. It accommodated harbor workers, who unloaded the ships' cargoes, porters of the many warehouses, sailors, and also workers from the brickyards on the Vatican slopes. . . . Shopkeepers and small craftsmen were drawn by the harbor and its imported goods—ivory carvers, cabinet makers, and potters. Millers from Trastevere ground the imported grains unloaded in the harbor. . . . Knacker and tanner operations spread a penetrating odor: The "dog's skin that hangs in Trastevere" (Martial 6.49) stank pervasively. (50)

Seven brick basins from the Coraria Septiminiana, a leather factory where urine collected from the public latrines was used for tanning, were discovered under Trastevere's Church of Santa Caecilia. The area around the Via Appia was similar, filled with traders, craftsmen, and transport workers, the latter carting their wares on city streets by law only at night. It was a noisy and boisterous district. Judging from the names of several neighborhoods, many worked there with wool and linen in the textile industry, weaving, dying, or possibly making leather tents or linen awnings. That is of course exactly the kind of area where one would expect to find Prisca and Aquila, the Jewish tentmaking couple so important in Paul's life. They might have made sails or tents for the Roman army in Corinth, but in Rome they probably made those many awnings used in theaters, amphitheaters, the circus, or private homes. This social location also fits with the names mentioned by Paul in Romans 16 because about two-thirds of those names are Greek rather than Latin. That suggests that they or their ancestors came from the East most likely as slaves and were later freed, but continued to prefer Greek to Latin names.

HOUSES. Trastevere was the area with the lowest ratio of villas to insulae in Rome. There were, in other words, fewer villas like those we saw at Pompeii and Herculaneum in Chapter 6 and far more apartments or tenements. But that does not imply a homogenous lower class. Like those Vesu-vian cities, Rome's urban neighborhoods, even those of lesser reputation, were made up of many little patronal pyramids. Though the Roman insula was more cramped and lacked an atrium or courtyard, it shared a certain commercial and domestic fluidity; its architectural structure was arranged vertically in tiered stories rather than horizontally in rows of rooms. As we see in the Insula Aracoeli (Figure 132), whose first-century outlines have

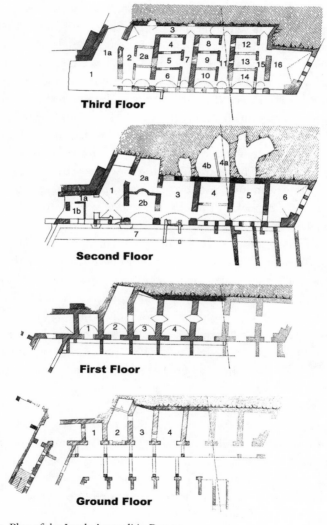

FIGURE 132. Plan of the Insula Aracoeli in Rome.

survived millennia of renovation and repair, the lowest story was made up of a row of shops that faced the street. Above them was a mezzanine level, some of whose rooms were interconnected. Those served as storage space, as workers' quarters, or as additional work space associated with the shops below. The next level up had large and spacious rooms, probably belonging to the insula's owner-paterfamilias, who was most likely an upwardly mobile freedman or a low-level freeborn; a room niche was apparently used as a *lararium* (2b). The floor above that contained a set of three corridors opening onto three small rooms apiece. They must have been dark if not dingy, and it is open to debate whether slaves, renters, or dependents lived there.

Archaeologists, unfortunately, can only uncover the lower floors constructed of stone, brick, and concrete in such four- to five-story tenements. Any upper stories made of wood, added by landlords to increase occupancy and revenue, necessarily elude them. Those buildings were proverbial in literary texts for being hot in summer and cold in winter, for being dim and fetid, and for being prone to fire or collapse. Juvenal mocks Rome for its dangerous high-rises: "Who at cool Praeneste, or at Volsinii amid its leafy hills, was ever afraid of his house tumbling down? . . . But we here inhabit a city supported for the most part by slender props: for that is how the landlord patches up the crack in the old wall, bidding the inmates sleep at ease under a roof ready to tumble about their ears" (*Satires* 3.190–96). Rather than the anonymity of modern urban apartments, those living in the close quarters of the ancient Roman insula would have felt keenly the pervasive patronal system, as the insula's owner-landlord-patron wielded considerable influence over its architectural, social, and economic structure.

The insulae and their neighborhoods are certainly the context in which the earliest Christian communities must be understood. So we ask, even though unable to give a definitive answer, where they would have met. Should we imagine a group of twelve to fifteen people meeting in the small shops after hours? Or up a flight of stairs in the mezzanine level, where those tending the shops lived? Should we imagine a group of twenty to thirty crowding the more spacious rooms of the insula's owner as the local patron? Or should we imagine a much smaller group huddling in the corridors or inside a tiny cubicle on the fourth floor, or worse, in the wooden shacks atop the roof? We wonder what a *house*-church meant in Rome and wonder, ultimately, if Paul could have himself imagined what it meant as he wrote to the Romans from Corinth.

The Rhetoric of Religious Polemics (Once Again)

In the sixteenth century Luther said two things about Paul's letter to the Romans, one fundamentally right, one fundamentally wrong, both fundamentally important. In the preface to his commentary on that letter he said,

> Faith is a living, unshakable confidence in God's grace; it is so certain, that someone would die a thousand times for it. This kind of trust in and knowledge of God's grace makes a person joyful, confident, and happy with regard to God and all creatures. This is what the Holy Spirit does by faith. Through faith, a person will do good to everyone without coercion, willingly and happily; he will serve everyone, suffer everything for the love and praise of God, who has shown him such grace. *It is as impossible to separate works from faith as burning and shining from fire.* (italics added)

That last sentence is both crucial and correct. In Romans 3:18 Paul says "justified by faith" and Luther's German translates that as "by faith alone." Of course. Because "faith alone" already includes works or it is not faith. *The room was lit by the fire alone* means exactly the same as *the room was lit by the fire's shining.*

But Luther then went on to argue that "the Jews" made that impossible disjunction between faith and works in three different ways. First, by *hypocrisy:* they claimed to do what was right, but did not actually do it. Such were "those who appear outwardly pious or who sin secretly." Second, by *externalism:* if they both claimed and did what was right, they did so only externally, but not internally. Such were those "who live virtuous lives but without eagerness and love; in their heart they are enemies of God's law and like to judge other people." Third, by *pride:* if they both claim and do what is right and also do it both internally and externally, they think to replace divine grace by human power. Such are those "who want to live virtuously by nature or by free will."

All of that would have been fair enough in the abstractly hypothetical case of *things some people might do.* We are composed of body and soul, flesh and spirit, inside and outside, intention and action. Disjunctions between those elements can and do take place. But because we can only see the externals, such accusations are also marvelous devices for polemical attacks against individuals, groups, nations, or religions we do not like. They are the standard tools of *us versus them,* the normal strategies of *othering* an opponent.

ʋse your vision or your program, we say that you talk the
alk the walk, or you do both but only externally, or that
d in both ways, but it is all for money, display, pride, or self-

ɪ a contemporary example. You display a large American flag on
ness. I dislike you and say you are doing it just to attract people, to
nore money, to fake patriotism, or to be like everyone else. It does
ome, I say, from the inside, from the heart, from true patriotism. If, to
ntinue that example, a law commanded such flag displays, the one who
ad always done it could claim *faith-works* and accuse those newly instituting
the practice of mere *law-works*. But how, short of actual evidence ("he admitted it"), could one tell for sure which was the case? Without such certain
evidence that accusation is simply the typical rhetoric of polemical defama-
tion. It was particularly useful, in Luther's day, for opposing Christians to
Jews and, through those surrogates, for opposing Protestant Reformers to
Roman Catholics.

All of that points to one conclusion. In Romans Paul is struggling hard
for a vision that *most* pagans, *many* Jews, and *some* Christians do not share.
He is struggling hard for the meaning of his own life and his own vocation
as "a servant of Jesus Christ, called to be an apostle, set apart for the gospel
of God" (1:1; read 1:1–6), a gospel about "salvation for everyone who has
faith . . . in the righteousness of God" (1:15–16). But *salvation, righteousness,*
and *faith* are words whose backs are bent if not broken by the weight of
post-Reformation theological controversy. They will need very delicate
and very accurate handling.

Finally, we cannot forget that Paul is also locked in controversy for "my
gospel" (2:16; 16:25). That means we can never ignore or forget the rhetoric
of religious polemics *by Paul* against direct or indirect Christian, Jewish, and
pagan opponents. We emphasize this not from political correctness, ecu-
menical courtesy, or post-Holocaust sensitivity, but from simple historical
actuality. Nothing is ever easier, in either political or religious polemics,
than that accusation of "works" against "faith," of externalism against inter-
nalism, of action against intention. If I do not like your external action, I
will attack your internal motivation as evil ("You just want money") or even
as totally absent ("You just want publicity").

Paul's accusation works well as long as it is read only by Christians and as
long as no Jews get to respond. If they did, their answer would be obvious.
Of course we Jews are justified only by God's grace, God's free gift of

covenant, and we both receive it initially and maintain it continually; we both accept it internally and live it externally through faith. Works are simply faith's external face. It is by the grace of faith that we receive the law, and it is by the grace of faith that we live the law. You, Paul, are making a separation of faith and works that we would never make. Any Jew and every Jew would have agreed with Paul's own injunction in Philippians to "work out your own salvation with fear and trembling; for it is God who is at work in you, enabling you both to will and to work for his good pleasure" (2:12–13). To will and to work, or faith and works, are two gifts or, better, a single gift of God's grace. Paul, however, is struggling with his native Judaism to convert its sympathetic pagan God-worshipers to Christ. In that struggle he gives no quarter, takes no prisoners, and considers the strongest external attack the best internal defense.

The Unity of Pagans and Jews: Romans 1–8

Luke's Acts gave Paul certain civil privileges, such as Tarsian and Roman citizenship, and certain religious privileges, such as descent from Pharisees and education under Gamaliel, that Paul probably lacked and certainly never mentioned. What Paul did receive, and it may well have been much more useful for his future, was a first-class education in the synagogue at Tarsus with a strong emphasis on apologetics for Judaism and polemics against paganism. He was educated, in other words, not just for debates within Judaism, but for debates with paganism or, better, for debates within Judaism about paganism.

God, World, and Judgment

God's ideal, says Paul in 1:16–3:18, is to create a unity from "the Jew first and also the Greek," a phrase repeated thrice in 1:16 and 2:9–10. But the argument is, to say the least, rather unusual in that it begins with the accusation that "all, both Jews and Greeks, are under the power of sin" (3:9), so that, between them, "there is no distinction, since all have sinned and fall short of the glory of God" (3:22–23). The unity of Jew and Greek, that is, of all the world, is already there, as it were, but it is a unity under sin. Notice, by the way, that, as Paul argues his case, he looks at the Greeks first in 1:16–2:16 and then at his fellow Jews in 2:17–3:18.

THE GREEK (1:16–2:16). First, Paul appeals to what we might call the *common law of humanity* by postulating that, with regard to idolatry and immorality, the covenantal law of Judaism written on biblical texts reappears as the natural law of paganism (un)written on human hearts, and in both cases, "it is not the hearers of the law who are righteous in God's sight, but the doers of the law who will be justified" (2:13; read 2:12–16).

Second, in his accusation of sin against pagans in 1:16–2:16 Paul cites the standard polemical apologetics of his native Judaism against paganism. *On idolatry:* pagans "exchanged the glory of the immortal God for images resembling a mortal human being or birds or four-footed animals or reptiles" (1:23). That, of course, is as inaccurate as saying that Jews worshiped an empty room in the Jerusalem Temple. Imagine what a pagan saint like Epictetus would have replied! *On immorality:* Paul asserts three times that, because of that idolatry, "God gave them up" to immorality (1:24, 26, 28). The list of vices is also fairly standard for both Paul and his contemporary Judaism, with homosexuality emphasized and in first place: "Their women exchanged natural intercourse for unnatural, and in the same way also the men, giving up natural intercourse with women, were consumed with passion for one another. Men committed shameless acts with men and received in their own persons the due penalty for their error"(1:26–27; read 1:26–31).

Paul, speaking from within Jewish Torah, singles out homosexuality alone for rejection as "unnatural" in Romans 1:26–27. But, in that tradition as in many others, sexual nature was determined by biology, body, and genitals. For many people today, however, sexual nature is determined by chemistry, brain, and hormones. So Paul never faced the question we must now ask. Yes, of course, sexual action follows sexual nature, but by what and by whom is sexual nature determined? And what if homosexuality is as "natural" for some as heterosexuality is for others?

THE JEW (2:17–3:18). Continuing his accusation of universal sin in 1:16–3:18, Paul turns from pagans in 1:16–2:16 to fellow Jews in 2:17–3:18. And, quite frankly, it is again a rather feeble accusation.

You, then, that teach others, will you not teach yourself? While you preach against stealing, do you steal? You that forbid adultery, do you commit adultery? You that abhor idols, do you rob temples? You that boast in the law, do you dishonor God by breaking the law? (2:21–23)

No doubt some Jews somewhere, sometime, somehow may have done such things. But pagan accusations against Jews were not about the hypocrisy of infidelity, but about the stupidity of fidelity.

Paul then points his criticism precisely at circumcision, repeating the same equation he made between externally written Jewish law and internally (un)written pagan law in 2:12–16 with regard specifically to circumcision, and he concludes, "A person is a Jew who is one inwardly, and real circumcision is a matter of the heart—it is spiritual and not literal" (2:29; read 2:25–29). But, of course, the obvious answer is that circumcision is both spiritual and literal for Jews, but only spiritual for pagans. The pagan becomes holy *with* but not *by* its absence and the male Jew becomes holy *with* but not *by* its presence.

When you first read that startling accusation of total global sin, it is very tempting to dismiss it as the cosmic hell-and-damnation hyperbole of the fervent preacher or even rabid apocalypticist. And the closer you look at those typical sin lists for pagans in 1:18–31 and Jews in 2:21–24, the more confirmed you might be in that dismissal. But beneath their artificiality or superficiality and especially behind their sexual emphasis, there lurks a deeper evil that validates Paul's global indictment. *There seems to be something profoundly wrong and seriously askew if not with human nature, then at least with human civilization.* We have, in a horrible evolution, moved from nineteenth-century imperialism through twentieth-century totalitarianism into twenty-first-century terrorism. We are now forced to wonder about civilization itself, and that makes us reread Paul's accusation of global sin today on a deeper level than when he first wrote it. Maybe, of course, he just saw the same global flaw, but expressed it in the only language given by his past and present tradition, while we must do it now in the more radical language given by our past and present experience.

Righteousness, Justification, and Christ

How can that global unity under human sin be replaced by global unity under some divine alternative? Paul's basic answer and its first three key words appear in 3:25–26: the *righteousness* of God is granted for the *justification* of humanity through the *sacrifice* of Christ. Here debates multiply and controversy abounds, because for each of those phrases a basic misunderstanding can occur.

RIGHTEOUSNESS: *DISTRIBUTION, NOT RETRIBUTION.* In the biblical tradition of poetic parallelism God's *justice* and *righteousness* are two words for the same concept. God does what is *just* by doing what is *right,* and God does what is *right* by doing what is *just.* God, indeed, *is* justice = righteousness, so that, in whatever format, the terms *justice* and *righteousness* always indicate the very character of that God.

But, as we turn to Paul on God's justice and righteousness a giant interpretive shadow falls across that biblical vision of God *in a modern confusion between distribution and retribution.* We use the term "justice" primarily if not exclusively for punishment, for retributive justice. Our law courts are often in the Hall of Justice, and individuals who have been wronged cry out on the evening news for justice, for wrong to be punished and right to be vindicated. But the primary meaning of justice is not *retributive,* but *distributive* justice. Think about it for a moment. If a wrongdoer who is rich, powerful, and important claims that status to avoid retributive justice, we would fall back on distributive justice by saying that legal sanctions have to be distributed fairly, equitably, justly. So also in the Hebrew scriptures—the primary and basic meaning of God's justice or righteousness is not retributive but distributive justice. In fact, you might even say that retribution is not so much the intervention of divine punishment as the inevitable result of human *dys*tribution. But with that *mis*understanding of divine righteousness primarily if not exclusively as human punishment, humans (for example, Luther!) tend to cower before the fear of divine justice as retribution rather than to celebrate the challenge of divine justice as distribution. And how is the former "good news" for anyone?

It is that divine insistence on global distributive justice with God's earthly administration matching God's heavenly character that Paul refers to as "the righteousness of God . . . attested by the law and the prophets" in 3:21. But what then?

JUSTIFICATION: *TRANSFORMATION, NOT IMPUTATION.* Paul's special term for that gift of divine righteousness is *justification* or *making just,* that is, the process whereby divinity makes humanity just. Thus, while *justice* and *righteousness* are used essentially of divinity and derivatively of humanity, *justification* is never used of God, but only of us. It is the process whereby the justice and righteousness of divinity becomes the justice and righteousness of humanity. God, therefore, is both the One who is "just" and also the One who "justifies" the world (3:26). How is that done? By

"Christ Jesus . . . whom God put forward as a sacrifice of atonement by his blood" (3:25). And here, once again, a shadow falls over Paul's vision *in a modern confusion between imputation and transformation.*

Imagine if a human judge went into the courtroom and immediately declared a defendant innocent. We would consider that totally invalid. Instead of such fictional imputation of innocence by a judge, there must be a factual establishment of innocence by a jury. When, then, divine righteousness becomes human justification, is it an act of fictional imputation or factual transformation? Is it, we might ask Paul, simply God treating the world *as if* it were just? And to that question Paul would have used his favorite negative in this letter: "By no means! For then how could God judge the world?" (3:6). Divine righteousness becomes human justification not by fictional imputation, but by factual transformation. Recall, from earlier, Paul writing in 2 Corinthians, "All of us, with unveiled faces, seeing the glory of the Lord as though reflected in a mirror, are being transformed into the same image from one degree of glory to another" (3:18) and, "If anyone is in Christ, there is a new creation: everything old has passed away; see, everything has become new" (2 Cor. 4:16; 5:17). That is transformation, not mere imputation.

Indeed, Paul repeatedly and redundantly pounds on the reality first of global sin and then of global holiness as transformation throughout all of Romans 6:11–23. At its start: "You must consider yourselves dead to sin and alive to God in Christ Jesus" (6:11), and at its end: "you have been freed from sin and enslaved to God" (6:22). But how does that transformation take place?

CHRIST: *PARTICIPATION, NOT SUBSTITUTION.* The world of Paul's time took it for granted that sacrifice was how you established and maintained peaceful unity with a god, a goddess, the gods, or God. You offered something that belonged to you to the divine. It could be as small as a libation, the first sip of wine poured out before a private banquet, or as large as a hecatomb, one hundred oxen slain before a public temple. Thereafter, the circle of human-divine and divine-human relationship was completed as you drank the wine or ate the meat now made sacred—hence "sacrifice," from the Latin *sacrum facere,* "to make sacred." Everyone in Paul's world, Jews and pagans alike, understood that "reconciliation" (5:11) could involve "a sacrifice of atonement by blood" (3:25). Even today we still use and understand the word "sacrifice" when, for example, firefighters rush into a burning house, save a family, but die in the attempt. We say those firefighters gave up their lives to save others, that they sacrificed their lives. On the one hand, all human life and death is sacred but, on the other, the deaths of those firefighters are especially, peculiarly, particularly sacred. Why? Because they died that others might live.

And however we explain that sacrificial death of Jesus, we must remember two points. First, in antiquity, nobody within that normal world of blood sacrifices thought that the slain animal was being vicariously punished by God. Nobody ever argued that the hecatomb was somehow a more preciously appropriate or more divinely demanded replacement for the inadequate human offerer who actually deserved such death. And in modernity, nobody would ever suggest that God wanted somebody punished by death in that burning house, if not the family, then those firefighters who would suffice as vicarious substitutes.

But what is most interesting is that Paul, having mentioned sacrificial atonement by Christ, does not develop it further in any way, but speaks instead of *participation in Christ,* which, as we say in Chapter 5, is the heart of his theology. And where *sacrificial atonement* got only one verse (3:5), *participation* gets a whole chapter (6:1–23). Paul probably saw that sacrificial atonement might explain the death of Jesus, but what about the resurrection? It was necessary to speak of both death and resurrection, of "Jesus our Lord . . . who was handed over to death for our trespasses *and* was raised for our justification" (4:25; read 6:3–5).

Finally, Paul speaks of the "death" of Christ in, say, 4:25, 5:10, and 6:3–10 rather than of the execution or crucifixion—recall how he emphasized that word throughout 1 Corinthians 1:23–2:8, for example: "Christ crucified . . . Jesus Christ, and him crucified . . . the rulers of this age . . . have crucified the Lord of glory."

On the one hand, his theology would not be the same if Christ had simply died in his bed and been raised thereafter by God. Jesus did not simply die; he was publicly, legally, officially executed by the contemporary authority of the Roman Empire, that is, by the normalcy of civilization's permanent violence in his own time and place. It was not simply death and resurrection. It was execution by *Rome* and therefore resurrection against *Rome.* It is there, maybe more than Paul or Christianity wants to consider, that participation will be fully accomplished. On the other hand, the advantage of using "death" rather than execution or crucifixion is that he can then contrast not crucifixion and resurrection but *death* and *life,* thereby emphasizing present Christian resurrection life. Paul can then contrast death *versus* life repeatedly in Romans 4–6 (read 4:17; 5:10, 17, 20, 21; 6:4, 8, 11, 13).

Grace, Faith, and Works

GRACE AS GIFT. The Greek word *charis,* or "grace," means a free gift. You can see that juxtaposition of grace and free gift rather clearly when Paul speaks redundantly and emphatically about being "justified by his grace as a gift" (3:24), about "the free gift in the grace of the one man, Jesus Christ" (5:15), and, climactically, about "the free gift . . . the grace of God and the free gift . . . the free gift . . . the free gift . . . the abundance of grace and the free gift of righteousness" (5:15–17).

Think, for a moment, of a physical example such as the air itself. It is there for us all the time, equally available for everyone in every place at every time. We do not need to do anything to obtain it. We could not do anything to obtain it. It is not a question of whether we deserve it or not. It is absolutely transcendent in the sense that we depend on it totally. It is absolutely immanent in the sense that it is everywhere inside and outside us, all around us. And we hardly notice it unless something goes wrong with us or with it. But air does demand the reaction of awareness, the reply of acceptance, and the response of cooperation. Or, better, it does not demand that we breathe so much as we need to breathe to avoid either asphyxiation or hyperventilation. And, if you choose asphyxiation or hyperventilation, do not say that the air is punishing you. It is only and always a matter of collaboration. A grace gift is like a free upgrade but, of course, there too, you need at least to download it.

Paul's good news is that God's righteousness is, like earth's air, a grace, a free gift offered us absolutely and unconditionally for our justification, for the making of a just world. But, then, like any gift, it is actuated by acceptance, and Paul imagines two possible modes of such acceptance, only one of which is appropriate. The right way he calls *faith,* the wrong way *works* (we prefer *faith-works* and *law-works,* as we shall see).

FAITH AS COMMITMENT. Here comes another major misunderstanding. Faith does not mean intellectual consent to a proposition, but vital commitment to a program. Obviously, one could summarize a program in a proposition, but faith can never be reduced to factual assent rather than total dedication. Faith (*pistis*) is not just a partial mind-set, but a total lifestyle commitment. The crucial aspect of faith as commitment is that it is always an interactive process, a bilateral contract, a two-way street. Faith is covenantal and presumes faithfulness from both parties with, of course, all appropriate differences and distinctions. So also for Paul in Romans. God and Christ are faithful to the world and so, in response, is the world to them. God's righteousness in Christ is faithfully consistent, and Christians are consistently faithful in response to that grace gift.

Once again, as with Galatians 3:6–29 in Chapter 4, Abraham is Paul's model and argument for faith as the primary and essential response to God's gracious offer of divine righteousness for human justification. Abraham believed God's promise in Genesis 15 (the covenant) before the command for circumcision came in Genesis 17 (the sign of the covenant). Fair enough, but as we say earlier, a Jewish opponent would have responded that, of course, faith in the covenant was primary, but so was circumcision as its sign. Just as, that respondent might continue, Christian faith is primary, but baptism is its sign, seal, and sacrament.

In Galatians 3:6 Paul cited that key text from Genesis 15:6, "He believed the Lord; and the Lord reckoned it to him as righteousness." This is repeated thrice in Romans 4:3, 9, and 22. But there is one much more important difference. In Romans, as distinct from Galatians, Paul insists that Abraham was the common ancestor of Gentiles who live by faith *without* circumcision as well as of Jews who live by faith *with* circumcision. "Or is God the God of Jews only? Is he not the God of Gentiles also? Yes, of Gentiles also" (3:29; read 4:11–12).

WORKS AS POLEMICS. You will recall also from Chapter 4, that Paul set up a repeated antithesis of faith *versus* works in Galatians 2:16–3:12. That disjunctive dyad is picked up again here in Romans 3:27–46 and again later in 9:11, 32 and 11:6. Compare, for example, Galatians 2:16, "We know that a person is justified not by the works of the law but through faith in Jesus Christ," with Romans 3:28, "We hold that a person is justified by faith apart from works prescribed by the law." Was the Jewish Paul rejecting his native Judaism by attacking it frontally in his letters to the Galatians and the Romans? But, of course, his fellow Jews would have told Paul that they were justified by the grace of covenant and that faith included works as its inevitable concomitant. You are, Paul, they would have accurately responded, simply caricaturing us polemically with this faith *or* works dichotomy.

It was, actually, not a two-way but a three-way argument, with a God-worshiper or pagan sympathizer between Paul and his fellow Jews. Here Paul does have a valid apologetic point and not just an invalid polemical point. What the God-worshiper does could very well be described as works *before* faith rather than works *from* faith. You, Paul would have said to that God-worshiper, are lost between worlds, are working not from pagan faith, from Jewish faith, or from Christian faith. You may be working merely from religious superstition or social association. And there certainly would be a polemical hint from Paul that any opposing Jews might be doing the same. In any case, and even without that last element, Paul's fellow Jews would be understandably furious at his territorial invasion, stripping from them the safety and security of a buffer group of female and male sympathizers crucially important in either a popular pogrom or an official persecution. *Paul's antithesis of faith versus works stands on that delicate interface between valid apologetic argument from a Christian to a God-worshiper and invalid polemical argument from a Jew to a fellow Jew.*

Law, Sin, and Death

FROM LAW TO SIN. In both Galatians and Romans Paul uses three expressions more or less synonymously, and always negatively, with all three opposed to faith. We have just seen the first term, *works,* in some detail. The second term is *law,* as in, for example, Galatians 3:12, "The law does not rest on faith," or Romans 10:5–6, "righteousness that comes from the law . . . righteousness that comes from faith." The third expression is *works of the law* in, say, Galatians 2:16 (thrice) or *works prescribed by the law* in Romans 3:28. Why does Paul create this opposition between law and faith especially since, in those same two letters, Paul can speak positively of "the law of Christ" in Galatians 6:2, "the law of faith" in Romans 3:27, and "the law of the Spirit of life in Christ Jesus" in Romans 8:2. Also, "The whole law is summed up in a single commandment, 'You shall love your neighbor as yourself' " in Galatians 5:14 and, twice, "love is the fulfilling of the law" in Romans 13:8–10. Is Jewish "law" bad but Christian "law" good? What, for Paul, is wrong with law? Or, from our contemporary point of view, if life under law is so good for sociopolitical life, how can it be so bad for religio-political life?

First of all, by law Paul means all law, *not just Jewish law but Roman law, not just human law but divine law.* So what is wrong with all law for Paul? The specific criticism is found in Romans rather than Galatians. Here is the key verse: "The law brings wrath; but where there is no law, neither is there violation" (4:15; read 5:13; 7:5, 7, 8).

Paul does not mean, surely cannot mean, that desire ("covetousness") only arises from, because of, in reaction to, and in opposition to the law against it, as if the desire for murder only arose from the law against it and would never have happened without that proscription. It is simply that law establishes knowledge, asserts that we now know this or that is wrong, this or that should not be done. If, for example, a people declare that all have equal and inalienable rights, they already know too much, have admitted that they know too much, and, unless thereafter they follow through, their very own law condemns them.

Second, then, although law gives the power of knowledge (*we should not do this*), it does not bring inherently with it the power of obedience (*we will not do this*). "I do not understand my own actions," says Paul in the name of law, "for I do not do what I want, but I do the very thing I hate" (7:15). This is not at all a personal or individual confession by Paul before Jewish Torah, but a structural or systemic confession by humanity before its best laws and most sincere ideals. Law establishes information but not transformation, says Paul. But he is both right and wrong on that one. He is right that law coming from the outside in does not establish faith from the inside out. Of course not. But imagine the case of discrimination against some minority. When the law finally forbids it, some say that law will not change people's minds. But might not their children or their children's children grow up with different minds?

Third, Paul's description of the human conscience as divided, so that it can say, personified, "I do what I do not want" (7:20), should not be understood as the subjective feeling of guilt, but as the objective status of sin. Earlier he equated or at least collated the written covenantal law of the Jews and the unwritten natural law of the pagans. That is still how law is understood throughout this entire section and its law/works *versus* grace/faith dichotomy. But the term that dominates Romans 5–8 is not the plural and lowercase *sins,* but the uppercase and singular *Sin.* Indeed, Paul never uses the plural, *sins,* anywhere in Romans save when quoting from scripture in 11:27. His focus is on *Sin,* that is, quite simply, on disobedience to God's law acknowledged as known and admitted as just.

Finally, Paul does not seriously consider that law and faith might be both from inside *and* from outside in a dialectical or reciprocal relationship. He said in Galatians 3:24, "The law was our disciplinarian until Christ came, so that we might be justified by faith." But maybe that law as disciplinarian and justification by faith are not just successive phases for any person or any religion, but are permanent dialectical interactions. Like two sides of the one coin?

FROM SIN TO DEATH. Paul said in 1 Corinthians 15:26, "The last enemy to be destroyed is death" and, in 15:56, "The sting of death is sin, and the power of sin is the law." The sequence there, as in Romans, is from law to sin and from sin to death. Is Paul speaking about ordinary death, the normal end of life for everything that lives on earth, human beings included? Is death really God's last enemy?

One preliminary thought. In preindustrial society about one-third of live births were dead by six, two-thirds by sixteen, and three-quarters by twenty-six years of age. In that ancient world and in all those places where the modern world is still ancient, death is not life's future and distant end, but its present and constant companion. Even apart from death by war, famine, and plague, there was death by injustice's disease, malnutrition's exhaustion, and infection's contagion.

On the one hand, then, Paul had already said in 1 Corinthians 15:22, "All die in Adam." Here in Romans 5:12–19 he reiterates that "sin came into the world through one man, and death came through sin, and so death spread to all because all have sinned," that "because of the one man's trespass, death exercised dominion through that one," and that Adam's "transgression" or "trespass" or "sin" or "disobedience" led to death as "condemnation" not just for himself but also "for all," even for "those whose sins were not like the transgression of Adam." That is certainly clear, but is it certainly right?

On the other hand, as we saw above, Christ's "death" always meant for Paul the terrible death of an unjust execution, the horrible death of a shameful crucifixion. It did not mean death as the normal end of life. His theology was not actually built on Christ's death and resurrection as if Christ had died at home in Nazareth and rose there on the third day. That death meant injustice and violence. Here, then, after two thousand years and especially as the twentieth-first century's terrorism replaces the twentieth century's totalitarianism, we ask this question: Is it death or is it violence the is the last enemy of God? Or, better, is it unjust and violent death that is the last enemy of God?

The Unity of Jews and Christians: Romans 9–11

Paul had originally imagined the unity of Jews and Christians (to use those terms) within the one community of Christian Judaism. God was calling that community "not from the Jews only but also from the Gentiles" (9:24), so that "there is no distinction between Jew and Greek; the same Lord is Lord of all and is generous to all who call on him" (10:12). But by the time he wrote this letter he already knew that something had, from his point of view, gone terribly wrong. "I have great sorrow and unceasing anguish in my heart. For I could wish that I myself were accursed and cut off from Christ for the sake of my own people" (9:2–3; read 9:1–5)

By the mid-50s, then, as that anguished confession proclaims, Paul had already decided that the unified community of (many? most? all?) Christian Jews and (many? most? all?) Christian pagans had not happened and was not going to do so within the normal parameters of Christian missionary activity. So, in Romans 9–11, he ponders this "mystery" from the double viewpoint of both divine and human causality. He considers divine causality in 9:1–29 and 11:1–36, thereby framing human causality in 9:30–10:21. A mystery, by the way, is something hidden in the heart of God and not just a puzzle, difficulty, or problem to be solved by human ingenuity.

Divine Causality

As always, in biblical tradition, whatever humans do, whether for good or evil, is understood within the control, plan, and intention of God. And to apply that principle to the present situation, Paul laces his argument with citations from the Greek translation of the Hebrew scriptures.

ROMANS 9:1–29. First, Abraham had children of flesh, but the children of promise were chosen (9:6–9). Rebecca had Esau the elder and Jacob the younger, but Jacob was chosen (9:10–13). Even the disobedience of a Pharaoh is within divine permission (9:17–18). It is all simply part, says Paul, of the inscrutable mercy of God who, as the divine Potter, can "make out of the same lump one object for special use and another for ordinary use" (9:19–21). That is certainly quite clear, but not exactly consoling. Furthermore, biblical prophets are cited announcing that God would choose a "people" from among the pagans (9:24–26), but only a "remnant" from among the Jews (9:27–29).

ROMANS 11:1–36. Second, the theme of the remnant then jumps from that frame in 9:1–29 to this frame in 11:1–36; but now the emphasis is on the *nonremnant,* the vast majority who have refused the gospel. It is important to note that, even from within the exclusivity of his Christian vision, Paul never says that "those others of Israel" are lost, condemned, and abandoned by God. He proceeds with a second emotional, personal statement: "I ask, then, has God rejected his people? By no means! I myself am an Israelite, a descendant of Abraham, a member of the tribe of Benjamin. God has not rejected his people whom he foreknew" (11:1–2). "At the present time there is," he repeats, "a remnant, chosen by grace. But if it is by grace, it is no longer on the basis of works, otherwise grace would no longer be grace" (11:5–6). That theme of grace *versus* works refers back to the section on human causality in 9:30–10:21, and we will return to it below.

The eschatological vision of earliest Christianity was for Jews and pagans in one ultimate community or, as Paul wrote in Romans 1:16, the Jew first and only then the Greek. But now, announces Paul, God has changed that final program, not to the Greek only or even to the Greek and some Jews but to a complete reversal, to the Greek first and only then the Jew (11:11–12).

Next, Paul gives a direct warning to Christian pagans about non-Christian Jews at Rome in a preview of Romans 12–16. "Now," he says, in an unusually explicit separation, "I am speaking to you Gentiles" (11:13) and then introduces the image of the olive tree. He does not say that God has planted a new gentile olive tree, but that certain branches of the Jewish olive have been broken off to allow the ingrafting of a new, pagan, "wild olive shoot" (11:17). In other words, the rootstock of Christianity is Judaism and Rome's Christian pagans are sternly warned not to "boast over the branches" they have replaced and "so all Israel will be saved" (11:18–25).

He does not say explicitly *saved in Christ,* but he certainly presumes it. Still, he at least admits it is a divine mystery rather than just a human failure and today, after two thousand years and counting, it is even more mysterious than Paul could ever have imagined. He said then, "As regards the gospel they are enemies of God for your sake; but as regards election they are beloved, for the sake of their ancestors; for the gifts and the calling of God are irrevocable" (11:28–29). We now say what Paul never imagined. *There are twin covenants, one Jewish and one Christian, both free gifts of divine grace, both accepted initially and lived fully by faith.* That is the only way, *by now,* to reread what Paul called God's plan before the face of continuing history.

Human Causality

We already noted opposition of *by grace* or *by works* in Romans 11:6 as a residual summary explaining why most Jews had refused the gospel. This contrast is now more fully developed in the section between those just seen frames of 9:1–29 and 11:1–36.

ROMANS 9:30–10:21. On the one hand, Paul offers a third emotional, personal statement: "Brothers and sisters, my heart's desire and prayer to God for them is that they may be saved. I can testify that they have a zeal for God, but it is not enlightened" (10:1–2). That unenlightened zeal is explained as seeking righteousness or fulfilling the law not *by faith,* but *by works* (9:30–32).

Put crudely, *action by faith* flows externally, naturally, spontaneously, inevitably from an internally empowering belief—like driving at 55 miles per hour to save natural resources and human lives because you are convinced that is the right thing to do and you want to do it. But *action by works* is exactly the opposite—like slowing from 70 to 55 miles per hour when you see that squad car up ahead. But is Paul's accusatory explanation accurate and valid or is it simply lie and libel? The answer demands a clear distinction between pagan God-worshipers and full Jews.

Imagine this hypothetical case. There are many "pagans" who like certain elements of Christianity. They say morning, evening, and meal prayers using the sign of the cross and they attend Sunday services, but they do not undergo official baptismal initiation or undertake full communal participation. What would most Christians think of their devotions? Would they call them actions by *faith* or actions by *works*? Would they consider them inappropriate superstitious practices or appropriate Christian observances?

Recall those God-worshipers or God-fearers who were simultaneously semipagan and semi-Jewish, those sympathizers who attended the synagogue, maybe even observed kosher regulations, but whose males did not accept circumcision and who also accepted pagan religio-political and socioeconomic normalcies. Paul considered such individuals as lost between worlds.

First, their selective Jewish observances were *works,* not *faith,* he said, and those sympathizers were in greater danger before God than either pure pagans or full Jews. Second, once converted to Christianity, they would be constantly pulled in two directions—one way by Paul and the other way by their former Jewish friends. If they retained or acquired Jewish observances, did they come from Jewish faith or from Jewish works? But how could their practices come from Jewish faith, since they were not full Jews? We will see below Paul's startling warning, "Whatever does not proceed from faith is sin" (14:23). In that struggle between Christian Judaism and non-Christian Judaism, Paul not only used strong apologetics for the former position, but equally strong polemics against the latter. He not only warned pagans and especially converted God-worshipers against *works* and for *faith;* he went over to the attack against his Jewish opponents and accused them of trying to live by *works* themselves. But was that accusation fair and accurate? Of course not. It was, as noted at the start of this chapter, the standard rhetoric of religious polemics.

The Unity of Jewish Christians and Pagan Christians: Romans 12–16

The third, final, and innermost circle of Paul's narrowing focus concerns the unity of Roman Christians with one another and, of course, with outsiders, as far as that was possible. Romans 12–16 starts with more general admonitions in chapters 12–13 and concludes with specific details and greetings in 13–16. Two sets of sentences serve as thematic emphases toward the start and conclusion of the section. "Live in harmony with one another," Paul says in 12:16 and 15:5 and, by the time you get to that second one, you know that the first was not just abstract generality. Furthermore, Paul advises them "not to think of yourself more highly than you ought to think, but to think with sober judgment, each according to the measure of faith that God has assigned" (12:3). Later, he speaks of "the faith that you have, have as your own conviction before God" (14:22). Harmony is required, it would seem, because *God has granted them* divergences *within* Christian faith or differences *of* Christian faith. What, then, was the exact situation inside and outside Roman Christianity that required such a long plea for peaceful unity?

"Do Not Be Conformed to This World"

For the sake of economy, we simply mention the contents of Romans 12–13, which lays down the moral foundations for Romans 14–16, and we focus on that latter section, which is a plea for unity between *weak* Christians, who observe Jewish kosher practices and calendar observances, and *strong* Christians, who do not do so. There are four separate units in Romans 12–13, and all must be read against the specific situation of Roman Christianity in the mid-50s with the old emperor, Claudius, very dead and the new emperor, Nero, very alive. The two framing units in 12:1–13 and 13:8–14 emphasize internal unity and love, while the two central units in 12:14–21 and 13:1–7 emphasize external unity and peace.

First, Paul repeats in summary his view from 1 Corinthians 12–13 about the "many members" of the "one body in Christ" and pleads that they "love one another with mutual affection" (12:10; read 12:1–13). Second, Paul pleads with them to "bless those who persecute you" and "if it is possible, so far as it depends on you, live peaceably with all" (12:14, 18; read 12:14–21). Third, he recommends obedience to human authority especially with regard to taxes (read 13:1–7). This is not an abstract theology of civil authority that can be generalized to all Christian situations, but rather concrete and prudent advice for Roman Christians, presumably the *weak* ones, not to rebel against civil authority for what happened to them under Claudius and for what awaited them when they returned a decade later under Nero. Even granted that, it does not sound very Pauline, as it has nothing whatever about Christ. Most likely, therefore, it is, like those catalogues of pagan sins seen earlier, a standard example of Jewish synagogue advice for survival in a potentially hostile environment. As such it would be especially appropriate for Christian Jews in Rome. But how terribly ironic that precisely at Caesarea Maritima in Judea, where Luke's Acts 23–26 says that Paul was imprisoned before he was sent for trial in Rome, a later Byzantine government building put on its floor a mosaic containing Romans 13:36, "Would you have no fear of him who is in authority? Then do what is good." (Figure 133)

There are, however, two deeper contexts for understanding Romans 13:1–7. One is *the hierarchy of the negative*—there is a time and a way to obey, a time and a way to disobey. There is a hierarchy within resistance, opposition, and negation. On June 17, 1940, according to Eberhard Bethge's *Dietrich Bonhoeffer: A Biography,* when the fall of France made everyone around him jump up to give the Nazi salute, Dietrich Bonhoeffer did likewise, saying, "We shall have to run risks for very different things now, but not for that salute!" (681) There is a time to be a taxpayer or a saluter and a time to be a martyr. Another and even more profound context is the *primacy of the positive,* but we save that for our Epilogue.

Figure 133. "Do you wish to have no fear of the authority? Then do what is good" (Rom. 13:3) on a Byzantine mosaic in Caesarea Maritima.

Fourth, the closing framing unit in 13:8–14 picks up and again emphasizes twice the theme of "love" from the first framing unit in 12:1–13: "Love does no wrong to a neighbor; therefore, love is the fulfilling of the law" (13:10). Finally, then, after those four foundational sections, Paul turns specifically to the *weak* and *strong* Christians in Rome's mid-50s. How is all that theoretical harmony to work out in communal practice for Paul's third, innermost, intra-Christian circle?

"Welcome One Another"

There are clearly two groups and two opposing views among Roman Christians, and Paul's intention in Romans 14–15 is to bring them together into one overall community for worship. For one group, whom Paul calls the *weak,* Jewish observance of kosher and calendar was still important. For the other, whom Paul calls the *strong,* it was not. In his own words, "Some believe in eating anything, while the weak eat only vegetables. . . . Some judge one day to be better than another, while others judge all days to be alike" (14:2, 5).

We sometimes call the *weak* ones Jewish Christians or Christian Jews and the *strong* ones Gentile Christians or Christian pagans. Those terms are not totally wrong, but neither are they completely accurate or fully helpful. It is not just a matter of ethnic origins, but of religious practices. A converted pagan God-worshiper might want to continue the observance of kosher and calendar within Christianity, while a Jewish convert might want to cease them within that same Christianity. But, within the Roman situation of the mid-50s, it is most likely that the *weak* were predominantly Christian "Jews" returning from the Claudian expulsion, and the *strong* were predominantly Christian "pagans" who had never left the city. In that historical context, of course, *strong* and *weak* applied not just to one's conscience or one's observance, but to one's communal power and one's economic standing. Similarly, in 1 Corinthians 8–10, the *weak,* who are shocked that the *free* eat meat in a temple's dining rooms, are likely to be *weak* not just in conscience but in power, since such meals were more possible or prevalent for haves than for have-nots. In that sense, a term like *weak* is not so much pejorative about faith or belief as accurate about class or status.

On the level of theory and his own position, Paul is quite clear. "I know and am persuaded in the Lord Jesus that nothing is unclean in itself; but it is unclean for anyone who thinks it unclean" (14:14). He puts himself, therefore, among the *strong,* who do not consider Jewish observances necessary for either Christian Jews or Christian pagans. "*We* who are strong," he says in 15:1, "ought to put up with the failings of the weak, and not to please ourselves."

On the level of practice and their own situation, however, he is equally clear. Speaking to both, he says, "Those who eat must not despise those who abstain, and those who abstain must not pass judgment on those who eat; for God has welcomed them" (14:3). The common basis for unity even in that disagreement is this: "Let all be fully convinced in their own minds. Those who observe the day, observe it in honor of the Lord. Also those who eat, eat in honor of the Lord, since they give thanks to God; while those who abstain, abstain in honor of the Lord and give thanks to God" (14:5–6). Therefore, he insists, the *weak* should not "pass judgment" on the *strong,* nor the *strong* "despise" the weak (14:4, 10, 13).

Speaking to the *weak,* he never asks, advises, or commands them to abandon their religious observances of kosher and calendar. Indeed, all he ever says to them is to "not pass judgment" on the *strong* (14:3, 4, 10, 13).

Speaking to the *strong,* however, is what takes up most of Paul's time. They are told repeatedly and emphatically, "If your brother or sister is being injured by what you eat, you are no longer walking in love. Do not let what you eat cause the ruin of one for whom Christ died" (14:15; read 14:20–21; 15:1). If, in other words, kosher and calendar are not important for you, then neither is their negation. If all food is good, then so is kosher food. If every day is good, then so is the Sabbath. Adjust, get over it, grow up, dear *strong* ones, "for the kingdom of God is not food and drink but righteousness and peace and joy in the Holy Spirit" (14:17). Paul asks each group to accept the other's religious differences so that they can worship together and share the Lord's Supper (15:6–7). But he also insists that either observance or nonobservance must proceed from faith and not from, say, discrimination, contempt, or judgment (read 14:22–23).

Those tensions and separations between *weak* and *strong* Christians over Jewish observances within Christianity may sound distantly irrelevant to us after two thousand years of disjunctive identities. But, in that time and place, they were *a* major issue, maybe even *the* major issue, and how Paul sought to resolve them may well be paradigmatic for later intra-Christian disagreements. In any such debates, the *strong* are those who *despise* the *weak,* while the *weak* are those who *judge* the *strong,* and to both Paul says, "Welcome one another, just as Christ has welcomed you, for the glory of God" (15:7) and "not for the purpose of quarreling over opinions" (14:1).

Finally, recall that list of Roman Christians already seen in Chapter 2. Both the *weak* and the *strong* may be included in that list since Paul urges them "to keep an eye on those who cause dissensions and offenses" (16:17–18).

A Gift to Preserve Unity

In Chapter 4 we saw the agreement that was forged at Jerusalem between Peter's mission to Christian Judaism and Paul's mission to Christian paganism. We suggest that James led an assembly in Jerusalem that practiced community life with regard to their possessions, just as Acts says. In 2:44–45 they had "all things in common," and in 4:32–5:11 "no one claimed private ownership of any possessions, but everything they owned was held in common." They were known, therefore, as the Poor Ones, just as Jesus had said, "Blessed are the poor." That program would be similar to the lifestyle of the

Qumran Essenes, that is, a divine share-life in opposition to the normalcy of human greed-life. The Jerusalem agreement of Galatians 2:10 was for donations from Christian paganism for the specific support of that ideal, utopian, eschatological model community in Jerusalem.

This is also the second major case in this book when it is absolutely necessary to *combine* Paul's letters and Luke's Acts, and the reason is the same. Our first chapter on the God-worshipers showed how Paul never mentions them, but Luke does so repeatedly. In this present chapter on the collection, we have the reverse, Acts never mentions that collection, but Paul does so repeatedly. Still, in both cases, each has material that only makes sense by adding in the other's data. That correlation on the collection is as follows:

(1) Agreement:	Galatians 2:10	
(2) Program:	1 Corinthians 16:1–4;	
	2 Corinthians 8–9	Acts 11:27–30
(3) Delivery:	Romans 15:25–31	Acts 20:4
(4) Condition:		Acts 21:17–26
(5) Disaster:		Acts 21:27–36

In other words, we know, from Paul, about gathering the collection, but only from Acts about its delivery. Paul collected the money from his four provinces, Galatia, Macedonia, Achaia, and Asia but, for obvious reasons of propriety, had representatives take each province's own contribution.

Here in the letter to the Romans is his final recorded statement on the collection as the great symbolic act of unity between Christian Judaism and Christian paganism:

At present, however, I am going to Jerusalem in a ministry to the saints; for Macedonia and Achaia have been pleased to share their resources with the poor among the saints at Jerusalem. They were pleased to do this, and indeed they owe it to them; for if the Gentiles have come to share in their spiritual blessings, they ought also to be of service to them in material things. So, when I have completed this, and have delivered to them what has been collected, I will set out by way of you to Spain; and I know that when I come to you, I will come in the fullness of the blessing of Christ. I appeal to you, brothers and sisters, by our Lord Jesus Christ and by the love of the Spirit, to join me in earnest

prayer to God on my behalf, that I may be rescued from the unbeliev-
ers in Judea, and that my ministry to Jerusalem may be acceptable to
the saints. (15:25–31)

Paul is now turning his mission from the east to the west with Rome as the
pivot of that shift. The letter, therefore, is not just an abstract discussion of
unity, but a practical appeal to the Roman communities to accept Paul's vision for a world united under the justice and righteousness of God and to
support him in working for its accomplishment. But first there is one final
duty to the east, and Paul prepares to return there for the first time since the
great disagreement and separation at Antioch in Galatians 2. As mentioned
in Chapter 4, we are not following Luke's suggestion of that too-swift visit
in Acts 18:22–23.

Paul is very much aware of two separate dangers at Jerusalem. One is that
the Christian Jewish community will simply refuse the collection. The other
is that non-Christian Jews will attack him. Paul was right to worry on both
counts, but from this point onward Paul himself is silent and our only information is from Acts.

First, James's community refuses to accept the collection *unless* Paul shows
that "you yourself observe and guard the law" by using (some of?) the money
to pay for a purification ritual in the Temple (Acts 21:24; read 21:17–24).
Paul apparently agreed to accept this admittedly rather ambiguous test.

Second, Paul was in Jerusalem with a group of Christian pagans carrying
the collection. Nothing whatsoever prohibited him and those Christian
pagan companions from entering the huge outer Court of the Gentiles, but
they would have to wait for him there while he and those other Christian
Jews passed the warning balustrade and entered the smaller inner courts reserved under penalty of death for Jews alone.

Third, once he had entered the Temple he was attacked by "Jews from
Asia" for violating that ban by bringing those pagan associates into the inner
Court of the Jews (Acts 21:27–28). Paul is then arrested and starts the long
journey to Rome.

Luke's Acts never tells us what eventually happened to Paul when he
reached Rome. Acts was written long after Paul's death, so Luke must have
known the outcome. And we do not need to presume a missing third volume. But, as we saw in Chapter 1, Acts is not just about Paul, but about the
Holy Spirit bringing the gospel from Jerusalem to Rome and establishing

Rome for Christianity as Jerusalem was for Judaism. Once Paul is openly preaching in Rome, the story Luke intended to tell is over. So he simply ends by saying that Paul "lived there two whole years at his own expense and welcomed all who came to him, proclaiming the kingdom of God and teaching about the Lord Jesus Christ with all boldness and without hindrance" (28:30–31). But what do we think happened to Paul after that ending?

The Martyrdom of Paul

There are two major alternative scenarios and, of course, various subsets within them. In both of them Paul dies a martyr under Nero, but the question is when and how. Although we argue for the second one, we emphasize that educated guesswork is the best any option can attempt.

One reconstruction argues that Paul was freed at Rome, went as planned to Spain, wrote those letters judged in this book as post-Pauline, and eventually returned to Rome and martyrdom under Nero. Toward the end of the first century C.E., the Christian letter *1 Clement* was sent from Rome to Corinth. In first place but more briefly, it mentions that Peter, and then in second place but more lengthily, that Paul both "gave testimony," that is, died as martyrs (*martyrēsas*). "Peter . . . went to the glorious place which was his due" (5.4). Paul, "a herald both in the East and the West . . . taught righteousness to all the world and when he had reached the limits of the West . . . passed from the world and was taken up into the Holy Place" (5.5–7).

Our own alternative reconstruction also begins at the end of Luke's Acts. On the one hand, had Paul been acquitted, freed, and gone westward to Spain, Luke could surely have added one or two more sentences to that effect. It would be hard to imagine a more fitting climax to all those Roman declarations of Christian innocence, that great theme of Acts seen in Chapter 1, than to say that Paul had been declared innocent and set free by the imperial tribunal itself. On the other hand, had he gone to an individual martyrdom after an imperial trial, it is also hard to imagine no clear and strong tradition of that event. Our best guess, therefore, and it can be no more, brings us back once more to the emperor Nero, but at an earlier moment in his reign. It also explains why Paul, and Peter as well, could have died as martyrs in Rome with very little tradition left behind about what actually happened. We return, in other words, to the great Roman fire seen at the start of this chapter.

Just after mid-July of 64 C.E. a great fire broke out at the west end of the Circus Maximus and blazed eastward and outward through the valley between the northern Palatine and southern Aventine hills. Of Rome's fourteen regions, three were totally destroyed, seven were severely damaged, and only four were left unharmed before the fire was finally stopped after a week of urban terror. Tacitus's *Annals,* written in the second century's second decade, tells of the immediate belief that Nero himself ordered the fire:

> Therefore, to scotch the rumour, Nero substituted as culprits, and punished with the utmost refinements of cruelty a class of men, loathed for their vices, whom the crowd styled Christians. . . . First, then, the confessed members of the sect were arrested; next, on their disclosures vast numbers were convicted, not so much on the count of arson as for hatred of the human race. And derision accompanied their end; they were covered with wild beasts' skins and torn to death by dogs; or they were fastened on crosses and, when daylight failed, were burned to serve as lamps by night. (15.44.2, 4)

Suetonius's *Lives of the Caesars: Nero,* written soon after Tacitus's *Annals,* listed the fire among Nero's vices: "he set fire to the city" and "some granaries near the Golden House, whose room he particularly desired, were demolished by engines of war and then set in fire, because their walls were of stone" (38.1). Earlier, however, he cited among Nero's virtues the fact that "punishment was inflicted on the Christians, a class of men given to a new and mischievous superstition" (16:2).

Our best historical guess, then, is that Paul, and presumably Peter as well, died among those many Christians martyred by Nero in 64 C.E. Paul's death was not a singular event. Paul's death was not that of a Roman citizen executed by a privileged beheading with the sword. Paul died among all those other Christians rounded up in Nero's scapegoat persecution. If that is correct, he died horribly, but he did not die alone, separate, special, or supremely important. In the terror of Nero's accusation and the horror of Nero's vengeance, few Christians were able to concentrate on what happened to Paul, Peter, or anyone else. His death is hidden among all those deaths described in the *Annals* of Tacitus. It is possible that the author of *1 Clement* knew of that inclusion although, as seen above, he presumed that Paul had reached Spain before his martyrdom—but was that just extrapolation from Romans 15:24–28? In any case, immediately after mentioning the execution of Peter and Paul, *1 Clement* continues by saying, "To these men with their holy lives was gathered a great multitude of the chosen, who were the victims of jealousy and offered among us the fairest example in their endurance under many indignities and tortures" (6.1). Notice, by the way, that Tacitus spoke above of "vast numbers" and *1 Clement* speaks here of "a great multitude . . . among us," referring, we suggest, to that same scapegoat persecution by Nero in 64 C.E.

There is here a first irony. Recall the fierce disagreement between Paul and Peter at Antioch in Galatians 2:11–14 from Chapter 4. They were finally reconciled, at least by later tradition, as martyrs under Nero. Also, recall the disagreement between the *weak* and the *strong* from Romans 14 earlier in this chapter. We do not know if Paul's plea for their unity was successful or not. But, once again, that discord was rendered moot by Nero's brutality. Peter and Paul, *weak* Christians and *strong* Christians, united in martyrdom, were finally able, as Paul prayed in Romans 15:6, "together with one voice to glorify the God and Father of our Lord Jesus Christ."

There is also a second irony. Paul did not know that the letter to the Romans would be his last will and testament. He did know that accompanying the collection to Jerusalem was personally very dangerous. But the letter and the collection were both about unity and, eventually, that search for unity would cost him his life. He accepted that possibility. You may disagree with him on pagans and Jews, on Jews and Christians, on Christian Jews and Christian pagans. You may also disagree with him on whether Christ is or is not the answer. But, of course and in any case, Christ is only the answer because he incarnates the nonviolent justice of God in his own life and death. So think not just of Christ, but of life within the transcendental imperative of global distributive justice. Read, then, Paul's explanation of that great collection for James's utopian community at Jerusalem in 2 Corinthians 8:13–14:

> I do not mean that there should be relief for others and pressure on you, but it is a question of a fair balance between your present abundance and their need, so that their abundance may be for your need, in order that there may be a fair balance.

We cite that text as applying not just to the original situation of the great collection, but to the present situation of our modern world. "It is a question of a fair balance."

The ideal of human unity under divine justice grounds Paul's theology of history in Romans. And, after two thousand years, we know it did not work out as he expected, but we also know that it must work out somehow if the earth is to have any future. What a world under justice looks like is already given in the citation from 2 Corinthians. Is it not clear by now that the safety of the world and the security of the earth demand the unity not of global victory, but of global justice? Otherwise, God will still be God, but only of the insects and the grasses.

Epilogue

The Lure of a Global Empire

Albert Beveridge (R-Indiana): "The Philippines are ours forever, and just beyond the Philippines are China's illimitable markets. We will not retreat from either. . . . We will not renounce our part in the mission of our race, trustees under God, of the civilization of the world. . . . God has marked us as his chosen people, henceforth to lead in the regeneration of the world. . . . He has made us adept in government that we administer government among savage and senile peoples."

George Hoar (R-Massachusetts): "I have listened, delighted, as have, I suppose, all the members of the Senate, to the eloquence of my honorable friend from Indiana. . . . Yet, Mr. President, as I heard his eloquent description of wealth and commerce and trade, I listened in vain for those words which the American people have been wont to take upon their lips in every crisis. . . . The words Right, Justice, Duty, Freedom were absent, my friend must permit me to say, from that eloquent speech."

—Debate in the U.S. Senate (February 1899)

To Romans the glory of their empire was even greater than that which Pericles could claim for Athens, because they had come to think that it properly embraced the whole world. Moreover, their dominion was ordained by the gods, whose favor Rome had deserved by piety and justice, and it was exercised in the interests of the subjects. . . . The Athenians too had liked to see themselves as protectors of peoples unjustly threatened or oppressed, and as benefactors of their subjects; it seems very doubtful if many of them acknowledged publicly or in their own hearts that their empire was a tyranny and unjustly acquired. What was most novel in the Roman attitude to their empire was the belief that it was universal and willed by the gods.

—Peter A. Brunt, in P. Garnsey and C. Whittaker, eds., *Imperialism in the Ancient World* (1978)

❧ ❧ ❧

First Victory, Then Peace

In Pamplona, Spain, it's the running of the bulls. In Ankara, Turkey, it's the running of the *taksis*. Especially at rush hour. Not jay-walking but jay-running, as people take their lives in hand and sprint across, say, Independence Avenue among cars, buses, and yellow Fiat taxis roaring to, from, and around the huge mounted statue of the great statesman Atatürk in Ulus Square. For young males it is an art form: do not look left or right, do not hesitate front or back, and do not move faster than necessary to make that sidewalk one second ahead of death. The *taksi* for bull, the briefcase for veronica.

It is about 4:00 P.M., Tuesday, September 17, 2002, as your NASCAR taxi takes you through the narrow crowded streets of Old Ankara and stops at an island of quiet serenity before the Hacı Bayram Mosque, built in the fifteenth and restored in the eighteenth century. That esplanade, elevated above the adjacent streets, is a peaceful place reserved for pigeons, pedestrians, and parked cars. Young mothers sit as their children play, and old men sit as their coffees cool. The sky is blue, the air warm, and a cooling breeze whips the Turkish flag above the distant Citadel. The mosque contains the tomb of the fourteenth-century Sufi teacher Hacı Bayram Veli and is a popular site for devotional visitation. Also for shopping, with a mall across the street to the right and another beneath the plaza behind. That afternoon a very plain wooden coffin draped in white-calligraphed green cloth (like the Saudi flag) sits in front of the main door, but all around stand honor guards of police and military personnel. At 4:20 P.M. you are standing outside at the minaret when all across the city, but especially and emphatically from the balcony right above you, sounds the late afternoon call to prayer.

You are not there, however, for mosque or muezzin, but because that single minaret at the mosque's southwest corner looks directly down on a roofless ruin cocooned in steel wiring, metal scaffolding, and a locked enclosure, which belatedly protect it after ancient destruction, modern pollution, and acid rain have worked relentlessly to destroy it. What that framework holds and hides is not just a temple built in the early 20s B.C.E. to Roma and Augustus, then the divine couple at the heart of a new world order, but the most detailed, complete, and important inscription in all the ancient Roman world. You are there to see that *Res Gestae Divi Augusti,* or *Acts of the Divine Augustus,* in both Latin and Greek versions still in their original positions despite time the destroyer.

The original Roman temple was a beautiful marble rectangle on an east-west axis with columned porticos surrounding a foyer and main chamber. The entrance, appropriately even if accidentally, faced west toward Rome. Today, after successive stages as temple, church, house, ruin, and quarry, the entrance wall of the foyer is gone, but its side and back walls are relatively intact. The south wall is also relatively intact, but with three small high windows recalling its time as a church. The east wall is completely gone to allow for that church's rounded apse. The north wall is abutted directly by the mosque building and mosque office at either end, is partially hidden behind them, is badly damaged with a gaping top-to-bottom hole, but is secured across that gap with mortared stones to halfway height (Figure 134).

The north wall is also the only one you can still approach directly, through the mosque's courtyard. The other three sides are inside a low wall surmounted by iron railings with the west and south walls further sheeted in shiny metal about 12 feet high. You are back again the next morning at that north wall inside the mosque's east-side courtyard at 11:20 A.M. when, once

FIGURE 134. Temple of Augustus in Ankara, Turkey, with the best-preserved inscription of Augustus's *Res Gestae,* now surrounded by the Hacı Bayram Mosque.

again, the muezzin calls to prayer from right above your head. With another funeral in front, there is an overflow crowd in the courtyard, and, as they bow down on their prayer rugs with the temple's gaping hole as perfect *mihrab* (pointer) to Mecca, you attempt respectful invisibility and are grateful for the Turkish courtesy that completely ignores your intrusive presence.

Before Augustus's death in 14 C.E. he deposited with the Vestal Virgins in the Roman forum his political autobiography, *Acts of the Divine Augustus*. The original was to be inscribed in bronze at the doors of his mausoleum in Rome's Campus Martius and copies in Latin or Greek were to be incised across the empire in the temples of Roma and Augustus. That is what happened, for instance, at Ancyra, then capital of the Roman province of Galatia, now Ankara, capital of the Democratic Republic of Turkey.

The Greek translation is along the bottom of the south wall, but the Latin original begins in three columns to the left of the foyer's entrance and finishes in another threesome to the right. It is about twenty-five hundred words long. The opening ones start so high up on the wall that you need a ladder to climb to the catwalk in front of them. They are also so enlarged above normal size that, once you know where to look, you can actually glimpse them from outside the locked fence's southwest corner. Those large prefatory words proclaim the following text as "[A copy] of the Acts of the Divine Augustus by which he placed the whole world (*orbem terrarum*) under the sovereignty of the Roman people." Augustus's divine rule was not just over Rome, Italy, or the Mediterranean, but over the whole world. It was all accomplished, of course, by military force, in Augustus's own words, "when victories had secured peace by land and sea throughout the whole empire of the Roman people" or in the more lapidary Latin, *parta victoriis pax,* "peace by victories" (13).

"The whole world" is not just introductory enthusiasm. That general global introduction at the text's start is matched by a detailed global accounting at its end. For nine of its thirty-five segments Augustus cites place after place and people after people who now submit to imperial control. Land and sea, east and west, Europe, Asia, and Africa "experienced the good faith (*fidem*) of the Roman people" (32). If the *Acts of the Divine Augustus* were but an isolated example, it could easily be dismissed as enforced imperial propaganda. But, across the empire, many other inscriptions appeared too swiftly and too widely for such a misreading. They emphasized both Augustus's divinization and Rome's globalization as two sides of the one coin (often, literally so).

A claim of global conquest is one thing; a claim of manifest destiny is much, much more. Virgil, who lived from 70 to 19 B.C.E., cited divine decree and prophetic promise to ground Rome's providential vocation for world rule. The *Aeneid* is a poem whose theme was suggested and whose manuscript was published by the emperor himself. It is an epic saga whose first word is "weapons" (*arma*), a glorious hymn to Augustan redemption, a splendid dialectic of poetry and propaganda no less either for being both. It claims that the divinely willed destiny of Aeneas is to "bring all the world beneath his laws" (4.231) in order that "glorious Rome shall extend her empire to earth's ends, her ambitions to the skies" (6.781–82). And Aeneas, with his father, Anchises, and his son, Julus, had fled the Greek destruction of Troy over a thousand years before their descendants Julius Caesar and Augustus Caesar became, respectively, god and son of god.

Above the earth, in heaven, Venus, the divine ancestress of the Julian family, reminds her father, Jupiter, of his promise that the Romans would be "rulers to hold the sea and all lands beneath their sway" (1.236). He reaffirms his promise because, "for these I set no bounds in space or time; but have given empire without end . . . [to] cherish the Romans, lords of the world, and the nation of the toga. Thus is it decreed" (1.278–83). On the earth, in Italy, King Latinus hears an oracle that proclaims, "Strangers shall come, to be your sons, whose blood shall exalt our name to the stars, and the children of whose race shall behold, where the circling sun looks on each ocean [i.e., east and west], the whole world (*omnia*) roll obediently beneath their feet" (7.98–101). Later he recognizes that Aeneas "must be the offspring, glorious in valour, whose might is to master all the world (*totum orbem*)" (7.257–58). Under the earth in Hades, Venus's human consort Anchises admonishes their son, Aeneas, about his vocation. "You, Roman," says his now dead father, "be sure to rule the world (be these your arts), to crown peace with justice, to spare the vanquished and to crush the proud" (6.851–53).

Rome's global destiny and world dominion came from divine ancestry, heavenly decree, prophetic promise, and, of course, most ancient tradition. As Homer's Greek *Iliad* ended with three related women, Hecuba, Andromache, and Helen, mourning for Troy after dead Hector's fate, so Virgil's Latin *Aeneid* began with three related men, Anchises, Aeneas, and Julus, fleeing from Troy after dead Hector's apparition. In other words, Virgil took Greek paganism's Old Testament, Homer's *Iliad* and *Odyssey,* and combined them to produce Latin paganism's New Testament, the *Aeneid*'s soaring manifesto of *Pax Romana* and Augustan revolution.

All of that glory is long in ruins, so mockery comes easily now. But, in any case, imperial globalization, the conscious claim, the intentional hope, the prophetic promise, and expected destiny of world rule is a heady ideology, no matter what actual limits of time and place may come upon it as history unfolds.

First Justice, Then Peace

We already saw Paul's command to obey earthly government in Chapter 7's comments on Romans 13:1–7 and recognized that it was not a general universal decree, but a specific Roman situation. How could it ever have been an unqualified mandate to human power from a Paul who had just recorded this cosmic indictment in Romans 8:19–23 (italics added)?

> For the *creation* waits with eager longing for the revealing of the children of God; for the *creation* was subjected to futility, not of its own will but by the will of the one who subjected it, in hope that the *creation* itself will be set free from its bondage to decay and will obtain the freedom of the glory of the children of God. We know that the whole *creation* has been groaning in labor pains until now; and not only the *creation,* but we ourselves, who have the first fruits of the Spirit, groan inwardly while we wait for adoption, the redemption of our bodies.

We talked in connection with Romans 13:1–7 of the *hierarchy of the negative* in assessing nonviolent resistance and turn now, as promised there, to consider the even more fundamental *primacy of the positive.* Our proposal is that *both Jesus and Paul are not so much trapped in a negation of global imperialism as engaged in establishing its positive alternative here below upon this earth.* If you are only against something, you are doomed to negativity, which is why imperial dictators are often replaced by postcolonial ones and foreign thugs are often replaced by local ones. Think, instead, of Jesus's Kingdom of God or Paul's Lordship of Christ in terms of these two examples from our contemporary world. One example is Mohandas Gandhi against the authoritarian imperialism of the British Empire in India. The other is Václav Havel against the totalitarian imperialism of the Soviet Empire in eastern Europe. They are not just *against* something, they are positively *for* something else.

In *The Unconquerable World,* Jonathan Schell's book about violence and nonviolence, he quotes Gandhi's statement about truth-force, or *satyagraha* (*sat,* "truth"; *graha,* "steadfastness"): "Satyagraha is not predominantly civil disobedience, but a quiet and irresistible pursuit of truth. On the rarest occasions it becomes civil disobedience." Opposition to the British Raj was necessary, but not primary. "Why worry one's head," said Gandhi, over a demise "that is inevitable? . . . That is why I can take the keenest interest in discussing vitamins and leafy vegetables and unpolished rice" (139–40). Opposition to the Raj was negative and secondary, even if necessary, but when the British were gone, India's fundamental problems would still be there. What were his primary and positive goals? "For Gandhi," concludes Schell, "ending untouchability, cleaning latrines, improving the diet of Indian villagers, improving the lot of Indian women, making peace between Muslims and Hindus—through all of which he believed he would find God—were such goals" (142). That is why Gandhi was assassinated not by a British imperialist, but by a Hindu fundamentalist.

Schell moves next from Gandhi's *steadfastness in truth* to Havel's *living within the truth*. After "the succession of defeated rebellions against Soviet domination in East Germany (1953), Poland (1956), Hungary (1956), and Czechoslovakia (1968)" three different author-activists, Adam Michnik in Poland, Gyorgy Konrád in Hungary, and Václav Havel in Czechoslovakia agreed on the "same practical counsel that . . . it was a mistake to try to overthrow the system. Activism should be directed at achieving immediate changes in daily life" through an "unshakable commitment to achieving modest, concrete goals on the local level" (191, 193). For more detail, we turn next to two essays by Havel himself. Both "The Power of the Powerless" (October 1978) and "Politics and Conscience" (February 1984) are available in the edited collection, *Living in Truth*.

First, Havel insists on the ordinary needs of life in the localized here and now. Activist struggle "must pose questions, as it were, *ad hoc,* out of a concrete consideration of the authentic needs of life." It consists of "a real, everyday struggle for a better life 'here and now'" (1978: 89). Because of its emphasis on the negative, he keeps the word *dissident* in quotation marks, but "an essential part of the 'dissident' attitude is that it comes out of the reality of the human 'here and now.' It places more importance on often repeated and consistent concrete action—even though it may be inadequate and though it may ease only insignificantly the suffering of a single insignificant citizen—than it does in some abstract 'fundamental solution' in an uncertain future" (1978: 99).

Second, there is the question of violent action to achieve those day-to-day, here-and-now objectives of living within the truth in ordinary life. He argues, "Generally, the 'dissident' attitude can only accept violence as a necessary evil in extreme situations, when direct violence can only be met by violence" (1978: 92). More fully,

> This ["dissident"] attitude is and must be fundamentally hostile to-
> wards the notion of violent change—simply because it places its faith
> in violence. . . . An attitude that turns away from abstract political
> visions of the future towards concrete human beings and ways of de-
> fending them effectively in the here and now is quite naturally accom-
> panied by an intensified antipathy to all forms of violence carried out
> in the name of "a better future" and by a profound belief that a future
> secured by violence might actually be worse than what exists now; in
> other words, the future would be fatally stigmatized by the very means
> used to secure it. . . . The "dissident movements" do not shy away
> from the idea of violent political overthrow because the idea seems too
> radical, but on the contrary, because it does not seem radical enough.
> (1978: 92–93)

That neither advocates pure pacifism in all cases nor accepts violence as perfectly normal in all instances. It simply recognizes that violence should always be the last, not the first, option and that it is ultimately the last enemy.

Third, Havel concludes that the "responsibility is ours, that we must accept it and grasp it *here, now,* in this place and space where the Lord has set us
down. . . . Christianity . . . is a point of departure for me here and now—
but only because anyone, anywhere, at any time, may avail themselves of it"
(1978: 104). That might seem to imply that anyone can find that responsibility—but only within Christianity. Any ambiguity is clarified in the second
essay from six years later:

> At the basis of this world are values which are simply there, perenni-
> ally, before we ever speak of them, before we reflect upon them and
> inquire about them. It owes its internal coherence to something like a
> "pre-speculative" assumption that the world functions and is generally
> possible at all only because there is something beyond its horizon,
> something beyond or above it that might escape our understanding
> and our grasp but, for just that reason, firmly grounds this world, be-
> stows upon it its order and measure, and is the hidden source of all the
> rules, customs, commandments, prohibitions and norms that hold
> within it. The natural world, in virtue of its very being, bears within it
> the presupposition of the absolute which grounds, delimits, animates

and directs it, without which it would be unthinkable, absurd and superfluous, and which we can only quietly respect. Any attempt to spurn it, master it, or replace it with something else, appears, within the framework of the natural world, as an expression of *hubris* for which humans must pay a heavy price. . . . We must honor with the humility of the wise the bounds of that natural world and the mystery which lies beyond them, admitting that there is something in the order of being which exceeds all our competence; relating ever again to the absolute horizon of our existence which, if we but will, we shall constantly rediscover and experience. (1984: 137–38, 153).

Christianity is, therefore, *and only at its theoretical and practical best,* but one manifestation of that far more fundamental grounding of the world in that which we ignore at our peril. Paul described that world grounding as the justice and righteousness of God offered to us as a free gift. He, like Jesus before him, had a divinely mandated program that secondarily and negatively resisted imperial Rome, but that primarily and positively incarnated global justice on the local, ordinary, and everyday level. Here and now. We can read Havel now to understand both Jesus and Paul then.

Epitaph for an Apostle

Rome was not the evil empire of its ancient time. Rome was not the axis of evil in its Mediterranean place. Rome was not the worst thing that had ever happened to its preindustrial world. Rome was simply the normalcy of civilization within first-century options and the inevitability of globalization within first-century limits. Rome was maybe even the cutting-edge of civilization, although hear in the background snickers from the Han Chinese at the other end of the Silk Road. But this is the crucial point for this book. Who they were there and then, we are here and now. We are, at the start of the twenty-first century, what the Roman Empire was at the start of the first century. Put succinctly: Rome and the East there, America and the West here. Put more succinctly: they then, we now. Put most succinctly: SPQR is SPQA.

That clash between Paul's Jewish covenant and Rome's imperial power was a radically transcendental one and was, therefore, both a first-century and also a twenty-first-century conflict. Imagine, on the model of plate tectonics beneath our geological earth, the metaphor of plate tectonics beneath our historical world. Deep below the surface of history is a giant tectonic plate that some have called macroparasitism, kleptocracy, or "the cage," but we call civilization itself. The normalcy or even the cutting edge of human civilization in all its imperial inevitability has as its chant: *First victory, then peace* or *Peace by victory.* On one side, another plate grinds relentlessly against that great central one. Some call it utopia, eschatology, or apocalypse, but we call it postcivilization and its chant is *First justice, then peace* or *Peace by justice.* On the other side of civilization's great central plate, a third one also grinds relentlessly against it. Some call it nihilism, totalitarianism, or terrorism, but we call it anticivilization and its chant is *First death, then peace* or *Peace by death.* Those plate tectonics of human history curve around as does our globe, so that those two smaller plates of anticivilization and postcivilization grind not only again civilization, but also against each other. In the first century, however, and indeed for most of the next two thousand years, postcivilization's nonviolent alternative seemed to many a sweetly romantic, politically irrelevant, and idealistically unreal dream. Now, at the start of the twenty-first century, it seems more like a terrible warning two millennia ahead of its time. "If you live by the sword, you will die by it" no longer applies minimally to Israel or maximally to Rome, but minimally to world and maximally to earth. So, then, there remain these three: anticivilization, civilization, and postcivilization, but the greatest of these is postcivilization.

We titled this book *In Search of Paul.* We did not say "St. Paul" lest that title prejudge the result. But now we know fully and clearly that we have found a saint not only for then, but for now and always. We therefore give the last word to St. Paul, from, appropriately, the letter to the Romans (8:35, 37–39):

> Who will separate us from the love of Christ?
> Will hardship, or distress, or persecution, or famine, or nakedness, or peril, or sword?
> No, in all these things we are more than conquerors through him who loved us.
> For I am convinced that neither death, nor life, nor angels, nor rulers, nor things present,
> nor things to come, nor powers, nor height, nor depth, nor anything else in all creation,
> will be able to separate us from the love of God in Christ Jesus our Lord.

References

For more images and places we recommend putting, for example, *Ancyra* or the *Gemma Augustae* or anything else that interests you into your Internet browser and following its leads. We also recommend very highly the Web site, image collections (*Pictorial Library of Bible Places*), and newsletters of Todd Bolen's BiblePlaces.com.

Primary Sources

Primary sources are from the Loeb Classical Library, Harvard University Press, Cambridge, MA. Bible quotations are from the New Revised Standard Version.

The following standard abbreviations are used in this book for epigraphic collections:

CIL	*Corpus Inscriptionum Latinarum*
CIRB	*Corpus Inscriptionum Regni Bosporani*
I. Ephesos	*Die Inschriften von Ephesos*
IG	*Inscriptiones Graecae*
IGR	*Inscriptiones Graecae ad Res Romanas Pertinentes*
ILLRP	*Inscriptiones Latinae Liberae Rei Publicae*
ILS	*Inscriptiones Latinae Selectae*
SEG	*Supplementum Epigraphicum Graecum*
SGDI	*Sammlungen der griechischen Dialekt Inschriften*
SIG	*Sylloge Inscriptionum Graecarum*

Secondary Sources

The major secondary sources used for this book are cited not just as suggestions for further reading but as acknowledgments of indebtedness and as expressions of gratitude.

Clifford Ando. *Imperial Ideology and Provincial Loyalty in the Roman Empire*. Classics and Contemporary Thought 6. Berkeley: University of California Press, 2000. The epigraph in Chapter 4 is from p. 411.

G. Bakalakas. "Vorlage und Interpretation von römischen Kunstdenkmälern in Thessaloniki." *Archaeologischer Anzeiger* 88 (1973): 671–84.

François Baratte. "Arts précieux et propagande impériale au début de l'empire romain: L'exemple des deux coupes de Boscoreale." *Revue de Louvre* 41 (1991): 24–39.

Mary Beard. "The Roman and the Foreign: The Cult of the 'Great Mother' in Imperial Rome." In Nicholas Thomas and Caroline Humphrey, eds., *Shamanism, History, and the State*. Ann Arbor: University of Michigan Press, 1996. Pp. 164–90.

Mary Beard, John North, and Simon Price. *Religions of Rome*. Vol. 1, *A History*. Cambridge: Cambridge University Press, 1998.

———. *Religions of Rome*. Vol. 2, *A Sourcebook*. Cambridge: Cambridge University Press, 1998.

Eberhard Bethge. *Dietrich Bonhoeffer: A Biography*. Rev. ed. by Victoria J. Barnett. Minneapolis, MN: Fortress Press, 2000. See p. 681. We are grateful to Marcus Borg for drawing our attention to this passage as a parallel to Romans 13:1–7.

Donald D. Binder. *Into the Temple Courts: The Place of the Synagogues in the Second Temple Period*. BLDS 169. Atlanta, GA: Society of Biblical Literature, 1999.

David C. Braund. *Augustus to Nero: A Sourcebook on Roman History 31 BC – AD 68*. Totowa, NJ: Barnes and Noble, 1985.

Christoph vom Brocke. *Thessaloniki—Stadt des Kassander und Gemeinde des Paulus: Eine frühe christliche Gemeinde in ihrer heidnischen Umwelt*. WUNT 2d Series 125. Tübingen, Germany: Mohr Siebeck, 2001.

Peter A. Brunt. "Laus Imperii." In Peter D. A. Garnsey and C. R. Whittaker, eds., *Imperialism in the Ancient World*. The Cambridge University Research Seminar in Ancient History. Cambridge Classical Studies. Cambridge: Cambridge University Press, 1978. Pp. 159–191. The epigraph in the Epilogue is from pp. 161–62.

E. Buchner. *Die Sonnenuhr des Augustus*. Mainz, Germany: Zabner, 1982.

Thomas Francis Carney. *The Shape of the Past: Models and Antiquity*. Lawrence, KS: Coronado Press, 1975. The epigraph in Chapter 6 is from pp. 63, 90, 171, 94, 121 (in that order).

Robert A. Caro. *The Years of Lyndon Johnson*. Vol. 3, *Master of the Senate*. New York: Knopf, 2002. The epigraph in the Epilogue is from pp. 35–36.

Richard J. Cassidy. *Paul in Chains: Roman Imprisonment and the Letters of St. Paul*. New York: Crossroad (Herder & Herder), 2001.

David Castriota. *The Ara Pacis Augustae and the Imagery of Abundance in Later Greek and Early Roman Imperial Art*. Princeton, NJ: Princeton University Press, 1995.

John K. Chow. *Patronage and Power: A Study of Social Networks in Corinth*. Journal for the Study of the New Testament Supplement Series 75. Sheffield, United Kingdom: Sheffield University Press (JSOT), 1992.

Amanda Claridge. *Rome: An Oxford Archaeological Guide*. Oxford: Oxford University Press, 1998.

John J. Collins. *Sibylline Oracles*. In James H. Charlesworth, ed., *The Old Testament Pseudepigrapha*. 2 vols. Garden City, NY: Doubleday, 1983–85. Vol. 1, pp. 317–472.

Diane Atnally Conlin. *The Artists of the Ara Pacis: The Process of Hellenization in Roman Relief Sculpture*. Chapel Hill: University of North Carolina Press, 1997.

Joseph Jay Deiss. *Herculaneum: Italy's Buried Treasure*. Revised and updated edition. Malibu, CA: J. Paul Getty Museum, 1989. Pp. 12, 14.

Gustav Adolf Deissmann. *Paul: A Study in Social and Religious History*. Translated by William E. Wilson. New York: Harper & Row, Harper Torchbooks, 1957.

———. *Light from the Ancient East. The New Testament Illustrated by Recently Discovered Texts of the Graeco-Roman World*. Translated by Lionel R. M. Strachan. Limited Editions Library. Grand Rapids, MI: Baker Book House, 1965.

Jared Diamond. *Guns, Germs, and Steel: The Fate of Human Societies*. New York: Norton, 1997. In our Epilogue he refers to civilization as "kleptocracy," entitles his Chapter 14 "From Egalitarianism to Kleptocracy" (pp. 265–92), and speaks also of "kleptocratic religion" (p. 288).

Karl Paul Donfried. "The Cults of Thessalonica and the Thessalonian Correspondence." *New Testament Studies* 31 (1984): 336–56.

———. *Paul, Thessalonica, and Early Christianity*. Grand Rapids, MI: Eerdmans, 2002.

———, ed. *The Romans Debate*. Revised and expanded edition. Peabody, MA: Hendrickson, 1991.

Charles Edson. "Cults of Thessalonica (Macedonica III)." *Harvard Theological Review* 41 (1948): 153–204.

Neil Elliott. *Liberating Paul: The Justice of God and the Politics of the Apostle*. Maryknoll, NY: Orbis Books, 1994. The epigraph in Chapter 2 is from pp. ix–x.

Kenan T. Erim. *Aphrodisias: City of Venus Aphrodite*. New York: Facts on File, 1986.

Louis H. Feldman. *Jew and Gentile in the Ancient World: Attitudes and Interactions from Alexander to Justinian*. Princeton, NJ: Princeton University Press, 1993. The epigraph in Chapter 1 is from p. 445; statistics on Menahem Stern's collection are from pp. 124, 498 n. 4.

———. "The Omnipresence of the God-Fearers," *Biblical Archaeology Review* 5 (September-October 1986): 58–69.

Paula Fredriksen. "Judaism, The Circumcision of Gentiles, and Apocalyptic Hope: Another Look at Galatians 1 and 2." *Journal of Theological Studies* 42 (1991): 532–64.

———. *Jesus of Nazareth, King of the Jews: A Jewish Life and the Emergence of Christianity*. New York: Knopf, Random House, 1990.

Rosanna Friggeri. *The Epigraphic Collection of the Museo Nazionale Romano at the Baths of Diocletian*. Rome: Soprintendenza Archeologica di Roma, 2001.

Karl Galinsky. *Augustan Culture: An Interpretive Introduction*. Princeton, NJ: Princeton University Press, 1966. The epigraph in Chapter 3 is from pp. 90, 91, 93, 100, 106, 107, 118.

Peter D. A. Garnsey and C. R. Whittaker, eds. *Imperialism in the Ancient World*. The Cambridge University Research Seminar in Ancient History. Cambridge Classical Studies. Cambridge: Cambridge University Press, 1978.

E. Leigh Gibson. *The Jewish Manumission Inscriptions of the Bosporus Kingdom*. Texts and Studies in Ancient Judaism 75. Tübingen, Germany: Mohr Siebeck, 1999.

Michael Grant. *Cities of Vesuvius: Pompeii and Herculaneum*. New York: Penguin, 1971.

Erich S. Gruen. *Diaspora: Jews Amidst Greeks and Romans*. Cambridge, MA: Harvard University Press, 2002.

Victor Davis Hanson. *The Western Way of War: Infantry Battle in Classical Greece*. 2d ed. Berkeley: University of California Press, 2000.

———. *The Wars of the Ancient Greeks and Their Invention of Western Military Culture*. Cassell's History of Warfare. General editor, John Keegan. London: Cassell, 1999.

James R. Harrison. "Paul and the Imperial Gospel at Thessaloniki." *Journal for the Study of the New Testament* 25 (2002): 71–96.

Václav Havel. *Living in Truth*. Twenty-two essays published on the occasion of the award of the Erasmus Prize to Václav Havel. Edited by Jan Vladislav. London: Faber & Faber, 1987. See especially pp. 36–122, 136–57.

Holland L. Hendrix. *Thessalonicans Honor Romans*. Ann Arbor, MI: University Microfilms International, 1984.

———. "Archaeology and Eschatology at Thessalonica." In Birger Pearson, et al., eds., *The Future of Early Christianity: Essays in Honor of Helmut Koester*. Minneapolis, MN: Fortress Press, 1991. Pp. 107–118.

Keith Hopkins. *Conquerors and Slaves. Sociological Studies in Roman History.* Vol. 1. Cambridge: Cambridge University Press, 1978. The epigraph in Chapter 5 is from pp. 198, 199, 202, 242.

Richard A. Horsley, ed. *Paul and Empire: Religion and Power in Roman Imperial Society.* Harrisburg, PA: Trinity Press International, 1997.

———. *Paul and Politics: Ekklesia, Israel, Imperium, Interpretatio.* Essays in Honor of Krister Stendahl. Harrisburg, PA: Trinity Press International, 2000.

———. *Paul and the Roman Imperial Order.* Harrisburg, PA: Trinity Press International, 2004.

Ann L. Kuttner. *Dynasty and Empire in the Age of Augustus: The Case of the Boscoreale Cups.* Berkeley: University of California Press, 1995.

Peter Lampe. "Kein 'Sklavenflucht' des Onesimus." *Zeitschrift für die Neutestamentliche Wissenschaft* 76 (1985): 135–37.

———. "The Roman Christians of Romans 16." In Karl Paul Donfried, ed., *The Romans Debate.* Revised and expanded edition. Peabody, MA: Hendrickson, 1991. Pp. 216–30.

———. *From Paul to Valentinus: Christians at Rome in the First Two Centuries.* Translated by Michael Steinhauser. Edited by Marshall D. Johnson. Minneapolis, MN: Fortress Press, 2003.

Irina Levinskaya. *The Book of Acts in Its Diaspora Setting.* Vol. 5 in *The Book of Acts in Its First Century Setting.* Grand Rapids, MI: Eerdmans, 1966.

Wolf Liebeschuetz. "The Influence of Judaism among Non-Jews in the Imperial Period." *Journal of Jewish Studies* 52 (2001): 235–52. The epigraph in Chapter 1 is from p. 52.

Robert S. MacLennan and A. Thomas Kraabel. "The God-Fearers: A Literary and Theological Invention." *Biblical Archaeology Review* 5 (September-October 1986): 46–53.

Ramsay MacMullen. *Romanization in the Time of Augustus.* New Haven, CT: Yale University Press, 2003. The epigraph in the Prologue is from pp. ix–x, 134.

William H. McNeill. *Plagues and Peoples.* Garden City, NY: Doubleday, Anchor, 1998 (reprint of 1977). In our Epilogue he contrasts the "microparasitism" of disease and the "macroparasitism" of war (pp. 109, 111, 119), and he cites, "the macroparasitic basis of civilization" (p. 25), "the parallels between the microparasitism of infectious disease and the macroparasitism of military operations" (p. 72), and "the fulminating sort of macroparasitism we call civilization" (p. 111).

Michael Mann. *The Sources of Social Power.* 4 vols. Cambridge: Cambridge University Press, 1986–). The epigraph in the Prologue is from Vol. 1, *A History of Power from the Beginning to A.D. 1760,* pp. 250, 293, 297. In our Epilogue he speaks repeatedly of civilization as "the cage" or "the caged" (vol. 1, p. 100; vol. 2, p. 252).

Troy W. Martin. "The Covenant of Circumcision (Genesis 17:9–14) and the Situational Antitheses in Galatians 3:28." *Journal of Biblical Literature* 122 (2003): 111–25.

James C. Miller. "The Romans Debate: 1991–2001." *Current Research: Biblical Studies* 9 (2001): 306–49.

Stephen Mitchell. *Anatolia: Land, Men, and Gods in Asia Minor.* Vol. 1, *The Celts in Anatolia and the Impact of Roman Rule.* Oxford: Clarendon Press, 1993. The epigraph in Chapter 4 is from pp. 100, 103–4.

Henry Vollem Morton. *In the Steps of St. Paul.* With a new introduction by Bruce Feiler. New York: Da Capo Press, 2002. Originally published in 1936. The epigraph in Chapter 4 is from p. 15.

H. G. Niemeyer. *Studien zur statuarischen Darstellung der römischen Kaiser.* Monumenta Artis Romanae 7. Berlin: Mann, 1968.

Peter Oakes. *Philippians: From People to Letter.* Society for New Testament Studies Monograph Series 110. Cambridge: Cambridge University Press, 2001. The epigraph in Chapter 5 is from pp. 74–76.

Carolyn Osiek and David L. Balch. *Families in the New Testament World: Households and House Churches.* Louisville, KY: Westminster John Knox, 1997. The epigraph in Chapter 6 is from p. 199.

Birger A. Pearson. "1 Thessalonians 2:13–16: A Deutero-Pauline Interpolation." *Harvard Theological Review* 64 (1971): 9–94.

Michael Pfanner. "Über das Herstellen von Porträts." *Jahrbuch des Deutschen Archäologischen Instituts* 104 (1989): 157–257.

S. R. F. Price. *Rituals and Power: The Roman Imperial Cult in Asia Minor.* Cambridge: Cambridge University Press, 1984. The epigraph in Chapter 7 is from pp. 247–48.

William Mitchell Ramsay. *Paul the Traveller and the Roman Citizen.* 1st ed. The Morgan Lectures for 1894 in the Auburn Theological Seminary & Mansfield College Lectures, 1895. London: Hodder & Stoughton, 1895.

————. *The Cities of St. Paul. Their Influence on His Life and Thought. The Cities of Eastern Asia Minor.* The Dale Memorial Lectures in Mansfield College, Oxford, 1907. New York: Hodder & Stoughton (Doran), 1907. The epigraph in Chapter 7 is from pp. 425–26, 428, 429.

B. M. Rapske. "The Prisoner Paul in the Eyes of Onesimus." *New Testament Studies* 31 (1991): 187–203.

Christopher Ratté and R. R. R. Smith. "Archaeological Research at Aphrodisias in Caria, 1999–2001." *American Journal of Archaeology* 108 (2004): 145–86.

Amy Richlin. *The Garden of Priapus: Sexuality and Aggression in Roman Humor.* Rev. ed. New York: Oxford University Press, 1992.

Richard P. Saller. *Personal Patronage Under the Early Empire.* Cambridge: Cambridge University Press, 1982.

Jonathan Schell. *The Unconquerable World: Power, Nonviolence, and the Will of the People.* New York: Henry Holt, Metropolitan Books, 2003. See especially pp. 139, 140, 142, 191–93.

R. R. R. Smith. "The Imperial Reliefs from the Sebasteion at Aphrodisias." *Journal of Roman Studies* 77 (1987): 88–138.

————. "*Simulacra Gentium*: The *Ethne* from the Sebasteion at Aphrodisias." *Journal of Roman Studies* 78 (1988): 50–77.

Ethelbert Stauffer. *Christ and the Caesars: Historical Sketches.* Philadelphia: Westminster Press, 1955.

Menahem Stern. *Greek and Latin Authors on Jews and Judaism.* 3 vols. Publications of the Israel Academy of Sciences and Humanities. Section of Humanities. Fontes Ad Res Judaicas Spectantes. Jerusalem: Israel Academy of Sciences and Humanities, 1974–84.

Robert F. Tannenbaum. "Jews and God-Fearers in the Holy City of Aphrodite." *Biblical Archaeology Review* 5 (September-October 1986): 54–57. The epigraph in Chapter 1 is from p. 57.

Gerd Theissen. "Social Integration and Sacramental Activity: An Analysis of 1 Cor. 11:17–34." In his *The Social Setting of Pauline Christianity. Essays on Corinth.* Translated by John H. Schütz. Philadelphia: Fortress Press, 1982 (from the original German article of 1974). Pp. 145–74.

Paul R. Trebilco. *Jewish Communities in Asia Minor*. Society for New Testament Studies Monograph Series, 69. New York: Cambridge University Press, 1991.

Antonio Varone. *Eroticism in Pompeii*. Los Angeles: J. Paul Getty Museum, 2001.

Andrew Wallace-Hadrill. "The Golden Age and Sin in Augustan Ideology." *Past and Present* 95 (1982): 19–36. The epigraph in Chapter 3 is from pp. 30, 33.

———. *Houses and Society in Pompeii and Herculaneum*. Princeton, NJ: Princeton University Press, 1994. The epigraph in Chapter 6 is from p. 118.

Francis B. Watson. "The Two Roman Congregations: Romans 14:1–15:13." In Karl Paul Donfried, ed., *The Romans Debate*. Revised and expanded edition. Peabody, MA: Hendrickson, 1991. Pp. 203–15.

Wiefel Wolfgang. "The Jewish Community in Ancient Rome and the Origins of Roman Christianity." In Karl Paul Donfried, ed., *The Romans Debate*. Revised and expanded edition. Peabody, MA: Hendrickson, 1991. Pp. 85–101.

Paul Zanker. *The Power of Images in the Age of Augustus*. Translated by Alan Shapiro. Jerome Lectures: Sixteenth series. Ann Arbor: University of Michigan Press, 1990. The epigraph in Chapter 2 is from pp. 4, 101.

———. *Pompeii: Public and Private Life*. Cambridge, MA: Harvard University Press, 1998.

Illustration Credits

Abbreviations

ANS   American Numismatic Society
DAII   Deutsches Archäologisches Institut, Istanbul
DAIR   Deutsches Archäologisches Institut, Rom
PLBL   Pictorial Library of Bible Lands

Figure 1. Ephesus, overview, Grotto of St. Paul, copyright Österreichisches Archäologisches Institut, Vienna, photo by N. Gail.

Figure 2. Ephesus, fresco in Grotto of St. Paul, copyright Österreichisches Archäologisches Institut, Vienna, photo by N. Gail.

Figure 3. Ephesus, fresco of Thecla in the Grotto of St. Paul, copyright Österreichisches Archäologisches Institut, Vienna, photo by N. Gail.

Figure 4. Philippi, looking southwest, photo by Todd Bolen, PLBL.

Figure 5. Rome, *The Conversion of St. Paul* in S. Maria del Popolo, by Michelangelo Merisi da Caravaggio (1573–1610), photo by Scala, Art Resources, NY.

Figure 6. Rome, *The Conversion of St. Paul* in Coll. Odescalchi Balbi di Piovera, by Michelangelo Merisi da Caravaggio (1573–1610), photo by Scala, Art Resources, NY.

Figure 7. Aphrodisias, theater, photo by Jonathan L. Reed.

Figure 8. Map of key sites in search of Paul.

Figure 9. Aphrodisias, reconstruction of Sebasteion from R. R. R. Smith, "The Imperial Reliefs from the Sebasteion at Aphrodisias," *Journal of Roman Studies* 77 (1987): 97.

Figure 10. Aphrodisias, Julio-Claudian Emperor, photo courtesy of New York University Excavations.

Figure 11. Aphrodisias, Claudius over Land and Sea, photo courtesy of New York University Excavations.

Figure 12. Aphrodisias, synagogue inscription, photo courtesy of New York University Excavations.

Figure 13. Aphrodisias, face *b* of synagogue inscription, photo courtesy of New York University Excavations.

Figure 14. Corinth, *bēma,* photo by Todd Bolen, PLBL.

Figure 15. Map of Delos in the Aegean.

Figure 16. Delos, approach, photo by Jonathan L. Reed.

Figure 17. Delos, overview of excavations, photo by Jonathan L. Reed.

Figure 18. Delos, plan of Sarapeion A, after Philippe Bruneau, *Recherches sur les cultes de Délos à l'époque hellénistique et à l'époque impériale.* Bibliothèque des écoles françaises d'Athènes et de Rome 217 (Paris: Éditions E. de Boccard, 1970), 460.

Figure 19. Delos, Room E of Sarapeion A, photo by Jonathan L. Reed.

Figure 20. Delos, plan of synagogue, after B. Hudson McLean, "The Place of Cult in Voluntary Associations and Christian Churches on Delos," in John S. Kloppenborg and Stephen G.

Wilson, eds., *Voluntary Associations in the Graeco-Roman World* (London and New York: Routledge, 1996), 194.

Figure 21. Delos, Seat of Moses in the synagogue, photo by Jonathan L. Reed.

Figure 22. Delos, plan of Sarapeion C, after Philippe Bruneau, *Recherches sur les cultes de Délos à l'époque hellénistique et à l'époque impériale.* Bibliothèque des écoles françaises d'Athènes et de Rome 217 (Paris: Éditions E. de Boccard, 1970), 460.

Figure 23. Pompeii, Isis, Museo Archeologico Nazionale, Naples, photo by Erich Lessing, Art Resources, NY.

Figure 24. Rome, Altar of Peace, DAIR 76.2385.

Figure 25. Rome, Augustan Forum, photo by Todd Bolen, PLBL.

Figure 26. Rome, Temple of Mars *Ultor,* after A. Boethius and J. B. Ward Perkins, *Etruscan and Roman Architecture* (London: Harmondsworth, 1970), 190.

Figure 27. Rome, Augustan Forum, after Paul Zanker, *Forum Augustum: Das Bildprogramm* (Tübingen, Germany: Ernst Wasmuth, 1968), 8.

Figure 28. Silver coin of Julius Caesar, ANS 1995.11.1651.

Figure 29. Luni, Italy, tombstone, Museo Archeologico Luni, DAIR 30.232.

Figure 30. Silver coin of Augustus, ANS 1944.100.38324.

Figure 31. Rome, Prima Porta Statue, Vatican Museums, Vatican State, photo by Erich Lessing, Art Resources, NY.

Figure 32. Rome, Offices of the Knights of St. John of Jerusalem, Fototeca Unione 3562.

Figure 33. Silver coins of Octavian, ANS 1001.1.24910, ANS 1944.100.39138, and 1001.1.22824.

Figure 34. Silver coin of Octavian, ANS 1937.158.439.

Figure 35. Rome, *Ara Pacis,* plan and axonometric view after J. B. Ward-Perkins, *Roman Imperial Architecture* (New Haven, CT: Yale University Press, 1992), fig. 5.

Figure 36. Rome, *Ara Pacis,* south frieze, DAIR 72.2400.

Figure 37. Rome, *Ara Pacis,* south frieze, DAIR 72.2403.

Figure 38. Rome, statue of Augustus, Museo Nazionale delle Terme, inv. 56230, DAIR 65.1111.

Figure 39. Silver coin of Nero, ANS 1944.100.39794.

Figure 40. Rome, *Ara Pacis,* Tellus Panel, DAIR 86.1448.

Figure 41. Rome, reconstruction of the *horologium* of Augustus, after E. Buchner, *Die Sonnenuhr des Augustus* (Mainz, Germany: Zabern, 1982), fig. 14.

Figure 42. Rome, pavement of *horologium,* after Amanda Claridge, *Rome: An Oxford Archaeological Guide* (Oxford: Oxford University Press, 1998), fig. 86.

Figure 43. Rome, statue of Augustus, DAIR 65.1111.

Figure 44. Naples, statue of priestess from Pompeii, Museo Archeologico Nazionale, inv. 6041, DAIR 76.1157.

Figure 45. Naples, Alexander mosaic from Pompeii, Museo Archeologico Nazionale, photo by Alinari, Art Resources, NY.

Figure 46. Coin of Augustus, Rome, ANS 1944.100.38345.

Figure 47. Coins of Augustus, Ephesus, ANS 0000.999.16782 and 1944.100.39182.

Figure 48. Vienna, the Gemma Augustea, Kunsthistorisches Museum, photo by Erich Lessing, Art Resources, NY.

Figure 49. Paris, Grande Camée de France, Bibliothèque Nationale, photo by Erich Lessing, Art Resources, NY.

Figure 50. Coin of Caligula, Rome, ANS 1001.1.12266.

Figure 51. Coin of Caligula, Rome, ANS 1967.153.111.

Figure 52. Coin of Claudius, Rome, ANS 1001.1.11952.

Figure 53. Central Greece, Egnatia Odos, photo by Jonathan L. Reed.

Figure 54. Philippi, Greece, Via Egnatia, photo by Todd Bolen, PLBL.

Figure 55. Thessaloniki, Greece, statue of Augustus, Archaeological Museum of Thessaloniki, photo by Todd Bolen, PLBL.

Figure 56. Thessaloniki, statue of Claudius, Archaeological Museum of Thessaloniki, photo by Todd Bolen, PLBL.

Figure 57. Rome, Prima Porta Statue, Vatican Museums, Vatican State, photo by Erich Lessing, Art Resources, NY.

Figure 58. Rome, altar, DAIR 59.168 and 59.172.

Figure 59. Hierapolis, Turkey, sarcophagi, photo by Robert E. Merritt.

Figure 60. Pisidian Antioch, Turkey, Tiberia Plateia, photo by George R. Swain (July 12, 1924), Kelsey Museum Archive 7.1358.

Figure 61. Pisidian Antioch, Turkey, Yalvaç Museum, photo by Jonathan L. Reed.

Figure 62. Caesarea Maritima, Israel, aqueduct, photo by Todd Bolen, PLBL.

Figure 63. Map of Romanization.

Figure 64. Pompeii, Eumachia Building, DAIR 66.638.

Figure 65. Naples, statue of Eumachia from Pompeii, Museo Archeologico Nazionale, inv. 6041, DAIR 76.1157.

Figure 66. Pompeii, plan of forum, after Paul Zanker, *Pompeii: Public and Private Life* (Cambridge, MA, and London: Harvard University Press, 1998), fig. 19.

Figure 67. Pompeii, plan of forum, after Paul Zanker, *Pompeii: Public and Private Life* (Cambridge, MA, and London: Harvard University Press, 1998), fig. 37.

Figure 68. Nicopolis, Greece, Odeon, photo by Vanni, Art Resources, NY.

Figure 69. Caesarea Maritima, Israel, Pontius Pilate Inscription, collection of the Israel Antiquities Authority, photo copyright the Israel Museum, Jerusalem.

Figure 70. Rome, *The Dying Gaul,* Museo Capitolini, photo by Scala, Art Resources, NY.

Figure 71. Map of Galatia.

Figure 72. Ankara, Turkey, reconstruction of imperial temple, after Martin Schede and Daniel Krencker, *Der Tempel in Ankara,* Archäologisches Institut des deutschen Reiches, Denkmäler antiker Architektur 3 (Berlin: de Gruyter, 1936).

Figure 73. Ankara, Turkey, Temple of Rome and Augustus, photo by Schede, DAII 23490.

Figure 74. Pisidian Antioch, Turkey, Tiberia Plateia, photo by George R. Swain (July 12, 1924), Kelsey Museum Archive 7.1358.

Figure 75. Ankara, Turkey, reconstruction of baths, after Fikret Yegül, *Baths and Bathing in Classical Antiquity* (Cambridge, MA, and London: MIT Press, 1992), 419.

Figure 76. Pisidian Antioch, Turkey, aqueduct, photo taken July 12, 1924, by George Swain, Kelsey Museum in Michigan, Archive 7.1113.

Figure 77. Priene, Turkey, the Athena Temple, photo by Robert E. Merritt.

Figure 78. Berlin, Antikensammlung, Staatliche Museen zu Berlin, Paulus Fabius Maximus Inscription, Inv. Nr. 105, copyright Bildarchiv Preussischer Kulturbesitz, Art Resources, NY.

Figure 79. Berlin, Antikensammlung, Staatliche Museen zu Berlin, Paulus Fabius Maximus Inscription, Inv. Nr. 105, copyright Bildarchiv Preussischer Kulturbesitz, Art Resources, NY.

Figure 80. Ephesus, Turkey, excavations by Austrian Archaeological Institute, copyright Österreichisches Archäologisches Institut, Vienna, Inv. Nr. EAR 777.

Figure 81. Ephesus, Turkey, Artemis in excavation, copyright Österreichisches Archäologisches Institut, Vienna, Inv. Nr. Pl 758.

Figure 82. Selçuk Museum, Turkey, Artemis, photo by A. Schiffleitner, copyright Österreichisches Archäologisches Institut, Vienna, Inv. Nr. EPH 12644.

Figure 83. Ephesus, Turkey, Pollio Aqueduct, copyright Österreichisches Archäologisches Institut, Vienna.

Figure 84. Selçuk Museum, Turkey, bull-head capital, copyright Österreichisches Archäologisches Institut, Vienna.

Figure 85. Rome, tombstone of a *gallus,* Musei Capitolini, inv. No. 1207, DAIR 5877.

Figure 86. Delos, phallus, photo by Jonathan L. Reed.

Figure 87. Malibu, California, J. Paul Getty Museum, Workshop of Boethos, Herm, 100–50 B.C.E., Bronze with ivory inlay; H: 103.5 cm; W of base: 23.5 cm, 79.AB.138.

Figure 88. Naples, relief from Pompeii, Museo Archeologico Nazionale, RP Inv. No. 27741, photo by Erich Lessing, Art Resources, NY.

Figure 89. Naples, Priapus fresco from Pompeii, Museo Archeologico Nazionale, photo by Scala, Art Resources, NY.

Figure 90. Naples, fresco from Pompeii, Museo Archeologico Nazionale, RP Inv. No. 110569, photo by Erich Lessing, Art Resources, NY.

Figure 91. Naples, bas-relief from Pompeii, Museo Archeologico Nazionale, RP inv. No. 27714, photo by Scala, Art Resources, NY.

Figure 92. Naples, Cameo, Museo Archeologico Nazionale, photo by Scala, Art Resources, NY.

Figure 93. Aphrodisias, Turkey, Sebasteion, photo by New York University Excavations.

Figure 94. Aphrodisias, Turkey, Sebasteion, photo by New York University Excavations.

Figure 95. Paris, Louvre, Boscoreale Cup, photo by Réunion des Musées Nationaux, Art Resources, NY.

Figure 96. Boscoreale Cup, copyright Valerie Woelfel.

Figure 97. Boscoreale Cup, copyright Valerie Woelfel.

Figure 98. Boscoreale Cup, copyright Valerie Woelfel.

Figure 99. Boscoreale Cup, copyright Valerie Woelfel.

Figure 100. Corinth, Temple of Apollo, photo by Todd Bolen, PLBL.

Figure 101. Plan of the Corinthian Forum, after C. K. Williams and O. H. Zervos, "Excavations at Corinth, 1989: The Temenos of Temple E," *Hesperia* 59 (1990): 327.

Figure 102. Plan of the Asklepeion, after C. A. Roebuck, *Corinth: Results of Excavations Conducted by the American School of Classical Studies at Athens.* Vol. 14, *The Asklepieion and Lerna* (Princeton, NJ: The American School of Classical Studies at Athens, 1951), Plan D.

Figure 103. Plan of the Asklepeion, after C. A. Roebuck, *Corinth: Results of Excavations Conducted by the American School of Classical Studies at Athens.* Vol. 14, *The Asklepieion and Lerna* (Princeton, NJ: The American School of Classical Studies at Athens, 1951), Plan C.

Figure 104. Sketch of the column of the Iobacchoi, after Jane Ellen Harrison, *Primitive Athens as Described by Thucydides* (Cambridge: Cambridge University Press, 1906), fig. 25.

Figure 105. Plan of the Iobacchoi's meeting hall, after Walther Judeich, *Topographie von Athens,* Handbuch der Altertumswissenschaft (Munich: Beck, 1931), 291.

Figure 106. Sketch of the House of the Comedians, after Philippe Bruneau and Claude Vatin et al., *L'îlot de la Maison des comédiens,* Exploration archéologique de Délos 27 (Paris: Éditions E. de Boccard, 1970), 18.

Figure 107. Sketch of the House of the Comedians, after Philippe Bruneau and Claude Vatin et al., *L'îlot de la Maison des comédiens,* Exploration archéologique de Délos 27 (Paris: Éditions E. de Boccard, 1970), 34.

Figure 108. Plan of Pergamum insula, after Monica Trümpler, "Material and Social Environment of Greco-Roman Households in the East: The Case of Hellenistic Delos," in David L. Balch and Carolyn Osiek, eds., *Early Christian Families in Context: An Interdisciplinary Dialogue* (Grand Rapids, MI, and Cambridge: Eerdmans, 2003), 36.

Figure 109. Pompeii, *lararium,* photo by Scala, Art Resources, NY.

Figure 110. Plan of the Villa of the Mysteries, after Brenda Longfellow, "A Gendered Space? Location and Function of Room 5 in the Villa of the Mysteries," in Elaine K. Gazda, ed.,

The Villa of the Mysteries in Pompeii: Ancient Ritual—Modern Muse (Ann Arbor: Kelsey Museum of Archaeology and the University of Michigan Museum of Art, 2000), 25.

Figure 111. Pompeii, Villa of the Mysteries, photo by Scala, Art Resources, NY.

Figure 112. Pompeii, Forum, photo by Todd Bolen, PLBL.

Figure 113. Herculaneum, Insula V, photo by Alinari, Art Resources, NY.

Figure 114. Plan of House of the Bicentenary, after Andrew Wallace-Hadrill, *Houses and Society in Pompeii and Herculaneum* (Princeton, NJ: Princeton University Press, 1994), 203.

Figure 115. Herculaneum, Hall of the Augustales, photo by Scala, Art Resources, NY.

Figure 116. Plan of House of the Faun at Pompeii, after Andrew Wallace-Hadrill, *Houses and Society in Pompeii and Herculaneum* (Princeton, NJ: Princeton University Press, 1994), 208.

Figure 117. Naples, mosaic from Pompeii, Museo Archeologico Nazionale, photo by Alinari, Art Resources, NY.

Figure 118. Corinth, Erastus inscription, photo by Jonathan L. Reed.

Figure 119. Rome, Arch of Titus, photo by Todd Bolen, PLBL.

Figure 120. Rome, Arch of Titus, DAIR 79.2026.

Figure 121. Rome, Arch of Titus, photo by Todd Bolen, PLBL.

Figure 122. Florence, Uffizi, altar from Rome, DAIR 65.2155.

Figure 123. Rome, altar, Capitoline Museums, Palazzo dei Conservatori, inv. 855 DAIR 60.1472.

Figure 124. Rome, altar, Capitoline Museums, Palazzo dei Conservatori, inv. 2144 DAIR 35.210.

Figure 125. Rome, altar, Museo Nazionale delle Terme, inv. 49481, DAIR 76.1783–5.

Figure 126. Rome, plan of Nero's Golden House, after J. B. Ward-Perkins, *Roman Imperial Architecture* (New Haven, CT, and London: Yale University Press, 1981), 60.

Figure 127. Rome, Golden House, photo by Scala, Art Resources, NY.

Figure 128. Rome, Palatine Hill, sketch after Graydon F. Snyder, *Ante Pacem: Archaeological Evidence of Church Life Before Constantine,* rev. ed. (Macon, GA: Mercer University Press, 2003), 60.

Figure 129. Location of early Christian catacombs, after Amanda Claridge, *Rome: An Oxford Archaeological Guide* (Oxford: Oxford University Press, 1998), 409.

Figure 130. Rome, Catacomb of Priscilla, photo by Scala, Art Resources, NY.

Figure 131. Reconstruction of St. Peter's tomb, after Peter Lampe, *From Paul to Valentinus: Christians at Rome in the First Two Centuries* (Minneapolis, MN: Fortress Press, 2003), fig. 6.

Figure 132. Plan of Insula Aracoeli, after Andrew Wallace-Hadrill, "Domus and Insulae in Rome: Families and Housefuls," in David L. Balch and Carolyn Osiek, eds., *Early Christian Families in Context: An Interdisciplinary Dialogue* (Grand Rapids, MI, and Cambridge: Eerdmans, 2003), 16–17.

Figure 133. Caesarea Maritima, Israel, mosaic, photo by Todd Bolen, PLBL.

Figure 134. Ankara, the Temple of Augustus, photo by Eckstein, DAII KB 12.086.

Color Insert

View from Philippi, photo by Todd Bolen, PLBL.

Philippi, alleged prison of Paul, photo by Todd Bolen, PLBL.

Aphrodisias, Sebasteion, Claudius Imperator, New York University Excavations.

Aphrodisias, Sebasteion, Augustus with trophy, New York University Excavations.

Aphrodisias, Sebasteion, Nero over Armenia, New York University Excavations.

Aphrodisias, Sebasteion, Claudius over Britannia, New York University Excavations.

Delos, statue of Roma, photo by Jonathan L. Reed.

Delos, phallus by the Temple of Dionysos, photo by Jonathan L. Reed.

Delos, overview, photo by Jonathan L. Reed.

Alexander the Great, Museo Archeologico Nazionale, Naples, photo by Alinari, Art Resources, NY.

Thessaloniki, excavations on the Roman Forum, photo by Todd Bolen, PLBL.

Statue of Augustus, Archaeological Museum of Thessaloniki, photo by Todd Bolen, PLBL.

Statue of Claudius, Archaeological Museum of Thessaloniki, photo by Todd Bolen, PLBL.

Thessaloniki, model of the Roman Forum, Archaeological Museum of Thessaloniki, photo by Todd Bolen, PLBL.

Pisidian Antioch, Temple of Augustus, photo by Todd Bolen, PLBL.

Pisidian Antioch, *Res Gestae* in Yalvaç Museum, photo by Todd Bolen, PLBL.

Pisidian Antioch, Sergius Paullus Inscription, Yalvaç Museum, photo by Jonathan L. Reed.

Rome, *The Dying Gaul,* Musei Capitolini, photo by Scala, Art Resources, NY.

Ephesus, fresco in Grotto of St. Paul, copyright Österreichisches Archäologisches Institut, Vienna, photo by N. Gail.

Ephesus, excavations by Austrian Archaeological Institute, copyright Österreichisches Archäologisches Institut, Vienna, Inv. Nr. EAR 777.

Ephesus, Augustus inscription, photo by Robert E. Merritt.

Ephesus, theater, photo by Robert E. Merritt.

Pompeii, Forum, photo by Todd Bolen, PLBL.

Herculaneum, House of the Bicentenary, photo by Alinari, Art Resources, NY.

Roman relief, Museo Archeologico Nazionale, Naples, photo by Scala, Art Resources, NY.

Phallus, stone relief, Museo Archeologico Nazionale, Naples, photo by Erich Lessing, Art Resources, NY.

Pompeii, tavern, photo by Todd Bolen, PLBL.

Isthmus and Corinth, photo by Todd Bolen, PLBL.

Corinth, overview of excavations, photo by Todd Bolen, PLBL.

Corinth, Erastus inscription, photo by Jonathan L. Reed.

Corinth, *bēma,* photo by Todd Bolen, PLBL.

Rome, the Arch of Titus, photo by Todd Bolen, PLBL.

Rome, the trophies from Jerusalem on the Arch of Titus, photo by Todd Bolen, PLBL.

Rome, the Golden House, photo by Scala, Art Resources, NY.

Rome, the Catacombs of Priscilla, photo by Scala, Art Resources, NY.

Jerusalem, Temple Mount, photo by Todd Bolen, PLBL.

Caesarea Maritima, photo courtesy of Zev Radovan.

Index

Biblical chapters and verses appear in bold type.
Page numbers of illustrations appear in italics.